THE HISTORY OF ARCHAEOLOGY

The History of Archaeology: An Introduction provides global coverage of the history of archaeology with chapters devoted to particular regions of the world. This approach allows readers to understand the similarities in the history of and approach to archaeology across the world, but also shows the distinct differences in certain aspects. Each chapter is written by a specialist scholar with experience of the region concerned. Thus the book focuses on the earliest beginnings of archaeology in different areas of the globe, and how it developed from being a pastime for antiquarians and collectors to a serious attempt to obtain information about past societies.

Woven into the text are various boxes that explore key archaeologists, sites and important discoveries in the history of archaeology enriching the story of the discipline's development. With such far-ranging coverage, including an exploration of the little-covered development of Russian and Chinese archaeology, *The History of Archaeology* is the perfect introduction to the history of archaeology for the interested reader and student alike.

Paul Bahn studied archaeology at the University of Cambridge and did his PhD thesis (1979) on the prehistory of the French Pyrenees. Then he held post-doctoral fellowships at Liverpool and London, plus a J. Paul Getty postdoctoral fellowship in the History of Art and the Humanities. He went freelance in the mid-'80s, and since then has devoted himself to writing, editing and translating books on archaeology, plus occasional journalism and as much travel as possible. His main research interest is prehistoric art, especially rock art of the world, and most notably Palaeolithic art, as well as the archaeology of Easter Island. Among his many books are *Archaeology: Theories, Methods and Practice, sixth edition* (with Colin Renfrew, 2012), *Archaeology: The Key Concepts* (with Colin Renfrew; Routledge, 2004) and *The Cambridge World Prehistory* (edited with Colin Renfrew, 2013).

THE HISTORY OF ARCHAEOLOGY

An introduction

Edited by Paul Bahn

Routledge
Taylor & Francis Group

LONDON AND NEW YORK

First published 2014
by Routledge
2 Park Square, Milton Park, Abingdon, Oxon OX14 4RN

and by Routledge
711 Third Avenue, New York, NY 10017

Routledge is an imprint of the Taylor & Francis Group, an informa business

British Library Cataloguing in Publication Data
A catalogue record for this book is available from the British Library

Library of Congress Cataloging in Publication Data
The history of archaeology: an introduction/edited by Paul Bahn.
 pages cm
 Includes bibliographical references and index.
 1. Archaeology – History.   2. Excavations (Archaeology) – History.
 I. Bahn, Paul G.
 CC100.H58 2013
 930.1 – dc23
 2013025672

ISBN: 978-0-415-84170-2 (hbk)
ISBN: 978-0-415-84172-6 (pbk)
ISBN: 978-1-315-87934-5 (ebk)

Typeset in Bembo and Stone Sans
by Florence Production Ltd, Stoodleigh, Devon, UK

Printed and bound in Great Britain by
TJ International Ltd, Padstow, Cornwall

CONTENTS

LIST OF FIGURES

LIST OF KEY ARCHAEOLOGIST BOXES

LIST OF KEY DEVELOPMENTS
BOXES

LIST OF CONTRIBUTORS

Caroline Bird studied archaeology at Cambridge University and completed a PhD at the University of Western Australia. She taught for several years at La Trobe University and in the Victoria Archaeological Survey's Site Officer training program. She has research interests in stone artifact analysis and landscape archaeology and has conducted research in Victoria and Western Australia. She is also interested in heritage and public education and has been involved in the development of curriculum and educational resources in archaeology, heritage and Aboriginal Studies, for students at all levels. She is currently research manager at Archaeaus, an archaeological heritage consultancy in Western Australia.

Peter Bogucki received his undergraduate degree from the University of Pennsylvania and his PhD (1981) from Harvard University. At Princeton University since 1983, he is associate dean for undergraduate affairs of the School of Engineering and Applied Science, having previously served as director of studies of Forbes College. His archaeological research interests lie in European prehistory, including the establishment of farming communities, zooarchaeology and household archaeology. Bogucki has conducted excavations of Neolithic settlements in Poland and collaborated with researchers on the chemical analysis of bones and artifacts from these sites.

Ann Cyphers obtained her PhD in 1987 from the National Autonomous University of Mexico (UNAM). She is a senior research scientist at the Institute for Anthropological Research-UNAM in Mexico City and has conducted research in Mesoamerica at the sites of Chalcatzingo, Xochicalco, San Lorenzo Tenochtitlán and Laguna de los Cerros with a specific focus on the Preclassic period and the Olmec culture.

Philip Duke studied archaeology at the Universities of Cambridge and Calgary. He is currently an Emeritus Professor of Anthropology at Fort Lewis College in Durango, Colorado, having taught there for twenty-nine years. He has published on diverse topics, ranging from Northern plains prehistory to the relationship between tourism and the archaeological past. His current research interests concern public archaeology, and heritage and repatriation issues.

David Gill studied archaeology and ancient history at the University of Newcastle upon Tyne and wrote his DPhil thesis (1987) on Athenian black-glossed pottery. He was a Rome Scholar at the British School at Rome, a Sir James Knott Fellow at Newcastle, a member of the Department of Antiquities at the Fitzwilliam Museum in Cambridge, and Reader in Mediterranean Archaeology at Swansea University. He was appointed Professor of Archaeological Heritage at University Campus Suffolk in 2011. His research interests include the history of Classical archaeology and archaeological ethics. He received the Archaeological Institute of America's Outstanding Public Service Award in 2012 for his work on cultural heritage.

Enrique López-Hurtado studied archaeology at the Pontificia Universidad Católica del Perú and completed his PhD in anthropology at the University of Pittsburgh in 2011. His research focuses on the role of ideology in the development of social power on the pre-Hispanic Peruvian Central Coast, and it has been published in English and Spanish. His research has been funded by, among other sources, grants from the National Science Foundation and the Howard Heinz Endowment for Latin American Archaeology. He is currently a staff researcher at the Institute for Peruvian Studies and teaches archaeology at the Pontificia Universidad Católica del Perú.

Jane McIntosh studied archaeology at the University of Cambridge and wrote her PhD thesis (1982) on the Iron Age megalithic tombs of South India. Her more recent research has focused on the Indus civilisation and particularly its trading relations with contemporary third-millennium cultures. She has worked on excavations in Britain, Europe and Asia and has taught at Cambridge, where she was recently a Senior Research Associate. Since the 1980s she has mainly worked as a freelance writer of books and articles on archaeology and prehistory for both the general public, including schoolchildren, and academic audiences.

Georgina Muskett specialises in the art of the ancient Greek world. She studied ancient history and archaeology at the University of Liverpool, obtaining a doctorate in Mycenaean art. She has undertaken museum research and teaching at the University of Liverpool and more recently has been Curator of Classical Antiquities with National Museums Liverpool. Her publications include books and articles that draw on her research in Aegean prehistory, Greek painted pottery and sculpture and subjects related to the collections of National Museums Liverpool.

Margarete Prüch studied East Asian Art History, Sinology and European Art History in Bonn and Heidelberg. For her thesis (1995) on Chinese Lacquer of the Han-dynasty she received a one-year German Academic Exchange Service scholarship at the Beijing University, followed by studies in Taiwan and the USA. Since then she has been teaching East Asian Art History and Archaeology, as well as Chinese, has held appointments as curator for several exhibitions, and received a grant from the Commission for Archaeology of Non-European Cultures (KAAK) in Bonn. In recent years she has contributed essays to several exhibition projects and books on East Asian Archaeology.

Colin Renfrew (Lord Renfrew of Kaimsthorn) is Emeritus Disney Professor of Archaeology at Cambridge University, where he is a Senior Fellow of the McDonald Institute for

Archaeological Research. He is the author of many influential books on archaeology and prehistory, including (with Paul Bahn) *Archaeology: Theories, Methods, and Practice*, which is one of the standard text-books on the subject.

Anne Solomon is an archaeologist who received her doctorate on South African rock art from the University of Cape Town in 1995. Before becoming an independent researcher she was a senior curator at a national museum and a Postdoctoral Research Fellow of the Getty Center for the History of Art and the Humanities (Los Angeles). Her specialist research field is the rock paintings attributed to southern African hunter-gatherer peoples and the ethnographies of San peoples that have aided understanding of the rock images. Among her current research interests are questions of visuality and the 'art' of rock art.

Igor Tikhonov studied archaeology at St Petersburg State University, where his thesis was devoted to the development of archaeology at St Petersburg University from 1724 to 1936. His 2013 doctoral thesis is on the institutionalisation of archaeology in St Petersburg (eighteenth to early twentieth centuries). Since 1986 he has been Director of the University History Museum at St Petersburg University. He has also taught in the university's Department of Archaeology. His main scientific interests are the history of archaeology, the history of universities, the history of human sciences, museology and the preservation of cultural and scientific heritage.

Joyce Tyldesley studied archaeology at the University of Liverpool, before moving to Oxford to study for a DPhil in prehistoric archaeology. After a year teaching prehistory at Liverpool University she went freelance in the late 1980s, devoting herself to writing books on archaeology and Egyptology, and developing a research interest in the women of ancient Egypt. In 2006 she started to direct the online Egyptology courses at the University of Manchester, where today she is Senior Lecturer in Egyptology and an Honorary Research Associate of The Manchester Museum.

PREFACE

Paul Bahn

The *Cambridge Illustrated History of Archaeology*, a volume edited by myself and with contributions by an outstanding international team of specialists, was published in 1996. It presented the history of the subject in chronological fashion and met with great success, even being translated into Chinese. Since it has now gone out of print, a new volume is needed; but rather than produce the same thing again, it seems like a good idea to tackle the subject in a different way – on a regional basis, with chapters devoted to different parts of the world, including Russia whose rich archaeological history is rarely included in such studies. Within this structure, however, the spotlight is placed on a whole series of noteworthy individuals, many of them familiar names to the public, others less so but nevertheless of great importance. Some of the major methods applied to archaeological research have also been included in separate spreads. Some of the specialists in this new volume also contributed to that of 1996.

In the seventeen years since the last study, many books have appeared on various aspects of archaeology's history – most notably the major five-volume *Encyclopedia*, edited by Tim Murray – and interest in archaeology's history continues to thrive through the *Bulletin* devoted to it, which has been appearing since 1990. Clearly, following the remarkable lead given by Glyn Daniel and others in the second half of the twentieth century, the history of archaeology has become an important subject in its own right. Biographies of notable scholars and collections of papers on historic themes are published with some frequency.

The term 'archaeology' today means literally the study of the ancient, and has come to denote the investigation of the remains of the human past, from the very first artifact all the way to yesterday's garbage. First coined, naturally enough, by the Greeks ('arkhaiologia' or discourse about ancient things), it was originally applied to remote periods of history – for example, in the reign of the emperor Augustus, Dionysius of Halicarnassus wrote a great history of Rome from its beginnings to the Punic Wars, and called it *Roman Archaeology*.

The term 'archaeologist', however, appeared in the first centuries AD and had a somewhat specialised meaning. In Greek lands it denoted a category of actors who recreated ancient legends on stage through dramatic mimes. Subsequently, both words disappeared, and were not reinvented until Jacques Spon, a seventeenth-century doctor and antiquary in Lyons with a great interest in Roman antiquities, introduced not only 'archaeology' but also 'archaeography'. The former persisted, and entered international vocabulary.

It may seem amusing to imagine 'archaeologists' as players, cavorting on stage and enacting ancient legends, but in fact little has really changed. The modern phenomenon of archaeology, as outlined in this book, can arguably be considered as two separate but parallel soap operas. The first involves the archaeologists themselves – their different personalities, their influences, friendships and alliances, their rivalries and hatreds – and of course, as in any soap, the constant deaths and the arrival of new characters who breathe refreshing new life into the storyline. There are cliques, power groups and mafias, saints and scoundrels, bores and bullies, insiders and outsiders . . .

The second is archaeology's view of the past, constantly changing as new evidence arises or as old evidence is reinterpreted, and always closely interwoven with the personalities and interactions of the archaeologists themselves; as in any good serial, there are sudden surprises, plot twists and red herrings. Neither soap opera will ever end, but they both require a perpetual stream of novelties – eccentric characters, glamorous or spectacular finds – to maintain the all-important interest of their audience, without which they might be cancelled when times are hard.

The first soap, that of the archaeologists and their personalities, is all too factual; the second, the account of the past they put together, is inevitably fictional. Most archaeologists strive to be objective about the past, to discover the 'truth' about what went on, but the best that can be achieved without a time machine is an accepted fiction – one deduced from, and perhaps even tested against, the data, but a fiction nonetheless. We can never know what happened in the past – even for historic periods the written sources are always subjective and often mutually contradictory – but for periods before writing, archaeology is our only means of producing even an informed guess.

The narratives presented by archaeologists are often supported and enhanced by pictorial reconstructions of the past, and in recent years we have become aware that many such images – e.g., those of different kinds of fossil humans – have not only entertained and instructed the public but actually played an important role in influencing archaeological debate and in enforcing favoured interpretations.

This 'literary bias', where science proceeds by telling stories both verbal and visual, has allowed a number of conventional myths to take hold, in which powerful words or vivid pictures are found to be more romantic and inspiring than the plain facts. For example, when little Maria Sanz de Sautuola first spotted the great bison painted on the ceiling of Altamira, she did not cry out 'Toros, toros!' – if anything, she cried 'Mira, Papa, bueyes!' ('Look, Father, oxen!'); the dramatic image of horses being driven over the cliff-top at Solutré was created for the first prehistoric novel and never appeared in the factual literature about the site, since no such drive would have been possible there; Howard Carter's reply to Lord Carnarvon, who asked at the entrance of Tutankhamen's tomb (p82) if he could see anything, was not 'Yes, wonderful things' – according to Carter's own notes, he replied 'Yes, it is wonderful' (the more famous version was actually written later by Arthur Mace from Carter's notes); Heinrich Schliemann was not fired by an image of Troy in flames in a book given to him as a child – his interest in the subject arose far later and more deliberately; nor did he dash off a telegram from his dig at Mycenae to the King of Greece, claiming 'I have gazed upon the face of Agamemnon' (see p43) – that was invented later; and the moving and heroic mass suicide of the defenders of Masada was more likely a massacre, later adapted by the Jewish historian Josephus for his own ends – ironically, it was the archaeological excavations at the site that revealed his artistic licence, although Yigael Yadin, the excavator, tried hard to fit the archaeological data to the historian's more inspiring version of events (p70).

This book chronicles the slow development of archaeology, from the crude fumblings of early antiquaries to the sophisticated multidisciplinary projects of the present day; from the days of the polymath to those of extreme specialisation; from a scramble for curiosities and treasures to the search for answers to specific questions. It is the story of the growing realisation that evidence can survive, be recovered and be made to reveal its secrets; of a steady increase in the care with which the evidence was sought and interpreted; and of the close relationship between archaeology's progress and that of technology – from aerial photography to dating methods and computers, and from bone chemistry to the recovery and analysis of ancient DNA. One overriding development has been the ability to do more with less: consider, for example, the wide variety of information that can now be extracted from a single potsherd – its date and decoration, its raw materials and their source, the temperature of its firing, and perhaps even the contents of the vessel. In the book's conclusion, Colin Renfrew outlines his vision of how archaeology will continue to develop in the twenty-first century and beyond.

Archaeology is no longer just about finding things – though that can still be of great importance – but focuses more on finding out things. Although this book provides a truly worldwide survey of archaeology's development, some readers may still find it excessively Eurocentric in its emphasis on the discipline in terms of the 'Western experience'. We make no apologies for this. Archaeology was not created by non-Western experience. It was initiated predominantly in Europe, as people tried to make sense of the most distant past of which they were aware. Europeans strove to understand the Greeks and Romans through study of the Classical world; and they originally turned to Egypt and the Near East in order to find traces of the civilisations that touched the Classical world and the history of Christianity. These areas were seen as the cradle of the intellectual and spiritual life of the West. It was much later that archaeological interest spread to other areas. The emphasis on Europe is therefore inevitable, the result of historical accident.

The greatest difficulty in putting the volume together was in choosing what to include and what to leave out. It goes without saying that the history of world archaeology is so vast a subject that it could not possibly be encompassed adequately in a book of this length: all contributors could easily have filled it with material from their own region. Instead we sought a balance between the well-known and the unfamiliar, between archaeology's 'greatest hits' and the events or finds which, though perhaps unspectacular, were of the greatest importance to the subject's progress.

Paul Bahn
April 2013

Further reading

Alcina Franch, J. 1995. *Arqueólogos o Anticuarios. Historia Antigua de la Arqueología en la América Española.* Ediciones del Serval: Barcelona.

Bahn, P. G. (ed.) 1995. *The Story of Archaeology. The 100 Great Discoveries.* Barnes & Noble: New York/Weidenfeld & Nicolson: London.

Bahn, P. G. (ed.) 1996. *The Cambridge Illustrated History of Archeology.* Cambridge University Press: Cambridge.

Bahn, P. G. (ed.) 2008. *The Great Archaeologists*. Southwater: London.

Bernal, I. 1980. *A History of Mexican Archaeology*. Thames & Hudson: London.

Bon, F., Dubois, S. and Labails, M-D. (eds) 2010. *Le Muséum de Toulouse et l'Invention de la Préhistoire*. Editions du Muséum de Toulouse: Toulouse.

Ceram, C. W. 1951. *Gods, Graves and Scholars: The Study of Archaeology*. Knopf: New York.

Ceram, C. W. 1971. *The First American. A Story of North American Archaeology*. Harcourt Brace Jovanovich: New York.

Chakrabarti, D. K. 1988. *A History of Indian Archaeology from the Beginning to 1947*. Munshiram Manoharlal Publishers: New Delhi.

Clark, G. 1989. *Prehistory at Cambridge and Beyond*. Cambridge University Press: Cambridge.

Cohen, G. M. and Sharp Joukowsky, M. (eds) 2004. *Breaking Ground: Pioneering Women Archaeologists*. Michigan University Press.

Daniel, G. 1967. *The Origins and Growth of Archaeology*. Pelican: Harmondsworth.

Daniel, G. 1975. *150 Years of Archaeology*. Duckworth: London.

Daniel, G. 1981. *A Short History of Archaeology*. Thames & Hudson: London.

Daniel, G. (ed.) 1981. *Towards a History of Archaeology*. Thames & Hudson: London.

Daniel, G. and Chippindale, C. (eds) 1989. *The Pastmasters. Eleven Modern Pioneers of Archaeology*. Thames & Hudson: London.

Daniel, G. and Renfrew, C. 1988. *The Idea of Prehistory*. Edinburgh University Press: Edinburgh.

Daux, G. 1966. *Histoire de l'Archéologie*. 'Que sais-je?' No. 54, Presses Universitaires de France: Paris.

Díaz-Andreu, M. 2002. *Historia de la Arqueología, Estudios*. Ediciones Clásicas: Madrid.

Díaz-Andreu, M. and Stig Sørensen, M. L. (eds) 1998. *Excavating Women. A History of Women in European Archaeology*. Routledge: London.

Duval, A. (ed.) 1992. *La Préhistoire en France. Musées, Ecoles de Fouille, Associations du XIxe Siècle à nos Jours*. Actes du 114e Congrès National des Sociétés Savantes (Paris 1989). Editions du Comité des Travaux Historiques et Scientifiques: Paris.

Dyson, S. L. 2006. *In Pursuit of Ancient Pasts. A History of Classical Archaeology in the Nineteenth and Twentieth Centuries*. Yale University Press: New Haven.

Elliott, M. 1995. *Great Excavations: Tales of Early Southwestern Archeology, 1888–1939*. School of American Research Press: Santa Fe.

Fagan, B. 1975. *The Rape of the Nile: Tomb Robbers, Tourists and Archaeologists in Egypt*. Charles Scribner's: New York.

Fagan, B. 1977. *Elusive Treasure. The Story of Early Archaeologists in the Americas*. Charles Scribner's: New York.

Fagan, B. 1996. *Eyewitness to Discovery*. Oxford University Press: Oxford.

Fagan, B. M. 2004. *A Brief History of Archaeology: Classical Times to the Twenty-First Century*. Prentice Hall: Upper Saddle River, NJ.

Fernández, J. 1982. *Historia de la Arqueología Argentina*. Asociación Cuyana de Antropología, Tomos 34/35, *Anales de Arqueología y Etnología*: Mendoza.

Gräslund, B. 1987. *The Birth of Prehistoric Chronology*. Cambridge University Press: Cambridge.

Grayson, D. K. 1983. *The Establishment of Human Antiquity*. Academic Press: New York.

Groenen, M. 1994. *Pour une Histoire de la Préhistoire*. Jérôme Millon: Grenoble.

Horton, D. 1991. *Recovering the Tracks. The Story of Australian Archaeology*. Aboriginal Studies Press: Canberra.

Hurel, A. 2007. *La France Préhistorienne de 1789 à 1941*. CNRS: Paris.

Kehoe, A. B. 1998. *The Land of Prehistory. A Critical History of American Archaeology*. Routledge: New York & London.

Klindt-Jensen, O. 1975. *A History of Scandinavian Archaeology*. Thames & Hudson: London.

Laming-Emperaire, A. 1964. *Origines de l'Archéologie Préhistorique en France*. Picard: Paris.

Lartet, Breuil, Peyrony et les autres. Une histoire de la préhistoire en Aquitaine. 1990. Ministère de la Culture: Paris.

Lloyd, S. 1980. *Foundations in the Dust: A Story of Mesopotamian Exploration* (2nd edition). Thames & Hudson: London.

Malina, J. and Vasicek, Z. 1990. *Archaeology Yesterday & Today*. Cambridge University Press: Cambridge.

Marsden, B. M. 1974. *The Early Barrow-Diggers*. Shire Publications: Princes Risborough.

Marsden, B. M. 1984. *Pioneers of Prehistory. Leaders and Landmarks in English Archaeology (1500–1900)*. Hesketh: Ormskirk.

Murray, T. (ed.) 1999. *Encyclopedia of Archeology. The Great Archaeologists* (2 vols). ABC-Clio: Santa Barbara.

Murray, T. (ed.) 2001. *Encyclopedia of Archeology. History and Discoveries* (3 vols). ABC-Clio: Santa Barbara.

Norman, B. 1987. *Footsteps. Nine Archaeological Journeys of Romance and Discovery*. BBC Books: London.

Orellana Rodríguez, M. 1996. *Historia de la Arqueología en Chile*. Bravo y Allende: Santiago.

Piggott, S. 1976. *Ruins in a Landscape: Essays in Antiquarianism*. Edinburgh University Press: Edinburgh.

Reyman, J. E. (ed.) 1992. *Rediscovering our Past: Essays on the History of American Archaeology*. Avebury: Aldershot.

Richard, N. 2008. *Inventer la Préhistoire. Les Débuts de l'Archéologie Préhistorique en France*. Vuibert/Adept-Snes: Paris.

Robertshaw, P. (ed.) 1990. *A History of African Archaeology*. James Currey: London.

Schavelzon, D. 1983. La primera excavación arqueológica de América. Teotihuacán en 1675. *Anales de Antropología* (Mexico) 20: 121–34.

Schlanger, N. (ed.) 2002. Ancestral Archives. Explorations in the History of Archaeology. *Antiquity* 76(291), March: 127–238.

Schnapp, A. 1993. *La Conquête du Passé. Aux origines de l'archéologie*. Editions Carré: Paris (1996. *Discovering the Past*. British Museum Press: London; Abrams: New York).

Silberman, N. A. 1982. *Digging for God and Country. Exploration, Archaeology, and the Secret Struggle for the Holy Land, 1799–1917*. Alfred A. Knopf: New York.

Sklenár, K. 1983. *Archaeology in Central Europe: The First 500 Years*. Leicester University Press: Leicester.

Stiebing, W. H. 1993. *Uncovering the Past. A History of Archaeology*. Oxford University Press: Oxford.

Tantaleán, H. 2013. *Peruvian Archaeology. A Critical History*. Left Coast Press: Walnut Creek, CA.

Trigger, B. G. 2006. *A History of Archaeological Thought*. (2nd edition) Cambridge University Press: Cambridge.

Van Riper, A. B. 1993. *Men Among the Mammoths. Victorian Science and the Discovery of Human Prehistory*. Chicago University Press: Chicago.

Willey, G. R. (ed.) 1974. *Archaeological Researches in Retrospect*. Winthrop: Cambridge, MA.

Willey, G. R. 1988. *Portraits in American Archaeology. Remembrances of Some Distinguished Americanists*. University of New Mexico Press: Albuquerque.

Willey, G. R. and Sabloff, J. A. 1993. *A History of American Archaeology*. (3rd edition). Freeman: New York.

Also the *Bulletin of the History of Archaeology*, since 1990.

There are innumerable biographies and autobiographies of individuals mentioned in this book – references can be found in the more general works listed above, as well as at the end of some chapters, or by searching on the web.

1

THE ARCHAEOLOGY OF ARCHAEOLOGY: PRE-MODERN VIEWS OF THE PAST

Paul Bahn

Introduction

Like any area of study, archaeology has no fixed point of origin. A certain curiosity about the past seems to be widespread among human beings and is by no means a new phenomenon. The marked interest in archaeology displayed by modern royalty, especially in Britain and Scandinavia, also seems to have remote and eminent precursors.

People have always been aware that others came long before them. Before archaeology or even antiquarianism had come into existence, knowledge of these past times came only from written records, oral histories, religious beliefs, legends and superstition – in many rural areas this remained true even into the twentieth century. The most obvious relics of the past were the standing monuments or ruins, often shrouded in mystery and folklore. They stimulated the imagination and were often attributed to the fabulous heroes of mythology, to demons or elves, with the larger ones naturally being ascribed to giants. In some Christian communities, ancient monuments were eventually linked to the devil, while prehistoric rock art sites and megalithic tombs in south-west Europe were often given names linking them with the Moorish conquerors of the early medieval period.

The fact that most people travelled little, and occupied or worked in the same places for generations, engendered a strong sense of lineage and continuity in the ancient world and an attachment to native soil; but neither in ancient times nor in the medieval world was there yet any grasp of the fact that this soil could be a source of information about the past. Most antiquities came to light accidentally, through ploughing or construction work; any digging for objects involved a search for treasure, or – in medieval Europe – for saints' relics. The first glimmerings of archaeology lay with the pioneers who not only took a closer interest in the past but also realised that a history different from that of, for example, Classical texts, could be gleaned from traces left behind in the soil and landscape.

The earliest known 'archaeological' probings are usually reckoned to be those of Nabonidus, last native king of Babylon. The Mesopotamians looked on their past with reverence and this prompted them to preserve and restore earlier monuments and temples, on occasion excavating to trace lost structures, and to search records in order to revive earlier traditions. Nabonidus (r. 555–539 BC) thus excavated a temple floor down to a foundation stone laid 3200 years earlier. He was concerned with tracing out the floor plans of ruined temples and collecting artifacts from these 'excavations'. Nabonidus was not an early archaeologist, however much his techniques may have resembled those of nineteenth-century archaeology. However, his daughter En-nigaldi-nanna had a special room in her house for her collection of local antiquities.

A fifth-century princess in Thrace (the eastern Balkans) had a collection of Stone Age axes in her grave; and even divine emperors were not immune to the attractions of 'archaeology' – the historian Suetonius informs us that the Roman emperor Augustus, in the first century BC, 'had collected the huge skeletons of extinct sea and land monsters popularly known as "giants' bones"; and the weapons of ancient heroes.' This interest in 'ancient heroes' can be traced back to Homer, often considered the 'Father of Archaeology' for his role in turning people's eyes to the past, through his descriptions of the Trojan War in the *Iliad*, and of different peoples in the *Odyssey*.

The Near East

Mesopotamia, the region of western Asia defined by the Euphrates and Tigris rivers, enjoyed a roughly 2500-year literary 'stream of tradition', with another 1000 years encoded in myth and oral tradition. The ancient prestige of Mesopotamia ensured that many of its traditions passed into the literature of adjoining regions, including the Bible. This literary tradition included a variety of ostensibly historical documents, such as king lists, chronicles, annals, epic poems, lamentations and other forms. This literature was accumulated from its third millennium BC beginnings, repeatedly copied as part of the training of scribes and disseminated through libraries. By the time of the great Assyrian kings (in northeast Mesopotamia) and of Nebuchadnezzar in the first millennium BC, educated Mesopotamians were heirs to a long historical consciousness. The Bible, Classical literature and early Christian writings preserved in the Western tradition a memory of Iron Age civilisations in western Asia. The historical sections of the Bible like Kings and Nehemiah describe the petty kingdoms of southern Palestine (Israel, Judea, Samarra and their neighbours) and their relations with the neighbouring Phoenician and Aramaean kingdoms to the north and with the Assyrian, Babylonian and Persian empires.

The Classical world

Classical literature provided another view of the 'oriental', and particularly of the Persians. The Greek perspective on the Persians combined admiration of social and military virtues with contempt for political subservience and 'oriental despotism'; after the failed Persian invasions of Greece in the fifth century BC, the Greek attitude also carried a smug conviction of Hellenic superiority. At the same time Classical literature established a western stereotype of 'oriental despotism', it also preserved a memory of eastern cities, civilisations and history. Herodotus, an admirer of the Persians, left a description of Babylon that guided antiquarian research well into the nineteenth century. Other Classical historians and geographers also recorded details of various places and cultures east of the Mediterranean as far as India, especially in the wake of Alexander's conquests and the later Roman sea trade. While their details are often literally fabulous, many of these descriptions have proven valuable sources. For example, *The Periplus of the Erythraean Sea*, an anonymous trading manual of the first century AD, inventories the goods available in the ports of the Indian Ocean from East Africa and Malaysia.

The body of Classical literature also contains information that was crucial to the eventual decipherment of cuneiform scripts and the early study of Mesopotamian political history. And a Babylonian priest named Berossus even wrote, in Greek, a history of his country from the creation to Alexander the Great's invasion in the fourth century BC.

The emergence of Greece from the so-called Dark Ages in the eighth century BC led to a renewed interest in the extant remains from the Bronze Age. In particular the monumental Mycenaean 'beehive' tombs were markers of groups who had gone before. As states tried to find their identity these tombs appear to have been seen as the burial places of the forerunners of the community. As a result many Mycenaean tombs seem to have attracted offerings that have been interpreted as veneration for heroes. One tomb where such Early Iron Age activity occurred was at Menidhi in Attica. Its contents include pots decorated in the Geometric style with scenes of processing chariots, an allusion to earlier periods reflected in heroic oral poems like Homer's *Iliad*.

These Mycenaean tombs were also used in subsequent periods. During building work in the Athenian agora, the market place of ancient Athens, a tomb was uncovered by accident during the fifth century BC and offerings in the form of oil containers were left. Likewise in the hellenistic period (the final centuries BC) tombs seem to have again attracted offerings.

The construction of new towns and the erection of new buildings sometimes brought to light remains of former times. When Julius Caesar laid out the new town of Capua (Casilinum) near Naples, the biographer Suetonius records that 'a number of vases of ancient workmanship' were found in 'very old tombs'; while the geographer Strabo tells us that when Caesar founded a Roman colony on the site of ancient Corinth in Greece, his soldiers discovered numerous sixth- and seventh-century BC pots and bronzes of such quality that every tomb was rifled and the objects were sold for high prices in Rome as 'Necrocorinthia' (i.e., from the tombs of Corinth) – an early example of grave-looting and trading in antiquities.

In Greece itself there was a continuing fascination for the past even when incorporated into the Roman Empire. In the second century AD the geographer and historian Pausanias wrote what was in effect a travel guide to the monuments in Greece. In some parts, monuments and artifacts were placed against one of the key events of Greek history – the defeat of the Persian invasions in the early fifth century. Elsewhere he came across ruined temples in the countryside, which in his view had been left derelict since their destruction by the Persian invader. He noted that the paintings in the fifth-century BC sanctuary of Theseus at Athens had deteriorated through the ravages of time.

The past continued to be revered even after the fall of the western Roman empire. As Christianity became established in the lands of the Mediterranean, pagan cults started to be abandoned. Yet in spite of this, church officials started to build up collections of ancient statuary. A Byzantine chronicler recorded an array of major statues from the Classical world in the palace of Lausus – destroyed by fire in AD 475 – at Constantinople: these included Praxiteles' famous statue of Aphrodite from Knidos, the statue of Lindian Athena given to the sanctuary by Amasis the Egyptian, and finally Pheidias' gold and ivory cult statue of Zeus from the main temple at Olympia.

Medieval Europe

The Europe of the Middle Ages saw a potent mixture of Christian belief and popular mythology. From the story in the Book of Genesis the geographical origin of the human race was placed in the Near East, both at the Creation and after the Flood when Noah's sons repopulated the earth. Paganism was thought to have developed by a process of degeneration as people moved away from the Near East and lost touch with the mainstream of Jewish and Christian belief. Pagan monuments were thus considered the work of degenerate peoples and wherever possible were destroyed, neutralised or Christianised. Standing stones or menhirs were sometimes Christianised by having a cross carved into their surface or on their top. Churches were built alongside major prehistoric ritual monuments such as Avebury, and many sacred springs were rededicated to Christian saints.

The standing stones or 'menhirs' erected in several regions of western Europe by Neolithic and Bronze Age societies, thousands of years before Christ, were seen by early Christian clergy as intolerable pagan symbols. Legends and beliefs still attached to them during the Roman period, even if they were no longer the focus for religious rituals. It was not always necessary to destroy them, however, since they could be rededicated as Christian monuments. The best examples are the menhirs of Brittany with tops recarved in the shape of a cross. In other cases, a cross was simply carved into the stone's surface. There is an example in the life of the sixth-century Welsh saint Samson. Landing one day in Cornwall, he saw people worshipping at a menhir and hastened to denounce their idolatry and convert them to Christianity. To set his seal on their conversion, he carved a cross in the menhir's surface with his own hand, using an iron tool.

Coupled with this was a general lack of historical awareness. The world was thought to have been created by God in a literal seven days, as part of a divine plan whose end was to be Christ's second coming and the Last Judgement. There was little understanding of long-term natural or cultural change. In medieval art, Old Testament prophets and New Testament characters alike are represented in the garb of contemporary medieval people. The idea that human technology and society had been constantly changing over the centuries barely registered in the medieval perception of time.

A third factor was the power of scholarly mythology. In the ninth century, the Welsh monk Nennius claimed that Brutus, a Trojan prince, had been the first to settle the British Isles after the ravages of the Biblical flood. A powerful argument in favour of this hypothesis was the proposed derivation of 'Britain' from 'Brutus'. Two centuries later, the Welsh chronicler Geoffrey of Monmouth, in his totally fictitious *History of the Kings of Britain*, felt able to put a precise date on the arrival of Brutus in the southwest: 1170 BC. Similar mythologies and speculative genealogies were developed on the European mainland, where the Goths, for example, were thought to descend from Gog, a grandson of Noah mentioned in the Bible.

There are cases of early and unusual interest in antiquities in central and eastern Europe. In some cases, this interest was mercenary: finds of ancient silver coinage enriched the state treasury. For instance, Gustav Vasa, king of Sweden, following a 1547 find of ancient coins in the Åland Islands, indicated that more such finds would be desirable. At other times, the way in which the finds manifested themselves provoked curiosity, as in the 'mysterious' appearance of pots: in his *Historia Polonica*, the chronicler Jan Długosz (1415–80) reported extraordinary occurrences near the town of Śrem, where whole ceramic vessels seemed to emerge from the ground as if by magic. At Śrem and other localities in western Poland such events had become commonplace and there was a long-standing folk tradition about the 'magic crocks' that sprang from the earth. In 1416, on the orders and in the presence of Władysław II Jagiello, king of Poland, excavations took place at Nochowo, which unearthed some of these vessels.

This event marked one of the first conscious efforts to investigate the remains of the prehistoric inhabitants of eastern Europe. We know today that the 'magic crocks' emerging from the ground were probably cremation urns from the Late Bronze Age (1200–700 BC): large urnfield cemeteries of buried vessels with ashes are distributed widely across east-central Europe. Legends of 'magic crocks' abounded throughout much of central Europe and corresponded closely with the area in which the Bronze Age Urnfield cultures flourished! The erosion of the soil that covered the shallow pits in which these urns were placed would have created an impression of their rising from the ground by themselves. Still, it is important to note that such reports engaged the interest of the monarch of what was then one of the largest states in this part of Europe.

Chroniclers, like Długosz, were especially common in eastern Europe, and they frequently set down tales and legends of cultural origins and homelands. Burial mounds were ascribed to 'pagans', while other excavated objects were curiosities. Długosz pondered the origins of two massive burial mounds near Kraków, speculating that they housed the remains of the legendary Krak, whom he identified as a Roman in an attempt to connect the early Poles with Classical antiquity. Megaliths (large prehistoric stone monuments) along the Baltic coast were also attributed to murky 'pagan' tribes or even to antediluvian giants. The German term *Hünenbett*, used to denote megalithic tombs, is derived from the Old German for 'giant's bed'.

There are also isolated incidents of what could be called 'historical archaeology'. For instance, in 1390 Prince Louis of Brzeg in Silesia undertook excavations at the Slavic stronghold at Ryczyn on the Oder in order to determine whether it was the seat of the bishops of Wrocław (Breslau) three centuries earlier. In 1091, excavations were carried out in Kiev in an attempt to find the grave of Theodosius, founder of the first Russian monastery. Battlefields were also subjects of study, with chroniclers noting the piles of slightly-buried human bones at some locations. But such excavations were rare in an era in which magic and mystery were the main explanatory tools.

Traces of Palaeolithic (Old Stone Age) people were encountered repeatedly in central and eastern Europe prior to the second half of the nineteenth century, but, as in western Europe, the interpretative framework was lacking to appreciate their significance. In eastern Europe, early finds were almost invariably linked to the discovery of mammoth bones of the last Ice Age. In 1679 a Cossack troop engaged in the digging of a mill dam near Khar'kov uncovered a collection of mammoth bones which, like finds of human and animal bones from caves and other sites in western Europe, were attributed to a giant. When the leader of the Cossack troop publicly exhibited a mammoth tooth several years later, Tsar Fyodor Alekseevich ordered a formal investigation of the site entailing excavation and measurement. But if artifacts and other traces of human occupation were encountered at this locality, they were not reported.

The Tsar's action set a pattern of state involvement in Russian archaeology that has continued to the present day. In 1718, Peter the Great issued instructions to civilian and military authorities throughout Russia to collect and record finds of 'ancient things in the soil, namely unusual stones, bones of animals, fish, or birds, unlike those we have now'. Among the various discoveries brought to Peter's attention were mammoth bones from the Don River, collected from what later became known as the famous concentration of open-air Palaeolithic sites near the village of Kostenki ('kost' being the Russian word for bone). The Tsar personally examined some of the mammoth bones from Kostenki, which he thought to be the remains of war elephants from a wandering army of ancient Greeks (similar interpretations were placed upon mammoth remains recovered in Germany during this period).

For centuries, European farmers had also been turning up humanly-flaked flints and polished stone implements as they ploughed their fields. Popular belief had explained them away as elf-shots or thunderbolts ('ceraunia', as the ancient Greeks had already christened them). The thunderbolt theory was even given scientific elaboration by some writers. In the mid-seventeenth century, for example, one authority described their origin as 'generated in the sky by a fulgurous exhalation conglobed in a cloud by the circumposed humour'. Such pseudo-scientific obfuscation did not help towards discovering the true nature of these strange objects, which gave rise to a wide variety of beliefs. Many virtues and marvellous powers were ascribed to these stones – Etruscans and Romans had used such ancient arrowheads and polished stone axes as amulets, and in southern France, until the late nineteenth century, shepherds would often put a polished stone axe in a bag around the neck of the leading ram to protect the flock, hang one in the sheepstalls or bury one on the threshold of the barn to protect the ewes from disease, or carry one themselves as an amulet.

Other continents

Similar beliefs existed in other parts of the world, such as Central Africa where polished axes were likewise thought to be thunderbolts and preserved by the inhabitants of the region for many generations, while in West Africa perforated stones were called thunderstones (kwes, sokpe, nyame akuma). Two bored stones from the western shore of Lake Tanganyika were given to E.C. Hore, a Master Mariner of the 1877 London Missionary Society Expedition to Central Africa, by local people who regarded them as messages from ancestors and kept them carefully in baskets or small huts. Indeed oral traditions throughout the dark continent indicate that an interest in ancestors and relics from the past existed long before the arrival of Europeans.

The first recorded finds of polished stone axes in India, from the 1840s to the 1860s, all came from beneath trees in villages: Mahadeo or Mahadeva is generally worshipped in Indian villages under a peepul tree and any polished stone axes found in the area are placed under this tree even today. In North America, Iroquoian sites of the fifteenth and sixteenth centuries AD were discovered to contain projectile points, stone pipes and native copper tools that had been made thousands of years earlier – clearly the Iroquois must have found and kept them as very special objects. Similarly, mammoth molars had been found and kept in the prehistoric, multi-storey pueblo of Paquime, in Chihuaha, Mexico, which was abandoned c. AD 1400. An Olmec stone mask was found as an offering at the Aztec Great Temple of Tenochtitlán, despite being 2000 years older than the temple; and it is said that some Inka emperors kept collections of centuries-old 'pornographic' Moche pottery!

Whereas commoners may display some curiosity about the past, it is the elites of any society which have an intrinsic and vested interest in their own origins: the ruling class in any emerging or fully fledged state society will have institutionalised attitudes to the past in order to maintain the separation of the elite classes from the peasantry. In the Far East for instance, as in other early state societies, incipient antiquarianism can be found in the earliest complex societies of the region. Usually this took the form of a literary and philosophical interest in the semi-legendary past, but the earliest example of a focus on material culture can be found in the Song Dynasty (AD 960–1279) of China. Confucianism, which had grown out of the great philosopher's teachings of the fifth century BC but was subsequently eclipsed by the tenets of Buddhism from the first century AD, was undergoing a revival in Song China. To give greater authority to the current regime, a reverence for the Golden Age of the past – an attitude developed by Confucius himself in the fifth century BC – was reinstated in Song China through the study and imitation of ancient bronzes preserved in court collections. These imitations of past forms were then used in current court rituals to legitimise and strengthen the rule of the government. Catalogues documented the artifact collections and included descriptions and line drawings of the objects; 119 titles of catalogues are known from literature and thirty actual catalogues have survived, the earliest written by Lu Dalin in 1092 documenting 210 bronzes and thirteen jades dating from the Shang to Han dynasties (1700 BC–AD 220) existing in both private and imperial Song-dynasty collections. Neo-Confucianism is still practised today in the annual festival cycle of South Korea, using objects such as the ocarina vessel flutes or suspended stone chimes copied from the Shang and Zhou Dynasties of China.

Such continuity in material cultural and ritual was possible because of the presence of texts and imperial collections of artifacts from previous ages. Interest in more mundane objects such as arrowheads or stone axes used by early inhabitants awaited later generations of scholars who were nevertheless influenced in their studies by the principles of Confucian analysis: that is, rational explanation of the natural world and its contents, accompanied by measurement, description and illustration. Several groups of incipient naturalists, concentrating their interests variously on rocks, herbs, fossils and artifacts, thus emerged in Edo-period (1603–1868) Japan within the Neo-Confucian philosophic traditions. The important aspect of these antiquarian interests, however, was that the artifacts found on the ground were assigned either to various 'primitive' peoples mentioned in the earliest chronicles of Japan dating to the early eighth century AD or to the aboriginal groups of Ainu who were only becoming known to Edoites at that time through the settlement of Hokkaido Island by urban emigrants. This means that the objects were not recognised as 'prehistoric' but only as 'primitive'. By relating all archaeological features and artifacts to peoples known through the early texts, Japanese scholars committed the same mistake of the British antiquarians who assigned all such prehistoric remains to the Greeks, Phoenicians, Celts or other historically known peoples.

For example, the Confucian historian Arai Hakuseki attributed the stone arrowheads in Japan to the 'Shukushinjin', ancient inhabitants of Manchuria according to Chinese historical works, not yet knowing of the prehistoric Jomon peoples who made them between the tenth and fourth centuries BC. It took half a century of psychologically wrenching research to sever the link with the historical texts; acknowledgement of the fully prehistoric nature of such artifacts was not accomplished in Japan until 1936, even though by that time the periods themselves had been named and quite well described through excavation and artifact analysis.

Archaeology as a discipline is usually thought to have been imported to East Asia from the West; yet the earliest excavations were conducted on tombs by local elites interested in their own family histories before Western influence. In 1692, before the introduction of the discipline of archaeology from the West, the first recorded excavations in Japan took place when a regional daimyo (feudal lord) dug two tombs to investigate a stone inscription. A similar excavation was undertaken in 1748 in southeastern Korea by the father of a local governor (see p152).

The search for a timescale

Although the idea that humankind was tens of thousands of years old had existed among the Greeks, Egyptians, Assyrians and Babylonians, as well as in ancient Mesoamerica, there was as yet no conception of prehistory in the scholarship of either West or East. The only framework for human affairs and the origins of the world lay in written documents and, especially in the West, in the Bible. The claim published in 1650 by James Ussher, Archbishop of Armagh, that the world was created at noon on 23 October in 4004 BC has often been the subject of ridicule in modern times. However, such attempts to develop a chronology for all of human history were a major focus of seventeenth-century scholarship and Ussher was by no means the first to put forward such a date: the Jewish calendar still places the creation of the earth at 3761 BC, while the Venerable Bede, the eighth-century English theologian, had estimated 3952 BC.

For its time, Ussher's figure was quite conventional. Contrary to a popular misconception, he did not produce it by adding up ages and dates of lineages in the Old Testament – this would have been impossible. It was simply an example of a comparison of the six days of God's creation with 6000 years for the earth's potential duration ('one day is with the Lord as a thousand years'), a widely accepted scheme which meant that the earth was created 4000 years before the birth of Christ and might endure 2000 years after it; Ussher's extra four years came from the fact that Herod died in 4 BC, making that (paradoxically) the year of Christ's birth. While some scholars such as Bede had argued for world creation in the spring, an appropriate season for birth, others supported autumn (the Jewish year began then and Hebrew scriptures were the basis of the whole scheme). Ussher chose the first Sunday after the autumnal equinox (October in the old Roman calendar) and arbitrarily began his chronology with the creation of light, which he assumed must have been at noon. Other scholars would equally arbitrarily choose the morning, as in this seventeeth-century quotation by Dr John Lightfoot in his book *A Few and New Observations on the Book of Genesis, the Most of them Certain, the Rest Probable, All Harmless, Strange and Rarely Heard of Before*:

> Heaven and earth, centre and circumference, were created
> all together in the same moment and clouds full of water . . .
> this took place and man was created by the Trinity on
> October 23, 4004 BC at nine o'clock in the morning.

To modern generations, the calculations of Ussher and Lightfoot appear grossly naive on a number of counts (though there are still some who regard the date of the Creation as fixed by faith). Yet these men were intelligent scholars and their conclusions came to be widely accepted in educated circles. Their naivety may largely be excused on two grounds. First, it was a feature of the age in which they lived to regard the Bible as God's infallible word, a text of supreme and unquestioned authority; and second, Ussher and Lightfoot were living in a pre-scientific age, before techniques had been developed enabling a chronology to be built up on the basis of natural science rather than hallowed text.

These were the first glimmerings of an attempt to understand the ancient past and place it within a firm chronological framework. Some pioneers were becoming aware that the soil could 'speak' about the past, as clearly as, and perhaps even more reliably and truthfully than, written texts.

Renaissance and reformation: old worlds and new

The period from the sixteenth to the eighteenth centuries saw the rise of antiquarianism – an increasing awareness of the remains of the past, coupled with unprecedented revelations about far-off, exotic societies around the world, some of which were equated with ancient peoples in appearance, behaviour and lifestyle.

By the end of the fifteenth century, European contact with the New World was increasing. When Columbus landed on the shores of the New World, it caused an intellectual upheaval of, literally, biblical proportions. Nowhere in the Bible was there mention of either the New World or its inhabitants; debate immediately centred on whether or not the Native Americans (misnamed Indians) were human beings, and if so, how their presence could be explained within the confines of the biblical paradigm. One popular theory was that the Indians were descendants of one or more of the so-called Lost Tribes of Israel, a position maintained to this day by the Mormon Church. The question of Indian humanity had hardly been addressed when the Europeans received an even greater shock: the discovery of civilisations as advanced and as powerful as their own in both Mesoamerica and South America (see Chapters 11 and 12). As early as 1675, the first archaeological excavation of the New World was carried out by Carlos Sigüenza y Góngora – a tunnel dug into the Pyramid of the Sun at Teotihuacan.

Early contact with North America was marked by the European powers attempting to exploit the continent for different reasons and using local tribes as mercenaries in their wars. The Spanish who came en masse into North America during the sixteenth century were primarily after gold and also after souls that could be converted to Catholicism: the Papal Bull of Paul III in 1537 decreed Native Americans to be human and therefore convertible. The French, who first sent the explorer Jacques Cartier (1491–1557) into the Gulf of St Lawrence, were interested in developing commercial resources such as fishing and the fur trade, although their own priests were not far behind. The English were interested in the lands of Canada for the fur trade, but their interest in the Eastern seaboard was primarily for land and settlement.

The attitudes of early Europeans to the American aboriginals they met varied between considering them as inhuman savages incapable of even the veneer of civilisation, and portraying them as noble savages, imbued with all the natural qualities that decadent Europeans had lost. For example, on the one hand, Cotton Mather (1663–1728), an American clergyman, believed the Indians to be too inhuman even to be convertible to Christianity. On the other hand, early nineteenth-century painters like George Catlin of Pennsylvania (1796–1872) portrayed the Plains Indians he met along the Middle Missouri as noble and romantic warriors, filled with a natural dignity and courage. Both of these attitudes were unrealistic and either way the Indian was treated unfairly. Earliest contact with Native Americans was filled with incomprehension on both sides and certainly there were few attempts, on the European side, to deal with Native Americans as equals. Moreover, European impressions of the Indians were coloured by judging them by European, rather than Indian, values.

Contact with the east

First-hand European acquaintance with contemporary and ancient Asia was intimately tied to trade and politics. By the end of the fourteenth century Venice enjoyed a near-monopoly of the trade in the eastern Mediterranean, while Genoa largely controlled access to the overland routes through the Black Sea. The commercial, military and diplomatic contacts between

Europe and Asia sparked in Europe a gradual accumulation of information about Asia. Commercial travellers to China, the Venetian Polo family in the thirteenth century being the best known example, reported economic and social conditions in Mesopotamia, Persia and India; diplomatic missions (e.g., Papal embassies to the Mongols in the thirteenth and fourteenth centuries) also returned with reports. While most accounts addressed existing conditions, some also contained references to ancient places. Benjamin of Toledo, a rabbi in Moslem Spain, undertook a world tour in the years 1160–73; while in Mesopotamia, he identified and described Nineveh and Babylon.

The pace of discovery accelerated sharply after 1498, the year Vasco da Gama landed in Calicut on India's southwest coast. There was an increased exploration of the overland routes from the eastern Mediterranean to the Indian Ocean and Central Asia, and so, despite the Portuguese direct sea route, during the sixteenth century much of the trade between Europe and Asia still moved overland between the Persian Gulf and the Mediterranean. European merchants normally purchased goods in Levantine caravan and port cities, for shipment home, while a smaller number travelled into Mesopotamia and Persia. Some of these merchant travellers reported the ruined ancient cities of these regions, in the light of the Biblical and Classical literature. Indeed, identification of Assur, Nineveh, Babylon and Persepolis became a common theme in Western travellers' literature.

Leonhart Rauwolff (1535–1596), a physician from Augsburg, visited Syria, Palestine and Mesopotamia between 1573 and 1576, describing Nineveh (Kuyunjik), and identifying Aqar Quf (the ancient Dur Kurigalzu, whose ruined ziggurat still rises about 57m above the ground) as the Tower of Babel. Passing through the area a decade later, the English merchant John Eldred described the Tower of Babel as covering a quarter of a mile to a side and constructed of sun-dried bricks laid with a mat of reeds between courses; Eldred compared the ziggurat's height to that of the newly built St Paul's in London. John Cartwright, another English merchant and cleric, visited Nineveh in 1603 and described the enormous size of the place and its general layout. Thomas Herbert visited Persepolis in 1628 as a member of an English embassy to the Persian court that was negotiating access to the Silk Road. The seventeenth-century Spanish ambassador to Persia, Don Garcias da Silva e Figueroa, also visited Persepolis and made copies of the cuneiform inscriptions there.

The accumulation of information was haphazard, responding to the individual whim of the traveller. Nevertheless, the first stirring of a more systematic antiquarian interest in the Near East appeared in the mid-seventeenth century. The learned societies of Europe increasingly adopted the practice of giving lists of appropriate questions to travellers going east. In some cases, these questions showed an antiquarian interest. For example, the Royal Society in London drew up questions about Persepolis in 1667 for a merchant who was going to Shiraz in Persia. Other merchants, seized with curiosity, took the initiative themselves. Two such men, on hearing rumours of a ruined city in the Syrian desert, attempted to travel there. Blocked in their first attempt (in 1678), by unsettled conditions, they eventually reached (in 1691) the ancient caravan city of Palmyra and their account of this journey, published by the Royal Society in 1695, describes the monuments they encountered; this might be considered the first specifically archaeological 'expedition' in the Near East.

First encounters with South Asia

Europeans encountered India and its past while colonising the subcontinent, and by the end of the seventeenth century they had firmly established themselves in South and Southeast

Asia. The colonial presence first of the Portuguese and then of the East India Companies had the obvious consequence of facilitating the investigation of ancient monuments in South Asia. The direct control over an increasing amount of Indian territory permitted European scholars access to Indian antiquities, unimpeded by the uncertain politics of the Ottoman and Persian empires. Just as elsewhere, the initial European introduction to Indian monuments came from travellers' reports. Impressionistic notices of ancient monuments, notably the rock-cut temples in the Bombay area (e.g., Elephanta, Kanheri and Ellora, dating to the later first millennium AD), appeared during the sixteenth and seventeenth centuries at the hands first of Portuguese and then of English authors. These accounts presented a mixture of admiration and disgust for the Indian monuments, so alien to the Biblical and Classical expectations more suited to western Asia.

Portuguese excursions beyond the Indian Ocean in the seventeenth century also brought them into contact with several state-level societies in southeast Asia. Rather than destroying them, however, as the European explorers had done with the high cultures in the New World, they negotiated trading treaties with the local courts, sometimes after forceful takeovers of existing ports. Some of the earliest Portuguese visitors in the early 1600s who encountered the remains of the earlier Khmer monuments in Cambodia, for example at Angkor Thom, had difficulty in recognising their indigenous nature: one author attributed them to Alexander the Great while another credited the Jews 'who settled in China'. This reflected the general Western reluctance to acknowledge that Easterners also had the power and capacity to create high civilisation and art.

The first antiquaries

In Europe, the ever-growing interest in national origins did not long remain satisfied with legends and fanciful stories, and with the expansion of education and literacy people began to look for more solid grounds for historical belief, despite Francis Bacon's observation that 'the most ancient times (except what is preserved of them in scriptures) are buried in silence and oblivion.' A crucial change in northwest Europe came in the sixteenth century, when people for the first time began to recognise that information about the prehistory and early history of their homelands could be gained from the study of surviving field monuments. This new interest led to the appointment of John Leland as King's Antiquary by Henry VIII in 1533. His promising start was followed by the Tudor antiquary and historian William Camden (1551–1623), who in 1586 published *Britannia*, the first general account of early British remains, including both Stonehenge and Hadrian's Wall (see Chapter 2).

These, the first British antiquaries, formed the beginnings of a tradition that was to last over 200 years. It was a development soon mirrored in other parts of northwest Europe. In Scandinavia, national awareness was heightened by the political separation of Denmark and Sweden in 1503. By the following century, both countries could boast distinguished antiquaries – Johan Bure in Sweden and Ole Worm in Denmark – who documented ancient remains (notably stones bearing the Viking script known as runes) and made important collections of antiquities. In Germany, too, the sixteenth and early seventeenth centuries witnessed a new interest in national antiquities. Here they had the advantage of a helpful Classical text: the *Germania*, an account of the early Germans written at the beginning of the second century AD by the Roman historian Tacitus. This formed the basis for the first accounts of early German history. It was to be some time yet before the Biblical chronology of the Creation was to be superseded by a strictly archaeological approach, but the foundations for a new understanding of the European past had been laid.

The early antiquaries of central and eastern Europe followed a pattern similar to that of western Europe, collecting relics and investigating monuments, although the megaliths (large prehistoric stone monuments) that focused much of the attention of the antiquaries of the Atlantic coasts of Britain, France, Spain and Scandinavia were generally absent from central and eastern Europe. Instead, antiquaries investigated barrows (burial mounds), of which there were many across this entire region; Iron Age and Slavic strongholds with their bank-and-ditch fortifications that were distinctive features of local landscapes; and, in the area along the Roman frontier, the forts and camps of the limes, the Roman boundary with the barbarian world.

Prehistory emerges

In 1685, at Cocherel in southern Normandy, a local nobleman, Robert Le Prévôt, was seeking stone to repair a lock gate on the River Eure. Near the top of a south-facing slope, overlooking the river, two slabs of stone were poking out of the soil. Assembling a band of workmen, Le Prévôt soon had these disinterred, only to find a third slab, previously hidden, alongside. This, too, was dug out, to reveal human bones two metres below the surface. At this point the stone-breaking operation became transformed into a careful archaeological excavation, as Le Prévôt and his team, consumed by interest in their discovery, abandoned their original intention and embarked on a painstaking recording and recovery of a prehistoric chambered tomb. By the end of the work they had found remains of twenty skeletons together with stone axes, pottery vessels and a mass of cremated ash.

Le Prévôt's discovery at Cocherel is remarkable not just for what he found – a Late Neolithic collective tomb constructed of megalithic slabs – but also for the way he performed the excavation, with a painstaking care worthy of modern techniques, and the minute detail in which he recorded what he found. Unlike so many of his contemporaries, Le Prévôt was not attracted by lust for buried treasure, but by a genuine desire to understand the monument he had unearthed. It is this, above all, which marks his discovery as a major landmark in the history of European archaeology.

The significance of the Cocherel excavation lived on into the following century. In 1719 Le Prévôt's brother, the priest Dom Bernard de Monfaucon, drew on the discovery of stone axes at the site to ascribe all tombs of this kind to 'some barbarous Nation, that knew not yet the Use either of Iron or of any metal'. This recognition of a pre-metal age formed the cornerstone on which the chronology of European prehistory was to be built.

It was a recognition that depended upon the discovery of the true nature of early stone tools. Yet the clues had long been there, not least in the flaked and polished stone artifacts brought back by European explorers from the Americas. This did indeed lead some people to realise that stone tools found in Europe were human artifacts, notably the Italian geologist Georgius Agricola (1490–1555), and Michel Mercati (1541–93), Superintendent of the Vatican Botanical Gardens and physician to Pope Clement VII. Mercati undertook an inventory of the Vatican's collections, which included 'ceraunia' and flint arrowheads, and he decided that they were humanly made, in a time before iron: a plate in his *Metallotheca*, published posthumously in 1717, includes a fine, typical Upper Palaeolithic blade.

However, such ideas only achieved general acceptance towards the end of the seventeenth century. Le Prévôt's discoveries at Cocherel provided important confirmation that these were indeed early stone tools. Conversely, they indicated the great antiquity of the monuments in which such tools were found. In 1720, the German antiquarian A.A. Rhode published his pioneering experiments in making flint objects in order to reconstruct the manufacturing techniques of the ancients. As mentioned earlier (p6), 'thunderbolts' had been collected and kept for centuries, ending up in 'cabinets of curiosities' from the Renaissance onwards. In 1723 a Frenchman, Antoine de Jussieu, compared the 'thunderstones' in such cabinets with stone axes from Canada and the Caribbean, and attributed the thunderbolts to a remote period when iron was unknown. Hence this Stone Age was established by applying ethnographical observations to the prehistoric remains – a method that would not become common until the publication a few years after Darwin's *Origin of Species*, of Daniel Wilson's *Prehistoric Man* in 1862 and John Lubbock's influential book of 1865, *Pre-historic times, as illustrated by ancient remains and the manners and customs of modern savages*.

A different application of New World ethnography is that of the artist John Wick who, in 1585, went with Raleigh to Virginia and drew not only Indians but also some ancient Britons and Picts who were all given many features in common. Native Americans were thus being used as sources of analogy and information on the appearance and the tools of ancient Europeans: in fact, John Aubrey wrote in 1659 that the ancient Britons of Wiltshire 'were 2 or 3 degrees, I suppose, less savage than the Americans.'

London's Society of Antiquaries was founded in 1707 by a small group of men interested in the study and publication of antiquarian research and became formally constituted in 1717, with William Stukeley (see Chapter 2) its first President. It began the publication of the journal *Archaeologia* in 1770. The British Museum was started with the purchase of a collection of coins, antiquities, paintings and a 5000-item library owned by Sir Hans Sloane who died in 1753. The museum was originally located in Montague House, bought specially to house the Sloane collection, but later moved to a purpose-built home that was completed in 1847. This grandiose building, on Great Russell Street, has been added to since then as the museum's collections and library have grown.

First inklings of a remote past

Flint tools from the Palaeolithic (Old Stone Age) were being discovered sporadically, but their importance was not yet recognised: for example, in c.1690 a big point of black flint was found in a gravel pit in Grays Inn Lane near London by John Conyers, a London pharmacist and antiquary. We now know that it was an Acheulian handaxe (several hundred thousand years old), and it was in some kind of association with 'elephant' (perhaps mammoth) bones; but at the time it was assumed to be a weapon used by a Briton to kill an elephant brought over by the Romans in the reign of Claudius.

The conception of early periods could not go beyond written memory: megalithic monuments, for example, were attributed to the Celts or pre-Roman Gauls, or other local peoples. It is true that the Roman writer Lucretius (98–55 BC) did allude to a 'time before writing which escapes us', a notion that has been called a 'non-archaeological prehistory'. Progress on the concept of the remote past was not long in coming, however.

The early antiquarians were, literally, 'Renaissance men' – polymaths, scholars with deep curiosity and profound knowledge about a wide range of subjects such as medicine or astronomy. But towards the end of this period, one can discern a transition towards something which, while not yet archaeology, was taking shape as a separate discipline: the construction of knowledge about the remote past through its material traces, and a means of explaining those traces as well as describing them. Scholars were edging towards the realisation that the ground and the landscape could be interrogated and read like a document.

2

ANCIENT EUROPE

The discovery of antiquity

Peter Bogucki

As we saw in Chapter 1, in *Historia Polonica* the Polish chronicler Jan Dlugosz (1415–80) reported extraordinary occurrences: whole pottery vessels emerged from the ground as if by magic. Throughout central Europe, long-standing folk traditions described 'magic crocks' springing from the earth. Less than two centuries later, Jan Johnston (1603–75), a physician of Scottish descent born in northwestern Poland, wrote in his 1632 *Thaumatographia Naturalis* 'the clay vessels found in the ground were burial urns, inside are the bones of the dead. In all . . . were ashes, and in some, rings. The ancients, we know, had the custom of burning the body and burying the cremated bones.' We know today the 'magic crocks' were Bronze Age cremation urns buried in shallow pits. Erosion of the soil around them created the impression that they rose spontaneously from the ground. The transition from their interpretation as magical occurrences to the recognition that they were burial urns reflects the stirring of European archaeological inquiry. Johnston's use of the term 'the ancients' indicates emerging realisation of a human past before texts and tales.

Chroniclers in Medieval and Renaissance Europe frequently set down tales of cultural origins and homelands. Large stone monuments were attributed to mythical figures. The tomb at Wayland's Smithy near Oxford was believed to be the forge of the Anglo-Saxon god Volund. William Camden (1551–1623) approached sites more analytically, writing in 1586 'artificial hills both round and pointed . . . called burrowes or barrowes . . . bones are found in them', thus correctly identifying them as tombs. In Sweden, King Gustavus Adolphus appointed Johan Bure (1568–1652) to be State Antiquary. In the seventeenth century, John Aubrey (1626–97) attempted a classification of Britain's prehistoric remains and correctly attributed them to pre-Roman peoples. Later, William Stukeley (1687–1765) attributed many prehistoric monuments to Druids known from Classical authors. Roman camps along the *limes*, the Roman boundary with the barbarian world, attracted attention in central Europe.

The principal framework for addressing human antiquity in the seventeenth and eighteenth centuries came from the Bible. Observations undermining the Biblical view were beginning to be made, however. Niels Stensen (1638–87), a Danish scholar known as Steno, drew the first geological profile in 1669 and concluded that lower layers pre-dated upper ones. Steno's Principle of Superposition is fundamental to all archaeological research and interpretation.

Another development of the sixteenth and seventeenth centuries was contact with non-European peoples in the Americas and the Pacific. The idea that rational beings (so established by papal decree in 1537) had practices, beliefs and technology different from those of Europeans was revolutionary. Perhaps ancient people also had a way of life different from that known from the Bible.

During the late eighteenth and early nineteenth centuries, we see the first glimpses of archaeology as an empirical science. The Enlightenment provided an appreciation of evidence as the basis for conclusions. Romantic speculations about Druids and Britons were complemented, although not replaced, with the quest for facts. Graves were rich sources of information. The Reverend Bryan Faussett (1720–76) dug into more than 700 Anglo-Saxon burial mounds in Kent during the mid-eighteenth century. Later, William Cunnington (1754–1810), under the patronage of Sir Richard Colt Hoare (1758–1838), excavated hundreds of mounds near Stonehenge in Wiltshire. One of the most important was Bush Barrow, containing a male skeleton with well-crafted copper, bronze and gold artifacts.

An important supporting art in the emergence of field archaeology was making detailed drawings of finds and their context. Today, these drawings may be all the information that survives. When the immense burial mound at Kivik in southern Sweden was opened in 1748, drawings were made of carved stone slabs along the entrance. The slabs are now lost, but the drawings survive. Depictions of people, tools and wheeled vehicles date the Kivik tomb to approximately 1000 BC.

Early mound-diggers did not worry about Steno's Law. John Frere (1740–1807), however, did follow this principle in his observations at a brick quarry at Hoxne in eastern England. At a depth of four metres, Frere recorded bones of extinct mammals in the same layer as worked stones, now known to be handaxes made by the earliest Europeans. He described his findings in the journal *Archaeologia*, concluding that they were of a 'very remote period indeed; even beyond that of the present world'. He accompanied his article with a drawing of the side of the clay pit, another example of early archaeological draughtsmanship.

The emergence of archaeology

The main conceptual breakthrough in European archaeology during the early nineteenth century came from the natural sciences. Here, too, the Bible posed constraints, particularly Noah's Flood. Bones of extinct animal species appeared to corroborate the flood story, creatures that did not make it onto the Ark and drowned. The zoologist Georges Cuvier (1769–1832) believed that local catastrophic events had shaped both geological structures and animal populations. Others believed that the Flood, or floods, were global events that required new episodes of creation. William Buckland (1784–1856), Anglican minister and Oxford professor of geology, wrote an 1823 book 'attesting the Action of a Universal Deluge', based on finds of 'antediluvian' mammal bones in caves. Stone and ivory artifacts and a human skeleton associated with these finds did not seem to trouble him.

A pharmacist from Narbonne in southeastern France, Paul Tournal (1805–72), posed the heretical proposition that associations among these finds were significant. Tournal's digging in caves yielded bones of extinct and modern animals, human bones and stone tools. In 1833, he coined the term 'antehistoric' to suggest an epoch before historical (i.e., Biblical) time. This revolutionary insight is the first documented instance of the concept of 'prehistory', a time of human existence prior to written records.

Eventually, the catastrophist school of earth science was superseded by the notion that geological processes observed in the present (sedimentation, erosion, etc.) took place continuously in the past and shaped the geological structure of the planet. It was no longer necessary to invoke floods to explain what was observed in the strata. William Smith (1769–1839), a canal builder, spent twenty years piecing together observations throughout England into a geological map. Later, Charles Lyell (1797–1875) formalised the notion of 'uniformitarianism' and accepted that extinct mammals co-existed with humans.

During the second quarter of the nineteenth century, a French customs official named Jacques Boucher de Perthes (1788–1868) began poking around railway and canal cuts along the Somme near Abbeville and recognised the same association of stone tools and animal bones that others had observed in caves. In the large open-air exposures, the stratification was clear and it was duplicated from one exposure to the next. He interpreted his finds in traditional catastrophist fashion and attributed them to people who lived before the flood, but the soundness of Boucher de Perthes' field observations and the fact that they could be replicated by other investigators resonated with intellectual trends in geology. Geologists visiting Abbeville, including Lyell, could see with their own eyes the association between flints and bones and draw their own secular conclusions. Excavations by William Pengelly (1812–94) in Brixham Cave in southwestern England were visited by geologists, again including Lyell, who saw animal bones and stone tools beneath an intact layer of stalagmite.

In the 1860s, once the concept of prehistoric people had begun to be accepted, a number of pioneering scholars began to unearth portable art objects from the last Ice Age in rock shelters and caves in southern France. Most prominent among these researchers were the

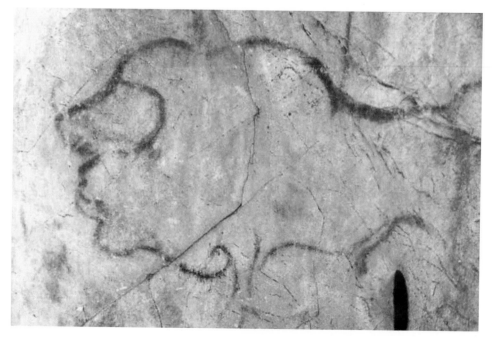

FIGURE 2.1 A bison drawn in outline in the cave of La Pasiega, Cantabria, northern Spain. Photo © Paul Bahn.

French scholar Edouard Lartet (1801–71) with the Englishman Henry Christy (1810–65), working primarily in the Dordogne, and the great French prehistorian Edouard Piette (1827–1906) in the Pyrenees. Eventually, artworks began to be noticed on the walls of caves and shelters – most notably in the Spanish cave of Altamira in 1879 – but it was not until 1902 that the existence of Ice Age cave art was finally accepted by the sceptical archaeological establishment. The most important figure in the study and recording of Ice Age art in those early days was a French priest, Henri Breuil (Box 2.1).

BOX 2.1 Henri Breuil (1877–1961)

Henri Edouard Prosper Breuil was one of the towering figures in Old World prehistory during the first half of the twentieth century, and was the pioneer of the study of Ice Age cave art.

Although he trained as a priest in his youth and remained a priest till his death, it was only a title since he was allowed to devote his whole existence to prehistory, undertook virtually no religious duties and made almost no contribution to the reconciliation of prehistory's findings with religious teachings.

The son of a lawyer, his childhood in northern France infused him with an intense love of Nature – especially of insects which remained a lifelong interest. An important

FIGURE 2.2 Henri Breuil.

early influence was his relative, the well-known geologist and archaeologist Geoffroy d'Ault du Mesnil, who showed him his collection of fossils and took the youth to the ancient sites of the Somme region. Here he also met Louis Capitan, who introduced him to the study of prehistoric tools.

He had the supreme good fortune, as a young man with a talent for drawing animals, to make the acquaintance of Edouard Piette and Emile Cartailhac (1845–1921), two of France's greatest prehistorians at the turn of the century, when they needed help with the study and illustration of Palaeolithic portable and cave art respectively. This led to Breuil becoming the world's leading authority on Palaeolithic art until his death. He discovered many decorated caves or galleries himself, and copied their art – by his own reckoning he spent about 700 days of his life underground. Although now seen as excessively subjective and incomplete, his tracings are nevertheless recognised as remarkable for their time. In some caves they constitute our only record of figures that have since faded or disappeared.

Breuil concentrated not only on Palaeolithic art, but also on the megalithic art of France and (during the First World War) the Iberian peninsula. In World War II he began a long campaign of copying rock art in parts of southern Africa. His concept of two cycles in the development of Palaeolithic art, the 'Aurignaco-Perigordian' followed by the 'Solutreo-Magdalenian' – two essentially similar but independent cycles, each progressing from simple to complex forms in engraving, sculpture and painting – was inconsistent and unsatisfactory, and was eventually replaced by the four 'styles' of André Leroi-Gourhan, themselves now in the course of abandonment. Breuil saw Palaeolithic art primarily in terms of hunting magic, thanks to simplistic use of selected ethnographic analogies, and he generally considered decorated caves to be accumulations of single figures, unlike Leroi-Gourhan who saw them as as carefully planned compositions.

An irascible and egotistical man, Breuil nevertheless had a lasting influence on numerous devoted friends and pupils. So ingrained was his image as the 'Pope of Prehistory' that he was often thought virtually infallible. It is only in recent years that it has become possible in France openly to criticise and re-examine his work like that of any other scholar. His huge legacy of publications and tracings has been found to contain many errors and misjudgements, but equally an abundance of profound insights that are only now being supported by new finds.

Recognition of human antiquity through natural science opened intellectual room for the study of prehistoric finds. No longer were antiquarians constrained by the short Biblical timescale. Humans were ancient and their technology changed dramatically over time. The challenge became to organise finds into the order in which they appeared in the past.

The three ages

In Denmark, a Royal Committee for the Preservation and Collection of National Antiquities was established in 1807 to protect archaeological sites and to act as a repository for artifacts found throughout the country. Within several years, its museum was filled with finds, primarily from graves and votive offerings in bogs. Christian Jurgensen Thomsen (1788–1865) got the job of organising the collections in 1816.

Thomsen grouped tools by material, with the earliest group made of stone, followed by bronze and finally iron. The concept of three successive ages of stone, bronze and iron had been proposed by the Roman writer Lucretius in the first century BC and subsequently by Renaissance scholars such as Michel Mercati (1541–93). Thomsen's brilliant touch, however, was recognising that the context of the stone, bronze and iron tools enabled other finds, such as pottery, to be linked to the three categories. Similar finds not found with cutting tools could be fitted into the same logical scheme of Stone Age, then Bronze Age and finally Iron Age.

The past could now be measured against a chronological yardstick, however imprecise, and organised sensibly. No longer were collections a confusing jumble. Most importantly, the public could make sense of them by seeing changes over time. When the Danish National Museum opened in 1819, displays were organised according to the simple and elegant Three-Age System. Later, Thomsen's protégé, J.J.A. Worsaae (1821–85) validated the sequence by stratigraphic excavations.

Archaeologists have since relied on the Three-Age System to provide a general structure for European prehistory. During the mid-nineteenth century, it allowed finds such as those of Ramsauer (Box 2.2) at Hallstatt to be related chronologically to discoveries elsewhere in Europe. It has been subdivided and refined, but it is the benchmark to which European archaeologists return for the most general divisions of human cultural development. Despite now being nearly 200 years old, the importance of Thomsen's contribution to European prehistory cannot be overestimated.

Swiss lake dwellings

Archaeology got a lucky break during the cold and dry winter of 1853–54. In the foothills of the Alps, water levels at lakes dropped up to 30 centimetres. Residents of Meilen in Switzerland noticed that receding water revealed a layer of black sediment and sticking out of this layer were stubs of wooden posts in rows. The dark sediment also contained animal bones, as well as pottery and tools made from wood, bone, antler and flint. A local schoolteacher contacted Ferdinand Keller (1800–81), president of the Antiquarian Society of Zürich.

Keller recognised the posts as the remains of houses and the artifacts as objects discarded or lost by their inhabitants. Their location at lakes triggered speculation about the nature of these settlements. Keller proposed that the houses were built on platforms over shallow water, connected to the shore by gangplanks. He referred to these settlements as 'pile dwellings', whose inhabitants dropped their rubbish into the surrounding water. More commonly, these sites are known as 'Swiss Lake Dwellings', although they are also found in Alpine parts of Germany, Austria, Slovenia, Italy and France.

Keller's romantic interpretation of the lake sites was embraced by both the public and archaeologists. Paintings and models propagated the notion of wooden islands. Artifacts from these sites were determined to be from an early farming society that we now know flourished between about 4000 and 2000 BC. In the late nineteenth century, they provided the definitive view of early European farmers, the benchmark to which other finds were compared.

The quantity and variety of artifacts from the lake dwellings were staggering. Wooden artifacts included picks, hoes, sickles, ladles, axe-handles, arrows, wheels and yokes. Water-logging had preserved objects made from plant fibres such as nets, baskets and ropes. Antler sockets were used to anchor stone axes into their wooden handles. Although domestic animals such as cattle, sheep and goats were present, many bones came from wild species such as red deer, beaver and boar. Plant remains included wheat and barley, wild fruits and nuts (crab apple, acorns, beech nuts and hazelnuts), vegetables (peas, beans, lentils), weeds and marsh plants.

Excavations in the early twentieth century led to abandonment of Keller's concept of wooden islands. Advances in geosciences made it possible to trace the pattern of rising and falling lake water and traces of floors and hearths were identified among the posts. By the early 1950s, archaeologists accepted that the settlements were built on the soft soil of lake shores, and the posts were both footings to keep the structures from sinking and vertical structural elements supporting walls and roofs. As lake levels rose, abandoned settlements were covered by silt, which preserved the rubbish layer and bottoms of the posts.

BOX 2.2 Johann Georg Ramsauer (1795–1874)

J. G. Ramsauer, Bergmeister in Hallstatt, geb. 1797, gest. 1876.
(Nach einer alten Photographie).

FIGURE 2.3 Johann Georg Ramsauer. From K. Kromer, *Das Gräberfeld von Hallstatt*, 1959.

Near Salzburg in Austria, mining engineer Johann Georg Ramsauer began excavations of the Early Iron Age cemetery at Hallstatt in 1846. Hallstatt is an idyllic lakeside town in the Salzkammergut, whose mountains conceal vast concentrations of rock salt, of value for the preservation of meat and fish. Salt mining began in the Salzbergtal, a narrow valley above Hallstatt, at least 3000 years ago. Ramsauer started working for the state salt mines as an apprentice at the age of thirteen. By 1831, he had become *Bergmeister* in charge of mining operations. Ramsauer lived adjacent to the mines in a medieval fortress, the Rudolfsturm, sired an enormous family (twenty-two children survived childbirth), and indulged his passion for archaeological excavation.

Between the Rudolfsturm and the salt mine lay an immense Iron Age cemetery, where Ramsauer excavated about a thousand graves between 1846 and 1863. About fifty-five per cent of the graves are skeletal burials and forty-five per cent are cremations. They yielded thousands of artifacts, including lavish grave offerings of bronze and iron. Each grave was cleaned, sketched and described in writing. Examples of remarkable water-colour drawings by the painter Isidor Engel can be seen on display at Hallstatt today.

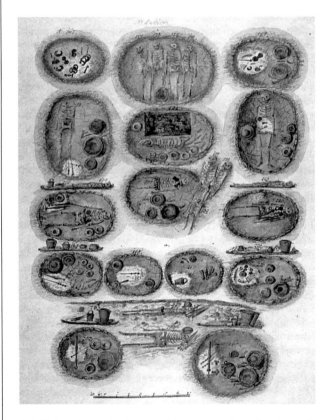

FIGURE 2.4 A sample of the striking watercolour drawings of both skeletal and cremation burials at Hallstatt made by Ramsauer's assistant Isidor Engel, showing the locations of vessels and other grave offerings in relation to the skeletons or cremated bones.

Unfortunately, Ramsauer's meticulousness did not extend to cataloguing pottery or bones, nor did he manage to prepare the information for publication before he died in 1874.

The handwritten documentation from Ramsauer's excavations disappeared after his death only to resurface in a Vienna used-book store in 1932. The finds were finally published in 1959 by Karl Kromer (1924–2003). Other fragments of documentation, including brochures prepared for visits to the site by Ludwig I of Bavaria in 1861 and the Emperor Franz Josef in 1855 and 1856, introduced inconsistencies that cast doubt on the reliability of Ramsauer's notes. Nonetheless, as F.R. Hodson notes (*Hallstatt, the Ramsauer Graves: Quantification and Analysis*, Bonn, 1990), 'pioneer failings in excavation and recording are not sufficient to obscure the abundance of useful information that Ramsauer managed to transmit to posterity.'

Making sense of the past

By the last decades of the nineteenth century, archaeology was firmly established as a field of scholarly inquiry. Organised excavations were routinely undertaken, not only in caves and burial mounds but also on ancient cemeteries and settlements across Europe. While techniques and documentation may have left something to be desired, many were carried out systematically and the finds stored in museums, where they could be studied. Archaeologists began to share information at congresses and in publications. Standards for recording of archaeological data were advanced by field research such as that of Pitt Rivers (Box 2.3) at Cranbourne Chase. The ability to compare finds from one site to another led to refinement of the framework provided by the Three-Age System and the development of regional sequences of artifact types.

The Industrial Revolution uncovers sites

Beginning in the nineteenth century, strong motivation for archaeological research in Europe came from a desire to recover evidence of the past in the face of industrial development. Cutting through hillsides and banks for roads and train lines exposed prehistoric sites while expansion of towns disturbed sites previously untouched under farmland. Deeper ploughing brought up increasing amounts of archaeological material.

An important factor in the explosion of archaeological discovery in the late nineteenth and early twentieth centuries was the use of reinforced concrete. Builders such as François Hennebique (1842–1921) and Robert Maillart (1872–1940) pioneered the use of reinforced concrete for many types of buildings, including bridges, gas holders and warehouses. Structural concrete is a mixture of cement and gravel, and pits were opened all across Europe to extract the aggregate. Farmers could often earn more from gravel under their fields than from crops. Gravel digging exposed archaeological finds and many sites were discovered (and quite a few destroyed) in this manner.

The only locations still relatively immune to human disturbance were infertile rocky soils, forested expanses of Russia and Scandinavia, barren zones of northern and western Europe and the mountains of central Europe. Forested areas present great problems for site discovery, since the only major disturbances are tree falls and rooting by wild boar. The archaeological record of Europe is thus highly biased towards finds in areas that have been built up or cultivated.

The discovery of archaeological sites was further advanced by the use of aerial photography after World War I. Archaeological features produce characteristic patterns that can be observed from above. For example, buried ditches hold more moisture than the surrounding natural soil, causing crops to grow higher over them. Buried walls, on the other hand, inhibit plant growth. Such patterns are especially visible under oblique sunlight early or late in the day. The British archaeologist O.G.S. Crawford (1886–1957) pioneered the use of aerial photography for finding sites and the technique continues to be important today, especially in central and eastern Europe.

BOX 2.3 Augustus Henry Lane-Fox Pitt Rivers (1827–1900)

Ramsauer's detailed recording of the Hallstatt finds was the exception rather than the rule during the middle of the nineteenth century. Sloppy digging methods prevented accurate observation of the positions of artifacts in the ground and soil layers. Field documentation was almost never published. Not until the last two decades of the nineteenth century did a retired British general set archaeological field research on a professional footing.

Born in Yorkshire in 1827, Augustus Henry Lane-Fox entered the Royal Military Academy at Sandhurst in 1841. After his commission in the Grenadier Guards in 1845, he served in the Crimea, Malta, England, Canada and Ireland, retiring in 1882 as a lieutenant general. At his posts, Lane-Fox began to collect artifacts and eventually excavated archaeological sites.

In 1880, under the will of his great uncle, Lord Rivers, Lane-Fox inherited a large estate in southern England and a comfortable annual income. The will also required him to assume the name of Pitt Rivers. Pitt Rivers' estate, Cranbourne Chase, was full of unexcavated Bronze Age barrows and other prehistoric sites. He devoted the rest of his life to their meticulous excavation.

Pitt Rivers organised his excavations as if they were military campaigns, planned them carefully and hired a staff of foremen, surveyors, excavators, draughtsmen and clerks. He ordered slow, precise excavation under trained supervision and paid as much attention to discarded potsherds as to whole vessels. Such organisation enabled timely publication of his results in four immense volumes entitled *Excavations in Cranbourne Chase*. Pitt Rivers also applied his orderly thinking to artifact classification, echoing work elsewhere by scholars such as Montelius.

By his death in 1900, Pitt Rivers had established standards for documentation and publication that transformed archaeology, in the words of Glyn Daniel, 'from a pleasant hobby . . . to an arduous scientific pursuit.' Sir Mortimer Wheeler (Box 2.6), himself a military man, praised the excavation techniques and publication standards used by Pitt Rivers as the inspiration for his own fieldwork.

A patchwork of cultures

The avalanche of archaeological data led to advances over the Three-Age System for dating finds. As the Swedish archaeologist Oskar Montelius (1843–1921) examined finds from closed contexts such as burials, he noted recurring associations of artifact types that he ordered in sequence. In the 1880s, Montelius proposed a six-part division of the Bronze Age. He subsequently divided the Neolithic into four periods and the Iron Age into ten. European prehistory became a chest of drawers into which new discoveries could be assigned a slot based on similarities to known types. Montelius also linked his sequences to finds from the Aegean and Egypt with known calendrical dates and proposed that innovations 'diffused' from there throughout Europe.

Danish prehistorian Sophus Müller (1846–1934) extended Montelius' approach to characterise broad complexes of finds, including artifacts and their associated architecture and graves. In Müller's *Urgeschichte Europas* (1905), he used the term *Kultur* to describe related groups of finds. Later, the Prussian archaeologist Gustav Kossinna (1858–1931) and others adopted this term to describe archaeological finds that repeatedly occurred together. In their 'culture history', the emergence and disappearance of such cultures and their mutual influences provided the narrative of prehistoric life. A noted culture historian was the German archaeologist Carl Schuchhardt (1859–1943) who stressed the heterogeneity of the archaeological record and studied finds throughout Europe during travels before World War I.

The contributions of Montelius, Müller, Kossinna and Schuchhardt provided the inspiration for the scholarship of V. Gordon Childe (1892–1957), perhaps the most celebrated European prehistorian of the twentieth century (Box 2.4). Working in the culture-historical tradition, Childe was a master synthesiser of the vast corpus of data that emerged from European soil during the nineteenth and early twentieth centuries. His seminal ideas – some have stood the test of time, others have not – still form the starting point for modern thinking in European prehistory.

BOX 2.4 V. Gordon Childe (1892–1957)

The contributions of V. Gordon Childe to archaeological scholarship are immense. Unenthusiastic about excavation (his only major fieldwork was excavating the Neolithic village of Skara Brae in Orkney), he was a voracious reader, traveller and conference attendee who was able to draw together vast amounts of information, organise it into a patchwork of cultures and produce a coherent narrative of later European prehistory. In addition, he presaged later developments in archaeological thought by developing models of the 'Neolithic Revolution' and 'Urban Revolution' to explain major transitions in prehistoric society.

Childe was born in Australia in 1892 and came to England in 1914 to study at Oxford, beginning his interest in European prehistory. After a brief sojourn in Australia, he returned to England in 1921 and began to read archaeological literature and travel widely, acquiring a working knowledge of several languages while visiting sites and museums. He rapidly began to translate this encyclopaedic corpus of information into books and articles.

The Dawn of European Civilisation, Childe's masterful overview of the European Neolithic, appeared in 1925 and went through seven editions and many translations before its last version was published in 1958. *Dawn* was complemented by *The Danube in Prehistory*, in which Childe defined his 'Danubian' sequence of cultures. Childe's synthesis of European prehistory was not entirely his own invention. The kernel of the Danubian sequence can be found in the Moravian chronology devised by Jaroslav Palliardi (1861–1922), his concept of the 'archaeological culture' echoed Müller's and Kossinna's, his diffusionism followed Montelius, and his sense of the heterogeneity of the archaeological record resonated with Schuchhardt's. Childe was truly the 'Great Synthesiser' of his era, not just of data but also of interpretative frameworks.

Professional recognition came quickly and in 1927 Childe was named Abercromby Professor at the University of Edinburgh. In 1946, the Institute of Archaeology at the University of London invited Childe to be its director and professor of European archaeology. Throughout these decades, he continued his career of teaching and prolific writing.

Much has been made of Childe's left-wing politics and their impact on his archaeological scholarship. His Marxist politics pre-dated his archaeological career and

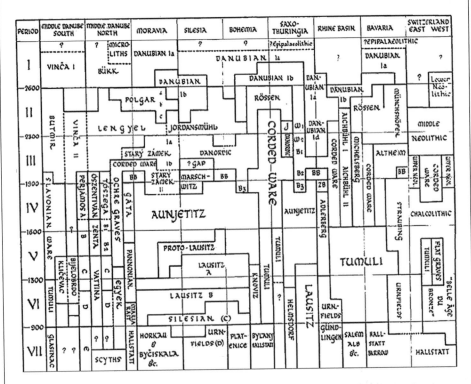

FIGURE 2.5 Childe's classic 1929 schematic depiction of the relationships among the Neolithic and Bronze Age cultures of central Europe that comprised his Danubian sequence. Chronologically, it reads from the top down, with the beginning set around 3000 BC, consistent with the pre-radiocarbon 'short' chronology then in use.

he held a sympathetic view of the Soviet Union, but Childe did not follow a consistent political approach in his writings. Some of his books, such as *Man Makes Himself* (1936) and *What Happened in History* (1942) are clearly products of an avowed Marxist, but other writings display little influence of Marxist thought.

Childe returned to Australia in 1956, where he leapt to his death from a precipice the following year. Over fifty years later, his legacy persists. His two major works of the 1920s, *Dawn* and *Danube*, still provide a foundation for the study of European social evolution, despite the tremendous volume of data that has been recovered in the intervening decades.

Archaeology in the service of nationalism

Political conditions during the nineteenth and early twentieth centuries in central and eastern Europe provided fertile ground for nationalist ideas and archaeology proved to be useful for their promotion. It was thought that ancient peoples maintained well-defined borders with neighbouring groups that were reflected in artifact styles and that these borders persisted into historical times. Modern distortions in national boundaries resulted from encroachments of alien neighbours. This 'injustice' could only be corrected through a return to ancestral boundaries defined through archaeology. Nationalist tendencies were particularly alive in Wilhelmine Germany.

The individual most identified with nationalist archaeology is Gustav Kossinna, mentioned above. Beginning in 1895, Kossinna (Box 2.5) used his 'settlement-archaeology' method to trace Germanic settlement between the Oder and Vistula rivers. Other German archaeologists, including Bolko von Richtofen (1889–1983), took up the issue of whether Germans or Slavs should claim ancestral rights in this area. Von Richtofen argued vehemently with Polish archaeologist (and Kossinna student) Józef Kostrzewski (1885–1969) throughout the 1930s about prehistoric Slavic or Germanic presence.

The ascendance of National Socialism and Adolf Hitler to the government of Germany in 1933 began perhaps the closest connection ever between archaeologists and a national government. The archaeologists were a mix of intellectual descendants of Kossinna and others who saw career opportunities in the Thousand Year Reich. They were cultivated by two offices in the Nazi regime, one led by Party ideologist Alfred Rosenberg and the other headed by the Reichsführer-SS Heinrich Himmler. Between 1933 and 1945, this alliance between archaeologists and the Nazi party resulted in one of the most egregious manipulations of the past to legitimise political ideology. Its goal was to establish the antiquity of Germanic presence over much of Europe and to demonstrate that the Stone Age roots of the German people had continued in a pristine line for several millennia.

Rosenberg's main archaeological associate was Hans Reinerth (1900–90), who assumed Kossinna's chair in Berlin. Reinerth served as an assistant in the 'Amt Rosenberg', the ideology office, as well as director of the Confederation for German Prehistory, which propagandised the past for political and patriotic ends. He also undertook strident personal attacks, in the tradition of Kossinna, against colleagues with whom he differed, including Gerhard Bersu (1889–1964) whose father had been Jewish.

In 1935, Himmler created a competing organisation to pursue his interests in Germanic heritage, the 'SS-Ahnenerbe' (Ancestral Inheritance). Multiple sections of the SS-Ahnenerbe covered virtually all historical sciences, including archaeology. Himmler was especially interested in the mystical, the occult and the romantic. For him, Germanic antiquity was part of an all-embracing national creed rooted in racial identity.

The SS-Ahnenerbe conducted or sponsored excavations, including at the Viking fortress at Haithabu and the Iron Age Hohmichele burial mound. Sometimes, SS members conducted the excavations themselves. Others were small projects by local archaeologists and amateurs. Himmler placed several archaeologists on his personal staff, including Alexander Langsdorff (1898–1946) and Werner Buttler (1907–40, killed in France). After the war, Nazi archaeologists were removed from professional posts or relegated to provincial backwaters and their damage to the field was quickly undone.

BOX 2.5 Gustav Kossinna (1858–1931)

The most imposing figure associated with German nationalist archaeology was Gustav Kossinna. His method, which he called *Siedlungsarchäologie*, or 'settlement-archaeology', relied on mapping characteristic types of finds to establish boundaries of their distribution. When the geographical distribution of a type could be established, it was taken as an expression of ethnic identity. The idea that cultural continuity equated with ethnic continuity did not originate with Kossinna, but he put it within a methodological framework, promoted it vigorously, and embedded it in nationalist and even racialist ideology.

Born in East Prussia in 1858, Kossinna studied linguistics and Germanic philology at several universities before taking an increasing interest in archaeology during the 1890s. In 1902, he was appointed professor of German archaeology at the University of Berlin. Kossinna himself did not excavate, except once in 1915. Instead, he relied on published sources and museum objects for primary data.

Kossinna focused on the evidence for Germanic settlement in East Prussia and Pomerania, maintaining that 'the Vistula area' was the ancient home of the German people. He presented his arguments forcefully, disparaging the study of non-Germanic populations, such as Celts and Romans. Over time, Kossinna's nationalist rhetoric became increasingly strident, as did his antagonism towards many contemporaries.

By the 1920s, Kossinna's views came to be viewed with alarm outside Germany. The Wilhelmine empire had ceased to exist in 1918. In Kossinna's research area, parts were replaced by new Slavic nations. His earlier nationalism took a chauvinistic tone: the presence of Germanic artifacts, no matter how distant from Germany itself, legitimised territorial rights. He began to promulgate a difference between innovating cultures (Germans) and passive, recipient cultures (all others, especially Slavs).

Kossinna died in 1931, before his nationalist ideology found expression in attempts by the Nazis to enlist archaeology in the service of the state. His disciples, including Hans Reinerth who held Kossinna's former chair in Berlin from 1934 to 1945, held prominent positions in the Nazi regime and his view of prehistory was taught in German schools.

A maturing discipline

After World War I, the emergence of research institutions and university departments put archaeology on a disciplinary footing equal to other academic fields. Archaeologists were more likely to be employed to practise archaeology rather than to pursue it as a pastime or ancillary activity. Archaeological finds could now be situated, at least stylistically, in time and space with a high degree of confidence, enabling archaeologists to ask questions beyond chronology, such as about settlement and diet.

The greatest generation

Modern European archaeology owes a considerable debt to archaeologists born mostly during the first quarter of the twentieth century. These scholars were younger contemporaries of Childe who came of age reading his syntheses and outlived him. Most are now dead, but their contributions to research and teaching made European prehistory the coherent and diverse discipline that it is today. All experienced World War II. To borrow Tom Brokaw's 1998 term, I call them 'The Greatest Generation' of European prehistory.

Members of the Greatest Generation saw each other frequently at international conferences, conducted excavations and visited each other's projects and corresponded about key research questions of the day. They were the first beneficiaries of radiocarbon dating. Journals and archaeological societies flourished under their leadership.

Most members of the Greatest Generation were inveterate excavators. P.-R. Giot's eulogy for Michael J. O'Kelly (1915–82), an Irish member of this cohort, sums it up: 'O'Kelly was a man of the field, an expert excavator, an experimental archaeologist, not at all involved in pseudo-marxist, pseudo-freudian, or pseudo-structuralist interpretations.' They published extensive excavation reports, often within months of completing a project, with lavish illustration of artifacts and site plans. Stuart Piggott (1910–96), another important contributor to field techniques and interpretation, helped establish standards for the presentation of finds in publication.

Archaeology as an environmental science emerged in the 1950s and 1960s. An important figure in this area was J.G.D. (Grahame) Clark (1907–95) of Cambridge University, whose 1952 book *Prehistoric Europe: The Economic Basis* was translated into many languages. His excavations at Star Carr and his innovative interpretation of the results excited the imagination of many younger scholars. Clark's interest in prehistoric subsistence was advanced further by Eric Higgs (1908–76), another Cambridge researcher, who oversaw training of students who did fieldwork in many European countries.

Each country had giants of archaeology among the Greatest Generation. In England, Clark, Piggott and Christopher Hawkes (1905–92) provided leadership after Childe. Glyn Daniel (1914–86) made the journal *Antiquity*, founded by O.G.S. Crawford, into a forum for world archaeology. In France, François Bordes (1919–81) developed systematic typologies of Palaeolithic tools, while André Leroi-Gourhan (1911–86) made contributions to the study of Ice Age art and settlements. In the Netherlands, P.J.R. Modderman (1919–2005) and H.T. Waterbolk excavated Neolithic settlements and burials. Hermann Schwabedissen (1911–94), Werner Krämer (1917–2007), Wolfgang Kimmig (1910–2001) and Werner Coblenz (1917–95) played important roles in German post-war archaeology. In central Europe, archaeologists like Richard Pittioni (1906–85), Konrad Jażdżewski (1908–85), Jiří Neustupný (1905–81), Jan Filip (1900–81), Pál Patay and Laszlo Vértes (1914–68) participated in a lively scholarly community. Carl Johan Becker (1915–2001) and Berta Stjernquist (1918–2010) were instrumental in the development of post-war Scandinavian archaeology.

Among the members of the Greatest Generation must be counted those who participated from overseas, especially from the United States. In the 1920s and 1930s, the Harvard-based American School of Prehistoric Research conducted excavations in both eastern and western Europe. Hugh Hencken (1902–81) and Hallam Movius (1907–87) worked in Ireland with the Harvard Archaeological Mission in the 1930s. After the war, Movius' excavations at the Abri Pataud in France provided a model strategy for investigating Palaeolithic rock shelters. Lithuanian-born Marija Gimbutas (1920–94), working first at Harvard and then at UCLA, played a critical role in bringing the archaeological record of eastern Europe before western eyes and also investigated Neolithic sites in southeastern Europe.

BOX 2.6 R.E.M. Wheeler (1890–1976)

One of the most colourful archaeologists of the twentieth century, Robert Eric Mortimer Wheeler was born in Glasgow in 1890. After education at the University of London and military service in World War I, Wheeler was appointed Keeper of Archaeology at the National Museum of Wales, subsequently becoming director in 1924. He excavated several Roman sites, including forts at Caernarfon and Brecon and an amphitheatre at Caerleon. Wheeler then became the director of the London Museum in 1926 and excavated several Roman sites, including Verulamium (St Albans).

A participant in the Verulamium excavations was Kathleen Kenyon (1906–78). Wheeler and Kenyon developed and refined the system of excavating along a grid and leaving baulks between excavated squares that bear their names. Wheeler professed admiration for the meticulous excavation techniques pioneered by Pitt Rivers and promoted precise stratigraphic observation and accurate drawing as indispensible prerequisites for archaeological interpretation. During the early 1930s, Wheeler was also central to the establishment of the Institute of Archaeology at the University of London.

During the 1930s, Wheeler turned his attention to the Iron Age fortress at Maiden Castle in Dorset, the largest hillfort of its time in Europe. Maiden Castle, consisting of several huge chalk ramparts on a steep hillside, had been attacked by Romans in AD 43. One of his most memorable discoveries was the skeleton of one of the defenders in which the projectile of a Roman *ballista* was found embedded in the spine.

During World War II, Wheeler returned to military service, but before long he was asked to direct the Archaeological Survey of India, where he introduced his techniques of stratigraphic excavation at sites such as Arikamedu. Returning to Britain after the war, Wheeler was appointed a professor at the Institute of Archaeology and resumed his interest in Iron Age and Roman archaeology. He was also named secretary of the British Academy, a position he held until 1968, and was knighted in 1952.

Wheeler used the new medium of television to popularise archaeology for the public. The show, 'Animal, Vegetable, Mineral?' ran on the BBC between 1952 and 1960 and involved a panel of three experts who tried to identify objects from British Museums. Wheeler's witty personality and erudite appearance led him to be named 'British TV Personality of the Year' in 1954.

How old is it?

By the middle of the twentieth century, archaeologists understood the diversity of prehistoric remains and their relative ages, but they simply had no idea how long cultures persisted. Any timescale on the chronological chart was mostly guesswork. Correlations between the historical record of the Near East and Europe, imperfect as they are, could only be taken back so far. The imprecision of the narrative of cultural development was frustrating.

Early attempts to derive calendrical ages used pollen associated with archaeological remains. Palaeobotanists had developed the analysis of pollen counts to reconstruct vegetation communities. They noticed that pollen sequences were characterised by similar vegetation communities at roughly the same time and could be divided into 'pollen zones' that served as a timescale. Pollen dating was widely applied in Scandinavia and Britain by researchers such as Harry Godwin (1901–85), Johannes Iversen (1904–71) and Jørgen Troels-Smith (1916–91).

A classic example of pollen dating was applied to an antler point dredged up from the North Sea floor by the trawler *Colinda* in 1931. Godwin determined that pollen associated with the point belonged to the Boreal pollen zone, correlating it with finds in Scandinavia. Re-dating in the 1990s using radiometric techniques established that the point was several millennia older than the Boreal, but in the 1930s even dating a find to a general span of time was a breakthrough.

Other dating techniques, such as the counting of annually laminated lake sediments called 'varves', or the counting of tree rings in preserved timber, had limited applicability outside of certain localities and periods. Archaeologists continued to rely on tenuous assumptions of the rate of change in artifact forms and decorative styles. It was not until after World War II that archaeologists received the dating tool that enabled them to obtain dates that resembled actual calendar years: carbon-14, or radiocarbon (Box 2.7).

BOX 2.7 The radiocarbon revolutions

The most significant advance in archaeological research was the discovery of radiocarbon dating by Willard F. Libby (1908–80). One carbon isotope, carbon-14, is radioactive and like all radioactive materials, decays at a known rate. Carbon-14 is absorbed by plants through photosynthesis. Animals eat plants, so they also ingest carbon-14. When an organism dies, it stops absorbing carbon-14 and the clock starts. From that moment, carbon-14 in the remains of the organism is no longer replenished, so it is possible to calculate the period between the death of the organism and the time a sample is tested to determine how much remains.

Initial applications of radiocarbon dating in the early 1950s revolutionised archaeology by providing calendrical ages for artifacts and sites. The first European labs were established at the British Museum in London, Oxford, Cambridge, Gif-sur-Yvette near Paris, Groningen, Uppsala, Copenhagen, Heidelberg, Berlin and Leningrad. Soon dates issuing from the labs caused sensations as well as consternation. For example, radiocarbon dramatically changed the dating of the spread of farming across Europe. Previously, archaeologists had estimated that farming began in the Near East around 4500 BC, spread to southeastern Europe about a millennium later and reached the British Isles around

2000 BC. This traditional 'short' chronology appeared in all textbooks prior to the 1950s. Radiocarbon dates, however, indicated that agriculture reached southeastern Europe by at least 6000 BC and England before 3000 BC. Suddenly, the time available for changes in pottery, houses and burials observed in the archaeological record became substantially greater.

Some archaeologists had made a great investment in the old chronology by devising sequences of cultures that changed rapidly within the 'short chronology'. They had also traced patterns of 'influence' and population movement based on assumptions about relative ages of pottery styles in neighbouring areas. Radiocarbon changed the order of the appearance of some artifact types or disconnected styles thought to overlap in time. Vladimir Milojčić (1918–78) was an outspoken doubter of radiocarbon dating. His 1949 book, *The Chronology of the Later Stone Age in Central and Southeastern Europe*, tied early farming cultures in southeast Europe to the Aegean Bronze Age chronology, which was linked to historical dates from Egypt. The new 'long' chronology did not fit his conception and he maintained that the technique was flawed.

Most archaeologists accepted radiocarbon dating and the changes it forced in their interpretations. The most compelling argument was the consistency of dates as they accumulated. Yet there were still problems. Some dates still did not coincide with dates derived from tree rings or historical records. Although radiocarbon had fulfilled its initial promise by providing a first approximation of calendrical dates, it became clear that its dates did not equate with solar years.

Crosschecking of samples of known age led scientists to conclude that the assumption that atmospheric concentrations of carbon-14 were constant through time was flawed. Variations in atmospheric carbon-14 resulted in different proportions of carbon-14 from other carbon isotopes in living organisms depending on when they died. Further research, using samples from ancient bristlecone pine trees in California, established the sequence of these variations. Algorithms were developed to convert raw radiocarbon dates into calendar years. Such 'calibration' has now become standard procedure for expressing radiocarbon dates.

The calibration revolution of the 1970s had further dramatic effects. In western Europe, dates for megalithic tombs were pushed back far earlier than Mediterranean monumental architecture from which they had hitherto been thought to be derived. Copper metallurgy in southeast Europe, once believed adopted from Anatolia, was also revealed to be a local innovation. The transition to calibrated dates was not entirely smooth, however. Archaeologists could make a hash of their arguments by mixing calibrated and uncalibrated dates. Moreover, atmospheric carbon-14 had fluctuated so much that a single radiocarbon date could yield multiple ranges of calendar years.

Early radiocarbon dating used a statistical method counting instances of the decay of carbon-14 atoms during a certain length of time to extrapolate how much remained. This resulted in large standard deviations, the span during which a date can be presumed to be sixty-five per cent accurate. As archaeologists sought finer dating resolution, a search began for techniques to determine how much carbon-14 actually remained in a sample.

In the early 1980s, scientists developed such a method using an accelerator mass spectrometer. AMS dating enables measurement of the remaining carbon-14 rather than relying on the detection of its decay. It also permits the use of very small samples. Only a gram or less of charcoal is sufficient and, more importantly, bones, seeds and even soil can be dated directly. Such high precision and small sample sizes have immense benefits. For example, the death of Lindow Man, a preserved body from an English bog, can be placed with ninety-six per cent confidence (two standard deviations) between 2 BC and AD 119. Small samples of tissue from the Copper Age glacier mummy known as Ötzi the Iceman could be used for multiple dates. Before AMS, a single sample would have destroyed much of Ötzi's body.

Postwar transformations

By the 1960s, carbon-14 dating was widely accepted. Moreover, the European frame-work of cultures established by Montelius, Childe and the Greatest Generation had been exhaustively subdivided and refined. Archaeologists began to ask whether they could learn more from the rich information at their disposal but were initially undecided about which direction to take.

One response was to treat archaeology as long-term history of technology, and efforts began to study how artifacts were produced and modified. Some archaeologists learned to make stone tools and to examine them under microscopes to study traces of damage and wear. Experimental earthworks were constructed to see how they deteriorated over time. Research centres at Lejre in Denmark and Butser Farm in England tried to duplicate pre-historic living conditions. Another short-term response was for archaeologists to immerse themselves in fieldwork and develop large-scale regional research programmes. Continuing threats to archaeological remains from construction and erosion spurred much of this work.

Settlement and subsistence

The last half of the twentieth century saw the emergence of archaeology as a way of studying relationships between people and their environments. Two major strands of scholarship converged: the development of settlement pattern studies and connections between archae-ology and the biological sciences. Settlement pattern study involves intensive regional field surveys to locate sites of different periods. Maps are then studied for spatial patterns, such as clustering or dispersion, relationship to drainage systems and soil types, and locations within the landscape. Changes in patterns are then hypothesised to correlate with factors such as climate change, subsistence change or sociopolitical change.

Before the 1960s, archaeologists who found animal bones and seeds sent them to zoologists and botanists whose identifications were appended to excavation reports. The interpretative potential of bones, seeds and other organic remains came to be recognised during the 1960s and 1970s, and specialised fields like archaeozoology and archaeobotany developed. Common standards for data recovery and reporting evolved as well as novel interpretative approaches. In archaeobotany, sieving and flotation demonstrated that carbonised seeds are often preserved, while archaeozoological techniques were developed for determining the sex and age of animals and for assessing the relative importance of different species.

Social process

During the 1960s and 1970s, archaeologists expanded their interpretative horizons. In North America, the so-called 'New Archaeology' sought to position archaeology as a science by focusing on hypothesis formulation and testing to 'explain' (in a strict scientific sense) social processes (see p189). Some winds of change blew across the Atlantic, but the transformation of European archaeology during the 1960s and 1970s was largely home-grown. American self-consciousness about research design and hypothesis testing was generally thought unnecessary with the data-rich European record. Nonetheless, archaeologists began to think about processes of change and how past societies functioned. They also began to pay more attention to methods of data recovery and the rigour of their analyses, particularly with regard to the quantification of data.

In Britain, two figures associated with processual initiatives were Colin Renfrew and David Clarke (1938–76). Renfrew was, and continues to be, a prolific scholar on many aspects of prehistory, but his major processual contribution during the 1970s was to the study of the emergence of complex societies in the Aegean. Clarke, who died prematurely young, was influenced by innovations in the field of geography. Among other contributions, he was a proponent of systems theory to generate models of social systems.

Elsewhere in Europe, archaeologists approached new orientations in archaeological thought with caution. Thinking about prehistoric society in terms of models was alien to most continental scholars, who believed that interpretations that did not spring directly from data at hand were not admissible for discussion. Over time, however, more extreme aspects of the processual agenda were pared away, particularly as it came to be realised by the late 1970s how impossible its demands were. Younger archaeologists came to feel comfortable discussing processes of prehistoric change without fear of disapproval from older colleagues.

Bringing the story up to date

Recent decades have seen a plurality in approaches to archaeological interpretation and the emergence of new methods for the recovery and analysis of archaeological data. Many archaeologists have become fascinated with 'theory', like their colleagues in the other humanities and social sciences, drawn from social philosophy and literary critisicm. On one hand, this has enabled archaeologists to think more broadly about the lives of prehistoric people and their motivations and values. On the other, it has given license to speculation in the absence of evidence and the introduction of modern agendas into the study of the past. At the same time, there has been an explosion of new scientific, technological, mathematical and computational approaches to the study of prehistoric remains. In some cases, the application of these techniques has reinvigorated the study of research questions that had stagnated due to the inability of traditional archaeological data to provide answers.

Post-processual archaeology

At the beginning of the 1980s, some European archaeologists reacted against what they saw as the overweening scientism of 1970s processual archaeology, particularly its emphasis on human behaviour as determined by environmental factors and the extremes to which societies were viewed as faceless systems. Primarily in England, but also in other countries, many archaeologists explored symbolic and ideological aspects of prehistoric human activity. The basic premise is that all human activity, even as mundane as making pots or discarding rubbish, is charged with symbolic meanings that reflect social relationships. Archaeologists can discover these meanings and make inferences about the social relationships that produced them. Clearly, the evidence for such meanings is much more elusive than that for diet and trade.

Initiatives in this direction provided a useful counterbalance to the cause-and-effect studies dominating processual archaeology. Observations from ethnoarchaeological research indicated that human behaviour and social relationships are intertwined with material culture. The problem was that many archaeologists embraced the post-modernist 'hermeneutic' paradigm popular in literary and cultural studies. It became fashionable to invoke theorists such as Derrida, Foucault, Habermas and Heidegger as if they provided insight into archaeological data not available from the archaeologist's imagination. Moreover, the archaeological record came to be seen as a social construction at the data recovery and analysis stage as well, not just at its prehistoric formation. As a result of this denial of the objectivity of scholarship, subjective visions of prehistoric life were seen as equally valid to those supported by empirical data and rigorous analysis.

Such 'post-processual' archaeology has had several salutary effects on archaeological scholarship, however. The emphasis on 'reflexive' self-scrutiny has led archaeologists to question and analyse their intellectual biases and preconceptions. In many respects, it is an intellectual analogue to the emphasis on methodological rigour that processual archaeologists stressed in the 1960s and 1970s. Archaeologists have identified gaps in their understanding of the past, such as in the study of gender relations and roles in prehistory, often biased by the assumption that males were accorded more importance in society. Post-processual archaeology has also made it possible to approach the archaeological record in terms of human agency, the cumulative effect of decisions made by individuals, rather than as faceless cultures. Another benefit of post-processual archaeology has been a growing emphasis on prehistoric landscapes, for they reflect the active role of people in constructing their environment by choosing where to locate monuments and how to channel movements and sightlines, which eventually may shed light on ideology and cosmology.

New scientific techniques

Major advances in archaeology still come primarily from new analytical techniques, especially the creative application of methods from the natural sciences. Ancient DNA preserved in skeletal remains can establish the relationships among individuals in cemeteries. Trace elements in skeletons enable the reconstruction of diets and the tracing of migrations (Box 2.8). Organic residues embedded in pottery and other artifacts can be identified, leading to insights about ancient practices such as dairying.

The fact that computers are ubiquitous and cheap permits the analysis of data with many variables and the visualisation of archaeological finds and their contexts. Widespread availability of Geographical Information Systems (GIS) software and the power of personal computers to run it has allowed archaeologists not just to make prettier maps but also to find new insights in spatial data. An important recent example of the power of computing to provide knowledge about prehistoric Europe has been the digital reconstruction using seismic survey data from oil and gravel companies of the drowned landscape under the North Sea populated by Mesolithic foragers until about 8000 years ago.

BOX 2.8 Testimony of the bones: Mobility, diet and DNA

The chemical and genetic composition of human skeletal remains can give archaeologists a remarkable amount of information on the lives of prehistoric people. Over the last several decades chemical techniques for studying human skeletal remains has improved markedly and in many respects has energized the study of certain research questions, such as the transition to agriculture and human mobility. Of particular importance is the fact that isotopes, the forms of an element that have the same atomic number and similar chemical properties but different atomic weights, can be differentiated and their ratios compared. Techniques for extracting and studying ancient DNA have also been refined considerably and have been combined with knowledge of the human genome to produce important breakthroughs.

Evidence of movement is provided by strontium isotope ratios in teeth. The ratio of strontium-87 to strontium-86 is constant as it moves from weathered rocks into soil, then into the plants and animals that people eat, ultimately to be preserved in human teeth. Different geological regions have different strontium isotope ratios. Since adult teeth form between four and twelve years of age, they contain a record of the geological region inhabited during those years. If strontium isotope ratios in teeth match those in the local geology, then the individual grew up nearby. A difference means that the person spent childhood elsewhere before moving to the area where he or she died.

Strontium isotope ratios have been used to trace a number of cases of prehistoric mobility in Europe. For example, isotope ratios from skeletons in Neolithic cemeteries at Schwetzingen, Flomborn and Dillingen in southwestern Germany showed a high percentage of non-local individuals. Most were women from uplands without Neolithic settlement, possibly coming from upland hunter-gatherer bands that intermarried with the lowland farmers. Another celebrated example of the use of strontium isotope ratios is that of the so-called 'Amesbury Archer' found near Stonehenge in southern England. Strontium isotope ratios in his teeth indicate that this man, whose burial suggests an elite individual, grew up somewhere in central Europe, perhaps in the foothills of the Alps.

Analysis of stable isotopes of carbon and nitrogen from bone collagen shows dietary pathways and sources of protein. Bone continually remodels during life, so stable isotope analysis reflects the last decade or so of an individual's life. Carbon isotopes permit the differentiation of protein from marine, terrestrial and freshwater sources, as well as between photosynthetic plants and the animals that ate them. Nitrogen isotopes indicate the trophic level of an organism in the food chain. In addition to determining the proportions of different sorts of food in the diet, stable isotope analysis is also useful to investigate whether there were differences in diet according to gender or age. Another application of stable isotope analysis has been to study the teeth of domestic cattle to determine the age of weaning, which has implications for the study of prehistoric dairy production.

One of the major scientific breakthroughs of recent decades has been the ability to recover and characterise DNA from prehistoric bones and teeth. The extraction of ancient DNA is not easy, and laboratory contamination issues took a very long time to overcome. Nonetheless, it has the promise of illuminating differences and similarities between individuals and populations. For example, DNA from Neolithic skeletons at Vedrovice in the Czech Republic indicated the presence of different genetic haplotypes, suggesting various ancestries. DNA analyses also indicate that early European domestic cattle originated from domestication in Anatolia, overturning claims for local domestication from wild cattle in different parts of Europe. The lineage of European domestic pigs, however, is revealed by DNA to be much more complicated.

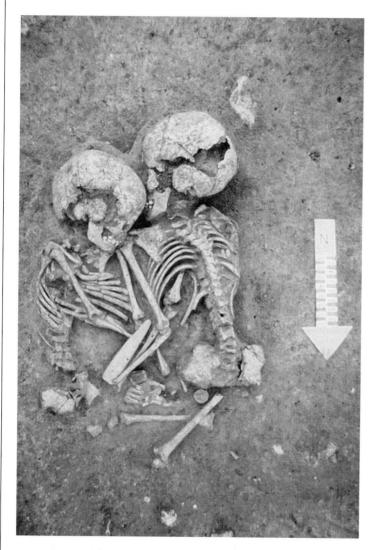

FIGURE 2.6 Skeletons of children from the Neolithic site of Osłonki in Poland have been analysed for stable isotopes of carbon and nitrogen to investigate whether there were differences between the diets of individuals of different ages, while skeletons of adults will be studied to see whether there were differences between diets of men and women (photo by Peter Bogucki).

At the beginning of the twenty-first century, the recent theoretical pendulum swings seem to be lessening in amplitude, with an emerging realisation that archaeology is really a very big tent that accommodates many different ways of looking at the past. At the same time, infrastructure development makes the rescue of archaeological remains more urgent than ever. Beneath European soil lie many more discoveries waiting to be made.

Further reading

Arnold, B. 1992. 'The past as propaganda: How Hitler's archaeologists distorted European prehistory to justify racist and territorial goals'. *Archaeology* July/August: 30–37.

Brodrick, A.H. 1963. *The Abbé Breuil, Prehistorian*. Hutchinson: London.

Daniel, G.E. 1975. *A Hundred and Fifty Years of Archaeology*. Duckworth: London.

Daniel, G.E. 1986. *Some Small Harvest: The Memoirs of Glyn Daniel*. Thames and Hudson: London.

Fagan, B.M. 2001. *Grahame Clark: An Intellectual Life of an Archaeologist*. Westview: Boulder, Colo.

Harris, D.R. (ed.) 1994. *The Archaeology of V. Gordon Childe: Contemporary Perspectives*. University College London Press: London.

Hauser, K. 2008. *Bloody Old Britain: O.G.S. Crawford and the Archaeology of Modern Life*. Granta: London.

Hodson, F.R. 1990. *Hallstatt, the Ramsauer Graves*. Rudolf Habelt: Bonn.

Murray, T. and Evans, C. 2008. *Histories of Archaeology: A Reader in the History of Archaeology*. Oxford University Press: Oxford.

Rowley-Conwy, P. 2007. *From Genesis to Prehistory: The Archaeological Three Age System and its Contested Reception in Denmark, Britain, and Ireland*. Oxford University Press: Oxford.

Trigger, B.G. 1980. *Gordon Childe, Revolutions in Archaeology*. Columbia University Press: New York.

Trigger, B.G. 2006. *A History of Archaeological Thought*. Cambridge University Press: Cambridge.

3

THE AEGEAN WORLD

Georgina Muskett

In archaeology, the 'Aegean world' refers to the societies of Palaeolithic, Mesolithic, Neolithic and Bronze Age Greece, both mainland and islands. Our knowledge of the societies of the Aegean world is comparatively recent, with the first excavations taking place only in the later part of the nineteenth century. Furthermore, it was not until the 1950s that one of the Aegean scripts, Linear B, was deciphered. This rediscovery of the Aegean world was set against the background of the development of archaeological techniques, discussed throughout this book, and the political changes that had occurred in Greece in the mid-nineteenth and early twentieth centuries.

The discovery of antiquity

The Ancient Greeks considered their past against a backdrop of a rich mythological tradition. Although it is apparent that many people in Ancient Greece considered the myths to be historical fact, others were more sceptical. The historians Herodotos and Thucydides, both writing in the fifth century BC, questioned and interpreted elements of mythology in relation to contemporary events. For example, Thucydides' description of the rule of the sea by King Minos of Crete, sometimes called the 'Minoan Thalassocracy', was a reflection of Thucydides' own experiences. As an Athenian he accordingly placed the sea at the centre of his history. In doing so, Thucydides was comparing the situation of fifth-century BC Athens, which could be considered an 'Athenian Thalassocracy', with the Minoan period.

By the Roman period, much of the area of modern-day Greece was part of the Roman empire and the ancient remains provoked interest from travellers, most notably Pausanias, writing in the second century AD. Pausanias' detailed description of his visit to Mycenae is still a useful source, although some of his interpretations are no longer considered correct. For example, the structure still popularly called the 'Treasury of Atreus' was not then recognised as a tomb but rather interpreted as the treasure house of Atreus, a legendary king of Mycenae.

FIGURE 3.1 The 'Treasury of Atreus'. Photo © krechet/istock.

The emergence of archaeology

From about 1750 onwards, an increasing number of travellers visited the ancient Greek sites, including those dating from the Aegean Bronze Age. One of the most famous, known through the accounts of his travels, is Edward Dodwell, who visited Greece between 1801 and 1805. Dodwell used literary sources to help him identify the sites, including Mycenae. At this time, scientifically conducted excavations were unknown, although this changed with the establishment of the Greek Archaeological Service in 1833 and the Archaeological Society of Athens in 1837, shortly after the founding of the modern Greek nation. This was followed by the foundation of overseas archaeological institutions, frequently referred to as 'foreign schools' in Greece. The first was the French School of Archaeology in Athens (École française d'Athènes) in 1846 followed by the German Archaeological Institute (Deutsches Archäologisches Institut) in 1847. The American School of Classical Studies opened in 1881, and the British School in Athens in 1886. The Italian School of Archaeology in Athens (Scuola archeologica italiana di Atene) did not open until the early twentieth century, in 1909, and more foreign schools and institutes of archaeology have followed.

Making sense of the past

Archaeological work that led to the discovery of Aegean Bronze Age societies began on the Greek mainland in the 1870s with archaeologists such as Heinrich Schleimann (Box 3.1) and was continued in the following decade by Christos Tsountas (Box 3.2) and others. On Crete, the discovery of the pre-Classical societies of the island was hampered by the political situation in the late nineteenth century. The work of early archaeologists on Crete was facilitated by the Syllogoi (Societies for the Promotion of Education). From 1883, the president of the Syllogos in Heraklion was Joseph Hazzidakis, whose support resulted in overseas archaeologists being able to work on the island.

BOX 3.1 Heinrich Schliemann (1822–1890)

In the middle of the nineteenth century, the Homeric epics the *Iliad* and the *Odyssey* were not considered to have any historical basis. Although travellers in antiquity, most notably the Roman traveller Pausanias writing in the second century AD, had linked the visible remains at Mycenae with the Trojan War, later travellers to Greece did not connect the monuments with Homer. By contrast, Heinrich Schliemann had the firm belief that Homer was a sound historical source and that archaeology could prove this.

Heinrich Schliemann was born in Germany in 1822 and pursued his interest in the ancient past only after achieving significant financial success as a merchant. Fired by his interest in Homer, Schliemann first visited Greece in spring 1868. His goal was to find the palace of Odysseus on the Ionian island of Ithaca. Although Schliemann succeeded in finding cremation burials, he did not find the impressive architecture he was seeking. From Ithaca, Schliemann travelled to the area of the Dardanelles in modern-day Turkey in his search for Troy. The diplomat Frank Calvert, who had previously excavated at the

FIGURE 3.2 Heinrich Schleimann.

site of Hisarlik, persuaded Schliemann that Troy could be found through excavation of the mound there. Schliemann conducted separate excavations at Hisarlik, which he quickly identified as Troy, from 1871 until 1890. Between 1871 and 1873, a massive team of workers, led by Schliemann, dug a series of trenches through the mound. Schliemann was keen to associate his finds with objects described in the Homeric epics. Accordingly, a type of cup with two handles was associated by Schliemann with the *depas amphikypelion*, a two-handled cup mentioned by Homer. This type of cup was subsequently dated to around 2300 BC, about a thousand years earlier than the supposed date of the Trojan War.

Schliemann's infamous discovery of 'Priam's Treasure' in 1873, given publicity through photographs of his wife Sofia wearing some of the jewellery, sealed Schliemann's fame but also gave him a more unwelcome reputation. It is said that, on sighting the hoard of objects made of precious metals, Schliemann dismissed the team of workmen and, along with Sofia, excavated the 'treasure' himself and arranged for it to be sent to Germany without the customary distribution to the Turkish authorities.

In 1874 Schliemann conducted some trial soundings at Mycenae, and in 1876 he continued work at Mycenae on behalf of the Greek Archaeological Society, which held

FIGURE 3.3 Sofia Schleimann wearing 'Priam's Treasure'. Gold jewellery unearthed at the site of Troy.

the excavation permit. Using the writings of Pausanias to guide him, Schliemann's excavations focused on the area inside the Lion Gate, where Pausanias suggested Agamemnon and his companions were buried. Schliemann found the burials inside what is now called 'Grave Circle A', where the deceased were buried accompanied by lavish offerings of weapons, jewellery, items imported from Crete and, most unusually, five men were buried with face masks made from gold. Schliemann is said to have sent a telegram proclaiming that he had 'gazed on the face of Agamemnon' when he saw one of the masks found in Grave V. Although Schliemann never associated this highly accomplished mask with Agamemnon, the anecdote is still connected with this mask. The burials in 'Grave Circle A' date from the sixteenth century BC whereas Agamemnon, if he ever existed, would have lived some three hundred years later. Schliemann's excavations of Mycenaean sites continued at Orchomenos in 1880 and at Tiryns from 1884.

Schliemann died in Naples in December 1890. His body was returned to Athens for burial in a tomb built in the Neo-Classical style, surrounded with a sculpted frieze showing his excavations. The *Iliou Melathron*, Schliemann's home in Athens, has from 1984 housed the Numismatic Museum of Athens.

Despite the controversy surrounding some of his claims, Schliemann's greatest achievement was his success in bringing the archaeology of the Aegean Bronze Age to a wide audience.

BOX 3.2 Christos Tsountas (1857–1934)

Christos Tsountas was a Greek archaeologist, who worked on both mainland Greece and the islands of the Cyclades, one of the first archaeologists to do so. He was also a pioneer in the field of maritime archaeology.

Tsountas was born in 1857 in an area that is now part of Bulgaria. He began his career as a Classical archaeologist and in 1884 led a pioneering project to investigate the site of the ancient sea battle of Salamis. This was perhaps the earliest known archaeological survey conducted under water. The team of divers were hampered by poor weather conditions, and Tsountas did not consider this survey to be a success.

From 1884 until 1902 he undertook excavations at Mycenae, where 'Grave Circle A' had been previously excavated by Heinrich Schliemann (see Box 3.1). Tsountas' work focused on other parts of the site, including semi-subterranean circular *tholos* tombs and a large group of chamber tombs outside the walls surrounding the citadel. He also found the remains of the palace and the remarkable staircase that leads to an underground cistern securing the water supply when the citadel was under attack. Tsountas is best remembered at Mycenae for the excavation of the area that was named after him, 'Tsountas' House', a shrine which is part of the Cult Centre.

Simultaneously Tsountas embarked on a major programme of fieldwork in the Peloponnese, the Cycladic islands and Thessaly. One of his most important excavations was of a *tholos* tomb at Vapheio, near Sparta. Although the chamber of the tomb had been looted in antiquity, Tsountas found a pit in the floor that had remained undiscovered. It contained the burial of a man accompanied by lavish offerings including a large group of engraved seal-stones, a dagger whose decoration was made using small pieces of precious metals and the 'Vapheio Cups', two gold vessels with decoration showing the capture of bulls. The following year, Tsountas excavated a Mycenaean shrine at the nearby Amyklaion, pre-dating the more famous sanctuary of the Archaic period.

In the early twentieth century, Tsountas worked in Thessaly in northern Greece. His two most important excavations were at the Middle Neolithic site of Sesklo from 1901 to 1902 and at the Late Neolithic site of Dimini in 1903. Although Tsountas' conclusions were subsequently superseded, his work helped to establish Thessaly as the focus of research on Neolithic Greece.

He is perhaps best known for his pioneering excavations of cemetery sites on several of the Cycladic islands. As a result of excavations conducted in 1898 and 1899, Tsountas identified a particular material culture that characterises the Early Bronze Age society of the Cyclades during the third millennium BC (approximately 3000 to 2000 BC), which he called 'Cycladic'. Some of the most notable excavations by Tsountas are the graves at the cemetery of Chalandriani on the island of Syros. He also excavated cemeteries on the islands of Siphnos, Paros, Despotiko and Amorgos.

Tsountas' book *Mycenae and the Mycenaean Age* was published in 1893. It made a crucial contribution to Mycenaean studies, so it was soon translated into English and, in collaboration with the US scholar J.I. Manatt, was expanded and republished in 1897, enabling wider appreciation of Tsountas' work.

Tsountas was most active as a field archaeologist for the first two decades of his career. In 1904 he was appointed Professor at the University of Athens and he died thirty years later in 1934.

The first Minoan remains at the palace of Knossos were brought to light in 1878 by the aptly named Minos Kalokairinos. Kalokairinos was an antiquary who lived in Heraklion (then known as Candia). He uncovered a section of the west part of the palace, including the storage magazines, and produced a rough sketch of the throne room. However, an edict of the ruling Ottoman government led to Kalokairinos having to abandon his work, although he continued to discuss his findings with other archaeologists, including Arthur Evans in 1894. Kalokairinos spread knowledge of Knossos throughout Europe by his donation to several European museums of examples of the large Minoan storage jars known as *pithoi*, which he had excavated in the west magazines of the palace. After Kalokairinos, several other archaeologists were keen to continue investigations at Knossos, including Heinrich Schliemann, W.J. Stillman (American Consul in Greece), the French archaeologist André Joubin and the British archaeologist John Myres, before Arthur Evans eventually purchased the land that included the site of the palace (Box 3.3).

BOX 3.3 Arthur Evans (1851–1941)

Arthur Evans is the most famous archaeologist to have worked on Crete, although not the first. He was born in 1851 into a fairly prosperous family. Evans did not initially pursue a career in archaeology, but travelled to the area then known as Illyria, approximately corresponding to modern-day Croatia. Basing himself in Ragusa (modern-day Dubrovnik), Evans worked as a journalist, writing articles for the *Manchester Guardian*. Illyria was then part of the Austro-Hungarian empire and Evans was a champion for its independence. As a result of his stance, Evans was imprisoned and then forced to return to England.

In 1883, Evans and his wife began a five-month visit to Greece, taking in Mycenae, Orchomenos and Tiryns, the prehistoric sites excavated by Schliemann (see Box 3.1). Indeed, Schliemann was happy to discuss his findings with Evans. On Evans' return to England he was offered the post of Keeper of the Ashmolean Museum in Oxford, which he held from 1884 until his resignation in 1908. Evans completely refurbished

FIGURE 3.4 Bust of Arthur Evans at Knossos.

the museum by acquiring much new material that was housed in a new building opened in 1894.

Evans' particular interest in Crete began at this time, the catalyst being the acquisition by the Ashmolean Museum of inscribed seal-stones from the island. He first visited Crete in 1894 to study the scripts on the seal-stones, and the following year published a study of these inscriptions, his first publication on the archaeology of Crete. Evans identified two distinct scripts, which he initially referred to as 'Pictographs' and 'Prae-Phoenician', now known as Linear A and Linear B respectively.

Evans travelled widely in Crete, one of his first visits being to Knossos, and it was at this time that he began his acquisition of the Kephala Hill that included the site of the palace of Knossos. The end of the Ottoman rule of Crete in 1899 allowed Evans to complete this purchase. Evans' excavations of the palace of Knossos began at precisely 11.00 am on 23 March 1900, and the first artifacts were exhibited in London in 1903. Excavations in the Knossos area, which included the buildings known as the 'Little Palace', 'Royal Villa', 'House of the Frescoes' and 'Caravanserai' continued for the next thirty-one years. The scope of the project encouraged Evans to commission the building of the Villa Ariadne as a base for his excavations at Knossos.

The discoveries at Knossos made Evans famous for the rest of his life and he received a knighthood in 1911. Not all of his work has been well-received by archaeologists. In particular, the substantial reconstructions of the 'Palace of Minos' at Knossos, completed in 1930, have been criticised. Evans paid his last visit to Knossos in 1935, when a bronze

FIGURE 3.5 The palace at Knossos.

FIGURE 3.6 The throne room at Knossos.

bust commemorating his achievements was unveiled in the West Court of the palace. That year also saw the publication of Volume IV of his monumental work *The Palace of Minos*. Evans died in 1941, a few days after his ninetieth birthday.

Until the excavations of Evans, almost the only knowledge of the palace of Knossos was confined to mythology and the legendary tale of Theseus, Ariadne and the Minotaur. Evans' legacy extends beyond his contribution to Minoan archaeology. In 1936 Evans met Michael Ventris, then aged fourteen, at an exhibition of Minoan objects at the Royal Academy in London. It is said that a chance remark by Evans that the Aegean scripts had not been deciphered inspired Ventris to solve the mystery of Linear B almost twenty years later.

The drive to continue the exploration of the Aegean Bronze Age continued in full force in the first decades of the twentieth century. On Crete, palatial buildings were revealed in the southern part of the island, at Phaistos and the neighbouring site of Aghia Triada, by Italian archaeologists led by Federico Halbherr. Excavations in the eastern part of Crete were dominated by American archaeologists, with work at Gournia in 1903 led by Harriet Boyd Hawes and at Vasiliki, Pseira and Mochlos by Richard Seager.

A maturing discipline

Archaeological techniques throughout the 'great age' of excavation of the late nineteenth and earlier twentieth century had developed significantly and the use of trial trenches, stratified excavation on a large scale and dating by pottery were soon adopted as the norm. All archaeologists working on Crete had adopted the three-part scheme devised by Arthur Evans, who had divided the development of Minoan society into three periods – Early, Middle and Late Minoan – with each period further subdivided. For sites on the Greek mainland, a similar scheme had been devised in 1918 by the British archaeologist Alan Wace and the American archaeologist Carl Blegen. Wace and Blegen developed the 'Helladic' classification system by analysing and comparing groups of pottery from different mainland sites. The Helladic classification, so called because Wace and Blegen wished to highlight the mainland origins of the pottery styles, was used to establish a relative chronology for the Bronze Age on the Greek mainland. It is still the accepted framework for dating finds from mainland sites.

Alan Wace (1879–1957), who was Director of the British School in Athens from 1914 until 1923, first excavated at Mycenae from 1920 until 1923. His findings led to conclusions that were at odds with the belief of Evans that the advanced Mycenaean society was the result of settlers from Minoan Crete. By contrast, Wace's excavations led to the deduction that Mycenaean society, although owing some debt to Minoan Crete, had developed on the mainland. Furthermore, Wace showed that the most intense period of monumental building at Mycenae was during the time when the Minoan palace society had collapsed. He observed

FIGURE 3.7 'Grave circle A' at Mycenae.

that there was strong Mycenaean influence on the last phase of occupation of the palace at Knossos, and even suggested a Mycenaean take-over of part of the island of Crete. In addition, Wace's continuing excavations of chamber tombs at Mycenae confirmed that the burials in 'Grave Circle A' should not be considered in isolation, but were part of a larger cemetery.

Evans was angered by Wace's stance and his influence was such that in 1923 Wace's appointment as Director of the British School at Athens was not renewed and his work at Mycenae stopped. The feud continued in a bitter debate between the two scholars conducted via a series of articles in the *Journal of Hellenic Studies* in 1925 and 1926. It was not until 1939 that Wace eventually returned to excavate at Mycenae.

This interwar period also saw the development of interest in connections between the Aegean world and other contemporary Bronze Age societies. In 1930, John Pendlebury (1904–41), whose interests spanned both the Aegean and Ancient Egypt, published a catalogue of Egyptian objects found in the Aegean area. As the excavation seasons in Egypt and Crete were different, Pendlebury was able to excavate in both locations. He directed excavations in Egypt, most notably at Tell el-Amarna from 1930 until 1936. At the same time, Pendlebury was curator of the site at Knossos. He also excavated several Minoan sites, most notably at Mount Dikte in the east of Crete, as well as the Temple Tomb at Knossos, the latter with Evans in 1931. Pendlebury was one of the first archaeologists to take account of sites within their landscape and walked the length and breadth of Crete, recording the location of sites.

Carl Blegen (1887–1971) worked at several sites on the Greek mainland, which dated from the Neolithic period onwards, although he is best known for the discovery of the Mycenaean palace of Pylos and for his excavations at Hisarlik, the presumed site of Troy. Blegen was also at odds with Evans' view that the language of Mycenaean Greece was Minoan. Blegen, by contrast, believed that the inhabitants of the mainland, from the Early Bronze Age onwards, spoke the Greek language. Blegen's work at Hisarlik is noted for his attempts to identify the stratigraphical layer equivalent to the city of Troy described in Homer's *Iliad*. In addition, his work at Hisarlik helped to confirm chronological correlations with the rest of the Aegean world.

The most significant contribution by Blegen to understanding the Aegean Bronze Age was his excavations, alongside his Greek colleague Konstantinos Kourouniotis, at Ano Engliano, site of the Mycenaean palace of Pylos. The first day of excavations in 1939 by the joint Greek–American team saw dramatic discoveries. The remains of a sizeable structure decorated with wall paintings were revealed. However, the most important discovery was a group of inscribed clay tablets, part of a large archive that had been preserved by fire. The text was written in a script called Linear B, until then known only from Knossos on Crete. This discovery would prove to be the crucial factor in the eventual decipherment of Linear B.

World War II (1939–45) had a major effect on archaeology in Greece and fieldwork was interrupted for virtually a decade. Among other projects, the excavations at the palace of Pylos and at Mycenae were effectively stopped, as were the plans by Spyridon Marinatos to investigate the causes of the destruction of the Minoan palace economy (Box 3.4).

Post-war transformations

The post-war period saw the decipherment of the Linear B script. The clay tablets written in Linear B had been photographed prior to being placed in safe storage in Athens during the wartime hostilities. The excavations at Pylos, resumed in 1952, had revealed further clay

BOX 3.4 Spyridon Marinatos (1901–1974)

The Greek archaeologist Spyridon Marinatos is best known for his excavations at the site of Akrotiri, covered during a volcanic eruption in the Late Bronze Age.

Born in 1901 at Lixouri on the Ionian island of Kephalonia, Marinatos was an archaeologist throughout his life. Starting his career on Crete, he was appointed Director of Heraklion Museum in 1929 where he met Sir Arthur Evans (see Box 3.3). Marinatos became Director of the Archaeology Division of the Education Ministry in 1937 and two years later was appointed Chair of Archaeology at the University of Athens. Marinatos' contribution to archaeology was recognised by the Academy of Athens, being elected as a member in 1955 and as President in 1971. However, his career was not without controversy, when in 1967 the military junta took power in Greece and he accepted the post of Inspector-General of the Greek Archaeological Service, although he was later relieved of the post.

Marinatos was a very active field archaeologist. He excavated several sites on Crete and on the Greek mainland, most notably Mycenaean tombs at Marathon in Attica and at Routsi, in the southwest Peloponnese, as well as the site of the battle of Thermopylae. However, he is best remembered for his excavations on the Cycladic island of Thera, also known as Santorini.

In 1939, Marinatos had been excavating the Minoan villa at Amnisos on the north coast of Crete. His findings led him to propose a radical theory to explain the fall of the Minoan civilisation, which resulted in the majority of sites on the island being destroyed. He suggested that the destruction, at that time considered a single event, was caused by a natural disaster – the eruption of the volcanic island of Thera, approximately 100 kilometres north of the island of Crete. Late Bronze Age material from Thera, some of which was revealed during the removal of volcanic ash used in the construction of the Suez Canal in the previous century, had already confirmed the presence of ancient remains on the island.

The outbreak of World War II prevented Marinatos from attempting to prove this through excavation on Thera and it was only in 1967 that excavation began. The heavy layer of volcanic ash that covered part of Thera as a result of the huge eruption in antiquity prevented excavation on much of the island. However, in the south part of Thera, erosion of the ash layer enabled excavation of an area close to the modern village of Akrotiri.

The excavations conducted by Marinatos produced spectacular results. A whole section of a Late Bronze Age town was revealed, not merely the buildings, which in some cases were two or three storeys high, but also their contents, preserved by the layer of ash and pumice. In some buildings, the ash had preserved the shape of wooden furniture and the painted walls of many of the rooms had their designs substantially complete. Although the painting technique was the same as found on Crete, many of the scenes were of a type not previously known. In particular, the 'Ship Procession Fresco' from the West House shows a complete landscape of the countryside, two coastal towns and some of their inhabitants. Most notably, the fresco depicts a group of ships, ranging in size from small canoe-type craft to elaborately decorated vessels with a sizeable crew, their passengers protected from the elements by awnings. Marinatos worked with his team at Akrotiri until his sudden death on the site in 1974. He was buried at Akrotiri, the only person to be accorded this honour.

tablets written in Linear B, and the first Linear B tablets from Mycenae were found by Wace in the same year. The discoveries of Linear B tablets on the mainland were crucial to the decipherment of the script. The first Linear B tablets had been found at Knossos by Arthur Evans between 1900 and 1904, but access to the 1500 examples was difficult as Evans had not published the information because he had hoped to decipher the script himself. The initial studies of Linear B were made by the American scholars Alice Kober and Emmett L. Bennett, Jr, the latter a student of Blegen. Bennett's analyses of the Linear B script were vital to the final decipherment in 1952 by the amateur British scholar Michael Ventris. Bennett's lists of words that he had deciphered increased the number of examples that could be used to test the sounds of the syllables and the way in which the words were formed. The decipherment revealed that the Linear B script preserves the form of the Greek dialect in use during the later part of the Aegean Bronze Age, from approximately the middle of the fifteenth century BC to the end of the thirteenth century BC. Linear B developed from a script now known as Linear A, which was used by the Minoan palace society on Crete, and remains undeciphered. John Chadwick, a philologist from Cambridge working on the early Greek language, contacted Ventris on hearing of the decipherment and offered collaboration. Their joint publication appeared in 1956, shortly before Ventris' death. The Linear B tablets have been of invaluable assistance in providing additional information on Late Bronze Age society on the Greek mainland and on Crete that could not be obtained from archaeological fieldwork.

At the same time, archaeologists on the mainland continued to make great strides in understanding Mycenaean palatial society. Excavation of the palace of Pylos resumed in 1952 and in the same year the Greek archaeologists George Mylonas and John Papadimitriou uncovered a second grave circle at Mycenae, which they named 'Grave Circle B'. The excavation of buildings, conventionally called 'houses', outside the citadel at Mycenae during the 1950s and 1960s shed more light on the workings of the Mycenaean palatial economies. Discoveries continued on the island of Crete in the 1960s, most notably a fourth building complex identified as a palace at Zakro, in the extreme east of the island. Nicholas Platon, the excavator of the site at Zakro, had proposed in 1958 a new system of chronological classification that he considered to be a more accurate reflection of the development of the Minoan palace economies than Arthur Evans' three-part system based on pottery. Accordingly, Platon named the period before the development of the Minoan palaces as 'Prepalatial', the time of the first palaces as 'Protopalatial' and the time of the second palaces as 'Neopalatial'. The three-part system devised by Evans has not been discarded completely and continues to be used for dating pottery.

After the spate of excavations in the Cycladic islands at the end of the nineteenth century, the pace of archaeological work in this region had slowed. However, new projects began in the 1960s and 1970s, including the excavations at Akrotiri that led to spectacular discoveries (see Box 3.4). Another important excavation took place at Ayia Irini on the island of Keos. Its location on the ancient shipping route between the Greek mainland and Crete led to the development of a settlement that was strongly influenced by external contacts, particularly Minoan Crete. The findings of the project, conducted by the University of Cincinnati, showed that the development of Ayia Irini is key to understanding the effects of 'Minoanisation' on the Cycladic Bronze Age societies. Another important site in this respect has been Phylakopi on the island of Melos, initially excavated from 1896 to 1899 and again in 1911. The excavations directed by Colin Renfrew from 1974 to 1977 for the British School at Athens have made a significant contribution to understanding the links within the Bronze Age Aegean. Knowledge of the nature and extent of connections between the Aegean world and other societies continues to develop. One of the most important contributions comes from the survey and excavation projects at Tell el-Dab'a in the eastern part of the Nile delta in Egypt. Archaeological work has been taking place at intervals since 1885, the most recent being from 1966 by the Austrian Archaeological Institute in Cairo. The Austrian excavators found fragments of wall paintings showing themes similar to those found on Crete. It has been suggested that the Minoan-style wall paintings from Tell el-Dab'a may have been the work of itinerant Minoan artisans.

Until the 1960s, most knowledge of the Aegean Bronze Age had been acquired through traditional land-based excavation. This changed with the development of underwater archaeology (Box 3.5) and archaeological field survey techniques.

Archaeological field survey, sometimes called field walking, has developed from its inception in the early part of the twentieth century, and projects have taken place in several areas of Greece since the mid-1970s. The technique has proved very successful in locating prehistoric sites, as it is possible to find not just monuments but the detritus of human activity. Field survey is a non-invasive activity and consists of walking over the ground looking for surface debris, in particular scatters of pottery, stonework and metalwork. The maquis landscape, with its dense vegetation, found in many parts of the Aegean world, results in aerial photography being of limited use in locating archaeological sites. By contrast, the Greek landscape is ideal for field survey as it is an environment with much surface erosion that leads to archaeological sites being exposed. Current archaeological thinking is to treat sites as part of the overall landscape rather than the earlier approach where they were considered in isolation. Accordingly, the importance of the results from field surveys are crucial to evaluating the Aegean Bronze Age landscape.

BOX 3.5 Underwater archaeology

There has been a long history of interest in evidence of the past that is found under water. This falls into two main categories: the discovery and excavation of shipwrecks and the exploration of sites that are now under water. Our knowledge of the Bronze Age Aegean has been greatly advanced in recent years by investigation of examples of both types of underwater site, most notably the shipwreck at Ulu Burun and the town of Pavlopetri. However, the earliest investigations of shipwrecks were salvage ventures.

Although there are written accounts in the Roman period attesting to *urinatores* (salvage divers), it was not until the Medieval period that an antiquarian interest developed in shipwrecks. One of the earliest investigations was at Lake Nemi, in the Lazio region of Italy, where two imperial pleasure barges were sunk in the first century AD. Their location was known through fishing and they were first reported to Church authorities in Rome in the middle of the fifteenth century. In 1446, Cardinal Colonna commissioned the architect Leon Battista Alberti to conduct a salvage operation, although he failed to raise the hulls. In 1535, Francesco de Marchi surveyed the vessels by using a rudimentary form of helmet and retrieved some artifacts and hull remains. A further unsuccessful salvage attempt in 1827 was followed by a more systematic survey in 1895, which confirmed the existence of two vessels. From 1928 to 1931, Lake Nemi was drained at the instigation of Benito Mussolini, and the hulls were raised. This provided valuable information about Roman ship construction. The hulls no longer survive, destroyed as a result of wartime bombing.

The development of underwater archaeology was aided by the introduction of 'hard hat' diving: that is, the development of brass diving helmets that could withstand water pressure. Although very cumbersome, the diving helmet allowed sponge divers to explore the seabed, with the consequence that more shipwrecks were discovered and reported. One of the shipwrecks found in this way was a wreck off the Greek island of Antikythera, discovered in 1900. The ship, which had sunk in the first century BC, had carried a rich cargo of statuary in bronze and marble, ranging in date from the fourth to the first century BC, together with the device known as the 'Antikythera Mechanism', a machine to calculate astronomical positions. The use of diving helmets also allowed archaeological surveys to be conducted under water. An example of this was the pioneering project in 1884 to investigate the site of the ancient sea battle of Salamis by Christos Tsountas (see Box 3.2).

'Hard hat' diving had disadvantages in terms of archaeology, being costly and cumbersome, and accordingly not conducive to recording archaeological remains. Consequently, underwater archaeology did not develop until the commercial development of a system that used a demand valve, which delivers breathing gas only when the diver is breathing in, coupled with a high pressure cylinder. The Aqua-Lung (also known as SCUBA, self-contained underwater breathing apparatus) was developed by Jacques-Yves Cousteau, a French naval officer, and the engineer Emile Gagnan. The use of the Aqua-Lung in the 1940s had led to chance finds of ancient shipwrecks and their cargo in the Mediterranean by sport divers. It was not until 1960 that the first underwater excavation, using the same techniques as on a land excavation, of a shipwreck from the time of the Aegean Bronze Age was conducted. The excavation was directed by the American archaeologist George Bass, who had learned of a shipwreck off Cape Gelidonya, in southwest Turkey. The ship, dated to around 1200 BC, carried a cargo of copper and tin ingots along with the crew's personal possessions. An even more spectacular discovery was made in 1982, when another underwater shipwreck was found at Uluburun, to the west of Cape Gelidonya. The wreck, excavated between 1984 and 1994 by the Institute of Nautical Archaeology, initially led by George Bass and subsequently by Cemal Pulak, dated to 1310 BC. The ship's varied cargo included large quantities of raw materials, which would be rare finds on land archaeological sites, including logs of blackwood, unworked elephant and hippopotamus tusks, and ingots of glass, copper and tin. It is generally considered that the vessel, of which some remains of the cedarwood hull were preserved under the cargo, was sailing around the Eastern Mediterranean in an anti-clockwise direction.

The ruins of the submerged town of Pavlopetri, in the extreme south of Greece, were initially discovered in 1967 and surveyed in 1968 by a team from the University of Cambridge. The settlement was initially thought to have been Mycenaean in date (mid-seventeenth to twelfth centuries BC). A new collaborative project between the University of Nottingham and the Ephorate of Underwater Antiquities of the Hellenic Ministry of Culture, which began in 2009, used not only conventional underwater archaeological

FIGURE 3.8 Underwater archaeologist at Pavlopetri examining the spread of storage
vessels. ©Jon Henderson, University of Nottingham.

techniques, but also employed recent developments in digital mapping technology to
survey the site. They discovered that occupation began as early as about 3500 BC and,
in addition, found evidence that suggested that the inhabitants of Pavlopetri had trading
links with Minoan Crete.

Further reading

Bowens, A. 2011. *Underwater Archaeology: the NAS guide to principles and practice* (2nd edition).
    Blackwell: Oxford.
See also the following journals:
ENALIA. Journal of the Hellenic Institute of Maritime Archaeology
International Journal of Nautical Archaeology
Journal of Maritime Archaeology

Bringing the story up to date

In the late twentieth century and at the start of the twenty-first, field-based projects of excavation and survey remain at the heart of ongoing research into the Aegean Bronze Age. On Crete, there is increasing evidence of occupation from the Palaeolithic period. In addition, more Minoan buildings based around a central court have been discovered at sites including Petras and Galatas, leading to a reconsideration of the term 'palace'. As well as new discoveries, sites such as Pavlopetri at the southern tip of the Greek mainland (see Box 3.5) and Phylakopi on the Cycladic island of Melos are being re-examined. At Phylakopi, alongside re-evaluation of the earlier archaeological work, a British team have been developing the ongoing management of the site. The late twentieth and early twenty-first centuries have also witnessed the development of artifact studies using scientific techniques to analyse the classes of artifacts such as pottery and wall-paintings to increase the understanding of how and where artifacts and pigments were made. For example, radiocarbon dating of an olive tree preserved by the eruption of the island of Thera (see Box 3.4) has been crucial to the debate on the precise dating of the eruption, and is seen by some to provide a fixed date in the relative chronological framework of the Aegean Bronze Age. Likewise, the analysis of lead isotopes associated with tin has suggested the possible origins of the metal ores and hence enabled trade routes of the Aegean Bronze Age to be tentatively identified.

The late twentieth and early twenty-first centuries have also witnessed the construction of new museums and the refurbishment of existing museums in Greece. They have provided the opportunity for new displays of finds from the Aegean world using artifacts from older and more recent archaeological work, as well as providing an opportunity for more modern interpretations.

The study of Aegean archaeology has developed from the writings of Roman authors through the recordings of eighteenth- and early nineteenth-century travellers and the early excavations led by pioneers such as Schliemann, Tsountas and Evans. Although the basic archaeological methods in use today have essentially remained unchanged for more than a century, there has been an increasing shift towards considering the way in which the sites were integrated into the overall ancient landscape. Advances in scientific techniques and methods have further enhanced the understanding of their society and economy. Research and fieldwork continue apace and will no doubt shed further light on the way of life of the peoples of the Aegean Bronze Age.

Further reading

Fitton, J.L. 1995. *The Discovery of the Greek Bronze Age*. British Museum Press: London.
Huxley, D. (ed.) 2000. *Cretan Quests: British explorers, excavators and historians*. British School at Athens: London.
McDonald, W.A. and Thomas, C.G. 1990. *Progress into the Past: The rediscovery of Mycenaean civilization*. Indiana University Press: Bloomington.
Wood, M. 1985. *In Search of the Trojan War*. British Broadcasting Corporation: London.

Specialist topics

Allsebrook, M. 2002. *Born to Rebel: The life of Harriet Boyd Hawes*. Oxbow Books: Oxford.
Becker, M.J. and Betancourt, P.P. 1997. *Richard Berry Seager: Pioneer archaeologist and proper gentleman*. University of Pennsylvania Museum of Archaeology and Anthropology: Philadelphia.

Brown, A. 1994. *Arthur Evans and the Palace of Minos*. Ashmolean Museum: Oxford.

Chadwick, J. 1958. *The Decipherment of Linear B*. Pelican: Harmondsworth.

Davis, J.L. (ed.) 1998. *Sandy Pylos. An Archaeological History from Nestor to Navarino*. University of Texas Press: Austin.

Demakopoulou, K. (ed.) 1990. *Troy, Mycenae, Tiryns, Orchomenos. Heinrich Schliemann: The 100th anniversary of his death*. Ministry of Culture of Greece: Athens.

Grundon, I. 2007. *A Rash Adventurer: A life of John Pendlebury*. Libri: London.

Robinson, A. 2002. *The Man Who Deciphered Linear B: The story of Michael Ventris*. Thames and Hudson: London.

Sherratt, S. 2000. *Arthur Evans, Knossos and the Priest-King*. Ashmolean Museum: Oxford.

Traill, D. 1995. *Schliemann of Troy. Treasure and deceit*. Penguin: London.

4

THE CLASSICAL WORLD

Antiquarian pursuits

David Gill

Classical remains were still visible in the medieval period. The Renaissance fostered a renewed interest in the Classical past and literature. Visitors to Rome and Italy observed the major monuments and some desired to remove key sculptures to display in their homes. One of the earliest English collectors was Thomas Howard, Earl of Arundel (1585–1646). He visited Italy in 1612 and acquired a number of sculptures that were sent back to England to be displayed in a special gallery at Arundel House in London.

During the eighteenth century Italy was frequently visited by English gentlemen on their Grand Tour. During this period sites such as Hadrian's Villa at Tivoli were explored on a regular basis to provide these visitors with major pieces to add to their collection. The sculptures were shipped back to England and placed within the setting of grandiose Classical houses. These included the displays at Holkham Hall in Norfolk, Petworth House in Sussex and Newby Hall in Yorkshire.

This period coincided with the influential work of the German scholar Johann Wincklemann (1717–68). He worked in Rome for the papal authorities and made important studies of Classical Roman sculpture that laid the foundations for the modern discipline of Classical archaeology. He also saw the value of bringing together the extensive range of Classical texts that mentioned ancient art with the surviving objects. In this way he was able to use the ancient sources to explore the origins of Classical art in the Greek world through the Roman custom of making copies.

In Italy Sir William Hamilton (1730–1803) had been acting as British Envoy and Plenipotentiary at the court of Naples. He arrived in 1763 and soon started to amass a major collection of antiquities largely drawn from the extensive Greek colonial cemeteries in Campania around the Bay of Naples. Other material was purchased from existing Italian collections. One of the main elements was figure-decorated pottery either imported from Athens or made in the Greek colonies of southern Italy. Hamilton commissioned Pierre d'Hancarville to produce volumes showing his collection and preparing the way for its sale. Hamilton's first collection of Greek pottery was sold to the British Museum in 1772 for 8000 guineas. Part of the second collection was lost when HMS *Colossus* was sunk off the Isles of Scilly in 1798. Much of the residue from the second collection was sold to the merchant

Thomas Hope in 1801 and placed on display in his home in Duchess Street, London. The Hope Collection was dispersed at auction in 1917, and parts of the Hamilton collection were dispersed to major collections in England and North America. Hamilton's collection was influential as the illustrations were used for designs by Josiah Wedgwood on his 'Etruscan wars' produced at his 'Etruria' factory in Staffordshire.

More intrepid travellers started to make their way into the eastern Mediterranean. One of the great draws was the famed city of Troy. Robert Wood (1716/17–71) made a study of the topography of the Troad in 1750. The Society of Dilettanti was founded in 1734. They commissioned James Stuart and James Revett to make a study of the remains of Athens in the early 1750s. Their multi-volume work, *Antiquities of Athens*, is a significant record of architecture that has since been destroyed or damaged.

One of the most significant developments was in May 1801 when Thomas Bruce, the seventh Earl of Elgin, obtained a permit that led to his removal of the architectural sculptures from the Parthenon, the main temple of the patron goddess Athena at Athens. The sculptures were sent back to England and then purchased by the British Government. The subsequent display of this material, consisting of large sections of the continuous frieze as well as the more fragmentary pedimental sculptures, did much to foster a British interest in Greek culture. These sculptures were supplemented by the frieze removed from the temple of Apollo at Bassai in the western Peloponnese. This remote building, described by the Roman travel writer Pausanias, was visited by Charles Robert Cockerell (1788–1863) during 1811. Cockerell also visited the temple of Aphaia on the island of Aegina; the pedimental sculptures were removed and sent to Munich.

The creation of universal museums: Exploration in Greece and Turkey

The Napoleonic Wars disrupted European travel in the late eighteenth century. Easy access to Italy and the eastern Mediterranean was denied. The Greek War of Independence started in 1821 and this encouraged a great spirit of Philhellenism. Greece was freed from the Ottoman Empire in 1832, and one of its first appointments was to make Ludwig Ross responsible for archaeological remains. A Central Archaeological Museum (now the National Museum) was opened in Athens in 1834 and the Archaeological Society of Athens was founded in 1837. The potential for excavating in Greece was realised with the opening of the French School in 1846 'for the study of the Greek language, history, and antiquities', in part as a cultural response to Britain's growing political interest in the country. Although part of the role of the French School was to study the archaeological remains of Greece, its members were also involved in linguistic and historical studies.

The nineteenth century saw the development of state museums that reflected national standing. Such collections were drawn from numerous countries and cultures reflecting imperial ambitions. The British Government had already purchased the Parthenon marbles from Greece and it then looked to Turkey as a possible source of Classical material.

As archaeological excavations were developing in Greece, Charles Fellows (1799–1860) was travelling through western Turkey in 1838. This took him to Lycia where he explored the remains of the city of Xanthos. He enlisted the help of Royal Navy sailors and removed fragments of the funerary sculptures. These were sent back for display in the British Museum.

Charles Newton (1816–94) joined the Department of Antiquities at the British Museum in 1840 and subsequently became British vice-consul at Mytilene (the island of Lesbos) in 1852. In 1856 he used sailors from HMS *Gorgon* to remove architectural slabs from Halikarnassos in western Turkey. This was the location of the great funerary monument of Mausolus dating to the fourth century BC. Newton and his team recovered large sections of the frieze as well as a number of free-standing portrait sculptures. Newton also went to the site of the great oracle at Didyma (Branchidai) outside Miletus and was able to recover a number of sculptures, including lions from the processional way.

The temple of Artemis at Ephesus was also a focus for attention. The main exploration took place from 1863 and was carried out by John Turtle Wood (1821–90). This exploration provided a record of the sanctuary's location. The Society of Dilettanti also supported the investigation of the major planned city of Priene, to the north of Miletus, and recovered a number of architectural elements from the temple of Athena Polias. Fragments from both these sites were shipped back to London.

The Louvre in Paris also started to benefit from the work of French scholars. The famous 'Venus de Milo' was discovered on the island of Melos in the Aegean. Such works were placed in the context of a wider art museum reflecting an interest in world culture and art.

Italy

During the 1840s George Dennis (1814–98) started to explore the ancient remains to the north of Rome. His *Cities and Cemeteries of Etruria* (1848) drew attention to the undocumented pre-Roman cultures of Italy. Imported Greek pottery found in the rock-cut tombs was acquired for collections in the Vatican as well as in northern Europe. The tombs were highly decorated inside and they attracted the attention of a number of artists including Carlo Ruspi. These nineteenth-century drawings have been invaluable in showing how the decoration has faded or been lost over the subsequent years. Dennis himself went to work in Benghazi in North Africa where he explored the Classical cemeteries. Many of his finds were presented to the British Museum.

The emergence of scientific archaeology

The second half of the nineteenth century saw a shift towards a more scientific approach to archaeology. In Britain there was a growth of local archaeological societies, which recorded the remains of Roman settlements and military installations. This recording started to have an impact on the way that Classical sites in the Mediterranean were perceived and explored. In Greece members of the French School were involved in the excavation of the major sanctuary of Apollo on the island of Delos in the southern Aegean. Initial excavations were conducted in 1864, followed by more systematic work in 1873. In 1874 the German Archaeological Institute in Athens was established.

The German Institute started work on the major sanctuary of Zeus at Olympia in 1875. One of the aims was to uncover the remains of the great Doric temple dating to the fifth century BC, which was 64m long and had contained the colossal gold and ivory statue of Zeus that had been described in some detail by the Roman travel writer Pausanias. They also uncovered the marble pedimental sculptures that showed the myth relating to the founding of the Olympia Games, as well as the battle between the Lapiths and Centaurs featuring the axe-wielding Athenian hero Theseus. Subsequent excavations by the Germans in the sanctuary also found remains of the workshop created by the sculptor Pheidias to create the great statue. The Germans also found remains of the athletic installations associated with the Panhellenic games that took place every four years. These included a series of treasuries in which individual cities could display valuable dedications to Zeus. A series of dedications, dating back to the eighth century BC, have been recovered, showing how the sanctuary was visited by people from across the Greek world. Among the finds was an inscribed helmet dedicated by Miltiades, the Athenian general at the decisive battle of Marathon of 490 BC.

These activities by the French and German schools chastened the British Classical community, and following a visit to Greece in 1878 by Richard Claverhouse Jebb (1841–1905) there was a move to establish a British School of Archaeology at Athens. Although there was a suggestion that the School should be established in Smyrna in western Turkey, it was felt that Athens would make a better centre. This opened in 1886 on a plot adjacent to the American School of Classical Studies (established in 1882). One of the perceived roles of the British School was to train future generations of archaeologists. Ernest Gardner (1862–1939), the first Cambridge student of the School and its second director, had excavated with Flinders Petrie (p79) at the Greek trading settlement of Naukratis in the western delta of the Nile. David Hogarth (1862–1927), the first Oxford student and a later director, subsequently went to excavate in Egypt with the Egypt Exploration Fund and then conducted a number of major surveys of eastern Anatolia, recording in particular Hittite monuments. The first major fieldwork conducted by the British School was on Cyprus and included the cemeteries of Marion, containing imported Greek material, and the gymnasium in the Roman city of Salamis in the eastern part of the island.

The development of the city of Athens saw the tidying up of the Acropolis with its centuries of post-Classical occupation. From 1885 to 1891 there was a series of major excavations on the sanctuary that exposed the remains of the temples that were constructed prior to the Parthenon. Among the most striking finds were groups of sixth- and early fifth-century sculptures, still carrying traces of their painted decoration. Some of the female statues have highly patterned costumes and one of the male figures had painted hair and is now known as 'The Blond Boy'. A number of associated inscriptions found with the statues have allowed the names of the sculptors to be identified. These statues seem to have been deliberately buried by the Athenians in the reconstruction of the Acropolis after its destruction by the Persian invaders in the autumn of 480 BC.

The French School made an application to excavate at the major sanctuary of Delphi in central Greece. This was the location of the famous oracle of Apollo that featured prominently in the historical accounts of the Greek historian Herodotus. These included the tales of King Croesus who bestowed a series of rich dedications on the sanctuary. The French had hoped to excavate on the site in the 1860s, but in 1891 a bid for a ten-year project was submitted. This involved the removal of the modern village that had grown up in the ruins of the ancient sanctuary. The excavations were assisted by the ancient account by Pausanias that allowed the French to identify the foundations of various buildings. One of the key buildings was the treasury dedicated by the Athenians and said, by Pausanias, to have been constructed from the booty won at the battle of Marathon. This structure was decorated with a series of relief panels showing the parallel myth of Herakles and Theseus. The French also recovered the remains of the long colonnade (stoa) adjacent to the supporting terrace wall of the temple of Apollo in which trophies from the Persian wars were displayed. One of the most exciting

FIGURE 4.1 The Akropolis (Photo author's own).

individual finds was the life-size bronze of a charioteer that formed part of a group dedicated by Polyzalos, the tyrant of Gela in Sicily in the 470s BC. To the east of the temple of Apollo the base of the twisted bronze serpents was found, that the alliance of Greek cities dedicated to mark the defeat of the Persians at the battle of Plataea in 479 BC. The monument itself, inscribed with the names of the cities, was removed to Byzantium (Istanbul) in late antiquity and put on display in the Hippodrome. The entwined bodies of the snakes have survived in situ, and one of the heads that had been severed was recovered during excavations.

The British turned their attention to the Classical site of Megalopolis in the central Peloponnese. These had been established in the 360s BC as a centre for the Arcadian Confederacy, and as such formed one of the cities hemming in Sparta. The work directed by Ernest Gardner explored the remains of the Classical theatre. This led to a heated debate with members of the German Institute about the function of different elements of the structure and the implications this had for the performance of Greek drama.

The Americans chose to excavate at Corinth, a site important during the Classical period but which was destroyed by the Romans in 146 BC. It had been re-established by Julius Caesar in 44 BC and became the seat of the Roman governor of Achaia. The site was also associated with the establishment of a Christian community described in the biblical Acts of the Apostles. The work concentrated on the central administrative area around the Roman forum and the adjacent sixth-century temple. Other work explored the theatre and the colonnaded streets leading to the main harbour areas.

The British then turned to prehistory, notably the excavation of the Bronze Age site of Phylakopi on the island of Melos (see p55), and then a series of sites on Crete through the work of the Cretan Exploration Fund. However, such activities failed to attract sufficient funds and Robert Carr Bosanquet (1871–1935) decided to investigate the possibility of exploring the territory of Laconia and conducting excavations at Sparta. This work, continued by his successor Richard M. Dawkins (1871–1955), uncovered remains of the sanctuary of Athena of the Brazen House, as well as the sanctuary of Artemis Orthia near the banks of the River Eurotas. The latter contained some exotic offerings including carved ivory dedications.

Anatolian explorations

Britain had long-standing interests in the Aegean area. In the early 1880s the Asia Minor Exploration Fund was established to explore some of the Classical sites in western Anatolia and to record their inscriptions. One of its most active members was the Scotsman William Mitchell Ramsay (1851–1939) who held the chair of Classical archaeology at Oxford for a year (1885–86) before moving to Aberdeen. Ramsay became a key figure in the identification of the Roman provincial background to the documents of the New Testament.

The Germans were active in Anatolia. In 1878 Carl Humann started work on the spectacular royal capital at Pergamon in northwest Turkey. This had been the base of the Attalid kingdom that had defeated the Gauls of central Anatolia (that subsequently became the Roman province of Galatia). Humann discovered the remains of a dramatic monumental altar of Zeus decorated with a continuous frieze showing the battle between the gods and the giants. These reliefs were removed from the site and sent back to Berlin where they continue to be displayed in the Pergamon Museum. The remains were also uncovered of the Classical theatre that clings to the slope of the Acropolis. The work at Pergamon, which also involved Wilhelm Dörpfeld (see Box 4.1), helped to make sense of the Attalid monuments erected in the public spaces of Athens.

In Britain there was a growing interest in the archaeology of the Roman occupation, by scholars such as Francis Haverfield (see Box 4.2). Students trained in Greece applied their knowledge to archaeological sites in Britain and beyond. Robert Carr Bosanquet, who had excavated on the island of Melos, returned to England and helped to excavate the Roman fort of Housesteads on Hadrian's Wall on behalf of the Society of Antiquaries of Newcastle upon Tyne. After serving as director of the British School at Athens, Bosanquet held the chair of Classical archaeology at Liverpool University. In 1908 the Liverpool Committee for Excavation and Research in Wales and the Marches was formed and took part in work at a number of Roman sites including the legionary fortresses at Chester and Caerleon and the smaller fort at Caersws in mid-Wales. The Society of Antiquaries also sponsored the excavation of the major Roman city of Silchester in northwest Hampshire. This investigation found remains of a carefully planned settlement along with substantial civic buildings. The Silchester work inspired the excavation of further towns at Wroxeter in Shropshire and Caerwent in southeast Wales.

Between the wars

World War I interrupted work in the Mediterranean. Soon after the cessation of hostilities the British initiated work at Mycenae under Alan J.B. Wace (1879–1957), but after several seasons this was abandoned for Sparta. Arthur M. Woodward focused on the area around the ancient theatre and the recovery of a series of inscriptions that revealed the organisation of

BOX 4.1 Wilhelm Dörpfeld – German who worked at Olympia, pioneer of large-scale excavations

Wilhelm Dörpfeld (1853–1940) was born in Barmen in Germany and trained as an architect in Berlin. He was appointed as architect of the German Archaeological Institute in Athens and became involved in a series of major projects in the eastern Mediterranean. He initially assisted with the major German excavations at Olympia, making sense of the foundations of the temples within the sanctuary of Zeus. He then joined Carl Humann in the excavations of the Great Altar of Zeus at Pergamon. He was subsequently engaged by Heinrich Schliemann (see p41) to work at Troy (1882). His work there reflected a change in attitudes whereby the emphasis was on the uncovering of major structures and their precise measurement, rather than the careful noting of stratigraphy and the contextual interpretation of objects. Schliemann and Dörpfeld then turned to the Bronze Age citadel at Tiryns in the Argolid. The German Archaeological Institute had been invited to excavate on the Athenian acropolis, and Dörpfeld made sense of the substantial foundations of the predecessor of the Parthenon, the Old Temple of Athena. Shortly afterwards Dörpfeld became involved in a bitter dispute over the interpretation of the remains of the theatre at Megalopolis that was being excavated by a British team under Ernest Gardner. On the eve of World War I he helped Wilhelm II, the German Kaiser, to excavate on Corfu. After World War I he resumed his interest in 'Homeric' archaeology and he settled on the island of Leukas. The appointment of an architect reflects a change in attitudes in archaeology whereby the emphasis was on the uncovering of major structures and their precise measurement, rather than the careful noting of stratigraphy and the contextual interpretation of objects.

FIGURE 4.2 The ruins at Olympia. Photo © Ed Siasoco/Wikimedia Commons.

BOX 4.2 Francis Haverfield – excavated many Roman sites in Britain, including Corbridge at Hadrian's Wall

Francis John Haverfield (1860–1919) was educated at Winchester College, a school that produced a number of archaeologists and museum curators in his generation. He read classics at Oxford and subsequently pursued a career as a schoolmaster at Lancing College, but retained a strong interest in Roman inscriptions and was invited by the German scholar Theodor Mommsen (1817–1903) to contribute to a project that was compiling a Corpus of Latin inscriptions. Haverfield contributed two supplements to the *Corpus* covering recent finds in Britain (1890, 1913).

Haverfield's work brought him back to Oxford in 1892 and he took on responsibility for recording Roman remains in Britain. Mommsen, whose study of *The Provinces of the Roman Empire* was translated into English in 1886, seems to have suggested to Haverfield the importance of a study of the Roman provinces. Haverfield travelled extensively and encouraged local archaeological societies to excavate and publish local remains. One of his Oxford students, Thomas Ashby, joined the excavation of the Roman town of Caerwent in south Wales and later became the director of the British School at Rome. He was also a guiding hand in the excavation of the Roman city at Wroxeter in Shropshire. Haverfield's great skill was encouraging local enthusiasts to engage with a major international research project. He initiated an annual report on finds from Roman Britain in the *Jahrbuch* of the German Archaeological Institute. A study of Roman sculptural finds

FIGURE 4.3 Roman ruins at Corbridge (Corstopitum). Photo © Glen Bowman/ Wikimedia Commons.

from Britain was made with Henry Stuart-Jones (1867–1939), a former director of the British School at Rome (and a scholar better known for his work on the *Greek Lexicon*). Some of Haverfield's findings were published in the definitive *Victoria County Histories* of England.

In 1907 Haverfield was elected the Camden professor of Ancient History at Oxford and this gave him the opportunity to encourage further exploration. One of the major projects was the excavation of the Roman supply station at Corbridge (Corstopitum) just to the south of Hadrian's Wall. He found remains of major granaries and workshops that were intended to support the Severan expedition into southern Scotland. One of the team was Leonard Woolley (1880–1960) who went on to excavate in the Near East (see p98). Another was Leonard Cheesman who worked on Roman auxilia but was killed at Gallipoli. Haverfield was an instrumental figure in the foundation of the British School at Rome and the establishment of the Society for the Promotion of Roman Studies in 1910. Haverfield moved the study of Roman Britain from an amateur pursuit to a full scientific study.

the city in the Hellenistic and Roman periods. Such work failed to capture the public imagination as it was overshadowed by the discovery of the tomb of Tutankhamun (see p82).

One of the major Classical projects to be initiated in 1931 was the American work on the Agora in the heart of the city of Athens, a project strongly associated with Homer Thompson (see Box 4.3). This had formed the political heart of the Athenian democracy and was the location for its law courts and the buildings in which the council of 500 met (*bouleuterion*). Although there had been interest in excavating the area prior to World War I most had been deterred by the high cost involved as it would have meant relocating local residents. However, during the 1920s the population of Athens had been swollen by the exchange of populations with Turkey following the destruction of Smyrna (Izmir). Money from the Rockefeller family was used to fund this undertaking. Work continued until 1940 when it ceased during the war years and occupation, and then resumed after the cessation of hostilities. The interpretation of the finds was greatly assisted by the walks through the second-century AD agora described by the Roman travel writer Pausanias. The excavations have uncovered a series of political buildings along the west side of the area, as well as the Roman insertion of the temple of Ares in the centre of the open space during the reign of the emperor Augustus. This temple had originally been constructed in a rural town in Attica during the fifth century BC. On the south side of the agora were a series of rooms that have been interpreted as committee rooms as they seem to have been laid out for dining. The law courts yielded evidence for water-clocks used to time speeches, as well as the casting of ballots in cases. Some of the more unusual finds included the ostraka, pieces of broken pottery, inscribed with the names of politicians who had been selected for ostracism. On the edge of the areas was the state prison in which Sokrates is likely to have drunk hemlock in 399 BC. After World War II, the American School reconstructed the monumental two-storeyed Stoa of Attalos on the east side of the agora. This had been given to the city by Attalos II, king of Pergamon (159–138 BC). This was used as a museum and store for the finds.

BOX 4.3 Homer Thompson – Canadian responsible for the American excavations of the Agora in the heart of Athens

Homer Armstrong Thompson (1906–2000) was born in Ontario, Canada. He was educated at the University of British Columbia and the University of Michigan. He was appointed to a fellowship at the American School of Classical Studies at Athens just as it was starting its excavations in the Athenian Agora. Thompson's first major excavation (with the Greek archaeologist K. Kourouniotes) was on the site of the Pnyx where the Athenian assembly met. In the Agora he worked initially with T. Leslie Shear, taking responsibility for the publication of lamps and Hellenistic pottery. Thompson took charge of the excavation of the public buildings associated with the democracy on the west side of the Agora. Among his studies was the unusual circular building known as the Tholos where members of the *prytanis* in charge of Athens for the month resided. At the same time he was a member of the University of Toronto and an assistant curator at the Royal Ontario Museum. During World War II he served in the Royal Canadian Navy and, on Shear's death in 1945, succeeded him as acting Director of the excavations (Director from 1947). He continued in this role until his retirement in 1967. During this period the American School helped to reconstruct the monumental colonnade presented to the city of Athens by the kings of Pergamon in the second century BC. This building, the Stoa of Attalos, became the museum and store for the finds from the excavation. He was also

FIGURE 4.4 The Agora (Photo author's own).

responsible for initiating the landscaping of the excavated area that introduced trees and shrubs to what could have become a sterile part of the modern city.

Thompson was responsible for regular reports on the progress of the excavations and in 1972 published a major study of the area with Richard E. Wycherley from the University of Wales. This formed Volume 14 of the *Athenian Agora* monograph series that Thompson had initiated.

The Italian expansion in North Africa led to a series of excavations at Classical sites. The work included the extensive Libyan sites of Leptis Magna, Sabratha and Cyrene. Leptis Magna was the birthplace of the Roman emperor Septimius Severus (AD 193–211) whose victory arch dominates the north end of the forum in Rome. The re-assertion of the Classical origins of these provinces vindicated Mussolini's imperial ambitions.

In Britain the National Museum of Wales organised the excavation of the Roman amphitheatre at the legionary fortress of Caerleon initially under the direction of Mortimer Wheeler (see pp30 and 114). Wheeler, who moved to the Museum of London, later excavated the Roman city of Verulamium near St Albans. This revealed a number of houses decorated with mosaics and wall paintings, as well as the Roman theatre. His work at the Iron Age hillfort of Maiden Castle outside Dorchester uncovered evidence for the Roman attack during the invasion of Britain. This included the graphic evidence of a ballista point embedded in the skeleton of one of the defenders (see p30). Wheeler's vision led to the creation of the Institute of Archaeology in London.

The interwar period saw a growing interest in the study of the material culture of the Classical past. One of the main areas was research into the pottery workshops of ancient Athens. A key figure in this area was the Oxford art historian Sir John Beazley (1885–1970). He attributed thousands of Athenian black- and red-figured pots to largely anonymous potters and painters. At the same time the major international publication of the *Corpus Vasorum Antiquorum* was launched to record largely decorated pottery in an agreed illustrated format.

Post-war excavations

Excavations in Greece resumed on a limited basis after the war, with much of the initial focus being on the Athenian Agora. Members of the occupying allied forces in North Africa took over responsibility for the Classical sites in what had been Italian-occupied Libya – most notably John Ward-Perkins. During the early 1950s the Ashmolean Museum in Oxford initiated the excavation of the planned Greek colony at Euesperides on the edge of Benghazi. The site had been identified from wartime aerial photographs and excavations have demonstrated that it had been established in the early sixth century BC. Coin evidence suggests that the site was abandoned in the early third century BC when the new Ptolemaic city of Berenice was formed.

Excavations by foreign archaeologists had not been permitted in Italy. After the war the American Academy at Rome under Frank Brown started a major research project at Ansedonia, the site of the Roman settlement of Cosa. It hoped to demonstrate the impact of this colony on the local countryside. As excavations in Greece were limited by political unrest, French archaeologists started to explore the Greek colonies of southern Italy and Sicily

---

BOX 4.4 John Ward-Perkins – British archaeologist who worked on major projects in North Africa, as well as excavating under the Vatican

John Bryan Ward-Perkins (1912–81) was educated at Winchester College. It was while he was at school that he was introduced to archaeology with the excavation of Buckley Priory. He subsequently studied classics at Oxford University. He developed an interest in the North European Iron Age and excavated at the fort of Bredon Hill in Gloucestershire with Thalassa Hencken (1935–37), and with Olwen Brogan at Gergovia in France.

In 1936 Ward-Perkins joined the staff of the London Museum where he worked alongside (Sir) Mortimer Wheeler. One of his early projects in 1937 was the excavation of the Roman villa at Lockleys near Welwyn in Hertfordshire. He also conducted work at the Iron Age hillfort of Oldbury in Kent. Ward-Perkins joined Wheeler's excavation at Camp d'Artus in Brittany. He was appointed to the chair of archaeology on Malta in early 1939 where he conducted a survey of the prehistoric monuments. Ward-Perkins returned to England to enlist in the Royal Artillery Anti-Aircraft Battery (Enfield's Own) commanded by Wheeler. Ward-Perkins served in the North African campaign that swept through the former Roman provinces of Cyrenaica and Tripolitania. There was considerable concern that the monuments would be damaged and Ward-Perkins was asked to draw up a plan for their protection. After the invasion of Italy Ward-Perkins became a member of the unit responsible for the protection of archaeological sites and fine art.

In 1946 he was appointed the Director of the British School at Rome. Ward-Perkins took an active role in the Roman sites of North Africa, in particular Leptis Magna and Sabratha. He was also invited by the Vatican authorities to explore the Roman cemetery under St Peter's Basilica. This included the putative burial of the remains of the apostle Peter. The British School at Rome had a long-standing interest in landscape studies and Ward-Perkins was involved in the survey of archaeological remains in southern Etruria. He retired in 1974.

---

through the French School in Rome. Among the sites excavated was Megara Hyblaea in eastern Sicily, part of the initial colonising movement in the eighth century BC. The work revealed the organisation and layout of the colonies as well as the cult activities. Subsequent work has started to shift onto the impact of the Greek colonists on local populations. Excavations in the area of the colony of Croton suggest that local settlements were replaced by a series of sanctuaries that appear to have been used to claim the new territory. One key site was at Pithekoussai on the island of Ischia in the Bay of Naples. This trading settlement seems to have been established from the island of Euboia in the eighth century BC. Among the finds is a short poem cut onto a clay drinking cup that celebrates 'Nestor's Cup', an object known from the Homeric poems. Excavations have revealed evidence of iron smelting on the island, and metallurgical analysis suggests that this was sourced from the island of Elba.

The use of aerial photography in wartime had brought an increasing interest in its application to archaeology (see Box 4.5). Kenneth St Joseph (1912–94) had worked on the interpretation of such photographs in World War II and on his return to Cambridge started using the technique to map unknown archaeological features. His identifications included the series of Roman forts that were constructed during the Agricolan and Severan incursions into Scotland. Many cities in Britain had suffered badly from bombing raids. William F. Grimes (1905–88) had initially worked in Wales before joining the Ordnance Survey just before the war. He assisted with the excavation of the ship burial at Sutton Hoo in Suffolk. During the war years he conducted emergency excavations prior to the construction of airfields. He pioneered rescue excavations in London including the uncovering of the rare temple of Mithras in the City of London, as well as recording a number of blitzed churches.

BOX 4.5 Aerial photography

Aerial photography is a remote sensing technique commonly used by archaeologists. From the earliest days of archaeological fieldwork scholars had realised that valuable information on a site could be gained from looking at it from above. Even something as simple as a tall ladder gave a different perspective. Cameras were rigged from balloons and then sent aloft. The earliest known aerial photograph in Britain of an archaeological site (Stonehenge) was taken by Lieutenant P.H. Sharpe in 1906 from an army balloon. By 1911 Italian archaeologists had photographed the Roman Forum and the ancient port

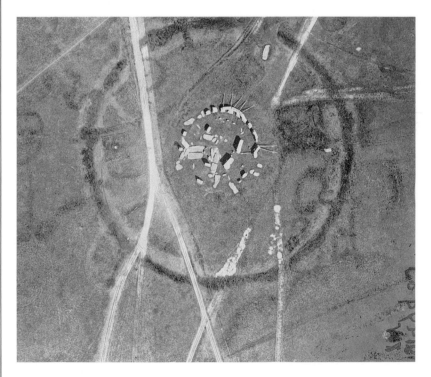

FIGURE 4.5 The first aerial photograph of Stonehenge. Photo © The Society of
        Antiquaries of London.

of Ostia. In 1922, the prehistoric site of Cahokia in Illinois was aerial-photographed (the first in North America). Balloon photography is still a valuable technique (e.g., see Myers *et al.* 1992) However, it was the invention of the aeroplane and the subsequent use of aerial photography by military planners in both World War I and II that unlocked the technique's full potential.

Aerial photography is used in two ways by archaeologists. The first application is on already known sites. Aerial photography allows the archaeologist to get a complete horizontal image of the site within its wider geographical setting as well as its spatial relationship to other nearby sites.

The second use is as a means of locating previously undiscovered sites. A plane will fly over a designated area and take photographs of the ground below. A single camera can record images vertically, or two cameras can obliquely overlap, providing a three-dimensional image when viewed through a stereoscope. This technique can, most obviously, record sites that – albeit above ground – are not readily visible to the naked eye. An example of this is Mayan sites located in thick jungle. However, it can also discover buried sites. This is because a buried site, which may contain features like walls or ditches, will affect the natural growth of the surface vegetation either by stunting root growth (in the case of walls) or by encouraging growth (in the case of buried ditches, which affect water drainage). These crop marks are easily visible from the air but invisible on the ground. In addition to traditional cameras, archaeologists now use highly sophisticated satellite imaging and infra-red photography. It was satellite imaging that revealed to archaeologists the numerous roads (over 180 miles in total length) that radiated out and around Chaco Canyon, a complex of Ancestral Puebloan sites. Most of the roads were constructed between AD 1000 and 1125.

Further reading

Myers, J.W., Myers, E.E. and Cadogan, G. 1992. *The Aerial Atlas of Crete*. Thames & Hudson: London.
Riley, D.N. 1987. *Air Photography and Archaeology*. Duckworth: London.
Wilson, D.R. 2000. *Air Photo Interpretation for Archaeologists* (2nd edition). Batsford: London.

The growth of archaeology in the 1960s saw an intensity of excavations in the former Roman provinces. This included the excavation of the Herodian site of Masada on the edge of desert to the west of the Dead Sea (see p103). The siege of this precipitous site at the end of the Jewish revolt had been described by the Jewish historian Josephus and excavations revealed remains of one of the most complex series of siege works to have survived from the Roman period.

The development of diving equipment has allowed the identification of Roman shipwrecks. These were often recognised by sports divers in the shallower waters around the coasts. Mounds of transport amphorae, the containers for wine, olive oil and fish paste (garum), were easily recognised. The stamped amphora handles allowed a sophisticated study of these containers to be developed in order to understand the long–distance movement of staples during the Roman period. One area of study has been the shipment of Spanish olive

FIGURE 4.6 The ruins at Masada. © Yossi Shwartz/Wikimedia Commons.

oil to the city of Rome, enhanced by a gigantic mound of amphora fragments known as the Monte Testaccio.

From excavation to survey

One noticeable change in Classical archaeology in the post-war period has been the move away from the prestige sites to excavations that are linked to settlements and their association in the landscape. In Greece this was pioneered by the Minnesota Messenia Expedition that looked at the region around the Late Bronze Age palace at Ano Englianos, the so-called Palace of Nestor. It looked at the impact of Sparta's annexation of the region during the archaic period, as well as Messenia's liberation in the fourth century BC. The area round Pylos has been resurveyed in a more detailed project. In recent years a more intensive multi-period survey has been conducted by the Pylos Regional Archaeological Project that has been able to re-evaluate the earlier results.

The southern Argolid project was linked to the excavation of the Classical settlement at Halieis. It showed how the region developed, especially the decrease in activity in the fourth century BC and the intensity of activity in Late Antiquity. The nearby survey of the Methana peninsula considered the use of the mountainous region during the establishment of a Ptolemaic base in the third century BC. This base was contemporary with a Ptolemaic base in Attica excavated by the American School. Both surveys detected an intensity of land use in Late Antiquity. The British School has also conducted a survey of Laconia, returning to sites first noted before World War I.

Threat to the archaeological record

Since the 1960s there has been a growing threat to the archaeological record from the activities of intensive illicit digging to provide material for the antiquities market (see p146). This has included the widespread looting of cemeteries in the Cycladic islands of the southern Aegean. It has been estimated that some eighty-five per cent of the corpus of figures have no indication of their archaeological find-spot. The acquisition of the Athenian red-figured calyx-krater by New York's Metropolitan Museum of Art in 1972 renewed the debate over looting. The krater showed the removal of the hero Sarpedon from the battlefield before Troy. Although it was claimed to have been acquired in the Lebanon, the Italian authorities suspected it had been removed from an Etruscan tomb in the vicinity of Cerveteri. This scandal caused the Archaeological Institute of America to issue a statement over the acquisition of antiquities by museums (1973). During the 1990s an investigation by Italian police led to the seizure of a major dossier of images in a warehouse at the Geneva free port in Switzerland. This led directly to the return to Italy of some 130 antiquities from North American public and private collections; among them was the Sarpedon krater. One of the significant groups of material returned consisted of South Italian pottery, particularly objects made for graves in Apulia. The debate surrounding such acquisitions has reminded the academic community of the intellectual consequences of removing objects from their archaeological contexts in an unscientific manner. One of the results of these investigations is that museums have started to become more diligent in their research before making significant acquisitions, and this appears to have reduced the destruction of archaeological sites to provide new objects.

Further reading

Dyson, S.L. 1998. *Ancient marbles to American shores: classical archaeology in the United States.* University of Pennsylvania Press: Philadelphia.

Dyson, S.L. 2006. *In pursuit of ancient pasts: a history of classical archaeology in the nineteenth and twentieth centuries.* Yale University Press: New Haven & London.

Freeman, P.W.M. 2007. *The best training ground for archaeologists: Francis Haverfield and the invention of Romano-British archaeology.* Oxbow: Oxford.

Gill, D.W.J. 2011. *Sifting the soil of Greece: the early years of the British School at Athens (1886–1919).* Bulletin of the Institute of Classical Studies, Supplement, vol. 111. Institute of Classical Studies: London.

Hood, R. 1998. *Faces of archaeology in Greece: Caricatures by Piet de Jong.* Leopard's Head Press: Oxford.

Huxley, D. (ed.) 2000. *Cretan quests: British explorers, excavators and historians.* British School at Athens: London.

Jenkins, I. 1992. *Archaeologists and aesthetes in the sculpture galleries of the British Museum 1800–1939.* British Museum Press: London.

Jenkins, I. and Sloan, K. 1996. *Vases and volcanoes: Sir William Hamilton and his collection.* British Museum Press: London.

Lord, L.E. 1947. *A history of the American School of Classical Studies at Athens 1882–1942: an intercollegiate project.* American School of Classical Studies at Athens: Cambridge, MA.

Marchand, S.L. 1996. *Down from Olympus: archaeology and Philhellenism in Germany, 1750–1970.* Princeton University Press: Princeton.

Mauzy, C.A. 2006. *Agora excavations 1931–2006: a pictorial history.* American School of Classical Studies at Athens: Athens.

Meritt, L.S. 1984. *History of the American School of Classical Studies at Athens 1939–1980.* American School of Classical Studies at Athens: Princeton.

Wallace-Hadrill, A. 2001. *The British School at Rome: one hundred years.* The British School at Rome: London.

5

EGYPT

Joyce Tyldesley

Earliest beginnings

The Arab invasion of AD 640 left Muslim Egypt more or less isolated from the western, Christian world. Those Europeans who wished to learn about ancient Egypt were forced to rely on the works of the Classical historians and the meagre information provided by the Bible, and this led to some strange misconceptions about life along the Nile. By the fifteenth century, however, Egypt had attained a greater accessibility and contact with the west was slowly increasing. This was an age of exploration and curiosity about the past, and travellers and missionaries started to publish Egyptian adventures that intrigued their readers. In 1646 the astronomer John Greaves published *Pyramidographia*, the first scientific analysis of the pyramids. In 1707 Father Claude Sicard travelled to the insignificant southern town of Luxor and realised that the Valley of the Kings was actually an ancient cemetery. He was followed by the Reverend Richard Pococke, the first Briton to journey south of Cairo. In 1768, the British explorer James Bruce also reached the Valley of the Kings, where he discovered 'Bruce's Tomb': the decorated tomb of the Twentieth Dynasty Ramesses III.

The emergence of archaeology

Napoleon's 1798 Egyptian campaign could not by any stretch of the imagination be considered a military triumph but, from a purely Egyptological viewpoint, it was a great success. The *Commission des Sciences et Arts d'Égypte*, a group of scholars charged with recording the natural and ancient history of Egypt, travelled to Egypt with Napoleon's soldiers; their work was eventually published as the *Description de l'Égypte* (1809–29). The *Description*, heavily illustrated with maps and plans, sparked a Europe-wide fashion for 'Nile-style'. This included a demand for genuine Egyptian artifacts, which were suddenly big business. Collectors like Henry Salt hired fieldworkers, such as the ex-circus strongman Giovanni Battista Belzoni (1778–1823), to acquire and export major pieces (colossal sculptures, stone sarcophagi and architectural elements) that the Egyptians, unaware of their value, were happy to send westwards. No one could read the curious inscriptions carved into these artifacts: they were therefore treated as curious *objets d'art* rather than historical documents.

Belzoni did not only recover colossal artifacts. He explored and excavated a variety of sites including the Abu Simbel Temples, the Giza Pyramids and the Theban area; here, in the Valley of the Kings, he discovered six royal tombs. His *Narrative of the Operations and Recent discoveries within the pyramids, temples, tombs and excavations in Egypt and Nubia* (1820) was a best-seller and his Egyptian exhibition, appropriately held in London's Egyptian Hall, was an equal success.

Gradually, the Egyptian authorities started to realise that their antiquities were a finite resource. The monuments, a valuable asset for a developing country, needed to be protected against those who would exploit them. This urge towards conservation was hastened by Champollion's 1822 decoding of the hieroglyphic script (see Box 5.1). Almost overnight, the once purely ornamental blocks of stone had context and meaning, and ancient Egypt's long and complex history was revealed.

BOX 5.1 Jean-François Champollion

Jean-François Champollion (1790–1832) was an exceptionally gifted French linguist with a flair for ancient languages: as a schoolboy he had studied Latin, Greek, Arabic, Hebrew, Syriac and Chaldean, and he later widened his range to include, among others, Sanskrit, Ethiopic, Chinese and Parsee. His interest in Egypt and its long-lost language was apparently sparked by a meeting with Jean-Baptiste Joseph Fourier, a member of Napoleon's Commission, when he was just eleven years old. Five years later Champollion wrote a paper arguing that Coptic, the language spoken by Christians in Egypt, was derived from the original Egyptian language. This was not an entirely new idea – Athanasius Kircher had first proposed it in 1636 – but so inspired was Champollion by his own argument that he started an in-depth study of the Coptic language.

Meanwhile others, too, were fascinated by Egyptian hieroglyphs and the problems inherent in their decipherment. The French Baron Antoine Isaac Sylvestre de Sacy, the Swedish Johan David Åkerblad and the British polymath Thomas Young all made important contributions to the subject, and Champollion was able to draw on their work. By late 1821 Champollion had confirmed to his own satisfaction that the ancient scribes had used three types of writing to record the same language: just as modern 'joined up' writing is a speedy form of printing, so in ancient Egypt hieratic writing was a simplified or shorthand form of the elaborate hieroglyphic writing, while demotic writing was a later, even more simplified version of hieratic.

The Rosetta Stone – a damaged, polished slab with a triple inscription in Greek, demotic and hieroglyphic scripts – was discovered in Egypt in 1799. As copies of the inscription circulated, it became clear that the Stone might serve as a key to deciphering the Egyptian scripts. The Greek version of the text explained that it was a decree issued by the priesthood at Memphis on 27 March 196 BC, in honour of Ptolemy V. More importantly, it confirmed that the two Egyptian scripts recorded identical messages. Simple counting showed that there were three times as many hieroglyphs as there were Greek letters. So, each glyph could not represent a single letter; there must be other elements to the script. Champollion already understood that the hieroglyphic script used determinatives – glyphs used to convey an impression of the sense of other glyphs – an idea developed by Young. And he knew that, in the hieroglyphic script, royal names were written in cartouches or ovals. As Champollion could read the name Ptolemy in the Greek text, he could find P, T, W, L, M, Y, S in the hieroglyphic cartouches. By combining this work with the examination of other bi-lingual inscriptions he was able to reconstruct a phonetic hieroglyphic alphabet that could be applied to Graeco-Roman royal names.

On 14 September 1822, while working on copies of texts carved into the Ramesside temples of Abu Simbel, Champollion found that the cartouches held more ancient Egyptian royal names: Ramesses and Thothmes, or Tuthmosis. Overcome with excitement, he shouted 'I've got it!' and fainted. On 27 September 1822 his results were presented to the Academy of Inscriptions, Paris, in the form of a formal *Letter to M. Dacier relating to the phonetic hieroglyphic alphabet used by the Egyptians*. In 1824 he published *A Summary of the Hieroglyphic System of the Ancient Egyptians*: this work provided a secure foundation for all future linguistic studies.

In 1826 Champollion was appointed curator of the Egyptian collection of the Louvre Museum. His first and only visit to Egypt occurred in 1828–29, when he accompanied the Italian Egyptologist Ippolito Rosellini. Champollion was appointed professor of Egyptian history and archaeology by the Collège de France in 1831. He died of a stroke in 1832.

FIGURE 5.1 Statue of Jean-François Champollion, by Frédéric-Auguste Bartholdi (marble, 1875).

Auguste Mariette (1821–81) taught himself to read hieroglyphs and Coptic from the texts published in the *Descriptions*. In 1850, when he was working as a curator at the Louvre Museum, Paris, he was sent to Egypt to obtain Christian era manuscripts. Inspired to excavate, Mariette started to work in the Sakkara cemetery; here, in 1850, he discovered the Serapeum, the catacomb designed by the Nineteenth Dynasty Prince Khaemwaset to hold the burials of the sacred Apis bulls. When, in 1858, Khedive Said Pasha, ruler of Egypt, established the National Antiquities Service, Mariette was appointed Director-General. The next year a national museum was established. Mariette was now the only archaeologist who could licence excavations in Egypt; finds from these licensed excavations would be displayed in the new museum. By the end of the 1870s Mariette's Antiquities Service had established a system for the practice of field archaeology in Egypt.

Egyptian archaeology at this time was primarily historical in outlook; the job of the archaeologist was to provide documents for the linguist to study. This bias was given a further twist in the 1880s with a series of excavations conducted by the Delta Exploration Fund (soon to become the Egypt Exploration Fund or EEF; later the Egypt Exploration Society, or EES) that sought to explore links between Egypt and the Bible. The Fund's first excavations (1883) were conducted by the Swiss Egyptologist Edouard Naville at the site of Tell el Maskhuta: this work was published as *The Store-City of Pithom and the Route of the Exodus*. The Delta, connected to the Near East by the Sinai land bridge, may have been the ideal place to look for Biblical evidence but, as the preservation of archaeological material was severely compromised by the damp soil, it did not hold out the prospect of spectacular or large-scale finds.

The moist Delta was just part of a wider problem of the selective preservation of Egypt's archaeological sites. The ancients constructed their houses and palaces of mudbrick, situating them close to the fertile land that fringed the River Nile. Stone was reserved for temples and tombs; buildings which were expected to last for all eternity. The first western visitors, accustomed to the European model of monarchy, found this hard to accept: they instinctively interpreted the ruined stone temples as once-splendid palaces. While temples might be located either in urban centres (cult temples) or at the desert's edge (mortuary temples), cemeteries were always situated away from the settlements and away from the damaging Nile waters, in the hot, sterile desert. Over time the mudbrick domestic architecture has almost completely vanished: dissolved into mud, flattened and built-over, or spread as fertile soil on modern fields. Only a few atypical domestic sites – those built, for example, in the desert, such as the workmen's villages of Kahun (Middle Kingdom) and Deir el-Medina (New Kingdom) – have survived. This means that the surviving archaeology – the temples and desert graves – presents a distorted and wholly incorrect view of the Egyptians as a people obsessed with religion and death. Untroubled by this, most of the earlier archaeologists preferred to work in the ruined temples and the desert cemetery sites where they hoped to find spectacular artifacts and interesting texts. Egypt's funerary traditions – mummification and the provision of extensive and valuable grave-goods – made the cemeteries particularly attractive to missions sponsored by museums or private individuals who expected to receive a share of the finds as a return on their 'investment'. The investigation of the ill-preserved mudbrick domestic sites was not high on anyone's list of priorities.

Making sense of the past

In 1879 Egypt was placed under joint British–French rule, with the British taking responsibility for finances and the French for justice and culture, including archaeology. When, in 1882, a failed nationalist revolt led to the imposition of British military rule, the French retained their control over all cultural matters. By convention, the Director-General of the Antiquities Service would always be French and this would occasionally lead to a conflict of interests with his British excavators. Mariette was succeeded by Gaston Maspero (1846–1916), Professor of Egyptology at the Collège de France and founder of the French School of Archaeology in Cairo. Maspero served as Director-General of the Antiquities Service and head of the museum from 1881 to 1886, and then again from 1899 to 1914. In 1882, the Egypt Exploration Fund was created in Britain, one of its founders being Amelia Edwards.

BOX 5.2 Amelia B. Edwards

Amelia Ann Blanford Edwards (1831–92) was a prolific journalist and popular novelist. Following the success of her travel journal *Untrodden Peaks and Unfrequented Valleys: A Midsummer Ramble in the Dolomites* (1873), she visited Egypt with the intention of writing an account of her adventures. *A Thousand Miles Up the Nile* (1877) allowed her readers to follow Edwards and her companion, Lucy Renshawe (known as 'L'), as they sailed southwards from Cairo to Abu Simbel, experiencing heat, sandstorms and cataracts, visiting ancient sites and, most thrillingly, meeting shady dealers in illicit antiquities. Written in an accessible and informative style, the book was extremely well received. It is still widely read today.

Edwards had no training as an archaeologist, yet she was struck by the poor condition of many of the monuments that she visited. It seemed clear that, while the west was becoming increasingly interested in Egypt's ancient civilisation, modern Egypt did not have the resources to protect her decaying heritage against the combined, and devastating, effects of neglect, tourism and modern development. The sites could be preserved through survey and excavation, but outside funding would be needed. And so, in 1882, in association with Reginald Poole, Keeper of the Department of Coins and Medals at the British Museum, and the surgeon Sir Erasmus Wilson, Edwards founded the Delta Exploration Fund, which soon became the Egypt Exploration Fund (EEF), a London–based society that today thrives as the Egypt Exploration Society (EES). The Fund aimed to finance and publish fieldwork conducted by properly trained Egyptologists, who would work with the full approval of the Egyptian authorities. Edwards and Poole served together as joint honorary secretaries.

The remainder of Edward's life was dedicated to Egyptology and to the Fund. Her fund-raising activities included numerous publications and, in 1889–90, a lecture tour of the United States. In recognition of this work she received three honorary degrees from American universities and a civil list pension. Edwards died on 15 April 1892. She left her library plus £2400 to University College London; an institution specifically chosen because it admitted women as well as men to its classes. The money was to finance 'a Professorship of Egyptian Archaeology and Philology including the deciphering and reading of Hieroglyphic and other Ancient Egyptian scripts or writings'. The Edwards chair was Britain's first chair in Egyptology.

With little money available for official excavations and a constant demand for antiquities, legally excavated or not, unofficial excavations and a thriving black market threatened to denude Egypt of her treasures. So when, in the late 1870s, the Luxor antiquities market was flooded with Third Intermediate Period funerary papyri, the Antiquities Service launched an investigation. The chief suspects were the el-Rassul brothers of the west bank village of Gurna, the notorious home of many skilled tomb robbers. However, nothing could be proved until Mohammed el-Rassul confessed. Ten years earlier his brother, Ahmed, had discovered the family tomb of the high priest of Amen, Pinodjem II. This tomb housed both the Pinodjem family burials and a collection of New Kingdom royal mummies, who had been gathered from their original tombs and stored in the Pinodjem tomb by the Third Intermediate Period necropolis officials. As the royal mummies had already been stripped of all valuables, the el-Rassul brothers had been stealing from the Pinodjem family.

On 6 July 1881 Mohammed led a group of officials along a mountain path behind the Deir el-Bahri bay on the Theban west bank. With Maspero absent, Émile Brugsch (1842–1930) represented the Antiquities Service. He was lowered down the shaft and, bent double, passed into a low corridor almost blocked by a large coffin. This led, via a short flight of steps, to a chamber packed with New Kingdom royal coffins, including those apparently belonging to Ahmose I, Tuthmosis I–III, Ramesses I, Seti I and Ramesses II. A separate chamber held the Pinodjem family. Stunned by his discovery, Brugsch decided that the tomb was to be cleared at once, without any recording or planning, and the mummies were to be sent straight to Cairo.

Jacques de Morgan (1857–1924) served as Director-General of the Antiquities Service from 1892 to 1897. He spent 1894–5 working intermittently at the pyramid site of Dahshur where, excavating in the Middle Kingdom cemetery, he cleared several elite tombs and recovered a collection of jewellery known as the 'Dahshur Treasure'. He moved on to excavate at Nagada, where he discovered a spectacular mastaba tomb attributed to Queen Neithhotep, mother of the first king of the unified Egypt, Narmer. He resigned from the Antiquities Service in 1897, and was replaced by Victor Loret (1859–1946).

Loret was interested in the Valley of the Kings, which had been more or less neglected since Belzoni's work. On 12 February 1898 he discovered the tomb of the Eighteenth Dynasty Tuthmosis III. The tomb had been emptied in antiquity and the king's mummy, recovered as part of the Deir el-Bahri cache, already lay in Cairo Museum, but the tomb yielded a beautifully carved quartzite sarcophagus. Less than a month later Loret discovered the tomb of Tuthmosis' son, Amenhotep II. Included in this tomb was a second cache of New Kingdom royal mummies including the Eighteenth Dynasty Tuthmosis IV and Amenhotep III, the Nineteenth Dynasty Seti II and Siptah, and the Twentieth Dynasty Ramesses IV–VI. Unlike Brugsch, Loret was well aware of the need to keep accurate records. The mummies were photographed and each of the finds was listed and plotted on the tomb plan. Loret went on to discover the tomb of Tuthmosis I, plus a further fourteen private tombs. In 1899 he retired from the Antiquities Service and Maspero returned as his replacement. During this second period of office Maspero supervised the transfer of the museum to the building in central Cairo where it remains today.

A maturing discipline

Theodore Davis (1837–1915) was a retired, and very wealthy, American lawyer determined to discover an intact royal tomb in the Valley of the Kings. Lacking the professional expertise to excavate alone, Davis financed excavations conducted by employees of the Antiquities Service, paying also for their lavish, but often sadly inadequate, publications. In 1902 Davis started to fund Howard Carter. Carter, then Chief Inspector of Antiquities for southern Egypt, was looking for the missing tomb of the Eighteenth Dynasty pharaoh Tuthmosis IV. In 1903, in association with Davis, he found it. Again working with Davis, Carter next explored the tomb of the female pharaoh Hatshepsut. When Carter was transferred to northern Egypt, Davis continued his association with the replacement southern Inspectors, working first with James Quibell (1867–1935), then with Arthur Weigall (1880–1934), both of whom had been trained by Flinders Petrie (see Box 5.3). On 5 February 1905 Quibell discovered the substantially intact double burial of Yuya and Thuya, parents of the Eighteenth Dynasty Tiy, consort of Amenhotep III.

BOX 5.3 W.M. Flinders Petrie

Flinders Petrie (1853–1942) became interested in ancient Egypt through reading *Our Inheritance in the Great Pyramid*, a book by the Astronomer Royal and family friend, Charles Piazzi Smyth. Smyth had developed the theory that the Great Pyramid (Khufu's pyramid at Giza) had been built under divine supervision using the 'pyramid inch' and that the proportions of its corridors and chambers could, if correctly interpreted, be read as a predictive text. The problem with Smyth's thesis was that it was unverifiable as the Great Pyramid had never been measured accurately. Petrie, an excellent practical mathematician and a man of steely determination, resolved to remedy the situation.

After practising by surveying Stonehenge in 1872, Petrie spent two seasons working on the Giza plateau. His work, which thoroughly discredited Smyth's 'pyramid inch' theory, set new standards for the surveying and recording of ancient monuments in Egypt. His abilities were recognised by the newly established Egypt Exploration Fund and he was contracted to excavate a number of Delta sites including Tanis (the capital of Dynasties 21 and 22) and Naucratis (a Greek colony during Dynasty 26) between 1884 and 1886. Subsequently, after a dispute with the EEF, his work was supported by a number of private benefactors and by the Egyptian Research Account, which later became the British School of Archaeology in Egypt. Eventually, in 1896, he was reconciled with the EEF and started to work with them again. His most important projects included the royal cemeteries of the First and Second Dynasties at Abydos, the Middle Kingdom pyramid-builder's town of Kahun, and the New Kingdom capital city Amarna.

One of Petrie's most important contributions to the developing science of Egyptological excavation was his belief in the value of small finds. While many early excavators deliberately sought monumental and valuable finds (inscribed stelae and gold jewellery, for example), Petrie paid attention to the less obviously valuable material, believing that humble pottery, so often disregarded, was the single most useful indicator for assigning a given site, or phase within a site, to a particular period.

His interest in pottery led him to develop the statistical technique of Seriation (or Sequence Dating). This development was a direct response to a particular problem. The 4000+ Predynastic (prehistoric) graves excavated at Nagada (1895), Abadiya and Hu (1898–9), had yielded vast quantities of pottery in different styles, some other grave-goods, but no writings. Determined to sort them into a relative chronological order, Petrie selected 900 graves, each containing at least five of the nine major pottery types. Each grave was represented by a cardboard strip, which was divided into nine sections representing the major pottery types: the numbers of each pottery type were then recorded on the slip. Next Petrie took the 900 strips and arranged them so that graves with similar pottery types were kept together. He then divided the sorted graves into fifty equal groups, to which he assigned 'Sequence Dates', numbering from thirty to eighty. This work

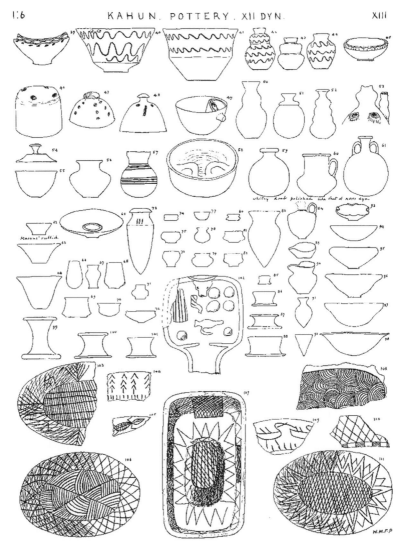

FIGURE 5.2 Drawings of pottery finds from Kahun. Plate XIII in W.M. Flinders Petrie, *Kahun, Gurob and Hawara*, 1890.

provided both the basic framework for discussing the Predynastic Period in Egypt and a significant analytical tool for modern archaeologists working with similar classes of material, although today the sorting is done by computer rather than by hand.

In 1892 Petrie became the Edwards Professor of Egyptology at University College London, a post he was to hold for forty-one years. He died Sir Flinders Petrie in Jerusalem on 29 July 1942. His body was buried in the Protestant cemetery on Mount Zion, but his head was preserved in a jar. Eventually it was shipped back to England so that, in accordance with his wishes, a scientific study might be made of Petrie's brain.

In late 1905 Davis stopped financing the Inspectors of the Antiquities Service and instead employed the freelance Edward Ayrton (1882–1914) to excavate on his behalf. This marked a downturn in the standard of Davis' work. Left to his own devices Ayrton was a competent, Petrie-trained excavator, but he found it impossible to resist Davis' demand for rapid results at the expense of proper record keeping and conservation. It is therefore unfortunate that, on 6 January 1907, the new team discovered a highly complex secondary burial in the tomb known today as KV 55. While Davis always believed that he had discovered the mummy of Queen Tiy, most Egyptologists today believe that he found either Tiy's son Akhenaten, or Akhenaten's successor Smenkhkare.

Davis went on to make more important finds including the royal tomb of Horemheb, last king of the Eighteenth Dynasty. But he was a disappointed man. He had always hoped to find the tomb of the late Eighteenth Dynasty Tutankhamen: a king whose name was known from several monuments, but who had neither a known tomb nor a body in either cache. Davis had, in fact, come very close. During the 1905–6 season Ayrton had discovered a faience cup bearing the king's name. In 1907 his team, again led by Ayrton, had found a small pit packed with Tutankhamen's embalming materials. Finally, in 1909, the team had discovered a small, undecorated chamber that yielded gold foil from a chariot harness, inscribed with the name of Tutankhamen and his successor Ay. Meanwhile, there were exciting discoveries being made in the nearby Valley of the Queens, the elite cemetery used by many New Kingdom consorts and their children. Official excavations did not start in this Valley until 1903, when Ernesto Schiaparelli (1856–1928), Director of Turin Museum, set to work. Schiaperelli's most important discovery was the empty, beautifully decorated, tomb of Nefertari, consort of the Nineteenth Dynasty Ramesses II.

In 1914 Maspero retired as Director-General of the Antiquities Service for the second time. His successor, Pierre Lacau, recognised that Egypt was undergoing rapid changes. In March 1922 Fuad I would be crowned king of Egypt; in April 1923 a new constitution would be put forward. With the British protectorate about to be abolished the Egyptians naturally wanted to take control over their own valuable antiquities. Lacau therefore decreed that all excavations would be strictly controlled by the state. The old practice of splitting finds between Egypt and the excavator on a 50:50 basis was to be ended; all finds would now remain in Egypt unless the authorities chose to make an exception. Not everyone was happy with this new rule. Excavators such as Petrie, who relied on private finance and who therefore needed to reward their backers with finds, suddenly started to find the prospect of working in the Sudan or the Near East appealing.

In 1922 Howard Carter and his patron, Lord Carnarvon, discovered the substantially undisturbed tomb of Tutankhamen in the Valley of the Kings. The tomb was packed with grave goods, while the king himself lay in the burial chamber, protected by a series of golden coffins. Carter was a skilled artist and a meticulous excavator and conservator, but he realised that he needed help if he was to empty the tomb without destroying its contents, so he halted work while he assembled an international team of experts: architects, a photographer, a conservator, an archaeologist, a linguist and others. Although the first Egyptologists had happily taken responsibility for all aspects of their sites – survey, excavation, planning, photography, pottery and bone analysis, mummy autopsy, etc. – this approach could no longer be justified. Today's excavators are both team leaders who supervise a diverse group of specialists and fund-raisers who work to raise the finances needed to support their work. Local workmen are still used to excavate the monuments, but not in the vast numbers employed by Belzoni or even Petrie. Work is far slower and much better supervised, with the Supreme Council of Antiquities insisting that only those with the appropriate training be allowed to work on archaeological sites.

BOX 5.4 Howard Carter

In 1891, the seventeen-year-old Howard Carter (1874–1939) started his Egyptological career as artist-assistant to Percy Newbury. Working for the Egypt Exploration Fund they recorded the decorated walls of the Middle Kingdom rock-cut tombs at Beni Hassan and el-Bersha. The next few years were spent acquiring valuable experience: there was a Christmas spent with Petrie at Amarna, a rescue excavation in the Delta and more recording work at the Deir el-Bahri mortuary temple of the female pharaoh Hatshepsut.

In 1899 Carter accepted a permanent position with the Egyptian Antiquities Service. As Inspector for southern Egypt he was responsible for the Valley of the Kings. He fitted metal gates on the tombs, installed electricity and even built a donkey park to accommodate the ever-increasing number of tourists. In 1903 he was transferred to Cairo, becoming Inspector for northern Egypt. The move was not a success and, following an unfortunate incident involving drunken French tourists, he resigned in October 1905.

After a few uncomfortable years living as an artist and antiquities dealer, Carter teamed up with the wealthy Lord Carnarvon. Both men were convinced that there was a royal tomb – that of the Eighteenth Dynasty Tutankhamen – waiting to be found in the Valley of the Kings. But, as the American amateur Egyptologist Theodore Davis held the sole concession to excavate in the Valley, they were powerless to act. It was not until 1917 that they could start to clear the Valley down to its bedrock. This was an expensive business and the results were so meagre that Carnarvon began to doubt the wisdom of continuing. It was agreed that there would be just one more season.

On 1 November 1922 workmen started to remove the debris lying beneath the tomb of Ramesses VI. Three days later they discovered a flight of steps leading to a sealed doorway. They had indeed, as they had predicted, discovered Tutankhamen's tomb! Following Carnarvon's untimely death, Carter spent a decade recording the tomb and its contents. He then started to prepare his work for publication. But his health was failing and he died on 2 March 1939. Tutankhamen's tomb remains substantially unpublished.

FIGURE 5.3 Howard Carter. Photo in the collection of the Library of Congress,
call no. LC-F8- 30481.

FIGURE 5.4 The temple of Hatshepsut at Deir el-Bahri, Egypt. © Matej Michelizza/istock.

The discovery of Tutankhamen fascinated the world's press and completely overshadowed all other archaeological discoveries for many years to come. In Middle Egypt, excavations at Amarna had started to reveal the complicated story of Akhenaten (Amenhotep IV) and his consort Nefertiti. Amarna was a vast, purpose-built site encompassing a main city, a workmen's village, two separate groups of elite tombs cut into the Amarna cliffs and a large royal tomb cut in a separate royal wadi (dried stream bed). The site had had been occupied for approximately thirty years and then abandoned; as it had never been built over, it preserved the mudbrick domestic architecture that other, longer-lasting cities lacked. Petrie had spent one season (1891–2) excavating the main city site. He was followed, in 1902, by an EEF expedition led by Norman de Garis Davies (1865–1941). Davies conducted a detailed epigraphic study of the rapidly deteriorating elite tombs in the Amarna cliffs and produced the invaluable six-volume *Rock Tombs of Amarna* (1903–8).

In 1907 a team from the Deutsche Orient-Gesellschaft (the German Oriental Society), led by Ludwig Borchardt (1863–1938), started to excavate the main city, concentrating on the suburbs. In December 1912 they discovered the studio workshop of the royal sculptor Tuthmosis. Tuthmosis had abandoned his studio early in the reign of Tutankhamen when the entire Amarna population relocated to Thebes. He left behind a series of broken, unfinished and unwanted works of art. Among these were twenty-three heads and faces of the Amarna royal family, including the painted limestone bust of Nefertiti that is today displayed in Berlin Museum. World War I put an end to the German excavations at Amarna, and in 1921 the EES resumed their work.

There were interesting developments in northern Egypt too. The Sakkara Step Pyramid built for the Third Dynasty king Djoser had been open, and empty, for many years. Its earliest

FIGURE 5.5 The step pyramid at Sakkara. © Steven Allan/istock.

modern investigators included Napoleon's soldiers, John Shae Perring and Colonel Vyse (1837) and Karl Richard Lepsius (1842). However, it was not until 1924, when Lacau and Cecil M. Firth (1878–1931) started to excavate around, rather than beneath, the pyramid, that the true extent of the king's mortuary provision was understood. We now know that Djoser's funerary complex, defined by a ditch and an impressive stone wall, included not only a pyramid but columned halls, chapels, ritual courtyards and a small-scale subsidiary tomb. In 1932 Firth was succeeded by the architect-turned-Egyptologist Jean-Philippe Lauer (1902–2001), who was to work at Sakkara for over seventy years, restoring the pyramid and its complex.

The Sakkara cemetery was already ancient when Djoser chose it as the site for his pyramid complex. At least two Second Dynasty kings had built tombs at Sakkara. The remaining kings of the Second Dynasty and all the kings of the First Dynasty had built their tombs at the equally ancient southern cemetery site of Abydos. The Abydos royal tombs had been investigated first by Emile Amélineau (1850–1915) and then, more scientifically, by Petrie. In 1935 Walter Emery started to excavate in the Sakkara cemetery. He uncovered an unprecedented series of rich mastaba-style tombs, which led him to conclude that Petrie may have been wrong in his interpretation of the Abydos cemetery. The kings of the First and Second Dynasties had, after all, been buried at Sakkara. This meant that the Abydos 'tombs' – undeniably inferior in size and content to the Sakkara tombs – were cenotaphs. This theory was a logical and attractive one, and it sparked intense academic debate. Today, however, we know that Emery had underestimated the scale of the Abydos monuments. The tombs may have been relatively small in size, but they were just one part of the royal mortuary provision. Nearby, on the edge of the cultivated land, the First and Second Dynasty kings built walled funerary enclosures housing shrines, sacred spaces and in at least one case a mound encased in mudbrick.

Another major figure working at this time was George Reisner.

BOX 5.5 George Reisner

The early twentieth century saw an increasing number of American archaeologists active in the Near East. Foremost among these was George Andrew Reisner (1867–1942). Reisner studied Egyptology at Harvard University, obtaining his PhD in 1893. He then studied Assyriology and Egyptology in Berlin, working with Adolf Erman and Kurt Sethe. Returning to the United States he embarked on an impressive academic career, eventually becoming Professor of Egyptology at Harvard.

Reisner had no formal training as an excavator. Nevertheless, he proved to be a systematic and methodical archaeologist, refining the techniques of scientific excavation developed by Petrie and devising his own detailed recording systems. He worked on a wide range of sites in both Egypt and Sudanese Nubia, where he excavated the royal burials of the Kingdom of Kerma. He is best known for his work on the Giza Plateau, where he surveyed and excavated many of the elite tombs in the mastaba cemeteries surrounding the three Fourth Dynasty pyramids. His excavation of the valley and mortuary temples of Menkaure (1908–10) yielded an unprecedented series of royal statues. These, all of extremely high quality, showed the king alone, the king and his consort, and the king and some of his gods.

Fifteen years later came another spectacular discovery. On 2 February 1925, when Reisner himself was home in the USA, his team was surveying to the east of the Great Pyramid of King Khufu. As the photographer set up his tripod, one leg sank deep into the desert sand. It had pierced the plaster covering a blocked shaft. Reisner's assistant, Alan Rowe, immediately started to excavate. The shaft proved to be 27m long, and was completely filled with limestone blocks. At the base was a simple, apparently undisturbed, chamber housing the grave goods of Queen Hetepheres, consort of King Snefru, and mother of Khufu. The tomb provided an archaeological mystery unsolved to this day. Although it yielded a wide range of grave goods, including the queen's alabaster sarcophagus and her canopic chest (complete with organs soaked in natron solution), the queen's body was missing.

Reisner made detailed written and photographic records of all his surveys and excavations, and it is therefore ironic that he died before he could complete the publication of his extensive fieldwork. After years of near-blindness, during which he dictated his work, Reisner died at Harvard Camp, Giza, on 6 June 1942.

In 1939, Pierre Montet (1885–1966) discovered the lost tombs of the Twenty-first and Twenty-second Dynasty kings at the eastern Delta site of Tanis (modern san el-Hagar). These Third Intermediate Period kings ruled northern Egypt from the Delta. They built their tombs in the securest place possible: inside the precincts of their temples. Tanis had been investigated by a series of excavators including Mariette (1860–80) and Petrie (1883–6), but Montet was the first to conduct a systematic survey of the site. He had started work in 1921 and had already made some interesting finds. On 27 February 1939, digging in the 'temple of Anta' (actually the smaller Mut temple), he discovered a royal tomb. Here, in a suite of four rooms, lay the burials of Shoshenq III, Takelot II, Osorkon II and his son Prince Hornakht. On 17 March he opened another tomb and discovered Siamun, Pseusenes and Heqakheperre-Shoshenq II, who lay in a remarkable falcon-headed silver coffin. A false wall and granite plug hid the entrance to the undisturbed burial of Pseusenes I. A second chamber held the intact burial of Amenemope. Two further chambers yielded the undisturbed burials of generals Ankhefenmut and Wendjebauendjedet. Montet continued to work at Tanis until 1951. French survey work continued at the site, first under Jean Yoyotte (1965–86) and then Philippe Brissaud (1987 to the present).

Bringing the story up to date

Today, conservation has become the Egyptian archaeologist's first priority, and excavation – essentially, the destruction of a site – is not a first response, but an extreme measure to be conducted either to answer a specific question, or to record a site that is under threat. There are many archaeological missions of all nationalities, Egyptian included, working in Egypt. Most of these are involved in long-term conservation projects, or in the re-excavation of sites that were inadequately excavated in times when Egyptologists specifically sought valuable and large-scale finds. The excavation and sieving of old spoil heaps often proves fruitful in this respect.

BOX 5.6 Unrolling the dead: The developing science of biomedical Egyptology

'Mummies' – artifically preserved human and animal corpses – have become a defining Egyptian artefact. While Egypt is not the only country to have yeileded deliberately preserved bodies, and while not all 'mummies' have been artifically preserved (some have been naturally conserved by ice, or by hot sand), Egypt has provided archaeologists with many thousands of ancient human bodies, hundreds of which are now housed in museums throughout the world. These mummies are allowing biomedical archaeologists to develop and refine sceintific techniques to allow a better understanding of the lives of the ancients.

The Egyptian mummies now housed in western museums are the legacy of nineteenth-century travellers who regarded the long-dead not as human remains worthy of respect, but as the ultimate holiday souvenir. Over time, many of these remains – wrapped mummies, unwrapped mummies and occasional body parts – were donated to local museums. These unprovenanced mummies were essentially archaeological 'dead ends' and, as such, were of little interest to professional Egyptologists. The public, however, were fascinated and paid to attend public mummy unwrappings. Belzoni, ever the showman, opened his London exhibition with the 'unrolling' of both a human mummy and a monkey. The surgeon Thomas Pettigrew found that he could make a good income from public unrollings, but he also kept detailed notes of his work and in 1834 published his popular *History of Egyptian Mummies*.

The discovery of the two royal mummy caches caused a change in attitude. Here was a group of well-known, well-provenanced individuals whose preserved corpses could perhaps, if investigated correctly, make a valuable contribution to the understanding of Egypt's history. Despite their obvious importance, the mummies were autopsied by Maspero, a man with no medical training. Maspero worked at a startling pace: Ramesses II, for example, was stripped to the skin in just fifteen minutes. The bodies were subsequently re-examined by anatomist Grafton Elliot Smith, whose 1912 publication, *The Royal Mummies*, remains the standard authority on this subject.

Ramesses, now displayed in the Cairo Museum, started to decay. Changes in temperature, humidity and light caused his skin to crack and he was invaded by bacteria, fungi and insects. In 1976 Ramesses was flown to the Musée de l'Homme in Paris. Here he was examined by a team of specialists. Samples were taken from his wrappings and body cavities, his skin was repaired and Ramesses was re-wrapped in his original bandages. Both king and coffin were sterilised and, after eight months abroad, Ramesses returned to Egypt.

In 1908, in Manchester, Margaret Murray assembled a team of experts to autopsy two Twelfth Dynasty mummies known as the 'Two Brothers'. Murray's multidisciplinary approach became the standard technique and her legacy has continued at Manchester where the KNH Centre for Biomedical Egyptology is dedicated to human and animal mummy research using a range of non-invasive procedures. Their work is typified by their 1999 investigation of the Late Period mummy of Asru, headed by Rosalie David. Asru had been donated, already unwrapped, to The Manchester Museum in 1825. She had no obvious signs of illness, but her fingers bore signs of arthritis and this, combined with

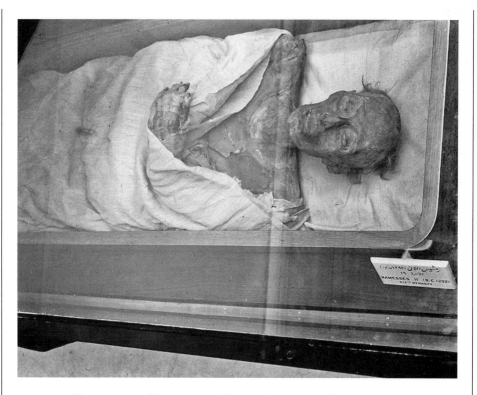

FIGURE 5.6 The mummy of Ramesses II. Library of Congress call no. LC–M31–14547.

signs of calcification in the aorta and the bronchi and in the lower legs and feet, and arthritis in the knee, indicated that she was between fifty and seventy years old at death. Finger- and toe-prints, however, suggested that she was probably in her late forties.

X-rays showed that Asru had bad teeth and that she had suffered a painful jaw infection. Asru's lung tissue showed the scars of sand pneumoconiosis, caused by the inhalation of sand particles. Her rehydrated intestines yielded the larval form of a parasitic worm. Her bladder tissue showed evidence of schistosomiasis infestation and her chest X-ray revealed a form of the dog tape-worm. A CAT (Computed Axial Tomography) scan allowed the scientists to make a solid polymer replica of Asru's skull and this was used as the core for a facial reconstruction. Asru was revealed as an elderly lady with high cheekbones, a protruding upper lip and deep-set eyes.

Supplementing this fieldwork, many projects are underway in museums and laboratories where finds made many years ago are being re-investigated using modern scientific techniques. This is particularly true of mummy studies: specialist departments are succeeding in extracting information from mummies that, not so very long ago, were regarded as essentially worthless. With these advances in scientific excavation, investigation and conservation techniques, Egyptian archaeology can no longer be considered the inferior, manual branch of Egyptology. It has become an important specialisation in its own right.

Further reading

Baird, K.A. (ed.) 1999. *Encyclopedia of the Archaeology of Ancient Egypt*. Routledge: London.

Clayton, P.A. 1982. *The Rediscovery of Ancient Egypt*. Thames & Hudson: London.

Dawson, W.R. and Uphill, E. 1972. *Who Was Who in Egyptology*. (second revised edition). The Egypt Exploration Society: London.

Drower, M.S. 1985. *Flinders Petrie: A Life in Archaeology*. Gollancz: London.

Edwards, A.B. 1877. *A Thousand Miles up the Nile*. George Routledge and Sons: London.

James, T.G.H. 1982. *Excavating in Egypt: the Egypt Exploration Society 1882–1982*. The Egypt Exploration Society: London.

James, T.G.H. 1992. *Howard Carter: The Path to Tutankhamun*. Kegan Paul International: London and New York.

Petrie, W.M.F. 1931. *Seventy Years in Archaeology*. Sampson Low, Marston and Co.: London.

Pringle, H. 2001, *The Mummy Congress: Science, Observation and Everlasting Dead*. Fourth Estate: London.

Reeves, N. 2000. *Ancient Egypt: The Great Discoveries*. Thames & Hudson: London.

Snape, S.R. 1997. *Decoding the Stones*. Weidenfeld & Nicolson: London.

Thomas, N. (ed.) 1995. *The American Discovery of Ancient Egypt, Catalogue and Essays*. Harry N. Abrams: Los Angeles.

Tyldesley, J.A. 2005. *Egypt: How a Lost Civilization was Rediscovered*. BBC Books: London.

Tyldesley, J.A. 2000. *Private Lives of the Pharaohs*. Channel Four Books: London.

6

WESTERN AND SOUTHERN ASIA

Jane McIntosh

West Asia

Antiquarians

Early European perceptions of West Asia were largely through the prism both of the Bible, focusing attention on the Biblical cities of the Levant and the empires at whose hands the Jews had suffered, and of Classical accounts that also painted an unfavourable picture of West Asian civilisations. Travellers were particularly interested in locating the remains of Babylon and the infamous Tower of Babel: they included the twelfth-century Rabbi Benjamin of Tudela and Pietro della Valle, who in 1616 acquired bricks with the first cuneiform inscriptions seen in Europe. The famous Persian city of Persepolis, where more cuneiform inscriptions were found, was also visited by many travellers.

The emergence of archaeology

By the later eighteenth century the interests of visitors in such sites was becoming more scholarly and systematic: there were tentative attempts, for example by the Dane Carsten Niebuhr, to distinguish and decipher different forms of cuneiform; plans of ruins were made, accompanied by detailed notes, and antiquities collected and described. Claudius Rich, appointed in 1807 as British Resident at Baghdad, was an outstanding exemplar of these new antiquarians, undertaking some excavation at Babylon and producing careful topographical plans and three volumes of descriptions of the structures and antiquities he found there, the latter forming the original nucleus of the British Museum's Western Asiatic collections.

In the Levant, the cities of the Holy Land had never ceased to attract the attention of pilgrims, but travellers also now described other ancient places, particularly Petra, the 'rose-red city' of the Nabataeans, rediscovered in 1812 by the intrepid Swiss explorer Johann Ludwig Burckhardt. In the 1840s and 1850s exciting discoveries greatly raised the level of public and scholarly interest in West Asian remains. Progress on the decipherment of cuneiform revealed that Mesopotamian texts named kings and told stories already familiar from the Bible, while initial excavations yielded impressive results. Spurred to greater efforts for national glory, British expeditions under Austen Henry Layard (1817–94) and Hormuzd Rassam (1826–1910) vied with French teams led by Paul-Emile Botta (1802–1870) and Victor Place (1818–75) to uncover spectacular antiquities from the great Assyrian cities of Nineveh, Nimrud and Khorsabad to swell the collections of the British Museum and the Louvre. These included monumental guardian figures of human-headed winged bulls and magnificent reliefs depicting scenes of Assyrian military victories and lion hunts.

BOX 6.1 Decipherment

Ancient texts contain a huge amount of useful and often fascinating information about past societies. Since, however, these are generally written in dead languages and scripts, unlocking this information requires decipherment.

Knowledge of the language is an essential part of decipherment: the early Indian Brahmi script, Chinese oracle bone characters, Egyptian hieroglyphs and the Mycenaean Linear B script were decipherable because they transcribed early forms of known languages spoken later in the same regions.

Etruscan, on the other hand, though written in a script very similar to the Greek alphabet, remains undeciphered because its language is unknown and unrelated to any known language. The same is true of Linear A, the Minoan script, whose signs are very similar to those of Linear B. The Indus script, with very short texts mainly on seals, its signs unrelated to any other known script and its language unknown, stands little chance of decipherment. However, Proto-Dravidian *might* be the underlying language (both for historical reasons and because its structure matches that identified by computer analyses of the Indus texts); it is being explored, though conclusive results may never be reached.

FIGURE 6.1 Brahmi script on Ashokan edict (photo © Jane R. McIntosh).

Decipherment is greatly facilitated when the unknown script evolved to a known script. Thus Brahmi syllabic signs and Chinese oracle bone writing were deciphered by tracing their evolution through later scripts in India and China. Known numerical and a few other signs borrowed from early Sumerian writing (proto-cuneiform) are helping in the slow decipherment of its contemporary and neighbour, Proto-Elamite. In general, however, comparison of sign forms between scripts is unjustifiable: many scripts draw from the universal pool of simple abstract and representational shapes to create their signs, and shared identity of sign values between scripts has to be demonstrated rather than assumed. To take an extreme example, many of the first alphabetic signs were based on Egyptian hieroglyphs – but their Semitic-speaking users gave them completely different sound values from those of the original hieroglyphs.

Analysing the signs' distribution in texts (such as their order, frequency and associations with each other) can provide important information, such as identifying numerical signs and the direction of writing, and segmenting texts into linguistic units from which language type may be deduced. Nevertheless, even identifying a script's signs can be problematic since it involves distinguishing discrete signs from allographs (variant forms of the same sign) and ligatures (combinations of two or more signs).

Both the nature of the script and its complexity play their part in the chances of its decipherment. Scripts that are purely alphabetic have a very small repertoire of signs (twenty to forty); identifying some yields incomplete words that provide clues to the identity of other signs. Syllabic scripts require more signs (thirty-five to 150) but deciphered signs similarly give the clue of partial words. Michael Ventris (1922–56), who deciphered Linear B, made grids of signs that behaved in similar ways, enabling him to group together signs containing the same consonant but different vowels; and the same vowel but different consonants. Guessing some Cretan place names in the texts gave him the sound value of a few signs: to his amazement, when he used these elsewhere in the texts, he found they spelt out words in early Greek – and full decipherment followed.

The majority of ancient (and some modern) scripts, however, are logosyllabic, combining hundreds and sometimes several thousand syllabic signs and logograms, often in complex ways. Since logograms represent the meaning and/or sound of whole words, they are deciphered one by one and usually offer no clues to the identity of other signs. Frequently logosyllabic scripts exhibit polyvalence (several meanings or sound values for a single sign or several ways of writing the same sound or word). Some scripts used determinatives to distinguish between polyvalent signs: these were unspoken, adding to the complexity facing the decipherer. Maya scribes fully exploited their script's many ways of writing individual words, one of the reasons it is still not completely deciphered; another is the large number of logograms.

Bilingual texts are invaluable in decipherment, the readable text giving the meaning of the parallel text in the unknown script. The publication of the Rosetta Stone, discovered in Napoleon's 1799 Egyptian campaign, enabled Jean-François Champollion (1790–1832) to begin his successful decipherment of Egyptian hieroglyphs (see p74). This inscription was written in Greek and Egyptian, using three scripts, Greek, demotic and hieroglyphic. Ptolemy was named in the Greek text: his name could be identified in the hieroglyphic text, written inside a cartouche (oval frame), using uniconsonantal signs (a small part of the hieroglyphic repertoire, which includes two- and three-consonant and other signs), and these could be matched with Greek letters. Other bilingual texts provided confirmation and the identification of further signs. Champollion correctly surmised that the underlying language was a form of Coptic, spoken later in the region.

Similar clues allowed the decipherment of cuneiform, the script used in West Asia from the third to late first millennia BC. Trilingual inscriptions of the Achaemenid King Darius at Persepolis in Old Persian, Neo-Elamite and Neo-Babylonian contained royal names and dynastic formulae.

FIGURE 6.2 Trilingual inscription of Xerxes on a pillar in the south portico of Darius' palace, Persepolis. Photo © شفرداینایواک Wikimedia Commons.

Georg Friedrich Grotefend (1775–1853) identified these in the largely alphabetic Persian text (a known language), obtaining the meaning of some of the cuneiform signs. Full decipherment was independently achieved by Henry Rawlinson (1810–95) using a much longer trilingual inscription of Darius at Behistun. From this Rawlinson and others could also identify names in the Babylonian text and begin the decipherment of its more complex, logosyllabic script: the underlying language belonged to the Akkadian branch of the Semitic family and could be reconstructed. This decipherment unlocked the rich archives of Assyrian, Babylonian and earlier Akkadian texts that were emerging from nineteenth-century excavations in Mesopotamia. These included numerous grammars, word lists and other bilingual texts that gave Akkadian equivalents for Sumerian words, providing the key to understanding Sumerian, apparently a language isolate, the language of the first writing in the region, from which cuneiform evolved.

Decipherment has made huge strides in the last two centuries and progress today is aided by the processing power of computers and by sophisticated modern imaging tools that allow accurate copying of poorly preserved texts on a variety of media, such as crumbling clay, weathered stone or faded manuscripts. Nevertheless, new scripts are still being discovered and some that have long been known still defy decipherment.

Further reading

Coe, M.D. 1992. *Breaking the Maya Code*. Thames and Hudson: London.
Coulmas, F. 1999. *The Blackwell Encyclopedia of Writing Systems*. Blackwell: Oxford.
Eglund, R.K. 2004. The state of decipherment of proto-Elamite, pp. 100–49 in (S.D. Houston, ed.) *The First Writing*. Cambridge University Press: Cambridge.
Moore, O. 2000. *Reading the Past. Chinese*. British Museum: London.
Parpola, A. 1994. *Deciphering the Indus Script*. Cambridge University Press: Cambridge.
Pope, M. 1999. *The Story of Decipherment* (Rev, edn.). Thames and Hudson: London.

Excavations in the earlier Assyrian capital at Assur and in southern Mesopotamian cities were initially considered disappointing, since their mud-brick architecture was often not recognised; by the 1860s, however, Assyrian and Babylonian texts could confidently be read, so in the last decades of the nineteenth century southern sites began to be mined for cuneiform tablets, both by archaeologists, such as the French consul Ernest de Sarzec (1837–1901) at Girsu and the Pennsylvania University expedition at Nippur, and by local officials who appreciated the growing market for tablets among European museums and scholars: one such was the Vali of Baghdad who plundered Sippar of 10,000 tablets, which he sold to local dealers, frustrating the authorised investigations of the British Museum's Wallis Budge (1857–1934).

In Iran, nineteenth-century investigations focused on Persian remains. Persepolis was visited and described, although no major excavation took place here until the 1930s. Susa was not so fortunate: it attracted the attentions of a French engineer, Marcel Dieulafoy (1844–1920) in the 1880s, who investigated Darius I's palace, and after him those of a geologist, Jacques de Morgan (1857–1924), who cleared massive quantities of earth in order to obtain antiquities. Little was learned of the structural history of the city.

Occasional discoveries of inscriptions in an unknown script, coupled with sculpture in an unknown style discovered at Boghazkoy in Turkey by the art historian George Perrot in 1861, presented a puzzle to which, by the 1880s, a solution was being offered: Dr W. Wright (1837–99), an Irish missionary, and the Assyriologist A.H. Sayce (1845–1933) both wrote books identifying these mysterious remains with the Hittites, a shadowy people mentioned in the Bible.

Making sense of the past

The late nineteenth century saw great advances in excavation techniques and the understanding of the significance of stratigraphy: leaders in this were Koldewey (see Box 6.2), Walter Andrae (1875–1956) and the great Egyptologist Sir Matthew Flinders Petrie (1853–1942) who in 1890–1 conducted scientific excavations in the Levant at Jerusalem and the 30-metre high tell of el-Hesy. Equally groundbreaking was the work of Raphael Pumpelly (1837–1923), an American geologist, and Hubert Schmidt (1864–1933), a German archaeologist, who conducted a stratigraphic excavation at the long-lived prehistoric mound of Anau in Turkmenia. They were remarkable in employing a multidisciplinary team of specialists, including botanists and animal bone experts, foreshadowing modern practices; in their concern with recording all material, however mundane; and in relating the fortunes of the settlement to changing local hydrology. Despite these fine examples, it took many decades before these new standards became the norm, particularly in French-monopolised Iran.

BOX 6.2 Robert Koldewey (1855–1925)

The formation of the Deutsche Orientgesellschaft (German Oriental Society) in 1898 marked a major turning point in the investigation of Mesopotamia's past, when the destructive mining of ancient cities for splendid sculptures and cuneiform tablets began to be replaced by the meticulous investigation and recording of the buildings within them. In the forefront of the Society's work was Robert Koldewey.

Born in 1855, Koldewey had already enjoyed a distinguished career as a lecturer in architecture and excavator of Classical sites in Europe and West Asia. By 1887 he was working on early sites in southern Mesopotamia where he developed the pioneering techniques that enabled him to identify and excavate the mud-brick architecture so widely employed in the region (which was still posing difficulties for some archaeologists eighty years later). His breakthrough techniques were adopted by his colleagues, such as Walter Andrae, greatly to the benefit of Mesopotamian archaeology.

In 1897 Koldewey visited Babylon, where he collected surface finds of magnificent glazed decorative tiles. This inspired him to return the following year, sponsored by Deutsche Orientgesellschaft: he devoted his remaining years in the field to uncovering the city, still famous as the capital of the Babylonian empire, and home of the ziggurat known as the Tower of Babel. Koldewey surveyed the city and excavated its principal monuments, including the magnificent sacred precinct containing the ziggurat and the temple of Marduk. His investigations showed that the Greek historian Herodotus had not exaggerated in describing the extraordinary width of the city's walls. Led by the tiles, Koldewey discovered the remains of the Ishtar Gate and the Processional Way, wonderfully decorated with friezes depicting lions, dragons and bulls.

In addition, Koldewey uncovered the palace of Nebuchadrezzar II, in which the throne room was also decorated with a magnificent frieze, and identified what he believed to be the remains of the Hanging Gardens of Babylon (the location of these remains a controversial issue: some scholars argue persuasively that they were located not at Babylon but at Nineveh). Koldewey also investigated part of the city's domestic architecture. Leaving Babylon in 1917 and meticulous to the last, Koldewey published his results in full by 1924, the year before his death.

FIGURE 6.3 The Ishtar Gate and throne room frieze from Babylon, reconstructed in Berlin's Pergamon Museum from the original glazed bricks. Photo © bpk/Vorderasiatisches Museum, SMB/Reinhard Saczewski.

Andrae's excavations at Ashur, the ancient political and religious capital of Assyria, meticulously uncovered the plan of the city and exposed mud-brick buildings. In a pioneering study, Andrae traced the temple of Ishtar from its final Neo-Assyrian form back some 2000 years to its origin as a small Sumerian shrine. A gifted artist, Andrae enlivened his thorough, detailed excavation reports with fine reconstruction drawings. Andrae and Koldewey were both members of the Deutsche Orientgesellschaft, which conducted many substantial investigations in West Asian sites, particularly the uniquely important site of Uruk, the 'first city', where its work continues to the present day, interrupted only by wars.

A maturing discipline

After World War I when the Ottoman Empire was carved up, Iraq came under British Mandate. Gertrude Bell (1868–1926), a veteran traveller and Orientalist, who was tasked with creating an Iraqi antiquities service, introduced regulations to protect the new state's past. Permits were now required for excavation, which had to meet the best standards of the time; appropriate specialists such as an epigrapher had to form part of the team; and finds were to be divided between the country funding the excavation and the Iraqi National Museum, which Bell set up. Similar regulations were adopted in other West Asian countries.

Southern Mesopotamia, the cradle of civilisation, was a major focus of archaeological attention. While the mud-brick architecture of Sumerian cities could not match the splendours of Assyria or Egypt, popular interest was stirred by Woolley's spectacular discoveries at Ur (see Box 6.3). In the 1930s the Chicago Oriental Institute under Henri Frankfort (1897–1954) undertook exemplary excavations at the major Sumerian sites of Eshnunna and Khafajeh in the Diyala valley, pioneering a technique for preserving the fragile clay tablets by baking them at the site. The huge numbers of tablets recovered from early Mesopotamian cities revealed in minute detail both the daily life and history of the Sumerians and their Old Babylonian successors and their rich literary, religious and mythological world. Excavations of the superimposed levels of the temple of Abu at Eshnunna yielded limestone figures depicting Early Dynastic worshippers, while the investigation of the city's houses uncovered material that brought the Sumerians to life. Thorkild Jacobsen (1904–93) and his wife Rigmor, members of the Chicago team, undertook an innovative survey of the Diyala valley, making a systematic record of the many ancient settlements there, which they were able to date from surface finds of pottery; the linear pattern of the settlements revealed the course of ancient rivers, streams and canals.

The Chicago Institute also worked outside southern Mesopotamia. For example, in 1933 Jacobsen and the British archaeologist Seton Lloyd (1902–96) rediscovered the remains of the Jerwan aqueduct, constructed by the Assyrian king Sennacherib to bring clean water from the mountains to his capital at Nineveh, a major engineering feat.

The antecedents of the early cities were still only patchily known from a few excavations, such as those of Max von Oppenheim (1860–1946) at Halaf in 1899–1929. In order to set such sites within a secure chronological framework, deep soundings were dug at a number of long-occupied sites, such as Uruk in the south, where occupation began in the fifth millennium BC 'Ubaid period, and Nineveh in the north, where in 1931 Max Mallowan (1904–1978) excavated a 21-metre-deep trench down to virgin soil, which established that the Halaf material occurred immediately before the 'Ubaid period. By 1943, excavations at sites such as Chagar Bazaar had identified two earlier periods, Samarra and Hassuna.

BOX 6.3 Sir Leonard Woolley (1880–1960)

Leonard Woolley's name is forever linked with the spectacular discoveries in the Royal Cemetery at Ur, where, among more than 2000 graves, he discovered sixteen richly furnished tombs from the dawn of Mesopotamian history. Some contained inscribed objects linking them to rulers named in the Sumerian King List, which refers to the city-states of the Early Dynastic period later unified in the Akkadian Empire. Many of the remarkable grave goods from the tombs were made of gold or inlaid with mosaic designs including pieces of lapis lazuli from distant Afghanistan. Several graves contained grooms, female attendants, musicians and guards, seemingly willing human sacrifices to accompany their ruler: one, the 'Great Death Pit', contained seventy-four of them. Woolley's vivid account of his discoveries brought the funerary scenes alive.

But it also shed light on his extraordinary skill and inspired excavation methods. Encountering the tiny fragments of surviving decorative elements, he devised techniques using wax, plaster of paris and inordinate patience to recover the form of the harps, gaming boards and other long-decayed wooden objects that they had once adorned. An experienced excavator, Woolley applied to Ur the archaeological techniques and principles that were gradually gaining acceptance: attention to stratigraphy; careful exposure of architecture, including the ubiquitous but difficult to recognise mud-brick structures; and the collection and analysis of pottery and other artifacts that could shed light both on the chronology of the city and the life of its inhabitants.

Born in 1880, Woolley began his archaeological career in Oxford's Ashmolean Museum, but soon became involved in excavations, digging in Britain and Nubia and in 1913 succeeding David Hogarth (1862–1927) at Carchemish, an important Neo-Hittite city in the Levant. From here he also conducted an archaeological survey of Sinai. An intelligence officer during World War I, he spent 1916–18 as a Turkish prisoner, returning in 1919 to complete the Carchemish excavations. Following a season at the Egyptian city of Amarna, he was appointed director of the joint British Museum–University Museum of Pennsylvania expedition to Ur, where he excavated from 1922 to 1934.

FIGURE 6.4 The reconstructed remains of the ziggurat of Ur.

This city was the capital of the Ur III empire, which reunited southern Mesopotamia about a century after the collapse of the Akkadian empire. Woolley uncovered the precinct of the moon god, Nanna, Ur's patron deity, at the heart of the city, within which were temples, the vaulted tombs of the Ur III kings and the magnificent and well-preserved ziggurat.

Outside the precinct Woolley exposed much of the residential area of the city and discovered quays: Ur had been a major port in the third millennium BC, though the coast later shifted far to the south. Woolley's excavations took the city's history into later times: of particular interest was an entire residential quarter of the succeeding Old Babylonian period. He also uncovered the remains of the earliest occupation here. To Woolley's excitement this was separated from the Early Dynastic levels by sterile alluvial deposits; a clergyman's son, with an enduring interest in theology, he concluded that these were evidence of the Great Flood, a divinely ordained catastrophe in Sumerian religious literature as it is in the Bible (though later scholars more prosaically assign these deposits to one or several localised episodes of flooding, to which the region was prone). Woolley also completed earlier excavations at the nearby settlement of 'Ubaid, occupied since the fifth millennium BC.

Knighted in 1935 for his work at Ur, Woolley went on to excavate later sites in the Levant: the important Bronze Age city of Alalakh (Tell Atchana) and the Greek colony at Al-Mina, retiring in 1949 to work on the reports of his findings: some of the ten volumes on Ur appeared after his death in 1960.

Although Halaf pottery was also found at Carchemish in the Levant, investigations in this region were largely concerned with later times: historical Jewish sites, the Iron Age Phoenician and Israelite cities known from the Bible, including the Israelite capital Samaria, and their Bronze Age Canaanite precursors, including Jericho. The Chicago Oriental Institute expedition to investigate Megiddo was planned and executed on a grand scale; like all American expeditions of the time it was funded on a level beyond the wildest dreams of the austerely equipped European ventures, its personnel enjoying facilities including a tennis court. The enormous size of the mound made the original plan of complete excavation impossible, but between 1925 and 1939 large parts of the upper cities were exposed and several deep trenches were sunk to explore the mound's lower levels. Particularly impressive were the remains attributed to the time of Solomon, when structures matching Biblical descriptions of his palaces and stables were traced across the settlement.

In 1929 the French under Claude Schaeffer (1898–1982) began long-running excavations at Ugarit, uncovering a large part of the later Bronze Age levels of the long-lived city, including palaces, rich tombs, private houses and temples, as well as Ugarit's port on the nearby coast. A great archive of tablets provided detailed information on life and culture and particularly on the administration of Ugarit, at that time a vassal of the Hittites.

The obscurity that had surrounded the Hittites themselves in the nineteenth century was by now largely dispelled. In 1906 Hugo Winckler (1863–1914) began excavations for the Deutsche Orientgesellschaft at Boghazkoy, which proved to be Hattusas, the Hittite capital. Here he exposed massive inner and outer fortifications, an outer town and a citadel with palaces and temples and a massive archive of cuneiform texts. Excavations were resumed under Kurt Bittel (1907–80) in 1931. Many of the texts were written in Akkadian, which was now well understood; others used the cuneiform script but were in the Hittite language. The Czech linguist Friedrich Hrozny (1879–1952), who tackled its decipherment, soon established that, unlike Akkadian and most West Asian languages, Hittite was not a Semitic but an early Indo-European language; by 1915 he had achieved success. A number of texts on monuments, however, were written in a different script, hieroglyphic Hittite. At first thought only to be a series of symbols, it was later identified as a script and finally deciphered in 1947 when a bilingual text in hieroglyphic Hittite and Phoenician was discovered at Karatepe.

The archives from Hattusas and from other Hittite sites reinforced and filled out the picture revealed some decades earlier by the Amarna letters, of the Hittite empire as a major player in the power politics of second-millennium BC West Asia, along with Egypt, Mitanni and the Kassites. The latter, who ruled Babylonia, remained a shadowy dynasty until 1942–45 when Seton Lloyd and the Iraqi archaeologist Fuad Safar discovered a substantial quantity of Kassite texts at Aqar Quf (ancient Dur-Kurigalzu), a short-lived Kassite palace and town.

A slightly earlier period of Mesopotamian history was spectacularly revealed by French excavations under André Parrot (1901–80) and his successors at Mari on the central Euphrates in Syria. Beginning in the 1930s, when tightened antiquities' export restrictions drove many foreign expeditions to transfer from Iraq to Syria, Parrot worked here until 1974. Occupied from the third millennium BC, the city-state of Mari saw its peak of prosperity in the eighteenth century BC under Zimri-Lim, whose 300-room palace has been the main focus of the excavations. An archive of more than 20,000 tablets uncovered here has yielded abundant information on all aspects of life, from the state's foreign relations and internal administration, through the daily management of the palace and its personnel, to the private life of the royal family.

Knowledge of early humans in West Asia was established by the remarkable British Palaeolithic archaeologist, Dorothy Garrod (1892–1968), who became the first woman to hold a chair in Cambridge when she was appointed Disney Professor of Archaeology in 1939. Her excavations in the Mount Carmel caves of Tabun, el-Wad and es-Skhul in 1928–34 revealed the cultural remains and bones of Neanderthals and modern humans, including deliberate Neanderthal burials, as well as a long sequence of stone tool industries stretching from the Lower Palaeolithic to the early Neolithic period, which could be related to the already well-established European sequence of climatic and faunal phases. Similar remains were found by other archaeologists at sites such as Qafzeh.

Post-war transformations

World War II saw a break in archaeological activity in most areas, though Seton Lloyd continued work in Iraq, and in the following decades there were fewer excavations. However, remarkable Neanderthal burials were discovered in the 1950s by the American archaeologist Ralph Solecki at Shanidar in the Zagros foothills: in one burial abundant traces of pollen suggested that the body had been buried with an offering of many flowers. Another individual was severely crippled: his survival to a considerable age indicated a level of care and cooperation hitherto unsuspected in Neanderthal behaviour. The discovery in the 1960s at Ubeidiyah in the Jordan valley of stone tools similar to those associated with early African hominins also revealed a surprisingly early human occupation of West Asia. Associated faunal material suggested a date around 1.4 million BP, indicating that this site belonged to the earliest spread of hominins out of Africa.

A major post-war focus was on the origins of agriculture, which had long been linked particularly with West Asia. Theories based on the inevitability of farming as a step up the ladder of human progress were beginning to give way to questions about the processes that had stimulated the development of agriculture and the mechanisms that had been involved. Several major American expeditions focused on these questions. For their investigations from 1948 onward, the Americans Robert Braidwood (1907–2003) and Bruce Howe selected the 'hilly flanks of the Fertile Crescent', an area in which wild wheat and barley grew and rain-fed agriculture was possible, so a likely place to hold evidence of early farming villages. In order to extract all appropriate data, they fielded a multidisciplinary team, including soil, bone and plant experts. They located a number of sites, of which they excavated one in Iraq, Jarmo, a small village whose inhabitants grew wheat and barley and raised sheep and goats, but also continued to exploit wild resources. Thanks to the recent invention of radiocarbon dating (1949), Jarmo could be assigned to the eighth to seventh millennium BC, making it the earliest farming site then known. Frank Hole and Kent Flannery's expedition, 1961–63, to investigate Ali Kosh in southwest Iran was also multidisciplinary, looking not only at bones and plant remains, which they recovered by the pioneering method of flotation, but also the local environment and regional ecology. Hole returned in 1974 to spend time with local pastoral nomads, using this innovative ethnoarchaeological study to gain many insights valuable for recognising and interpreting the material remains of pastoral communities.

Sites in the Levant and Syria also contributed to a growing understanding of early agriculture, among them Kenyon's (see Box 6.4) excavations at Jericho. It was becoming clear that sedentism, traditionally considered to be a result of agriculture, had actually preceded it in the Natufian period, due to the presence of wild cereals that could be harvested in quantity and stored: this prompted deeper consideration of the factors behind the adoption of agriculture. In the 1970s the British Academy project on the origins of agriculture, the brainchild of the British economist and archaeologist Eric Higgs (1908–76), focused attention on the complex and varied nature of human–animal and human–plant relationships, demonstrating that these form a changeable spectrum rather than the previously accepted clear-cut dichotomy between foraging and agriculture. Much of the work by this project's members was on West Asian sites, including Nahal Oren in Israel and Tell Abu Hureyra in Syria; the latter has provided substantial botanical evidence for the transition to agriculture.

Early agricultural sites were also found in Anatolia: one, at Çatalhöyük, excavated by James Mellaart 1961–5 and still under excavation by a team led by Ian Hodder, proved surprising in many ways. The settlement, occupied from around 7400 BC, extended over 21 hectares and was formed of closely packed mud-brick and timber houses, entered through the roof. Many of the rooms were decorated with colourful murals and some with modelled bull's heads. Comparable in size to a town, but apparently lacking a town's social and economic complexity, Çatalhöyük still poses a challenge in its interpretation. However, one important factor in its prosperity was probably its role in trading local obsidian, a material highly valued and widely exchanged in Neolithic times. Work on tracing the patterns of distribution of obsidian from different sources was made possible by the development during the later twentieth century of scientific methods for characterising materials, for example, by identifying the presence of different combinations of trace elements. Materials like obsidian that could be characterised provided markers identifying networks through which a far wider range of less distinctive materials had been exchanged.

BOX 6.4 Dame Kathleen Kenyon (1906–78)

The difficulties facing female scholars in a man's world meant that many women archaeologists of the earlier twentieth century, such as Tessa Verney Wheeler (1893–1936), operated as the equally active but frequently disregarded partners of their famous husbands. Not so a small band of unmarried women who single-mindedly rose to the top of the profession. Many were involved with West Asia, including Gertrude Bell, Dorothy Garrod and Kathleen Kenyon.

When Gertrude Caton-Thompson (1888–1985) investigated the ruins of Great Zimbabwe, dispelling popular myths by conclusively proving that they were the work of Africans, she took with her as assistant and photographer the twenty-three-year-old Kathleen Kenyon. The daughter of the Director of the British Museum, Kenyon was a keen archaeologist, elected first female president of the Oxford University Archaeological Society while a history undergraduate. On her return to Britain, Kenyon dug with the Wheelers at Verulamium, and was involved in their foundation of the Institute of Archaeology in London, becoming its acting Director during World War II.

In the 1930s she took her Wheeler-taught skills to Palestine, where she participated in John Crowfoot's (1873–1959) excavations of Samaria, capital of divided Israel in the early first millennium BC, sacked by the Assyrians and later reoccupied by the Romans. In 1951 she returned to the Levant where she reopened the British School in Jerusalem, becoming its honorary director and undertaking excavations.

The first was that for which she is best known: the ancient city of Jericho, where she worked from 1952 to 1958. Earlier work by John Garstang (1876–1956) had already revealed Mesolithic and early Neolithic settlement here, but had concentrated on understanding its Bronze Age history, the time of Joshua, when the Bible recounts the Israelite sack of a Caananite town. Kenyon's excavations shed more detailed light on the early settlement, revealing much that was surprising. The site was first occupied around 12,000 BC. In the early ninth millennium BC, when farming was beginning in West Asia, its inhabitants were already participating in an exchange network by which they obtained obsidian for tools from Çiflik in eastern Turkey. After a short break the site was reoccupied throughout the Pre-Pottery Neolithic period, c. 8500–6200 BC: not only was the settlement large, around 4 hectares (10 acres), but it was also surrounded by an astonishingly massive stone wall, 3.6 m (12 ft) high, with a substantial rock-cut ditch and a 9 m (30 ft)-high stone tower with an internal stair.

Kenyon interpreted these surprising structures as defences, against man or beast, while others have speculated that they were designed to impress contemporary communities, provide a barrier against rubbish dumped outside the settlement or act as flood defences. Their discovery overturned the previous impression of early farming communities as necessarily small and technologically limited. Kenyon's excavations traced the succession of later settlements at Jericho; demonstrated that there was unlikely to have been a walled settlement at the time of Joshua; but found evidence consistent with later, Iron Age, Biblical accounts of the city's history.

Later Kenyon turned her attention to Jerusalem, uncovering part of the City of David; her work here was ended by the Six-Day War in 1967. In 1962 she had been made Principal

FIGURE 6.5 The massive stone tower built by the people of Jericho in the Pre-Pottery Neolithic period. Photo © Reinhard Dietrich/Wikimedia Commons.

of St Hugh's College, Oxford; when she retired in 1973, she was made a Dame of the British Empire. She devoted her final years to publications, of which she already had many to her credit: these included site reports, fine synthetic works on the archaeology of the Levant as well as a volume, *Beginning in Archaeology*, on the field techniques of which she was an outstanding exponent, and which she had passed on to many who had worked with her.

In the southern Levant, the creation of the state of Israel turned the attention of its archaeologists, led by Yigael Yadin (1917–84), to sites of strong significance in Jewish history. For example, the Bronze Age city of Hazor, excavated in 1955–8, revealed well-defined thirteenth-century destruction and subsequent Iron Age reoccupation and fortification, which, following the Bible, were linked to the arrival of the Israelites during the Exodus from Egypt and subsequent fortification by Solomon. The palace-fortress of Masada, scene of a Jewish last stand against the Romans, had particular resonance: it was excavated in 1963–5. The accidental discovery in 1947 of ancient manuscripts hidden in a cave at Qumran led eventually, after much dubious activity, to the recovery of jars from eleven caves containing many copies of books of the Old Testament, dated c. 200 BC–AD 100, around a thousand years older than the earliest copies previously known to have survived. Hidden along with commentaries and some other works, these Dead Sea scrolls may have been the property of an Essene monastic community based at Qumran or of individuals fleeing Jerusalem during the Jewish revolt in AD 67.

Many travellers visited the impressive Nabataean city of Petra and some made detailed records of its monuments, but serious archaeological investigation did not take place until the 1950s. By this time, however, work in other sites of the region had built up a picture of the Nabataeans, who owed their prosperity to trade, particularly in incense from Southwest Arabia. Work in the latter region, which has gradually come to be identified with the fabled land of Sheba, began in the 1840s; more recent excavations have shed light not only on the monuments and settlements of the region's kingdoms but also on their magnificent irrigation works, such as the Marib dam.

Pioneering work on underwater archaeology, facilitated by the invention of the aqualung in 1943, was undertaken by Honor Frost, Peter Throckmorton, George Bass and others in the Mediterranean and Black Sea from the 1950s onwards. The discovery of several second-millennium ships, as well as many later ones, gave a whole new insight into ancient trade networks and activities, as well as providing fascinating details of ancient shipbuilding. The most spectacular discovery was a wreck found by Bass near Kaş (Uluburun) off the Turkish coast, dated to c. 1310 BC by dendrochonological analysis of logs in its cargo (see Box 3.5 pp52–3). This was probably a Canaanite vessel, regularly sailing on a circular route from the Levant coast to Cyprus, the Aegean and Egypt; its cargo, largely preserved, included ingots of copper, tin and glass, fine pottery, terebinth resin, ivory objects and fine timber.

In Mesopotamia, Max Mallowan's 1949 excavations at Nimrud uncovered 'Fort Shalmaneser', the arsenal and palace of King Shalmaneser, where he recovered many fine objects brought here as tribute or war booty, including a cache of exquisite ivory carvings preserved in the waterlogged deposits at the base of a well. British, Polish and Italian teams worked at Nimrud in later years, and in 1990 Iraqi archaeologists discovered the tombs of several Assyrian queens, buried with magnificent gold jewellery. Other important historical cities also saw new excavations in the post-war years and there was a new emphasis on conservation, for example the work of the Iraqi Antiquities Department at Babylon. At Nippur, Samuel Noah Kramer (1897–1990) and Thorkild Jacobsen excavated the scribal quarter: the thousands of tablets they recovered included copies of almost all known works of Sumerian literature.

Regional surveys became a more common feature of archaeological investigations in the post-war years. An exemplary survey of the Diyala region of Iraq by Robert MacCormack Adams collected data that enabled him to reconstruct the changing patterns of settlement distribution, density and location and their relationship to the local environment, economic activities and other factors, from the earliest occupation in the fifth millennium BC to medieval times. A follow-up study by Jacobsen in 1956 investigated soil salination, charting late-third-millennium BC environmental degradation due to over-irrigation and the consequent northward political and economic shift in Babylonia. Other surveys also provided important information on settlement, environment, economic development, communications and infrastructure. Excavations and surface scraping at Abu Salabikh, an unidentified Sumerian city (possibly Eresh), in the 1960s–'90s, have provided an interesting picture of its third-millennium BC development, including the prevalence of burial under house floors and subsequent tomb robbing after a decent interval. The city also yielded a collection of rare Early Dynastic documents.

Outside the Mesopotamian heartland, excavations continued at Mari and other major sites. The Italian excavations at Tell Mardikh in Syria in the 1960s exposed the remarkable remains of Ebla, capital of an important kingdom of the third and second millennia BC. Among its treasures was a huge adminstrative archive of clay tablets, preserved when the palace was destroyed by fire: many were written in the local language, Eblaite.

An even larger archive, around 25,000 tablets, has been recovered over the years from Kanesh (modern Kültepe), a small Bronze Age city in Turkey, by the eminent Turkish archaeologist Tahsin Özguc (1916–2005), who devoted fifty-seven years to its excavation until his death. Capital of a small kingdom, it was also the foreign trading headquarters of Assyrian merchants in the nineteenth and eighteenth century BC. Composed mainly of economic records but also including personal letters, these documents give an intimate and uniquely detailed picture of the trade in textiles and tin, brought from Assur by donkey caravan and exchanged for Anatolian silver, and also of the daily lives of the participants, including family troubles, smuggling and external political problems.

Some third-millennium BC Sumerian records referred to ships arriving in their ports from Dilmun, Magan and Meluhha, evidently lands accessed through the Gulf. In the 1950s, explorations in the Gulf began to give these names some archaeological substance. A Danish expedition to Bahrain, under Peter Glob (1911–85) and the English archaeologist Geoffrey Bibby (1917–2001), excavated Qala'at al-Bahrain, exposing a settlement of the later third and second millennia BC with imports from both Mesopotamia and the Indus, as well as distinctive local round stamp seals. Combined with investigations on the adjacent mainland and on Failaka at the head of the Gulf, these excavations revealed that Dilmun, land of sweet-water springs and home of Mesopotamia's counterpart to Noah, had been a major trading entrepôt, centred on Bahrain but at different times including various other parts of the northern Gulf.

Danish expeditions also began work in the Oman peninsula, uncovering tombs and towers from the third and second millennia BC, as well as a settlement on the island of Umm-an-Nar. More recently, this region has seen work by expeditions from various nations: among their important discoveries from the same era have been copper mining and processing sites, such as Maysar; coastal fishing villages, such as Ras al-Jinz; and a cache of bitumen pieces that provide detailed evidence of the construction of the reed vessels for which they had formed part of the outer caulking shell. There is little doubt now that this region was Magan in Mesopotamian sources, while Meluhha was the Indus civilisation.

The eastern, Iranian shore of the Gulf was less hospitable for shipping, with few anchorages and access points to the interior. One exception is the area around the centre of the Iranian coast. An important Sassanian and Islamic port was established here at Siraf: this was the subject of a major investigation by David Whitehouse in 1966–73, sponsored by the British Museum, which uncovered the houses of wealthy merchants, industrial areas and imported material reflecting Siraf's international connections with countries throughout the Gulf and Indian Ocean. In this arid area, the cisterns that the excavation uncovered were of crucial importance.

Iran's archaeology was badly neglected until the advent of Roman Ghirshman (see Box 6.5) and the lifting of the French archaeological monopoly in 1931, one immediate result of which was a major survey by Aurel Stein (see Box 6.7). The combination brought up-to-date techniques and principles, such as the importance of stratigraphy, and a growing interest in the early development of towns across the Iranian plateau, contemporary with those in Mesopotamia. To Ghirshman's own excavations at Tepe Giyan and Tepe Sialk were added those by foreign archaeologists at Tepe Yahya, Godin Tepe, Shahr-i Sokhta and elsewhere, and by the Iranian archaeologist Ali Hakemi (1915–97) at Shahdad. These opened up a new world, hinted at in Sumerian mythology, of communities in the fourth and third millennia BC engaged in long-distance trade in metal ores, chlorite, turquoise, lapis lazuli and other commodities, extending from Badakshan in Afghanistan, through Baluchistan, Turkmenia and the Iranian plateau to Mesopotamia where it joined the Uruk and Early Dynastic Sumerian networks that were known from excavations at Uruk and at sites elsewhere in West Asia such as Habuba Kabira South and Tepe Gawra. Many of the Iranian sites yielded a small number of tablets written in what was dubbed the Proto-Elamite script: with some similarities to early Sumerian but in a different language and different in many ways, this script is only now beginning, slowly, to be deciphered.

BOX 6.5 Roman Ghirshman (1895–1979)

Roman Ghirshman was born in 1895 in the Ukraine, but, fleeing the Russian Revolution, eventually settled in France. Here he met his wife Tania, who gave up dentistry to work alongside him. Her autobiography, *Archéologue Malgré Moi*, provides a fascinating account of their travels and life on excavations in Iran and Afghanistan.

Ghirshman transformed archaeology in Iran. Since 1894 the French had enjoyed an official monopoly on archaeological activity here, and had devoted themselves largely to excavating the great city of Susa, where they built themselves a comfortable headquarters, nicknamed 'Susa Castle'. Paying inadequate attention to the context of their finds, they focused on recovering impressive antiquities for museum display, among them the Lawcode of Hammurabi, brought here from Babylon as war booty by an Elamite king.

In 1931 Reza Shah revoked the monopoly, opening Iran to new foreign missions, though the French continued to dominate Iranian archaeology. Ghirshman was among the new wave of archaeologists sent out at this time to investigate beyond Susiana. One of the first sites he worked on was Tepe Sialk, a settlement occupied from the fifth millennium BC: in contrast to his predecessors, Ghirshman conducted the excavation methodically, relating objects to the deposits and structures within which they were found, for the first time identifying mud-brick architecture, and exposing a stratigraphic sequence that was to be the chronological template for Iranian prehistory thereafter. Ghirshman later applied his admirable techniques of recovery and recording to sites in Afghanistan, where France had also enjoyed an archaeological monopoly since 1922, working particularly at Begram, an Indo-Greek and Kushan city enriched by international trade.

In 1947 Ghirshman was appointed director of the French Institute in Iran and turned his attention to Susa, where he excavated until 1967, making sense of the chaos left by his predecessors. He established the city's stratigraphic sequence into Islamic times; exposed an Achaemenid palace, acropolis and royal town; and discovered the first mosque built in Iran. He also conducted excavations at Choga Zanbil, a city established by the second-millennium Elamite King Untash-Napirishu, centred on an unusually constructed and well-preserved ziggurat. Even after retiring in 1967, Ghirshman continued privately sponsored fieldwork. Publication of his findings was completed by Tania after his death at a conference in 1979.

FIGURE 6.6 Detail of a relief on the eastern staircase of the Apadana at Persepolis, Iran, depicting Lydian tribute bearers. Photo © Phillip Maiwald/Wikimedia Commons.

Other work in Iran inevitably focused on the major sites of the Persian Empire. From 1931, the Chicago Oriental Institute undertook work at Persepolis, beginning under the veteran German excavator and Iranologist Ernst Herzfeld (1879–1948) and continuing until 1939. They uncovered the eastern Apadana staircase with its famous reliefs and several of the major palace buildings on the royal terrace, as well as undertaking conservation work.

Subsequently, the Iranian Antiquity Service continued the excavation, but from 1964 entrusted conservation work to IsMEO in Rome. Other Achaemenid royal remains were investigated at Susa and Pasargadae. Susa was also the main focus of research into earlier times, when the city was the capital of Elam; a few other sites of this period were also explored, including Anshan (modern Tal-e Malyan).

Pumpelly's work at Anau for a long time remained in a vacuum, but in the 1950s V.M. Masson uncovered early farming settlements in southern Turkmenia, including Djeitun. These seemed to fit into the emerging picture of very early farming communities in West Asia expanding into adjacent areas in subsequent millennia: the sixth-millennium BC date of the Djeitun culture was consistent with this. Further work in this region uncovered Bronze Age towns at Namazga and other Kopet Dagh sites, which were in trading contact with the Indus cities and Iranian plateau towns.

Bringing the story up to date

Recent investigations in Yemen have focused on the development of early agricultural communities, particularly in the Dhamar region of the highlands and the adjacent lowlands.

These have revealed the impressive antiquity of the sophisticated agricultural terraces and water conservation techniques, such as dams and channels, which began during the fourth millennium BC and continued until disastrously superseded by modern agricultural methods in the twentieth century AD, which have brought erosion, aridity and loss of vegetation. Here, as in several parts of the world, archaeology is now being used to demonstrate the advantages of traditional 'backward' technology over modern mechanised methods.

In recent years, work by Russian archaeologists in the Oxus region has revealed a flourishing but still poorly understood civilisation, BMAC (Bactria-Margiana Archaeological Culture), a linked series of oases with irrigation agriculture and fortified urban settlements, dating to the late third and early second millennia BC. Thereafter its settlements were abandoned, but its distinctive material appeared in neighbouring regions, including Helmand and Baluchistan.

The accidental discovery of a rich tomb, followed by a year of systematic looting, recently revealed another important new culture, in the Jiroft area of Iran's Kerman province. At first known mainly from the plundered material surfacing on the international antiquities market, its identity, extent and cultural integrity were initially difficult to gauge, but ongoing excavations at Konar Sandal and other Jiroft sites have now established the culture's context among fourth- and third-millennium BC communities, when it was a major source of the highly prized and widely traded chlorite vessels. The story of the Jiroft culture illustrates a wider issue of great current importance throughout West Asia and beyond: although countries like Iran often devote considerable resources to the investigation and conservation of their past, the task of policing and adequately investigating all casual discoveries and known sites is frequently beyond the resources of the state, providing many opportunities for international criminal networks to operate within the illicit antiquities market.

In addition, in recent years political developments have taken their toll on West Asia's surviving past. Although work continued throughout the Iran–Iraq war of the 1980s, the Gulf War and subsequent sanctions seriously curtailed international work in Iraq, though the Iraqis themselves continued some archaeological activity, particularly rescue excavations on sites in the south. This was brought to a halt by the Coalition invasion that toppled Saddam in 2003 and the massive security problems that have followed; tragically, the breakdown of law and order has greatly facilitated the plundering of archaeological sites by looters feeding the huge international trade in illegally acquired antiquities and has allowed them with impunity to vastly increase the scale of their operations. Many Iraqi sites have been raided using massive earthmoving equipment, resulting in their almost total obliteration. Warfare has also provided the cover for massive looting in other parts of West Asia – for example, in Lebanon.

South Asia

Antiquarians

Early European travellers in India were forcefully struck by the cave temples, stupas, temples and other monuments they encountered and often recorded their observations in considerable detail. The unfamilar artistic conventions and subject matter of the carvings and architecture provoked admiration and revulsion in about equal measure.

The emergence of archaeology

By the late eighteenth century European polymaths had become strongly interested in India's cultural and intellectual past. Scholarly studies were advanced by the foundation of the Asiatic Society of Bengal in 1784 by Sir William Jones (1746–94), who first drew attention to the similarities between the Sanskrit, Avestan (early Iranian) and European languages. He and his colleagues, such as James Fergusson (1808–86), James Burgess (1832–1916) and James Prinsep (1799–1840), took a keen interest in antiquities, describing and recording monuments, inscriptions and chance discoveries, undertaking some excavation, studying coins and epigraphy, recording folk history and relating ancient texts to surviving remains. The megaliths of the south sparked much interest since they resembled those of Europe: the question of their relationship drew some extraordinary answers. Robert Bruce Foote (1834–1912) focused on earlier remains, identifying Palaeolithic and Neolithic tools comparable with those of Europe, and correctly surmising that the ash mounds were related to early cattle keeping.

Notable among these researchers, most of whom were antiquarians only in their spare time, was Alexander Cunningham (1814–93). Employed at first as a military surveyor, in 1871 he was appointed the first Director-General of the newly formed Archaeological Survey of India. Eclectic in his antiquarian pursuits, his chief interest lay in investigating Early Historic and Buddhist sites, following historical information contained in Classical Greek, Indian and Chinese literature.

A maturing discipline

In 1890 the post of Director-General of the Archaeological Survey of India was abolished and responsibility for archaeological conservation and investigation devolved to regional authorities, with the result that these became patchy and generally substandard. When Lord Curzon was appointed Viceroy of India in 1899, he made it a priority to rectify the situation, appointing John Marshall as DG, an inspired choice. Marshall (see Box 6.6) rose magnificently to the challenge, setting conservation on a firm and enlightened path and conducting and overseeing excavations and surveys throughout the subcontinent. His own work focused on Early Historic cities, Buddhist monuments and the great Indus city of Mohenjo-daro. Under his authority, however, a much wider range of investigations took place. Ernest Mackay (1880–1943), who succeeded Marshall as principal excavator at Mohenjo-daro, also excavated the Indus town of Chanhu-daro, where he uncovered industrial facilities including a bead-making factory. Mackay at Mohenjo-daro and the Indian archaeologist M.S. Vats at Harappa found material belonging to the final stages of Indus city life, revealing decay and civic disintegration.

The Indus towns and cities yielded many inscribed seals, and a much smaller number of other inscribed materials. These attracted attention from the start and several decipherments of the script were soon proposed. But in contrast to other important ancient writing systems, the Indus script, despite innumerable attempts, still defies decipherment.

Work on South Asia's earliest inhabitants was advanced in the 1930s by the Cambridge–Yale expedition to the Potwar plateau under the German geologist Hellmut de Terra (1900–81) and his British colleague T.T. Patterson. Through a detailed study of the gravel terraces and loess deposits of the Soan river here, and of their association with stone tools, it was possible to build up a sequence that could be correlated with the glacial sequence in Kashmir and the far better-known European sequence of Pleistocene climate change and cultural development.

BOX 6.6 Sir John Marshall (1876–1958)

John Marshall's appointment in 1902 as Director-General of the Archaeological Survey (ASI) ended a decade of archaeological neglect in India. With a Classics degree and excavation experience gained at the British School in Athens, Marshall was young and inexperienced – but extremely able. In his twenty-six years as DG he designed and executed an excellent conservation policy, saving many important monuments from decay or destruction; drafted comprehensive and enduring antiquities legislation; instituted the publication of annual reports on all aspects of the ASI's work and monographs on the most important; began the training of indigenous South Asian archaeologists and oversaw their excavations, as well as undertaking a number of important excavations himself.

These focused mainly on historical sites, including the Early Historic city of Bhita, the Great Stupa at Sanchi, and particularly the great cosmopolitan city of Taxila in the northwest, where Hellenistic and Indian traditions cross-fertilised to produce the famous Gandharan art style. Here Marshall uncovered large parts of the three successive cities, occupied by Indians, Greeks, Kushans and others, Buddhist shrines and monasteries and other important structures, and revealed a wealth of fine antiquities, including Roman imports and Buddhist sculptures, as well as the artifacts of everyday life.

However, Marshall is best remembered for the discovery of the Indus civilisation. It had been firmly accepted that urban society had not emerged in India until the first millennium BC. In the early 1920s Marshall instigated excavations that completely overturned this belief. Previous exploration at Harappa in the Punjab had turned up strange objects including a seal written in an unknown script; ASI excavations here and at Mohenjo-daro now revealed material unparalleled in the subcontinent and the remains of impressive baked-brick and mud-brick architecture: cities of a lost civilisation.

Marshall published a selection of the material in the *Illustrated London News* in 1924, hoping for clues to its date, and was immediately rewarded: Mesopotamian scholars had encountered similar architecture, seals, figurines and other objects in third-millennium sites such as Ur and Susa. It was clear that the people of the Indus civilisation, as it was soon named, were contemporary with the Sumerians.

Marshall himself took charge in the 1925–6 field season at Mohenjo-daro, the more rewarding site, since Harappa had been badly damaged by nineteenth-century railway engineers plundering its bricks. In this and later seasons at Mohenjo-daro, large residential areas were exposed containing well-built courtyard houses, straight streets and, most remarkably for the period, an efficient drainage system, while on the high mound on the west, a large rectangular brick basin, the 'Great Bath', was discovered.

Marshall was diligent in applying those archaeological techniques with which he was familiar, for example keeping records of the three-dimensional location of finds, but his unsatisfactory excavation methods using arbitrary, artificial levels measured from the (varying) ground surface have earned him the opprobrium of later generations, notably his eventual successor, Mortimer Wheeler. Nevertheless, the scale of his work at Mohenjo-daro, coupled with his thorough and prompt publication of his results, provided the solid foundations of data on the Indus civilisation while his intelligent and inspired interpretations, rooted in a thorough knowledge of Indian culture, created a picture of the Indus civilisation that still has much value.

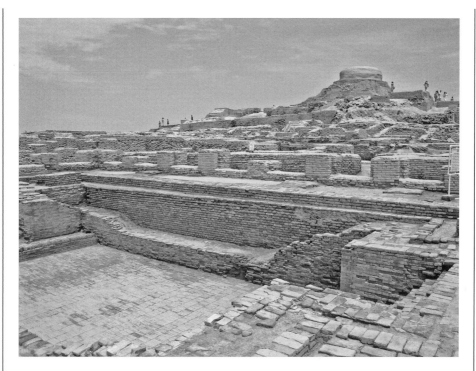

FIGURE 6.7 The 'Great Bath', Mohenjo-daro. Photo © Grjatoi/Wikimedia Commons.

Under Marshall's energetic and engaged authority, archaeological work and conservation were undertaken all over the subcontinent, firmly ensuring the preservation and appreciation of the visible heritage and shedding new light on the past. After retiring as DG in 1928, Marshall worked for the ASI until 1934, preparing the report on Mohenjo-daro; and much of the rest of his life was spent on the publication of both full reports and excellent popular guides on Taxila and Sanchi. He received many well-deserved honours including a knighthood in 1914.

The work on historical archaeology begun in the nineteenth century continued strongly in the twentieth. Excavations at Taxila and other cities in the northwest shed light on the development of the Gandhara art style, the Indo-Greek kingdoms that followed Alexander's conquests, the Kushans whose empire stretched from Inner Asia to central India, and the flourishing trade between China and the west that flowed through these northern cities. Aurel Stein's (see Box 6.7) explorations of Inner Asia revealed many of the cities along this trade route. In 1938 French excavations in the trading city of Begram revealed a treasury of imported material, including Roman glassware from Alexandria, Chinese lacquerware and exquisite Indian Buddhist ivory carvings. In the Ganges valley, excavations in the Mauryan capital at Pataliputra uncovered wooden and stone remnants of the magnificent buildings described in the contemporary accounts of the Greek ambassador Megasthenes and the Mauryan chief minister Kautilya.

BOX 6.7 Sir Mark Aurel Stein (1862–1943)

Mark Aurel Stein was born in Hungary in 1862 but took British nationality in 1904. Educated in languages and oriental studies, he also received invaluable military training in geography and surveying. In 1888 he took up a post at Punjab university and during his annual leave visited Kashmir, where he began the detailed explorations that were to become his lifelong passion: here he traced the topography described in the chronicle of the region's kings. He also established a mountainous tented camp at Mohand Marg near Srinagar, to which he returned after each of his later expeditions and which became his only real home.

Publication of the Kashmir work and his subsequent surveys in India having attracted favourable attention, he was able by 1900 to secure official funding for the first of his expeditions into Inner Asia. Accompanied, as on later expeditions, by a surveyor deputed from the Survey of India, a few assistants, pack animals and a fox terrier called Dash (the first of seven), Stein explored and excavated the ruins of Silk Road cities in Khotan and along the fringes of the Taklamakan desert. At sites such as Niya (China) he recovered antiquities preserved by the region's extreme aridity, including hundreds of documents written in Kharoshthi, Chinese and other scripts on bamboo slips and wooden tablets, and revealed the cosmopolitan Silk Road culture, which blended Indian, Chinese and Hellenistic influences.

The remarkable success of his first expedition was dwarfed by that of his second, in 1906–8. He traced the ancient Chinese military frontier in Central Asia, recovering hundreds of documents and personal possessions of Chinese soldiers stationed along it. But his greatest coup was the discovery at Dunhuang (China) of a huge cache of Buddhist documents in many languages, along with magnificent silk paintings and banners, carefully concealed during the eleventh century in one of the painted Caves of 1000 Buddhas.

Stein used subtle persuasion and bribery to acquire a large quantity of these from the cave's custodian. He obtained many more on his third expedition in 1913–6, during which he also made further significant contributions to the historical geography of Inner Asia. By 1930, however, when he organised a fourth expedition, with generous American financial backing, the international climate had changed. Chinese scholarship and nationalism had both grown significantly: the Chinese authorities forbade Stein to remove material from places he visited and raised other difficulties. In frustration he turned his attention elsewhere.

In the intervening years he had undertaken valuable survey work on the historical geography and archaeology of Swat, Punjab, Seistan, Baluchistan and Makran, tracing parts of Alexander the Great's expeditions and the antecedents and external connections of the Indus civilisation. He therefore turned his attentions and funds from the failed Central Asia expedition to an extended survey of Persia in 1931–6, from the Makran through south and west Iran to Khuzistan in the north, making a detailed record of topography, discovering sites of all periods, matching the landscape to historical records of Alexander's return journey and establishing a sound picture of previously uncharted archaeological territory. In 1938–9 he conducted a ground and aerial survey of Roman and Parthian

FIGURE 6.8 Mural from Cave 285 at the Caves of the Thousand Buddhas, Dunhuang.

remains in Iraq and Transjordan; returning to India in 1940–1 he surveyed the dried-up Saraswati river in Bahawalpur. He was about to embark on another expedition, in his eighty-first year, when in 1943 he died.

Stein was a remarkable scholar whose mastery of many languages and knowledge of many cultures gave him the ability to recognise the most significant material among the remains he encountered; whose tireless efforts and meticulous recording and publication secured and made available to scholars huge quantities of material of the first importance; and whose keen and insightful eye for the landscape enabled him to make a huge contribution to the historical geography of a vast region from West Asia through India to China.

The loss of Marshall's brilliant organisational abilities on his retirement, coupled with the economic depression of the 1930s, brought a steep decline in archaeological work in the subcontinent, from which it was rescued in 1943 by the appointment of Sir Mortimer Wheeler (see p30) as DG. Wheeler conducted investigations that spanned South Asia's past from the Neolithic into historical times, introduced new excavation techniques and trained a generation of archaeologists, many of whom subsequently occupied key posts in India and Pakistan's archaeological world: as a result Wheeler's methodology survived in the subcontinent long after it had been superseded elsewhere.

In the northwest Wheeler dug in 1944–5 at Taxila, where he focused on Sirkap, the Indo-Greek city, and its defences, and returned in 1958 to investigate Charsadda, ancient Pushkalavati, looking particularly for evidence of its siege by Alexander the Great in 327 BC. He worked in south India in 1945 and 1947, conducting training excavations at Arikamedu on the east coast, where he uncovered an important Roman trading station, and at Brahmagiri and Chandravalli, two sites in the plateau interior where he firmly established the south Indian prehistoric cultural sequence, from Neolithic villages, through Iron Age megalithic graves to the Early Historic contemporaries of the Roman traders.

Best known, however, is his work in the Indus cities: his 1946 training excavations at Harappa, and Mohenjo-daro where, as archaeological advisor to the Pakistan government, he dug in 1950. At both cities he exposed massive walls, which, following his military mindset, he viewed as fortifications; and at Mohenjo-daro he interpreted skeletons from the uppermost levels as victims massacred by hypothetical invaders. Subsequent investigations have shown the walls to be defences against flooding and the skeletons perfunctory burials, perhaps of victims of disease, but Wheeler's forcefully presented interpretations influenced views of the Indus civilisation for decades and still linger on in popular accounts.

Post-war transformations

With Independence came Partition, with the new nations following different archaeological trajectories. In Pakistan, many investigations have focused on the Indus civilisation and its antecedents. In the 1960s the American archaeologist George Dales (1927–92) employed drainage equipment to make a deep sounding at Mohenjo-daro, penetrating the lowest levels of the city, which the high water table had previously made inaccessible. More recently an Italian–German expedition under Michael Jansen and Maurizio Tosi re-investigated the city, conducting detailed surveys and attempting to match Marshall's records with archaeological stratigraphy: these studies greatly enhanced understanding of the settlement and in particular of craft activities and the construction and chronology of the massive platforms on which major parts of the city were built. Since the 1980s a joint Pakistan–American expedition (HARP) has been re-investigating Harappa, uncovering its development from a small settlement in the earlier fourth millennium BC to its final occupation in the second millennium.

The American archaeologist Walter Fairservis (1921–94) conducted excavations in the tiny town of Allahdino and George Dales in the coastal town of Balakot, shedding light on regional urbanism; both scholars also contributed to theoretical understanding of the Indus civilisation's development. In Bahawalpur a major survey by the Pakistani archaeologist Rafiq Mughal revealed the dense distribution of Indus sites along the course of dried-up rivers, showing that this region had in the Indus period been well watered and fertile, supporting many settlements and contributing significantly to the prosperity of the Indus civilisation.

The early stages of Indus development were uncovered in excavations at Kot Diji and Amri: from these and excavations in Baluchistan and India it became apparent that the Indus state had grown out of the amalgamation of several distinctive though related Early Indus cultures. Explorations in Baluchistan and the Indo-Iranian borderlands by a number of scholars, including the veteran British archaeologist Beatrice de Cardi, revealed many settlements antecedent to the Indus civilisation, such as Bampur and Mundigak. But it was the discoveries of a French team led by Jean-François and Catherine Jarrige at Mehrgarh in Pakistan that proved most exciting: by or before the seventh millennium BC, there were early farmers living here. Mehrgarh grew from the earliest farming village into a substantial town occupied until Indus times when it was replaced by nearby Nausharo; it was re-occupied briefly in the post-Indus period, when the nearby town of Pirak flourished, giving this small area an unbroken archaeological sequence of some six millennia.

Early Historic and Buddhist sites continued to attract major research attention in Pakistan and in neighbouring Afghanistan. This included further investigations at Taxila and Charsadda; work on Old Kandahar; and French excavations at the Hellenistic city of Ai Khanoum. Particularly spectacular were the Kushan burials, richly furnished with gold jewellery, discovered at Tillya Tepe in Bactria by the Russian archaeologist Victor Sarianidi in the 1980s while excavating a Bronze Age settlement.

Partition left India its share of the finds from Harappa and Mohenjo-daro but with no excavated Indus sites, a situation that Indian archaeologists immediately set about rectifying. Explorations in the two regions at the southern and eastern extremes of the Indus area, Gujarat and the eastern Punjab/Haryana, yielded spectacular results, including the important towns of Kalibangan and Lothal, the latter with an enigmatic basin identified by its excavator, S.R. Rao, as a dockyard. Kalibangan demonstrated particularly well the widespread sequence of an Early Indus town deliberately demolished and reconstructed as a planned settlement at the beginning of the Mature Indus period. The recent discovery and excavation of another city, Dholavira, in Gujarat, has been particularly exciting: while displaying some similarities with Harappa and Mohenjo-daro, it also has many distinctive features, including seven massive and magnificently engineered reservoirs. In addition to towns and cities, Indian archaeologists have in recent years paid considerable attention to small rural settlements, revealing not only pastoral camps but also specialised craft villages, for example processing seashells for bangles and manufacturing gemstone beads. Work in the Indian regions of the Indus civilisation has shown that the demise of the civilisation was not the cataclysm previously envisioned but a loss of urban features and disintegration of political unity, coupled with flourishing rural life and population growth in the south and east.

The subsequent growth of larger villages and towns, such as Inamgaon, in the Deccan plateau in the later second millennium was foremost among the many new chapters of South Asian prehistory revealed by the work of the great post-war Indian archaeologist, H.D. Sankalia (1908–89). He also advanced India's study of the past through his teaching at the Deccan College, Pune, still a major centre of Indian archaeological research. Among Sankalia's successors was S.B. Deo whose work on the stone circle graves of Vidarbha greatly advanced knowledge of the south Indian megaliths. These enigmatic and highly varied funerary monuments had attracted antiquarian attention from early times, and had been given a rough chronological position by Wheeler's excavations at Brahmagiri, but later twentieth-century excavations of burials and associated settlements finally allowed them to be anchored in their Iron Age cultural context.

Early interest and speculation had also focused on south India's ash mounds. In the 1950s the British Indologist Raymond Allchin (1923–2010) solved the mystery of their significance when he excavated the ash mounds of Utnur and Piklihal, revealing that they resulted from periodically burning dung accumulated by corralling large numbers of cattle. These and more recent investigations have shown that the inhabitants of south India in the third millennium BC were pastoralists, who also foraged and practised a little horticulture.

From their beginnings with the ash mound excavations, Allchin and his wife Bridget went on to become major figures in South Asian archaeology, conducting fieldwork in India, Pakistan and latterly, at the great early city of Anuradhapura in Sri Lanka. Equally importantly, they raised the profile of South Asian archaeology outside the subcontinent. With a few of their intimate colleagues they founded the Association of South Asian Archaeologists, now a major forum for the exchange of information and views; and Raymond used his post at Cambridge University to offer many South Asian scholars the opportunity to study in Britain.

Allchin was among many scholars also to focus on the archaeology of India's Early Historic cities. Here one of the main inspirations was the *Mahabharata*, India's great epic poem recounting the war between the heroic legendary dynasties of city-states in the Ganges valley and beyond. Investigating the historicity of this account was of major interest to many leading Indian archaeologists, including B.B. Lal, who excavated Hastinapura, capital of one of the warring dynasties. Other work has focused on the subsequent centuries, a time of major political and religious change in India, when city-states developed in the Ganges valley and neighbouring regions, were amalgamated by conquest and alliance into fewer, larger states and were finally united into the great Mauryan empire. Here and in Pakistan, archaeological studies of the historical period have been closely coupled with those of art history and architecture.

The origins of agriculture have been a major theme of archaeological investigation worldwide. In India nothing of the antiquity of Mehrgarh has yet been discovered, although for a few years it was thought that sixth-millennium BC rice cultivation might have been discovered in the middle Ganges region. Nevertheless, investigations have uncovered an extremely rich picture of development in the subcontinent, with separate hearths of agricultural innovation in Gujarat, south India, the middle Ganges and possibly other regions. In addition, work has revealed the complexity and durability of forager lifestyles in South Asia, with long-lasting and often mutually beneficial interactions between farmers and hunter-gatherers. Among the most impressive discoveries in India are the rock paintings of hunter-gatherer communities, particularly those found by V.S. Wakankar (1919–88) at Bhimbetka.

South Asia's remote past has continued to attract attention. In the 1970s–'90s a British archaeological mission further investigated the Potwar plateau, building up a picture of Palaeolithic activity in the region stretching back possibly to 2 million years ago.

Bringing the story up to date

Recent investigations in central and southern India have focused on the crucial period when modern humans first spread out of Africa: data from this region are critical to testing the hypothesis of a southern route along the Indian Ocean coast and assessing the impact of the eruption of Mount Toba 74,000 years ago.

The political developments of recent years have taken a terrible toll on South Asian archaeology. Warfare and religious extremism have been responsible for casual damage and deliberate destruction throughout the region, from Afghanistan to Sri Lanka, the most notorious examples being the tearing down of the Ayodhya mosque by Hindu extremists and the blowing up of the two magnificent, immense standing Buddha figures at Bamiyan by the fanatical Taliban, who also destroyed many fine figurative works of art in the Kabul Museum. That so many of Afghanistan's treasures survived the dark periods of the Soviet invasion and Taliban rule is due to the amazing heroism and foresight of the museum's curators, who at risk to their own lives hid them away in safe places, from which they were recovered in 2003 after the Taliban were overthrown. The continuing unstable conditions in Afghanistan and northern Pakistan, however, mean that little archaeological work is currently possible, and the many chance discoveries of material from the region's rich past are generally immediately looted, often by warlords or drugs barons; the Kabul museum's saved treasures are currently touring the world, to keep them safe for the future.

Further Reading

South Asia

Chakrabarti, D.K. 1988. *A History of Indian Archaeology from the Beginnings to 1947*. Munshiram Manoharlal Publishers Pvt Ltd: New Delhi.

Chakrabarti, D.K. 2003. *Archaeology in the Third World. A History of Indian Archaeology Since 1947*. D.K. Printworld: Delhi.

Cummings, J. (ed.) 1939. *Revealing India's Past*. India Society: London (reprint 2005, Cosmo Publications for Genesis Publishing Pvt. Ltd: New Delhi.)

Cunningham, A. 1875. Harappa, pp. 105–8 in *Archaeological Survey of India: Report for the Years 1872–3*.

Guha, S. (ed.) 2010. *The Marshall Albums. Photography and Archaeology*. Mapin Publishing Pvt Ltd: Ahmedabad.

Lahiri, N. 2006. *Finding Forgotten Cities*. Seagull: London/Berg: Oxford.

Marshall, J. 1924. First light on a long-forgotten civilization: new discoveries of an unknown prehistoric past in India. *Illustrated London News*, 20 September, 428–32 and 548.

Possehl, G.L. 1999. *Indus Age: the Beginnings*. Oxford University Press: Delhi.

Possehl, G.L. 2002. Fifty years of Harappan archaeology: the study of the Indus civilization since Indian independence, pp. 1–41. In S. Settar and R. Korisettar, (eds) *Indian Archaeology in Retrospect. II. Protohistory. Archaeology of the Harappan Civilization*. Indian Council of Historical Research. Manohar: Delhi.

Wang, H. (ed.) 2004. *Sir Aurel Stein. Proceedings of the British Museum study day, 23 March 2002*. British Museum Occasional Paper 142. British Museum: London. www.britishmuseum.org/research/publications/research_publications_series/research_publications_online/sir_aurel_stein_study_day.aspx

Wheeler, R.E.M. 1955. *Still Digging*. Michael Joseph: London.

West Asia

Bienkowski, P. and Millard, A. (eds) 2000. *Dictionary of the Ancient Near East*. British Museum Press: London.

Curtis, J. 1982. *Fifty Years of Mesopotamian Discovery*. British School of Archaeology in Iraq: London.

Daniel, G. 1981. *A Short History of Archaeology*. Thames and Hudson: London.

Ghirshman, T. 1970. *Archéologue malgré moi*. Albin Michel: Paris.

Jacobsen, T. 2000. Searching for Sumer and Akkad, pp2743–52. In J.M. Sasson (ed.) *Civilizations of the Ancient Near East*. 4 volumes. Hendrickson Publishers, Inc.: Peabody (reprint of 1995 edition. Scribner: New York).

Kuhrt, A. 2000. Ancient Mesopotamia in Classical Greek and Hellenistic thought, pp55–66. In J.M. Sasson (ed.) *Civilizations of the Ancient Near East*. 4 volumes. Hendrickson Publishers, Inc.: Peabody (reprint of 1995 edition. Scribner: New York).

Leick, G. 2001. *Mesopotamia. The Invention of the City*. Allen Lane, The Penguin Press: London.

Lloyd, S. 1980. *Foundations in the Dust*. Revised edition. Thames and Hudson: London.

Lloyd, S. 2000. Excavating the land between the two rivers, pp2729–41. In J.M. Sasson (ed.) *Civilizations of the Ancient Near East*. 4 volumes. Hendrickson Publishers, Inc.: Peabody (reprint of 1995 edition. Scribner: New York).

Martinez-Sève, L. 2001. Ghirshman, Roman, pp583–6. In *Encyclopedia Irania*. Vol. X, Fasc. 6. www.iranica.com/articles/ghirshman (last updated Feb 9, 2012).

Meyers, E.M. (ed.) 1997. *The Oxford Encyclopedia of Archaeology in the Near East*. 5 Volumes. Oxford University Press: Oxford.

Sasson, J.M. (ed.) 2000. *Civilizations of the Ancient Near East*. 4 volumes.Hendrickson Publishers, Inc.: Peabody (reprint of 1995 edition. Scribner: New York).

Woolley, L. 1950. *Ur of the Chaldees*. Pelican: Harmondsworth. (revised reprint of 1929 edition).

Woolley, L. 1982. *Ur 'of the Chaldees'*. The final account, *Excavations at Ur*, revised and updated by P.R.S. Moorey. Book Club Associates/Herbert Press: London.

www.mesopotamia.co.uk/tombs/home_set.html

For both

Bahn, P.G. (ed.) 1999. *Cambridge History of Archaeology*. Cambridge University Press: Cambridge.

7

AFRICA

Anne Solomon

No continent has a prehistory as deep as Africa. It is astonishing therefore to realise that thorough archaeological studies here are really little more than a century old and that, even today, the continent's rich archaeological record remains far from fully explored. Victorian scientists and collectors established the foundations of scientific research, finding, describing and classifying curiosities. It would be some decades before rigorous, systematic studies became firmly established. The first professional appointment in sub-Saharan Africa was in 1923. When the prehistorian J. Desmond Clark arrived to work in Zambia in 1938, there were still only two or three archaeologists in the entire subcontinent.

Archaeology in Africa can be viewed through many lenses, including the ideas about human behaviour and society that shaped its narratives, innovations in techniques and methods and a catalogue of exciting new finds through the years. The story of the African past is also a tale about the colonial enterprise in Africa and European ideas and attitudes, as well as an account of the pioneering efforts of a handful of dedicated individuals.

In its more recent forms, African archaeology is concerned with restoring the African past to its own peoples, although many of its most celebrated finds are of global interest, as part of the story of humankind.

The discovery of antiquity and the emergence of archaeology

The first glimmers of interest in African archaeology are evident in incidental comments by early travellers and extended in the activities of nineteenth-century antiquarians. Often keen naturalists and members of scientific societies, these first collectors were aware of the discovery of antiquity in Europe and several sent their finds to colleagues at home in order to extend the geographical focus of these enquiries.

In nineteenth-century thought, ideas of unilinear evolutionary stages prevailed, with supposed 'primitives' (Africans, commonly perceived as savages, being prime candidates) at the bottom of the ladder and Europeans inevitably at the top. By the early twentieth century, the idea that societies progressed from primitive to complex had given way to a 'culture history' approach, which explained similarities among archaeological materials in terms of diffusion:

the spread of ideas and material culture by migration and culture contact. Egypt loomed large as a supposed exporter of high culture to the continent and indeed, the wider ancient world.

In the earlier phases of African archaeology, marvels of the African past were repeatedly attributed to immigrants. Though it had been recognised in the nineteenth century that some stone artifacts had surely been made by the ancestors of indigenous peoples, the more spectacular the archaeological find, the greater the urge to assign it to some superior incoming 'race'. Candidates included Egyptians, Hamites, Semites, Phoenicians and other peoples as the supposed importers of Africa's great art and architecture. A 1900 article title (Delafosse) says it all: 'On the probable traces of Egyptian civilisation and men of white race on the Ivory Coast'. Let us not forget the contribution of France's abbé Henri Breuil (see p18) after seeing photographic enlargements of the San rock painting in Namibia dubbed 'the White Lady of the Brandberg': 'It was then that I saw that the Lady's face was Mediterranean'. In fact, it is not even a female figure! Despite enlightened individual participants whose work defended the intelligence of indigenous peoples, the racial thinking that permeates much early writing often makes shocking reading today.

These myths proved tenacious; some still believe the Iron Age centre of Great Zimbabwe was built by some superior, mystery 'race'. As archaeologists began to map, describe and analyse materials (initially stone artifacts in particular), another picture began to emerge. Detailed published descriptions of Stone Age finds appeared around the turn of the twentieth century, by investigators such as Johnson and Peringuey in the south of the continent, by Stainier in the Congo and by Pallary in North Africa. In 1906, Randall-McIver controversially but bravely claimed an African origin for Great Zimbabwe, thus challenging romantic and racist notions about lost cities and foreign architects.

Making sense of the past

Much of the groundwork for future African archaeological research was laid down between the late 1800s and World War I. Professional archaeologists were becoming active in the 1920s; by the 1930s, some full-length volumes had begun to accumulate. The energetic abbé Breuil provided an overview of the entire continent's prehistory in 1930. Other notable works were published by Miles Burkitt in 1928 and by A.J.H. Goodwin (1900–59) and Clarens Van Riet Lowe (1894–1956) in 1929, both dealing with southern African materials. Maurice Reygasse's work on North African archaeology appeared in 1931, as did a volume by Louis Leakey on the Stone Age of Kenya. Leakey followed his East African volume in 1936 with a study entitled *Stone Age Africa*, the first English language overview of the archaeology of the continent as a whole. One can only imagine the adventure of those years, when the archaeology of large swathes of the continent was virtually unknown and untold wonders awaited discovery (or re-discovery; after all, wonders such as the rock-hewn churches of Lalibela in Ethiopia had been part of the lives of African peoples for around a thousand years).

Dating the material was a key problem and much effort was spent on typologies, sequences and terminology. These studies began to reveal that African archaeological materials could not easily be squeezed into the schemes devised for classifying European finds. It became apparent relatively early that a new sequence was needed, since what came to be known as the African Early, Middle and Later Stone Ages did not mirror the European scheme of Lower, Middle and Upper Palaeolithic. Nor was there evidence of an African 'Bronze Age'. The term 'Neolithic', imported to describe herding peoples with pottery and domestic animals, remains the subject of debate today in relation to peoples of southern Africa.

FIGURE 7.1 Later Stone artefacts, including coarse grained pottery (right), a worked bone tube (bottom) and stone artefacts. Later Stone Age (LSA) stone artefacts are typically made using fine-grained materials. Microtools were designed to be mounted in a handle to create an effective cutting implement. Other commonly excavated artefacts include scrapers (for processing animal hides) and adzes for woodworking. Photo: author's own.

A notable development of the 1920s, running parallel to investigation of Early Stone Age artifacts, was a dawning recognition of Africa's hominin fossil heritage. Before World War I, two finds had attracted attention: the Boskop skull from South Africa, and fossils c. 1914 found by Reck at Olduvai Gorge, Tanzania (the latter attracted Louis Leakey to this most famous of African fossil sites). Raymond Dart's (1893–1988) discovery of the Taung 'man-ape' child in South African limeworks was a scientific sensation in 1924. It would, however, be some years before more *Australopithecus africanus* specimens from Sterkfontein Cave, near Johannesburg, convinced sceptics and directed palaeoanthropological attention towards Africa.

Scholars of all the European colonial powers were active in Africa. The abbé Breuil and Teilhard de Chardin, both French clergymen, are two well-known figures. The German adventurer-scholar Leo Frobenius (1873–1938) contributed to rock art research from 1904 to 1935. The Italian scholar Paolo Graziosi (1906–88) produced notable work on Saharan rock art and in 1935 undertook pioneering excavations at Gogoshiis Qabe, Somalia, a site that would reveal early evidence of mortuary practices in Africa.

Because archaeology always has an element of serendipity, non-professionals made many great discoveries in the early years (and indeed since). The terracotta sculptures of Nok, Nigeria, dated to c. 2300–1800 BP, were found by tin miners in 1928. Mapungubwe, the hilltop settlement of an Iron Age elite, and the precursor of Great Zimbabwe, was found by a farmer in 1932. From the 1920s and 1930s onward, a number of systematic surveys were undertaken across the continent. These surveys were no longer only about finding objects, but about investigating contexts, and time frames in particular, often in collaboration with geologists.

Notable expeditions at opposite ends of the continent included surveys and excavations in the Fayum Depression, Egypt, by the redoubtable archaeologist Gertrude Caton-Thompson (see Box 7.1) and the geologist Elinor Gardner, both striking a blow for women scientists.

BOX 7.1 Gertrude Caton-Thompson (1888–1985)

Gertrude Caton-Thompson's obituary in *The Times* in 1985 describes her as 'quiet, retiring and private; but in her pioneering field-work she was intrepid and absolutely indomitable, while her acute, methodical and incisive brain ... solved problems which others had not even formulated'.

Gertrude Caton-Thompson seized the career opportunities newly available to Edwardian women in Britain. After a stint as a civil servant, aged thirty-three she began studying archaeology under Sir Flinders Petrie, with whom she excavated at Abydos, Egypt, in 1921. Her first major contribution to African archaeology was at the predynastic site of Badari, near the Nile, where she instigated work on settlements rather than the cemeteries which had previously been the focus of much attention. Excavations yielded key information on the advent of African agriculture.

In 1925, with the geologist Elinor Gardner, Caton-Thompson surveyed and excavated in the Fayum Depression, a lake basin west of the Nile where they documented African Neolithic (hunter-herder-fisher) cultures dating back 7000 years. From 1930–3, they investigated open sites around Kharga Oasis. Subsequent researchers have described their contribution: they 'pioneered regional interdisciplinary research in Africa, covering all time periods and including geochronology, palaeo-environmental studies, geoarchaeology and aerial survey. Caton-Thompson also quantified attributes in order to seriate Pleistocene artifacts, possibly the earliest attempt to do so in Africa'.

In between these expeditions, Caton-Thompson was invited to re-investigate Great Zimbabwe. Building on McIver's important, but inconclusive work (1906), her systematic

FIGURE 7.2 The Conical Tower at Great Zimbabwe. © Chris Howes/Wild Places Photography/Alamy.

excavations allowed her to pinpoint the kingdom's rise to circa the end of the first millennium AD and provided evidence that its builders were indeed indigenous Africans. Her rigorous methods influenced other Iron Age research, including pioneering work on African pottery in the 1930s.

Her conclusions about Great Zimbabwe challenged colonial ideologies about Africans' incapacity to build such structures. Caton-Thompson gave critics short shrift, declaring that their speculations should be filed under 'insane'. This forthright side of her personality was mentioned in another of her obituaries: 'Gertrude terrified many men who did not realise that her firmness and clear criticism, her sincerity and honesty masked a great kindness and sympathy'.

Gertrude described herself as 'not easily alarmed'. Her intellectual courage and innovative work places her among Africa's most eminent archaeologists of all time.

In South Africa, surveys of the Vaal River gravels by Clarens ('Peter') Van Riet Lowe helped to establish a geomorphological context for Stone Age materials. In early research in Uganda, archaeology and geology came together in the persona of E.J. Wayland, whose surveys and research from 1919 onward had considerable influence on African archaeology of that era.

A maturing discipline

The 1930s through to the 1960s have been called the 'formative' period of African archaeological research. As bodies of material accumulated, it became possible to revise conclusions and refine methods and hypotheses. The need to break away from European models had become clear, though intellectual ties with metropolitan traditions remained close. The Ice Ages, with glacial and interglacial periods, loomed large as a chronological frame in European thinking, but proved irrelevant in Africa. Wayland formulated an equivalent model for Africa, the 'pluvial hypothesis', based on periods of higher and lower rainfall, inferred from geological evidence.

The pluvial hypothesis eventually went the way of other flawed, if ingenious, ideas, with work in the 1950s eventually demonstrating that high and low lake levels could be accounted for by unstable geology, rather than fluctuating rainfall. The pluvial hypothesis nevertheless exemplifies emerging ways of thinking about the African past and the recognition that it diverged from that of Europe. The quest was for scientific rigour and a matrix of dates. Along with surveys, increasingly careful excavations were being undertaken in order to get a much-needed grip on stratigraphy and sequence.

As well as exploring time and change, archaeologists became increasingly interested in environmental contexts, with material culture (though this term had not yet been coined) as evidence of economy and subsistence strategies adapted to particular places. The influence in the mid-twentieth century came strongly from Cambridge University-trained archaeologists. Though it was not without its limitations, a bonus of this 'functional' approach was that it diverted attention from tedious fantasies about Phoenicians and other foreigners as makers of the African past.

Meanwhile French archaeology, at home and abroad, remained rather mired in classificatory pursuits. In 1989 an authoritative writer on archaeological progress in Francophone West Africa had little positive to say about work up to 1940 (the word that recurs is 'limited'), prior to, and even after, the 1938 establishment of IFAN (Institut Français d'Afrique Noire). Whatever those limitations, this institute embodied the rejuvenating vision of a former civil servant, Raymond Mauny, who lobbied tirelessly for research funds and opened up new research areas in Francophone West Africa. Anglophone archaeologists played a key role in shaping African archaeology in these earlier years, although some French thinking, particularly in the fields of rock art research and stone tool analysis, would take centre stage in the 1960s.

With diffusionism increasingly old hat, researchers were starting to consider African societies as holistic systems with their own internal dynamics. From the 1930s to the 1950s, the African story focused more on diverse ways of living, animal and plant domestication, food production, metalworking, the development of settled societies and the rise of urban complexes. A.J. Arkell, working in Egypt and the Sudan from the 1920s to the 1940s, was one contributor. His work included surveys and excavations in Egypt and the Sudan, including investigating the evidence for large-scale iron working at the Kushite city of Meroe, Sudan, and exploring the shift from foraging to animal husbandry.

With growing respect for indigenous ingenuity, questions emerged about whether the domestication of plants and animals and innovations in technology were imported or independently invented in Africa. Work by Caton-Thompson and Arkell helped sketch a picture of changing ways of life from about 1000 BP in the Sahara and other northerly parts of the continent: of hunter-fisher peoples with pottery, less mobile than hunter-gatherers, and of pastoralists with domestic animals. The unique trajectories of African economies are still often the subject of intense debate today.

In these early years great effort went into developing methods and refining ideas and classifications, as well as building chronologies – no mean feat in pre-radiocarbon dating days. Excavations of diverse sites, in many countries, were elucidating the contours of African prehistory. Often, the key sites were not the spectacular ones that fired the public imagination, like Aksum and Great Zimbabwe, but sites with clear sequences that extended understanding of the range and time-depth of prehistoric African cultures. Few non-archaeologists know of the advances in excavation and understanding Stone Age sequences made by Goodwin at Oakhurst Cave in South Africa, or Caton-Thompson's path-breaking excavations at Great Zimbabwe. Staff from institutions like the Frobenius Institute in Germany and the Royal Museum for Central Africa in Belgium worked on African materials, transforming themselves through time from colonial museums exhibiting curiosities to research centres specialising in African prehistory and anthropology.

The year 1947 saw the first of a continuing series of Pan-African Congresses where archaeologists, geologists, zoologists, botanists and other specialists, many working separately in relative isolation, could compare notes. A turning point in African archaeology came in the 1950s, with the development of radiocarbon dating (see Box 2.7, p31). Early dates were by no means as reliable as they are today, before it was recognised that dates needed calibration, but absolute dating methods helped refine chronologies and narratives of African prehistory.

The impact of science was also felt in the allied field of palaeoanthropology, with potassium-argon and other dating methods being developed for older materials that lay beyond the reliable range of radiocarbon dating (c. 50,000 years). This revealed the unexpected antiquity of African

BOX 7.2 Louis and Mary Leakey

Among the most famous names in palaeoanthropology, Louis (1903–72) and Mary Leakey, nee Nicol (1913–96), made extraordinary contributions not only to the study of human evolution in Africa, but to several allied fields. Kenyan-born, Cambridge-educated Louis and his English second wife, Mary, are nevertheless best known for their work at Olduvai Gorge (now Oldupai), Tanzania, and other key East African fossil sites.

In the early years of studies of human evolution, controversy had erupted over the antiquity of a skeleton discovered at Olduvai in 1913. In the late 1920s Louis Leakey became convinced that hominin fossils of great age would be found there and led an expedition in 1931. Though Acheulean hand axes and animal fossils were found, the evidence he sought, at Olduvai and other East African sites, would be years in coming. The real breakthrough came only in 1959, when Mary Leakey found skull fragments they classified as 'Zinjanthropus' (now *Paranthropus*, a hominin not in the direct human lineage), nicknamed 'Zinj', or 'Nutcracker Man', because of the specimen's large teeth and robust anatomy. When the bed from which Zinj had eroded was dated, in 1960, to c. 1.75 million years, Leakey's conviction regarding the antiquity of hominin evolution in Africa was finally vindicated.

The find helped attract funding for intensive research in East Africa, which paid dividends. In the following few years, fossils of *Homo habilis*, which appeared about 2.4 million years ago, were found at Olduvai by the Leakeys and their team, which included their sons. Specimens of *Homo erectus* (or *ergaster*, as African examples are known),

FIGURE 7.3 Olduvai Gorge landscape. Photo © ChrisCrafter/istock.

successors of the habilines in the earlier Pleistocene, were also unearthed at Olduvai in the 1960s and after.

The impetus to palaeoanthropological research created by the Leakeys' work was enormous, and the Leakey phenomenon led to numerous new finds across East Africa in the years that followed. Louis Leakey had also contributed more generally to documenting the Stone Age of Kenya and exploring the geological and environmental contexts of East African prehistory. He and Mary also made notable palaeontological (non-human) finds, such as the rare Miocene primate, *Proconsul africanus*.

Years later, the Leakey marriage turned sour and both assumed separate careers. After Louis' death, Mary Leakey made one of the most spectacular finds of the twentieth century: a trail of fossilised footprints preserved by volcanic ash. Believed to be the 3.6 million-year-old tracks of three *Australopithecus afarensis* individuals, the Laetoli footprints are important evidence for the early adoption of an upright posture (bipedalism) in hominin evolution. Though Louis Leakey's biography was called 'Leakey's Luck', Mary's fortuitous finds are especially striking.

Both Leakeys had more strings to their bows. Louis was also a promoter of primatology and was influential in the careers of both the chimpanzee expert, Jane Goodall, and the ill-fated Dian Fossey, celebrated in the film *Gorillas in the Mist*. Mary Leakey, who began her archaeological career as an illustrator, also published a volume on Tanzanian rock art in 1983.

Without question, the Leakeys paved the way for the study of evolution in Africa, with their joint careers extending from a time when archaeology and palaeoanthropology were fledgling disciplines to the days when the world was regularly in thrall to exciting new finds and ideas about human origins. Their legacy is the Leakey Foundation, which continues to foster cutting-edge palaeoanthropological research. Their sons, Philip, Jonathan and, especially, Richard Leakey, along with the latter's wife, Meave, and their daughter, Louise, perpetuate the family tradition.

hominin fossils. Another of Africa's archaeological wonders created a sensation in 1959 and focused world scientific attention on East Africa. Mary Leakey, working with her husband Louis (see Box 7.2) at Olduvai Gorge, Tanzania, found the cranium of a heavily-built hominin that they named *Zinjanthropus* (now renamed *Paranthropus boisei*). Intensive excavations at Olduvai, and at other East African, Ethiopian and South African fossil sites, have since contributed enormously to our understanding of human evolution and the Early Stone Age.

East Africa also provided important new evidence for the history of African farming peoples who were accomplished in iron smelting. From the 1960s onwards, evidence from excavations, pottery analyses and historical linguistics accumulated, showing that Early Iron Age farmers in this region began to disperse rapidly southwards from around AD 100, with agriculturalists populating parts of South Africa, thousands of kilometres to the south, in only a few short centuries.

Iron Age research in East Africa and the Horn also opened up other new windows on past lives and economies and dismantled ideas of Africans as isolated primitives. Research on the East African coast was beginning to reveal extraordinary intercontinental contacts in the deep past: Arabian peoples settled in the Horn of Africa 2000 years ago and, by the second millennium AD, Swahili settlements in the region thrived on intercontinental trade with the Mediterranean and even the Far East, centred on the Red Sea. The Sahara and large swathes of Africa were criss-crossed by trade routes, with African products, including ivory, skins, metals and slaves exchanged for exotic goods, such as beads and porcelain.

The importance of archaeology in revealing the dynamic character of African prehistory, mainly in the absence of written records, has been immense. Finds in West Africa have played a key role in highlighting the technological and artistic prowess of African peoples. Cast brass sculptures from Ife and Igbo Ukwu, Nigeria, dated to around the end of the first millennium AD, confirmed this sophistication. Thurstan Shaw's (1914–2013) excavations (1959–60) at the latter site also revealed 'treasures' of the kind that archaeologists dream of: a remarkable burial of a high-status individual, surrounded by signs of his wealth and power. Equally evocative was the French scholar Théodore Monod's discovery in Mauretania a few years later: quantities of cowrie shells and over 2000 bronze bars, part of the otherwise archaeologically invisible Islamic trans-Saharan trade by camel caravan.

Of course, many of the most important finds in African archaeology were less spectacular, but no less significant. The story of Africa's past, though still tantalisingly incomplete, was now recognised as being many times more complex and fascinating than anyone could have guessed, covering almost every aspect of the human journey on one continent. By the late 1950s, with a suite of basic tools and methods in place, the broad contours of Africa's past had been sketched out and archaeologists across the world were taking note of developments.

The flowering of African archaeologies: The post-war period

African archaeology took off in the 1960s, in several directions. The creation of many new posts for professional archaeologists, in museums, universities and conservation agencies, fuelled research. Africa became an increasingly attractive destination for American and other researchers. By the late 1950s numerous African nations were gaining independence from their colonial masters, providing new impetus for Africa-centred (pre-)histories, especially studies of Iron Age societies and the more recent past.

Equally important was the influence of new ideas from global archaeological theory. Ecology was the new buzzword, and archaeologists embraced approaches that explained past human behaviour in relation to particular ecosystems and environments. Systems theory was also important in the so-called 'New Archaeology' (now renamed processual archaeology), associated especially with the work of American archaeologist Lewis Binford (see p189). In what now seems like a vain quest, the New Archaeologists aimed for scientific rigour in explanations of culture, seeking 'rules' governing cultural behaviours.

Ethnoarchaeology, which brought in anthropological studies of living peoples, played a key role, in which the celebrated San ('Bushman') hunter-gatherers of the Kalahari Desert loomed large. Studies that covered every facet of their lives served many purposes. On the one hand, that included modelling the subsistence strategies of African hominin ancestors. With apparent continuities between San technologies and ways of living and those of their Holocene hunter-gatherer forebears, ethnoarchaeological studies were also relevant for understanding Later Stone Age materials of the last 10,000 years: stone tools, bone debris, settlement patterns and rock art (though the Kalahari San did not themselves make images on rock). Experimental archaeology and replication exercises were hot stuff, with researchers enthusiastically doing things like carving up elephant corpses with stone tools to study patterns of wear on tools and cutmarks on bones, while statistical analyses and precision in recording methods became highly valued. Though perhaps not strictly 'archaeology', work by primatologists such as Jane Goodall, Dian Fossey and Irven De Vore made a strong impact, with observations of chimps and gorillas providing new insights into possible early human behaviour.

The attention to enhanced accuracy in recording and documentation is exemplified by one book. Harald Pager (see Box 7.3) and his wife, Shirley-Ann, spent two years in the 1960s in Ndedema Gorge (now Didima) in South Africa's Ukhahlamba-Drakensberg Moutains, recording all the rock paintings in 147 sites and analysing their associations in meticulous detail (see box). Also in the later 1960s, in the same region, Patricia Vinnicombe (1932–2003) began producing meticulous facsimile copies of paintings and devised an early system for computer-aided analysis of images.

BOX 7.3 Harald Pager (1923–85)

FIGURE 7.4 Harald Pager at work. Photo © R.Kuper, Copyright Heinrich-Barth-Institut.

The work of Czech-born Harald Pager and his wife, Shirley-Ann, is a beacon in world rock art research. After emigrating to South Africa, Pager developed a lifelong passion for hunter-gatherer rock art, created in sub-Saharan Africa until as late as the nineteenth century. Trained in art and design in Austria, Pager pursued his 'amateur' interest in rock art with extraordinary dedication and insight.

Pager's greatest contribution was recording rock paintings in Ndedema (now Didima) Gorge in the Drakensberg-Ukhahlamba Mountains, KwaZulu-Natal. Previous recorders had used various strategies: freehand 'cartoons' in the Victorian era, colour photography from the 1950s onwards; full-colour facsimile paintings in the 1960s and '70s; and, peculiarly, black and white tracings in the 1980s. With his artist's eye, Pager developed a new technique, first recording the imagery using black and white photographs. The Pagers then revisited the sites, where the full-size photographic prints were hand-painted with oil paints. Beginning in 1967, fully recording the images in the gorge's seventeen sites took the Pagers over two years.

The technique's advantage was that it allowed for more accurate colour reproduction than was the norm, while painting onto photographic prints preserved visually important

FIGURE 7.5 Winged creatures of various kinds are regularly imaged in the art of the Drakensberg-Ukhahlamba of eastern South Africa; they may display human, antilopine and avian features. In this example two so-called 'flying buck' are imaged (centre), along with an antelope (right) and a figure that seems to be predominantly human (left), though apparently with an animal head. Some examples of the motif may represent spirits in part-animal form. Photo: author's own.

details of the rock face. The results were published in the landmark 1971 volume *Ndedema*, a uniquely accurate record with meticulous additional analysis of the imagery and the archaeological, historical and environmental contexts of the sites and images. Owing to the decay of some of these paintings since, the Pager panels are records of rock art of unparalleled value.

The method's disadvantage was the cost of recording and publishing. Pager spent the last seven years of his life producing equally comprehensive recordings of the rock paintings in a 570 km² area of the Brandberg Mountains (Daureb, in the local language) in Namibia, in association with the University of Cologne. Cost dictated reliance primarily on black and white drawings of the paintings in nearly 900 sites, totalling around 43,000 individual images and comprising about eighty per cent of all the rock art in that area.

Pager's artistic appreciation and skill, precision recording and insights into prehistoric image-making have earned him a lasting place in the history of global rock art research.

FIGURE 7.6 This picture blends a photo of a Brandberg frieze (site C 10) with Pager's original tracing and with the final monochrome reproduction in the publication. Pager's tracing shows the extra data which he added to his recordings. Photo © Heinrich-Barth-Institut.

These records remain invaluable over forty years later. Other pioneering rock art researchers worked on the thousands of rock art sites in the Sahara (especially in Libya and Algeria) made by hunting and pastoralist peoples when the land was green and wet. Pager and Vinnicombe in South Africa, Mary Leakey in Tanzania, and Henri Lhote (1903–91) and Paolo Graziosi in the Sahara were all researchers who paved the way for future work on African rock arts. One major problem facing them, like rock art researchers everywhere in the world, was how to date the imagery (see Box 7.4).

BOX 7.4 Dating rock art

Dating rock art is a perennial headache for archaeologists. The long-standing assumption that paintings or petroglyphs could be dated by identifying sequences of styles has proved problematic. Though the principle may sometimes apply, styles are not necessarily unambiguous markers of time periods. Independent verification of proposed sequences is always necessary. Studies of super-positioning (overlapping sequences of images) have promise but have not yielded startling results.

Subject matter sometimes helps to date rock art; for example, historical subjects or animals known to have been introduced at a certain date can bracket the age of some images. Similarly, images of animals known to have become extinct by a certain period may provide broad dates (i.e., they are unlikely to be much younger than the date of extinction). However, datable subject matter of this kind in rock art is the exception, not the rule. Identifying species from visual images that, by definition, are always artistic interpretations of 'reality', are error-prone and may only be imprecisely correlated to vast time periods.

Indirect dating, such as radiocarbon dating of the strata deposited on site floors, in which *art mobilier* or painted flakes from cave walls sometimes occur, has been very useful. Its limit is that it provides only minimum dates (i.e., the materials cannot be younger than the layer in which they were found). Accelerator mass spectrometry has provided direct C14 dates on actual pigments, but it has never been practical to roll it out on a larger scale. Not all pigments contain carbon and the method requires that the paint is carbon-based (e.g., made from charcoal) or contains adequate carbon from other organic (plant or animal) sources. Environmental contamination, such as soot (carbon) deposits from fires in inhabited caves and rock shelters, can fatally skew results.

Even when sample selection is meticulous there is always an error margin, often of unknown proportions. For petroglyphs (carved, rather than painted, images), the method is irrelevant. Estimating petroglyph age via studies of patination (post-production weathering) depends on understanding specifics of local geology and environmental conditions that are rarely available. The reuse of paintings and petroglyphs, sometimes over millennia, introduces further complications.

Two newer indirect dating methods have attracted attention. Optically stimulated luminescence dating (OSL) is possible where paintings or petroglyphs have been buried beneath sediments, away from irradiation by sunlight. The crystals in some minerals, especially quartz, feldspar and calcite, absorb light energy at a known rate. OSL permits estimates of how long they have been deprived of light by comparing trapped light energy with what would have been present if they had not been buried.

FIGURE 7.7 Petroglyphs at Qurta, Egypt. Photo: Paul Bahn.

Dating the mineral crusts that can form naturally on top of paintings and petroglyphs is another novel method, recently used on calcite layers in some of the Ice Age decorated caves of northern Spain such as El Castillo, where a faded red paint dot has been nominated as the world's 'oldest known rock art', as the calcite covering it began forming about 40,000 years ago. The method measures the decay of natural uranium into thorium; their current ratios allow an estimate of time elapsed and provide minimum dates for the art beneath. This technique makes it possible for the first time to obtain minimal ages for engravings and non-organic pigments on cave walls. Dating methods and their calibration (error correction) are nevertheless a matter for ongoing research. What seems like 'hard' science is no guarantee of accuracy, until calibration tables based on many case studies and independent verifications are developed.

Further reading

Bahn, P.G. 1997. *The Cambridge illustrated history of prehistoric art.* Cambridge University Press: Cambridge (Chapter 6).

Pike, A. *et al.* 2012. U-series dating of paleolithic art in 11 caves in Spain. *Science* 336: 1409–13.

Strecker, M. and Bahn, P. (eds) 1999. *Dating and the earliest known rock art.* Oxbow Books: Oxford.

Processual archaeology and its anthropological dimension provided a necessary injection of theory and critical examination of methods, but its search for universal rules of cultural behaviour hardly highlighted history. Trigger, a historian of archaeology, has noted that in Africa, as in North America, it 'remained as remote from native peoples and their concerns' as previous approaches. In contrast, work on Iron Age societies in some countries was more explicitly geared to a post-colonial social and political agenda. This was especially so in West Africa, where the Francophone tradition had long been more closely tied to history. Even in apartheid South Africa and Zimbabwe (Rhodesia), progressive scholars contributed to undoing colonial myths of black inferiority, though this was not necessarily effectively communicated beyond white academe.

A fascinating development in the 1960s was the use of oral histories (direct recollections) and oral traditions (often mythical and poetic). Thanks to continuities in African traditions and culture, these have helped in locating sites, and providing information on their dates, function and symbolic architecture, as well as the identity and social organisation of their inhabitants. Oral sources were used early on by investigators at Bigo, one of three second-millennium AD Ugandan kingdoms, whose inhabitants built dams and great systems of earthworks and processed salt on a large scale. The use of oral materials here ultimately proved controversial and sometimes misleading. Yet elsewhere – for example at the early urban settlement of Jenne-Jeno in Mali (c. 300 BC–AD 900) – oral traditions about the site proved more accurate than written accounts by outside visitors. Using oral sources has further augmented African archaeology's multidisciplinary character and adds another, very human, 'insider' dimension to our understanding of the African past. In Iron Age research, objects such as pots came to be seen as more than objects, but rather as residues of social and political groups and living, breathing and thinking people.

Bringing the story up to date

African archaeology expanded in many directions in the years that followed, alongside the pursuit of traditional core tasks such as surveying new areas, excavating to refine chronologies and typologies and developing analytical methods. New finds, like the 3.2 million-year-old fossil known as Lucy (*Australopithecus afarensis*) assured Africa, as the cradle of humankind, ongoing world attention. However, in the twenty-first century Stone Age studies have lost the pre-eminent place they enjoyed in archaeology's early years, with the exceptions of evolutionary research and rock art studies. Excavations in the late 1960s and 1970s at South African sites, such as Klasies River Mouth Caves and Border Cave, injected new life into Middle Stone Age research and the origins of modern human behaviour, which are of central interest today. Evidence of possible ritual cannibalism at the Klasies River site fuelled debates about the emergence of modern human cognition.

For most of African archaeology's history, the majority of archaeologists were jacks of all trades, dealing happily across its remit, from Stone Age rock art and cave sites to farming settlements and human fossils. One of the doyens of African prehistory was J. Desmond Clark (see Box 7.5), who worked in Zambia, Ethiopia, Somalia, Malawi, Angola and Niger. He published several books and over 300 papers on diverse subjects and, as a professor at UC Berkeley, trained a generation of African archaeologists. Such polymaths are now rare, while amateur enthusiasts also play a lesser role. As knowledge accumulated, methods advanced and theory become more prominent, professionalisation and specialisation became more marked.

BOX 7.5 J. Desmond Clark (1916–2000)

One of many archaeologists who graduated from Cambridge University and headed from England to Africa, J. Desmond Clark played an important role in African archaeology over six decades. The range of his work, in almost all areas of African archaeology and across the entire continent, was truly remarkable.

Clark's first job was at Zambia's Livingstone Museum, where he remained for nearly a quarter of a century, bar military service in Somalia and Ethiopia during World War II. Clark took that opportunity to explore the archaeology of these regions. Much of his research was directed towards Stone Age materials, with a predilection for Early Stone Age research. His early publications were two classic volumes: one on the Stone Age of Zambia (1950) and another on the prehistory of the Horn of Africa (1954).

In the early 1950s Clark excavated at Kalambo Falls, on the Zambian-Tanzanian border. The long sequence begins with Acheulean artifacts (finely made hand axes and cleavers) dating to perhaps 400,000 years ago, while the uppermost levels contained evidence of an Early Iron Age settlement dating to around AD 300. Especially exciting was preserved organic material in the ancient layers, including items of worked wood – a spectacularly rare find. Three books documenting this unique site appeared between 1969 and 2001.

Clark's other legacy was in the archaeological community: helping organise the Pan-African Archaeological Congresses that began in 1947 and later, as a professor of anthropology at the University of California Berkeley, training generations of Africanist and indigenous African archaeologists. In later years he resumed his interest in early stone artifacts and the Horn of Africa, conducting important work in the hominin fossil-rich Middle Awash area (Ethiopia), alongside palaeoanthropological teams.

One of those palaeoanthropologists, Tim White, has said of Clark that he 'wrote the book on African prehistory'. Clark is remembered equally for his efforts to promote African archaeology around the world.

Several archaeological sub-disciplines were emergent in the 1970s. In southern Africa, rock art took on new interest, with several landmark volumes published. As was typical, infusions of new ideas came from Europe. André Leroi-Gourhan pioneered structuralist analysis to understand Upper Palaeolithic cave art in France (see p29). These and allied theoretical developments were especially influential in studies of African rock arts in the 1970s and beyond. Historical archaeology, sometimes defined more narrowly as the 'archaeology of colonialism', was also emergent in the 1970s and, alongside it, maritime archaeology. These sub-disciplines helped introduce social theory and addressed new subjects such as global capitalism and the slave trade. They contributed to sowing the seeds of a more socially and politically conscious archaeology in the 1980s, though this was sometimes controversial.

Major ripples stirred Anglophone archaeology in the 1980s, once again following trends in Britain and America. Post-processual archaeologies were in part a reaction to the long-standing tradition of environmental archaeologies and processual archaeology, with its search for laws of cultural behaviour. Now emphasis fell on society, symbolism and an 'archaeology of mind'. Rather than the science of the past, some writers emphasised the way that archaeologists are always creating historically situated narratives from the available facts, and highlighted the social and political uses of archaeological knowledge.

This resonated strongly with some African archaeologists, critical of African archaeology as an ivory-tower, colonial enterprise that remained remote from those whose history archaeologists study. The new insistence on archaeology as cultural and political practice was highlighted when South African archaeologists were controversially banned from the 1986 World Archaeological Congress, as an anti-apartheid statement. In southern African archaeology, Marxist (historical materialist), feminist and politically engaged heritage studies began reshaping the face of African archaeology, though more traditional programmes continued. In some parts of Africa (notably West Africa) indigenous archaeologists had been trained to lead research into their own histories for some years; in countries like South Africa, this took on new urgency.

Though initially resisted by many as unscientific, the new approaches of the decade left their mark. 'Social' and symbolic archaeologies explored the archaeological record as evidence of people's ideas, ways of thinking and human relationships, and remain important, though approaches have evolved. Early efforts drew heavily on structuralist ideas; examples include Huffman's analysis of symbolic space at Great Zimbabwe and other Later Iron Age sites, and Lewis-Williams' work on rock art. Though structuralist analyses took steps towards exploring ancient 'mind', their core flaw was insensitivity to history and change. For some critics, structuralism perpetuates an older view of African societies as static and timeless, and efforts have been made to address this by further emphasising history, process and change.

In this regard, much attention has been paid to 'interactions', contact with European colonisers and cultural exchanges. One of the most prominent debates of recent years has centred on the Kalahari Desert dwellers. Are recent hunter-gatherers exemplars of our ancestors' ways of life? Or have economies, cultures and identities irrevocably changed in the last two millennia, as Africa started to become part of a global economy and new political formations and intergroup contacts were formed? Combating residual primitivist ideas (such as the proposition that the San/Bushman are in any way 'living fossils') and understanding change in African societies through the millennia engages teams of researchers across disciplines.

In the arena of empirical research, African researchers have contributed notably to global archaeology by developing archaeometry. South African archaeometrists generated the first radiocarbon date for a rock painting in 1987, using accelerator mass spectrometry, though most rock paintings remain undated and at present it is impossible to use direct dating methods on petroglyphs. Stable isotope studies using carbon and strontium isotopes have also contributed importantly to investigating prehistoric diets. Genetic studies also promise to play an ever-increasing role in understanding African history, and movements and minglings of peoples.

'From peripheral to paramount'

The importance of African archaeology within global prehistory is now clear. Although debate continues, on the basis of fossil, archaeological and genetic evidence, most researchers today accept the idea that early humans evolved in Africa and migrated in waves to other parts of the world. A competing explanation (the multi-regional hypothesis) has challenged but not yet refuted that hypothesis, while new finds (such as *Sahelanthropus*, from Chad) continue to push back the dates for hominin evolution in Africa. The spotlight today still shines brightly on the African Middle Stone Age and the emergence of modern human consciousness, with controversial claims for the world's oldest 'art' at another South African site, Blombos Cave.

Studies in African rock arts also made a global impact in the 1980s and 1990s, with the hypothesis that San rock arts and other hunter-gatherer arts worldwide (including those of the European Upper Palaeolithic) derived from 'shamanic' altered states of consciousness. This 'neuropsychological' explanation found popularity in many quarters and focused attention on African rock arts. Though it has not stood up to close scrutiny, devotion to it remains in some quarters.

In social and cultural terms, African archaeology today plays an often vigorous role in debates about national identity and an 'African renaissance'. However, much remains to be done. Many key questions remain hotly debated. Research outside the currently popular focus areas, and in under-developed or volatile areas of the continent, remains under-funded, even neglected. Authorities often battle to control illicit antiquities trading. Yet, despite challenges, African archaeology remains a vibrant field, with exciting finds still proving Pliny's dictum: *Ex Africa semper aliquid novi* (Always something new out of Africa).

Further reading

Delafosse, M. 1900. Sur des traces probables de civilisation égyptienne et d'hommes de race blanche à la Côte-d'Ivoire. *L'Anthropologie* 11: 677–83.

Derricourt, R. 2011. *Inventing Africa: History, archaeology and ideas.* Pluto Press: London, New York.

Garlake, P. 2002. *Early art and architecture of Africa.* Oxford University Press: Oxford.

Le Quellec, J-L. 2004. *Rock art in Africa: Mythology and legend.* Flammarion: Paris.

Mitchell, P. 2002. *The archaeology of Southern Africa.* Cambridge University Press: Cambridge.

Phillipson, D. 2005. *African archaeology.* Third edition. Cambridge University Press: Cambridge.

Robertshaw, P. (ed.) 1990. *A history of African archaeology.* James Currey: London.

Stahl, A.B. 2005. *African archaeology: A critical introduction.* Blackwell Publishing: Oxford.

Trigger, B. 1990. 'The history of African archaeology in world perspective'. In P. Robertshaw (ed.), *A history of African archaeology,* pp. 309–19. James Currey: London.

Trigger, B. 2006. *A history of archaeological thought.* Second edition. Cambridge University Press: Cambridge.

8

THE FAR EAST

Margarete Prüch

History of Chinese archaeology

Earliest beginnings

For a long time traditional Chinese antiquarianism, also known as the 'jin shi xue' (the study of ancient Chinese bronzes and stone stelae) dominated the approach to researching the past. The Chinese term for archaeology, 'kaogu', which means the 'investigation of the past', had originally been used by Song-dynasty (AD 960–1279) antiquarians. One of the first palaeographical works, dating from 1092, was the 'Kaogu tu' (*Illustrations for Studying Antiquity*). The Chinese have always been interested in investigating their past, most notably through written sources and also in the rich collections of antiques assembled by the Chinese Emperors starting from the Song dynasty onwards.

Archaeology in the nineteenth and twentieth centuries

But it was only in the twentieth century that the connotation of the word 'kaogu' was used for what was known as 'archaeology' in Western terms. A series of important discoveries mark the end of the nineteenth and the first decade of the twentieth century, such as the so called 'dragon bones' in Anyang, Henan province, which proved to be Shang-dynastic oracle bones; and the Tang-dynasty manuscripts and paintings in the Buddhist caves of Dunhuang in Gansu province. After the political revolution of 1911 and the collapse of the last dynasty, Western palaeontology and geology together with traditional Sinology were the basis for a new concept of archaeological research; and it was only at the beginning of the twentieth century that investigations in specific territories and scientific excavation started. Initiated by Japanese, Russian and European explorers (mainly self-taught) and trained scholars, the focus was then on the Palaeolithic, the Neolithic and the beginning of the historical dynastic system. Among them were Aurel Stein (British, 1862–1943 – see p112), Paul Pelliot (French, 1878–1949) and Sven Anderson Hedin (Swedish, 1865–1952), who left their footprints in the northwest, mainly in Gansu and Xinjiang provinces, Mongolia and Tibet. They removed thousands of artifacts, today housed in museums all over the world.

The first modern scientific archaeological excavations were mainly conducted by the Swedish geologist J. Gunnar Andersson (1874–1960) and the young Palaeolithic archaeologist

Pei Wenzhong (see Box 8.1) at the cave site of Zhoukoudian, southwest of Beijing, occupied approximately 700,000 to 200,000 years ago. The fossils they found there later became known as 'Peking man'. Altogether six skull caps, bones and tools proved the importance of these excavations. In 1941, after being placed on transport to America, the fossils disappeared. It was also Andersson who in 1921 excavated painted pottery in the Neolithic settlement at Yangshao village, Mianchi, Henan province. This culture, henceforth named Yangshao, marks the beginning of post–Palaeolithic prehistory in China and, together with the Longshan culture, is said to be the foundation of Chinese civilisation.

BOX 8.1 Pei Wenzhong (1904–82)

Pei Wenzhong (also known as W.C. Pei) was born on 5 March 1904 in Fengnan, Hebei province. He was an eminent Palaeolithic archaeologist and palaeontologist and is considered to be the founding father of Chinese anthropology. He devoted himself to the growth of Chinese prehistory and the establishment of its theoretical system.

At the age of twenty-three he graduated from the Department of Geology at Peking University and, only a year later, in 1928 began to work for the newly established Cenozoic Research Laboratory of the Geological Survey of China, an association of Chinese and foreign research institutions aimed at doing research on the famous excavation site of Zhoukoudian, later better known as the Peking man site. In 1918 the Swedish geologist and archaeologist Gunnar Andersson first visited the site, after he was told that there were fossils on what the farmers called the 'Chickenbonehill'. Pei Wenzhong joined the excavation team in 1929 and soon after was named field director of the excavations and soundings at Zhoukoudian where he stayed until 1935. During that time four special localities and the so-called Upper Cave were excavated. On 2 December 1929 Pei Wenzhong was the first to excavate an almost intact cranium/skull cap of Peking man, the second specimen that constituted firm evidence of our hominin ancestor *Homo erectus* (the earliest being Java Man). He also discovered *in situ* stone tools and evidence for the use of fire by Peking man. This was also when he first published his excavation results and the research he had done on them. At Zhoukoudian he also reformed excavation methods, dividing the site into squares and establishing complete archives of the data unearthed.

In 1937 he started to study prehistoric archaeology in France and returned to China with a PhD degree from the University of Paris. In the meantime the excavations at the Zhoukoudian site had been stopped. Tragically none of the more than forty remains of Peking man survived the turbulent and insecure times that followed in Chinese history.

During the following years he devoted himself to the growth of Chinese prehistory and the establishment of its theoretical system. He also finished his studies on the stone assemblages of Zhoukoudian, such as microliths. From the 1940s onwards, he did pioneering work on the denomination, origin and periodisation of microlithic stone artifacts.

Pei Wenzhong worked at many other sites, for example Zhalainor, Inner Mongolia, and in Gansu province. In 1955 he was elected to the Chinese Academy of Sciences, became the first Chairman of the Chinese Association of Natural Science Museums, and the second director of Beijing's Museum of Natural History. Until his death, he worked

FIGURE 8.1 Pei Wenzhong (centre) with An Zhimin (right) at the Peiligang site, 1977.

at the Institute of Vertebrate Palaeontology and Palaeoanthropology of the Chinese Academy of Sciences. He also wrote several books, including the first on Chinese prehistory. He passed away on 18 September 1982 and his cremated remains are buried at Zhoukoudian.

In 1928 the first archaeological institute in the Academia Sinica, Beijing, was founded and the first priority of Chinese scholars was to locate the ruins of Yin at today's Anyang, Shanxi province, the place where the so-called 'dragon bones' (inscribed bones as tools for divination) had been discovered in the late nineteenth century. Li Ji (1896–1979), trained at Harvard University in the fields of geology, anthropology, geography and archaeology, became the key figure in the excavation (see Box 8.2). Eleven royal tombs and thousands of artifacts confirmed that Yin was the late Shang dynasty capital. In 1928 the first Central Committee of Antiquities Preservation was established, charged with protection of cultural goods and the prevention of unauthorised digging.

BOX 8.2 Li Ji (1896–1979)

Li Ji, regarded as the 'father of Chinese archaeology', was born on 12 July 1896 in the small city of Zhongxiang in Hubei province. He was the first archaeologist to apply the field investigation method to the study of both prehistory and early history and gave ancient Chinese historiography a new tool. He also established the basic methodology of studying ancient Chinese civilisation through the combination of archaeological excavations, epigraphic science and anthropology.

Although he first had an education in Chinese classics, Li Ji graduated from the first Western-style preparatory school established in China, the Chinghu (Tsinghua) Academy in Beijing. He belonged to the first generation of Chinese scientists to be trained by leading scholars in universities in Western Europe and the United States. From 1918 onwards he studied abroad, entering Clark University in Worcester, Massachusetts. He first graduated in sociology and psychology and continued with the study of anthropology, receiving a PhD from Harvard University in 1923. His dissertation was published by Harvard University Press as *The Formation of the Chinese People: An Anthropological Enquiry* (1928). He preferred to return to China where he taught at Nankai University. In 1925–6 he conducted excavations in Xiyincun, Shanxi, deciphering the origins of the Neolithic Yangshao culture. In 1926 he returned to his Beijing University roots and participated in the Freer Gallery of Art's expedition to China, publishing the results as the *Archaeological survey of the Fen River Valley, Southern Shanxi, China*, which was the first field survey published in China. In 1928, while working again on Neolithic material, he became the director of the Academia Sinica, the Chinese Institute of History and Philology.

In that same year he conducted preliminary soundings in the ancient Shang dynastic capital at a site called Yin (today's Anyang) in Henan province. This site became important in 1899, when hundreds of tortoise shells and cattle bones with Chinese characters came to light. Peasants dug them up, named them 'dragon bones' and sold them to pharmacies where they were ground into medicine. It was only by chance that Chinese scientists became aware of this 3000-year-old invaluable material. It was in the year 1929, under the newly established Academia Sinica, Beijing, that Li Ji began to organise the excavation site. He was the first Chinese archaeologist to carry out field excavations in situ, which continued intermittently from 1929 to 1937. Familiar with Western methods he had a major impact on the quality of field archaeology. One of the major focuses for his generation of Chinese archaeologists was to investigate the origins of Chinese civilisation and also to stop the looting of Chinese relics, which had started to spread throughout the world. The civil war in 1930 stopped all archaeological efforts for a year but, by the end of the excavations, more than 300 burial sites had been found, including four royal tombs with more than 100 skeletons and over 100,000 objects: the inscribed bones used as tools for divination provided invaluable information about the ancient rulers, their battles and, most importantly, their religious rites.

From 1937 onwards the Sino–Japanese war totally halted the excavation project and many remains and notes were lost. In 1948 political turmoil and the communist takeover of China forced Li Ji and some of his colleagues to flee to Taiwan, where he established the Department of Anthropology and Archaeology of the National University of Taipei and became director of the relocated Academia Sinica. From then on he did an enormous amount of research on the remaining materials from the Anyang excavation. He published numerous books, including *The Beginning of Chinese Civilisation* (1957) and the unsurpassed *Anyang* (1977). In his research Li Ji for the first time placed the ritual objects from the excavations in a broader scientific context, such as terminology, classification, typology sequence and also decorative art. During his late career he was also the teacher of a younger generation of archaeologists such as Kwang-chih Chang (1931–2001), who finally brought Chinese archaeology to the attention of the Western world (see Box 8.3).

World War II and post-war developments

World War II and especially the Sino–Japanese war led to an interruption of archaeological work until 1949. After the foundation of the People's Republic of China in 1949 archaeology was still considered in terms of the question of the rise of Chinese civilisation and its periodisation, but furthermore to categorise the archaeological material within the political parameters of Marxist cultural theory and associated with cultural patriotism, also influenced by Soviet archaeology. Political motivation, rather than scientific reason, caused some Chinese academic authorities to persist in a classic evolutionism and refuse to allow any open discussion. The highest goal at this time was to prove that ancient Chinese history followed Marxist social developmental theory, and to prove the inevitability of the extinction of the private economic system. In terms of the archaeological theory of the historical period, for example, Mao's idea of the 'class struggle as a key link' was actualised in archaeological practice. It was also the time when administration, excavation and research were systematised under state control. Archaeological research was therefore placed under the State Bureau of Cultural Relics (Guojia wenwuju); and in 1950 the Institute of Archaeology (Kaogusuo) attached to the Institute of Social Science was established. Xia Nai (1910–85) became its director and conducted the first excavations in Changsha, Hunan province, and laid the foundations for further research on the Chu culture in the so-called Warring States Period (475–221 BC). Neolithic archaeologists refined prehistoric chronology in the Yellow River valley and also obtained fresh knowledge from the Yangzi river basin. Across the Taiwan Straits many prehistoric vestiges were excavated.

Although planned archaeological excavations were scarce in the period of the Cultural Revolution (1966–76), accidental discoveries and salvage excavations brought to light the tomb of Liu Sheng (second century BC) with its spectacular jade shroud; the so-called 'Flying Horse' from Wuwei, Gansu Province (186 BC); and the tomb of Mawangdui (168 BC), an intact burial of a noblewoman with silks, lacquers and bamboo inscriptions.

Of all Chinese archaeological discoveries, the best known in the West are the spectacular pits of the life-size terracotta soldiers guarding the tomb of the First Emperor of China, Qin Shihuangdi (259–210 BC). Located at Lintong, Xi'an, Shaanxi province, it is also one of the world's longest excavation projects – started in 1974, it is still yielding tremendous finds today.

After 1976, archaeology underwent rapid development. The Archaeological Society was established in 1979. Among the foremost archaeologists working at this time were Kwang-chih Chang (see Box 8.3), based in America, and An Zhimin (see Box 8.4). Since 1991 cooperation between Chinese and foreign institutions has been regulated by law and has helped to introduce new technologies, such as underwater archaeology, into the expanding field of excavation.

FIGURE 8.2 The funeral suit of Princess Dou Wan (wife of Liu Sheng), plaques of jade sewn with gold thread, from Mancheng, Hebei Province, China. Han Dynasty, 2nd century BC. Photo © DeAgostini/Getty Images.

BOX 8.3 Kwang-chih Chang (1931–2001)

The development of Chinese archaeology in the West during the second half of the twentieth century would be unimaginable without the inestimable research work of the Chinese archaeologist Kwang-chih Chang (aka. K.C. Chang, Zhang Guangzhi). Starting with the first edition of his *The Archaeology of Ancient China* (1963) Chang introduced and interpreted the rich archaeological discoveries from China's mainland ancient civilisations through several influential books and articles. For example, his highly distinctive contributions to archaeological methods and theory covered, among others, new developmental models of early Neolithic cultures, carbon-14 dating and chronology, settlement archaeology, bronze inscriptions, urbanism and capitals. He endowed every topic on which he worked with a wider cultural significance, placing archaeological evidence in a broader anthropological perspective.

Kwang-chih Chang was born on 15 April 1931 in Beijing. His parents both originated from Taiwan and immigrated during the Republican era. When he started his early education in two of the most selective public schools in Beijing, the Sino–Japanese war was in full operation. In 1946 the family moved back to Taiwan. After he was blacklisted as a Communist sympathiser, he was arrested on 6 April 1949 and spent a year in detention. It was not until 1952 that he was able to resume a more or less normal life.

He began to study archaeology at the National Taiwan University in its new Anthropology Department, as one of the first cohort of students. Modelled on anthropological departments in the USA, particularly Harvard University, it provided seminars in physical anthropology, archaeology, ethnography and also linguistics. Professor Li Ji, considered to be the father of modern archaeology in China and trained at Harvard (see Box 8.3), became Kwang-chih Chang's mentor. Upon graduation in 1954 Chang underwent military training for a year. He then joined the anthropological department of Harvard University and spent time on the Abri Pataud excavation in France with Professor Hallam Movius, Jr, a Palaeolithic archaeology specialist. After this period of research and excavation experience he was sure that his primary duty should be to devote himself to Chinese archaeology and anthropology. In 1960 he earned a PhD, being the first to discuss 'Prehistoric settlements in China: A Study in Archaeological Method and Theory'. He then took a teaching position at Yale University in 1969, was promoted to full-tenure professor in 1969 and chaired its department of anthropology. In 1963–4, during a sabbatical year, he returned to Taiwan to participate in the Fenbitou, Dapenkeng (Taipei county) excavation project. After his dissertation he published research work in three major fields: archaeological synthesis, method and theory, and original fieldwork, such as *Settlement Archaeology* (1968). Recognition came to him in the form of an appointment as a fellow of the Academia Sinica in Taipei. In 1977 he moved back to Harvard to take a position as Professor of Anthropology, and Curator of East Asian Archaeology at the Peabody Museum, while at the same time teaching East Asian Languages and Civilisation. In that same year he made his first trip back to Beijing as a member of a group of palaeo-anthropologists to see excavations and some of the archaeological finds with his own eyes. In 1979 he was appointed to the United States National Academy of Sciences. He chaired Harvard's Department of Anthropology from 1981 to 1984. In 1984 he also received the status of a permanent guest professor at Beijing University. After years of profound study and research he produced the fourth edition of his bestseller *The Archaeology of Ancient China* and until 1989 served as the head of the Harvard Council on East Asian Studies.

Kwang-chih Chang wrote more than 350 publications. In 1980, *Shang Civilization* was an exceptional work that gave the Western world great insight into ancient China and explained how Chinese civilisation evolved. He later published *The Chinese Bronze Age*. He had long wanted to carry out an archaeological excavation in China's Yellow River valley. Finally in 1988, communications were opened concerning such an excavation. But in 1989 the trouble that erupted in Tiananmen Square caused the talks to be postponed. Shortly after that, Chang was diagnosed with Parkinson's disease. Though very ill, he became Vice-President of the Academia Sinica, Taiwan's leading research institution, in 1994. He passed away on 3 January 2001.

BOX 8.4 An Zhimin (1924–2005)

An Zhimin belongs to the third generation of archaeologists in China. He was born in Yantai, Shandong province and graduated from Beijing National University in 1948, with a history degree. Trained mainly by Pei Wenzhong (1904–82), Liang Siyong (1904–54) and Xia Nai (1910–85) he started his teaching career in 1949 at Yanjing University. His main focus of interest at this time was already on Chinese prehistory. He continued his studies at Beijing University, where he graduated in 1952. An archaeological department per se did not exist at that time, but the history department opened one in 1952. Most introductions to archaeology were imparted by adjunct faculty on loan from various institutes of the Chinese Academy of Social Science. These included the great Palaeolithic specialist Pei Wenzhong and the archaeologist, Egyptologist and later Director of the Institute of Archaeology, Xia Nai (1910–85). An Zhimin, who had already joined the Academy in 1950, started to teach at the University from 1953 to 1957.

An Zhimin was one of the leading people in field archaeology, which turned out to be his lifelong endeavour, and he was one of the protagonists in the New Archaeology. Altogether he published ten major archaeological compendia and over 400 scientific articles. But most of his research time was spent doing fieldwork, for example as a participant in major archaeological excavations such as at the Han dynasty tombs of Shaogou, Luoyang, Henan province.

During his academic career he worked on the agriculture of the prehistoric age and, most importantly, on the origins of rice cultivation, on early ceramics, and on the typology and production of bronzes. His geographical interests extended from Gansu province in the northeast to the upper and lower reaches of the Yellow River, mainly at Sanmenxia Reservoir, and southwards to the excavations at Changsha, Hunan province. He also did research on the cultural exchanges between Ancient Japan and China.

From 1950 onwards he took part in the excavations in Anyang, Shaanxi province, which proved to be the ancient capital of the Shang dynasty (c. 1570–1045 BC). The most important discovery was that of the richest royal tomb No 5 of Lady Fu Hao, the consort of the Shang dynasty king Wu (c. 1200 BC E) in 1976, which underlined the long-term potential for archaeology at Anyang. From Lady Fu Hao's tomb more then 200 bronze ritual vessels, 100 vessels with inscriptions of her name or offering texts, 750 jade objects, 560 bone carvings, three ivory goblets, ceramics and other objects came to light.

He continued his archaeological and research efforts in the northeast of China in 1962–5, but then the Cultural Revolution interrupted his work until 1971. After this period he was involved in the first publication of the two great archaeological journals *Archaeology* (chin. Kaogu) and *Archaeological Studies* (chin. Kaogu xuebao) in 1971, and from 1978 he became the chief editor of *Archaeology*.

But his main interest lay in the investigation of Chinese prehistory, its regional structure and trade. In this field his research endeavours focused on the investigation of the so-called microliths and microblades, small-sized stone flakes from the Neolithic period, thus helping to understand the use of such tools in this period.

One of his great areas of research was the Neolithic period in the northeast, through the excavation (from 1956 to 1957) and in-depth studies of the Miaodigou site

FIGURE 8.3 An Zhimin, 1981.

(3900–2780 BC) in Sanmenxia and Sanliqiao, Henan Province, Central China, from the 1950s onwards. These finds clarified the time sequence of the Neolithic Yangshao and Longshan cultures, as well as their mutual relationships. The Miaodigou site, covering an area of about 362,000 square metres, includes both the Yangshao and Longshan cultures. The Miaodigou culture, distributed over mid-Shaanxi, south Shanxi and the west of Henan provinces, was the most prosperous facies of the Yangshao culture. The Miaodigou II culture was the continuation of the Yangshao culture, and later developed to the Longshan culture in Henan Province. In the Miaodigou site a large quantity of stone wares, bone wares and pottery was excavated, which provide important references for research on the development of ancient Chinese culture.

Excavation at the Peiligang and Cishan sites in Henan and Hebei province also led to the assumption that they preceded the Yangshao and Longshan cultures, thus explaining the development of the Neolithic period in the Central Chinese region. In 1982 he published his results in *Research on China's Neolithic period*, which proved to be an outstanding scholarly work.

Two volumes in honour of his lifetime achievements were published: in 2004 *Essays in Honour of An Zhimin*, to commemorate his eightieth birthday; and in 2011 *A Lifetime of Archaeology – Essays in Honour of An Zhimin*.

The modern situation

From the end of the twentieth century until today archaeology has become one of the most important sciences in China with a strong political impetus. During the ninth Five-Year-Plan (1996–2000) and on the occasion of the fiftieth anniversary of the Foundation of the People's Republic of China, the State Council launched an interdisciplinary 'Periodisation Project of the Xia, Shang and Zhou Dynasties'. The research was based on a combination of extensive archaeological excavations (along with the salvage excavations on the 'Three Gorges Dam Project' on the Yangzi River), thorough textual interpretations and advanced data technology to find the origins of the respective dynasties.

In 2001 the Institute of Archaeology announced the final result of the selection of the 100 most important among nearly 10,000 archaeological discoveries in China over the past 100 years. The selection was the largest ever made in the country, involving experts from eight state-level archaeological research organs, twenty-eight provincial institutes and eleven prestigious universities across China. World-famous discoveries were included on the list, such as Peking man, the Neolithic site at Banpo Village on the eastern outskirts of Xi'an in Shaanxi Province, the Shang-dynasty Yin ruin excavations, the Dunhuang Mogao Grottos in northwest China's Gansu Province, the terracotta army at the mausoleum of Emperor Qin in Xi'an, the Sanxingdui pits, near Guanghan, Sichuan province, with their huge bronze statues, the Mummies of Xinjiang, the Ming tombs in Najing, Jiangsu province, the Tang emperors' tombs, Qian county, Shaanxi province, and the Ming emperors' tombs.

Within the last ten years planned excavations and field archaeology projects have been carried out with great care and success. Modern technology and scientific research methods were introduced by foreign joint venture projects, in which Western and Chinese

---

BOX 8.5 Tomb raiders and the antiquities trade

'Looting obliterates the memory of the ancient world and turns its highest artistic creations into decorations, adornments on a shelf, divorced from historical context and ultimately from all meaning.' R. Atwood.

Tomb robbery is probably the world's second-oldest profession and has been a major problem ever since emperors, kings or rulers commissioned large tombs to be built in their honour and memory. In fact it has long been a curse in Egypt, where not a single Pharaoh's tomb escaped robbery completely. Even the famous tomb of King Tutankhamen, in the Valley of the Kings, had been raided in ancient times, long before it was discovered in 1922. What is true for Egypt also applies to many other tombs of ancient cultures, for example in parts of South America, but few people realise the scale and importance of this crime in China. The antiquities trade is growing enormously everywhere in the world, with China being one of the worst-hit areas.

General Cao Cao would have hardly believed his eyes: When Chinese state television broadcast the live excavation of his tomb, the destruction found inside proved that tomb robbers had won the race against time: the archaeologists were too late, finding the tomb empty. Back in the time when the cruel warlord Cao Cao lived (AD 155–220), he himself had organised soldiers to form a treasure-hunting and tomb-raiding league.

Tomb raiding has a long tradition in China, whether for the purpose of destroying tombs of disagreeable previous rulers or to gain possession of the valuable treasures buried in the tomb. Such was also the case with Emperor Qin Shihuang's (r. 221–210 BC) grave site, which was partly looted only fifty years after his death. The intruders, mainly seeking high-quality weapons, even innovated new tools specifically to make their work more efficient.

Shanxi, Shaanxi, Henan, Hebei, Anhui and Jiangsu provinces have been the principal regions for this phenomenon due to their enormous number of tombs that are not well protected. Official statistics by UNESCO indicate that 1.64 million Chinese artifacts are stored in 200 museums in over forty-seven countries, while possibly another million are tucked away in private collections. The real number may well be far higher, if one includes the plundering that began during the colonial era of the nineteenth and twentieth centuries. Adventurers and scientists coming to China in those days plundered Buddhist caves and dug up graves in order to 'protect' the antiquities. Foreigners and Chinese fleeing after the collapse of the Qing-dynasty (1644–1911) also pilfered a large number of valuable objects.

Nowadays the looting of tombs is listed as a crime by China's Law for the Protection of Cultural Relics. Since the 1980s, after China's official policy of opening-up, there was a boom in tomb raiding. The antiquities collection market had always had an eye on Chinese cultural relics, but now it was possible to smuggle them out of the country. Over the past few decades up to 300,000 tombs have been raided all over the country and raiders have grown bolder: well equipped with specialised tools, explosives or earthmoving equipment, and more recently using metal detectors, gas chromatography and GPS, they open up the tombs and grab whatever seems to be of value. Smaller tombs are systematically looted, but even some larger ones have been attacked. In February 2006 a gang raided the Tang Imperial tomb of Wu Huifei (699–737), who was a concubine of Emperor Xuanzong (685–762). The 27-ton coffin and five 'grade one' murals were finally found in the USA and were brought back to China.

Excavated antiquities from tombs are regarded as National Treasures categorised in levels of importance and value. Their sale or exchange is prohibited. Nevertheless tomb raiders can circumvent the law by selling them to the black market or to fixed buyers. China has now ratified the 1970 UNESCO Convention on the Means of Prohibiting the Illicit Import, Export and Transfer of Ownership of Cultural Property and the UNIDROIT Convention on Stolen or Illegal Exported Cultural Objects from 1995. Bilateral agreements with fourteen countries make possible the joint tracking of stolen artifacts. China itself established the so-called SACH (State Administration of Cultural Heritage) as an administrative agency subordinate to the Ministry of Culture. It is responsible for the protection of cultural relics of national importance and for the management of museums.

Further reading

Atwood, R. 2004. *Stealing History, Tomb Raiders, Smugglers, and the Looting of the Ancient World*. St Martin's Press: New York.

Murphy, D.L. 1995. *Plunder and Preservation – Cultural Property Law and Practice in the People's Republic of China*. Oxford University Press: New York.

archaeologists can work together. The publication of excavation reports is not only done in archaeological periodicals and magazines, but also disseminated via the Internet. Sensational excavations are filmed and broadcast on TV. But despite all this progress, Chinese archaeologists have not yet opened their utmost treasure: while the side burials of Emperor Qin Shihuang's necropolis were excavated recently, the tomb itself remains untouched. Conversely, one of the greatest threats still facing Chinese archaeology is the looting of ancient tombs.

History of Japanese archaeology

The early beginnings

The oldest reference to a prehistoric site in Japan is contained in a volume called '*Hitachi fudoki*', a description of the Hitachi district (today's Ibagari prefecture) compiled around AD 713 and recording a find of shells at a place called Ogushi Hill.

   Two things shaped the view of Japan's archaeology: Classical Chinese historiography and early eighth-century Japanese historical chronicles. The most important ancient histories were the Kojiki (Record of Ancient Matters) and the Nihongi (Records of Japan) compiled in AD 712 and 720. They establish a rudimentary timescale for the study of Japanese antiquity by the 'Age of the Gods', and the time after around AD 660. Although recognition of ancient sites had a long tradition in Japan, it was not until the Tokugawa-Period (1603–1869) that real archaeological interest arose. This was a time when Japan was conducting a policy of isolation from the Western world, and only a small group of scholars had contact with archaeological remains, such as Arai Hakuseki (1656–1725) and Tō Teikan (1731–98), the latter combining his interest in archaeological remains with historical research. Travelling was very common in this period; one of the first such travellers was the writer and ethnologist Sugae Masumi (1754–1829) who ranged widely across Japan. He showed special interest in pottery (now known to be prehistoric) that farmers had dug from the ground.

The nineteenth and twentieth centuries

At the end of the Tokugawa period Japanese scholars realised the importance of archaeology for their own history. In the following Meiji-era (1868–1912) an official government edict was issued in 1871 for the protection of historical records, collections and objects; and plans for a National Museum were set up. Miyake Yonekichi (1860–1920) founded the Association for Japanese Archaeology and promoted the academic circle of historical archaeology through the journals '*Kōkaido*' (The World of Archaeology) and '*Kōgogaku*' (Journal of Archaeology).

   Collections of ancient pottery and stone tools were assembled but there was still little interest in sites or the context of excavations. Negishi Bunko (1831–1902) was an avocational archaeologist and wealthy landowner who possessed a large collection of pottery sherds. It was probably contact with him that led the American biologist E.S. Morse in 1877 to conduct the first scientific excavation at the prehistoric Omori shell midden near Tokyo. Thus he not only introduced modern archaeology to Japan, but also gave the new science recognition. Meanwhile Tsubei Shōgorō (1863–1913) established the Department of Anthropology at the Tokyo Imperial Science University.

Between 1900 and 1945 archaeologists published research that was the basis for many post-war excavations. As was also the case in China, early in the twentieth century Japanese scientists trained in the West brought back new techniques such as typology and stratigraphy.

At that time academic archaeology in Japan was undergoing significant changes in methodology and approach. This was mainly due to the controversy about the dating of the well-known Buddhist temple, the Hōryū-ji, in Nara prefecture, the oldest wooden construction in Japan and today on the UNESCO World Heritage list. Only scientific excavation proved that it dated to the seventh century AD. These first excavations of the underground structure of a historic building led to detailed research on Nara palace, which in 1922 was designated as a historical site. The excavations of the imperial palaces that served as the emperor's residence and domestic governmental offices as early as the fourth and fifth centuries was as important as the research on the large tomb sites, known as the Kofun tombs. Kofun (English, 'old mound') are megalithic tombs, constructed between the early third century and early seventh century AD, which have given their name to the Kofun period (250–538). Even though kofun tumuli took various shapes in history, most of them have a keyhole-shaped mound, when looked upon from a bird's eye view, which is unique in ancient Japan. No special North–South orientation was necessary. The tomb sizes range from four to several hundred metres in length. The largest kofun ever found is the so-called 'Daisen kofun' in Sekai city, Osaka prefecture, today named Nintôku-tennô-ryô, the tomb of Emperor Nintoku. The burial mound itself is 482 m long. It is surrounded by three formerly water-filled ditches and smaller concomitant tombs with mounds, the whole area measuring approximately 196 acres (80 ha). To build this tomb 2000 workers per day had to work for

FIGURE 8.4 Golden Hall and Five-storied Pagoda of Hōryū-ji, in Ikaruga, Nara prefecture. Photo © 663highland/Wikimedia Commons.

FIGURE 8.5 Aerial view of Nintôku-tennô-ryô, the so-called 'Daisen kofun', in Sekai, Osaka prefecture. Photo © Ministry of Land, Infrastructure and Transport Government of Japan.

fifteen years and eight months to finish the whole complex. Kofun tombs were constructed all over the Japanese islands. On and in some of the mounds so-called 'Haniwa' had been placed. Haniwa means 'pottery ring' and comprises all sorts of grave goods. Haniwa grave offerings were made in numerous forms, such as horses, chickens, birds, fans, fish houses, weapons, shields, sunshades and pillows. The placing of male and female human images had a spiritual reason, that of protecting the deceased in his afterlife, and thus these figures were arrayed above and in the surroundings to delimit and protect the sacred area.

In 1972, the unlooted Takamatsizuka tomb was found accidentally by farmers in Asuka village, Nara Prefecture. Inside the tightly assembled rocks, white lime cement plasters had coloured pictures drawn on them, depicting the court or heavenly zoomorphic figures. A stone coffin was placed in the chamber and accessories, swords and bronze mirrors were laid both inside and outside of the coffin.

At that time, other major excavations in progress included those of the Kawadera temple, the Otsu capital and several other temple sites (until 1937). New techniques that traced structures from underground foundations even in the absence of surface features were invented. Great progress was also made in the study of ceramic manufacture, which provided clues for ceramic production, trade and chronological dating. Research on Buddhist remains, such as buried copies of Buddhist scriptures, ritual objects and bells, gave an insight into the long tradition of religious belief in Japan.

The most spectacular discovery in 1961 – first at Nara, and then also in other palaces, capitals and government offices – was a large number of wooden tablets with characters on them. There are now over 40,000 tablets from fifty excavation sites.

Some major discoveries stimulated archaeological interest after World War II. One was the excavation of the Palaeolithic site at Iwajuku, starting from 1949, which suggested that human occupation of the Japanese islands was much older than previously believed. The second was a third-century village called Toro (excavated 1947–50), where complete rice paddies and wooden tools were discovered, followed by the excavation of the Sannai Maruyama settlement of the Jômon period in 1992 and hundreds of Kofun tombs from the Kofun period.

As early as 1950 the Cultural Property Preservation Law (bunka zai hogo hō) was enacted and excavations were allowed to take place prior to any construction. Land development began to change Japan in the late 1950s. With increasing industrial and economic growth, large-scale constructions were undertaken. Salvage and rescue excavations were necessary most of the time to avoid destruction of archaeological sites. It was only in the 1960s and early 1970s that archaeology was supported by the government and an administrative system was built up.

The modern situation

The 1980s could be called the heyday of Japanese archaeology. In 1987, for example, archaeologists excavated 21,755 sites throughout Japan. Of these only 409 were academic excavations, while the rest were administrative rescue projects. In the year 2000, 1437 archaeological discoveries were acknowledged as 'Historical Sites' under the protection of the State.

One of them is the largest Jômon period settlement, the so-called Sannai Maruyama site located in the Anomori Prefecture in northern Japan. A long-term excavation since 1992 revealed that the site dated to the Early and Middle Jômon periods (c. 5500–4000 BC).

Over 600 pit dwellings and twenty long houses were discovered, and over 120 post-hole patterns have been identified representing raised-floor six-pillared buildings. In 1994 six wooden poles belonging to a huge building were excavated. Numerous storage pits and large shell middens and hundreds of thousands of artifacts have been recovered from this site, including arrowheads, polished stone axes, stemmed scrapers, potsherds, bark baskets, grinding stones and mortars, net sinkers, clay figurines, and stone and bone ornaments. Lacquered plates, bowls and combs were mainly made of wood and mostly found in the wetland areas. Lacquer tree seeds were found, suggesting that lacquer manufacturing took place in this site. Bone and antler implements included harpoon heads, fishhooks, needles, awls and hairpins, most of them made from mammal rib bones. Burial pits for adults were arranged in rows, identified as oval-shaped holes. Some are marked with large stones and some had mounds. Altogether there were approximately 250 adult grave pits and 800 burial jars for children. In 2001 the site was designated as a special Historical Site of Japan.

Nihon Kokogaku Nempo (Archaeologia Japonica: Annual Report of Japanese Archaeological Studies and Excavations), published by the Japanese Archaeological Association, is one of the most important journals with information on recent excavations. The Tokyo National Museum houses the biggest collection of Japanese archaeological objects from the Palaeolithic to the Kofun Period.

In 2009 the oldest keyhole tomb and a water management facility were discovered in the San'in region, Honshu, Central Japan. Atop the Motodaka hill, on the western side of the Sendai river flowing through the Tottori Plain, lies the Motodaka tomb group, built with a total of twenty tombs. As a result of excavations undertaken in 2009, it became clear that

Motodaka No 14, thought to have been a round mound of the largest scale, is the oldest keyhole tomb in the San'in region.

In the year 2010 there were many excavations related to state-supported provincial monasteries. Carried out mainly for the purpose of their preparation as historic sites, these included the provincial monasteries of Aki and Izumo in western Japan, and those of Tōtōmi, Mikawa, Kai and Musashi in eastern Japan.

In recent years Japanese archaeology has rapidly grown as a field of research. Many important excavations have been conducted and exhibitions around the world present the results of a long-term archaeological history.

History of Korean archaeology

From early beginnings to the nineteenth century

In 1748, Chŏng Chi-hae, the father of a local governor from Jinju region, in today's South Gyeongsang Province, southeastern Korea, excavated six ancient tombs to see if they were the lost tombs of his ancestors from the Koryō dynasty (918–1392). His search remained a vain endeavour but it was probably the first attempt at archaeological excavation on the Korean peninsula.

But it took centuries before modern archaeology was established in Korea. It was during the Japanese occupation from 1910 to 1945 that the local Japanese government set up a committee for archaeological investigation. In 1915 a small museum was inaugurated to house the material from the excavations all over the country. As excavation projects at this time were more a political gesture, ancient Korean culture was regarded as an inferior culture, being more or less a bridge between China and Japan. In 1947, two years after the Japanese retreat from Korea, the well-known Japanese archaeologist Umehara Sueiji (1893–1983) published the achievements of Japanese archaeology in Korea.

Within the next few years Korean archaeology saw a renewal and scientists realised that it was important for understanding the unique sequence of prehistoric events in East Asia as well as cultural processes.

The twentieth century

In 1946 the National Museum of Korea, the sole archaeological institution in South Korea, started excavation work. The Korean war (1950–3) halted scientific work for over a decade and brought an end to archaeological work in what was henceforth called North Korea.

The National University in Seoul opened a department for archaeology in 1961 and was followed by other universities throughout the country. For the first time students published a small periodical *Kogo misul* (Archaeology and Art) and the National Museum added a bi-annual publication called *Misul charyo* (Materials in Art History). The Korean Cultural Heritage Administration (CHA) was founded in 1961. It is a governmental agency in charge of the preservation, management and promotion of Korean cultural heritage. Scientific archaeological work started around 1969 with the construction of a Carbon-14 laboratory. During the 1960s excavations were rather sporadic; but in the 1970s archaeological work improved due to contacts with foreign archaeological circles. In 1975 the Institute of Cultural Properties was established under the Ministry of Culture and Information. At the same time salvage excavations and surveys, necessitated by the great quantity of construction work throughout the country, called for the formation of an archaeological centre. This finally led to the production of various scientific journals, among others the annual review *Archaeology in Korea* and the *Journal of Korean Archaeological Studies*.

From the 1970s and especially from the 1990s onwards, archaeological management has played a key role in the cultural and political development of South Korea. Palaeolithic and Neolithic discoveries have been most important for knowledge of the development of Korean culture. Discoveries throughout the country prove the existence of human settlement in these periods. For example, discoveries in 1994 on Cheju Island, the southernmost island of Korea, proved that as early as 10,000 BC pottery was produced, formed of clay with some organic matter.

Significant discoveries were made in Gyeongju, south-east Korea. In 1971 the brick tomb of Korea's twenty-fifth king, Muryŏng, and his wife was discovered, untouched since it was sealed up in AD 529. Muryŏng was king of Baekje, one of the three kingdoms of Korea's greatest period, from the fourth to the ninth century AD. Almost 3000 relics were unearthed, one of the greatest finds showing the social and cultural aspects of the Baekje Kingdom.

In 1973 archaeologists discovered the tomb of the Heavenly Horse (Cheonmachong) and dated it to the fifth–sixth century. It probably belonged to a king of the Silla period (57 BC–AD 935) and is representative of wooden chamber tombs with stone mounds. A wooden coffin and a wooden chest for the funerary objects were placed on a flat floor; boulders were then piled on top and an earthen mound was built over the whole thing. A total of 11,500 artifacts were retrieved, including the famous gold crown and a pair of birch-bark saddle-flaps painted with a flying horse, thus giving the tomb its name.

The Korean National Research Institute of Cultural Properties excavated the Anapji historical site with the Pond of the Moon (Wolji) and nearby areas for about twenty-five years, beginning in 1975. The garden with all the buildings, totalling 15,658 m² in area, was completed in the year AD 674. Three building sites were restored. Five pavilion sites, twenty-six building sites, eight wall sites, one water intake and two water discharge facilities were uncovered. No fewer than 33,000 artifacts from Anapji were excavated, including bronze, pottery, roof tiles, and wooden and lacquered objects.

One of the most interesting and complete dwelling sites is the Sinchangdong Wetland Site located in Sinchangdong, Gwangju City and designated as Historic Site No 375. This site has been under excavation since 1963. It contains an abundance of agricultural remains originating from the period between the late second century BC to the third AD. In 1963, fifty-three ancient jar tombs were found in the area, thereby introducing the Sinchangdong site to the wider world. A survey and excavation project carried out by a Gwangju National Museum team in 1992 unearthed the remains of an earthenware kiln, ditched enclosures, dwellings and farming fields, revealing it to be a large multi-period archaeological site containing relics related to agricultural production, daily life and burial practices from around the beginning of the Common Era.

Recent developments

The organisations that are engaged in archaeological survey and excavation are foundations, university museums and the National Museums. The Korea Cultural Properties Investigation and Research Institute Association (KCPIA), founded in 2000, publishes the *Journal for Field Archaeology*.

However, since the 1990s South Korean archaeology has witnessed an explosive increase in rescue or salvage excavations because of intensive national land development accompanying economic growth. In Korea excavators are required to organise a Project Direction Committee (Chido Winwŏnhoe) for each project, reporting on the excavation and preservation of the site. There are on-site Explanatory Meetings at the excavations, to explain the details of the excavation results to the public, as well as the characteristic features and artifacts.

Bibliography

Atwood, R. 2004. *Stealing history, tomb raiders, smugglers, and the looting of the ancient world*, p9. St. Martin's Press: New York.

Barnes, G. 1999. *The Rise of Civilization in East Asia: The Archaeology of China, Korea and Japan*. Thames and Hudson: London.

Barnes, G. 2001. *State Formation in Korea: Historical and Archaeological Perspectives*. Curzon Press: Richmond, UK.

Byington, M. E. (ed.) 2008. *Early Korea – Reconsidering Early Korean History through Archeology*. Harvard University Asia Center: Harvard.

Byington, M. E. (ed.) 2009. *Early Korea The Samhan Period in Korean History*. Harvard University Asia Center: Harvard.

Byington, M. E. (ed.) 2012. *Early Korea – The Rediscovery of Kaya in History and Archaeology*. Harvard University Asia Center: Harvard.

Chang Kwang-chih and Xu Pingfang 2005. *The Formation of Chinese Civilisation. An Archaeological Perspective*. Yale University Press and New World Press: New Haven, London, Beijing.

Chang Kwang-chih 1986. *The Archaeology of Ancient China*. Yale University Press: New Haven, CT (4th edition).

Colcutt, M., Jansen, M. and Kumakura, I. 1988. *Cultural Atlas of Japan*. Phaidon: Oxford.

Goepper, R. and Whitfield, R. (eds) 1994. *The Tomb of King Munyong – Treasures from Korea. Art through 5000 years*. British Museum Publications: London.

Ikawa-Smith, F. 1980. Current issues in Japanese Archaeology. *American Scientist* 68 (2): 134–45.

Kim, Won-yong 1986. *Art and Archaeology of Ancient Korea*. Taekwang Publ. Co.: Seoul.

Kohl, P. L. and Fawcett, C. (eds) 1995. *Nationalism, Politics, and the Practice of Archaeology*. Cambridge University Press: Cambridge.

Pearson, R. J. (ed.) 1986. *Windows on the Japanese Past: Studies in Archaeology and Prehistory*. University of Michigan: Ann Arbor.

Robertson, J. (ed.) 2005. *A Companion to the Anthropology of Japan*. Blackwell: Oxford.

The Rise of a Great Tradition: Japanese Archaeological Ceramics from the Jomon through Heian Periods (10,500 BC–AD 1185). 1990. Agency for Cultural Affairs, Japan, and Japan Society: New York.

Yang Xiaoneng. 1999. *The Golden Age of Chinese Archaeology. Celebrated Discoveries from the People's Republic of China*. Yale University Press: London & New Haven, CT.

9

RUSSIA

Igor Tikhonov

Earliest beginnings and antiquarians

The peculiarity of the formation of Russian archaeology is the fact that before the beginning of the eighteenth century there was no antiquarianism in Russia, such as was important for Europe as a cultural phenomenon. This was partly due to the fact that Classical artifacts were not known and were not discovered on its territory until the last quarter of the eighteenth century. Interest in antiquities originally manifested itself in the collection of rarities and jewels in the princes' and tsars' treasure rooms, and in church vestries. The initial steps of Russian archaeology belong to the era of Peter the Great, though some mentions of archaeological sites can be found in earlier times. In 1714, the first Russian Museum – the Kunstkamera in St Petersburg – was founded on Peter's orders and acquired a collection of artifacts from the burial mounds of southern Siberia, which he had received as a gift. In 1718 he issued the following decree:

> if anyone finds in the soil or in the water any ancient things . . . also any ancient inscriptions on stones, iron or copper things, or any weapons, old and unusual at the present time, dishes and everything else that is old and unusual, this has to be brought and will be rewarded adequately.

This decree initiated the acquisition of archaeological collections.

The following year, the first antique statues were acquired in Italy by order of Peter the Great, including the famous Tauris Venus, a Roman copy from a Greek original. The first scientific archaeological excavations of burial mounds in Russia were undertaken in Siberia during the expeditions of the St Petersburg Academy of Sciences in 1719–27 (D.G. Messerschmidt) and in 1733–43 (G.F. Miller, I.G. Gmelin). In the 1760s in the publications of the Academy of Sciences, there appeared for the first time an article on archaeological discoveries in Russia, written by G.F. Miller, who developed a unique guide for the study of Siberian antiquities. The Empress Catherine the Great in 1764 marked the beginning of the imperial court art collection with the museum of the Hermitage, which included a collection of antique gems, bronzes and sculptures. Following the monarchs, aristocrats also began to collect antiquities, primarily Classical ones.

In the last quarter of the eighteenth century, the excavation and study began of Greek and Scythian cultural artifacts in the area of the northern part of the Black Sea coast, following the accession of these territories into the Russian Empire. The first explorers were often army or navy officers, engineers and enthusiasts. For example, the archaeological study of the Kerch region was carried out by a French emigrant, Paul du Brux, who described and mapped the plans of many cities in the Bosphorus area. In St Petersburg the antiquities recovered were studied by academician E.E. Köhler and the President of the Academy of Fine Arts, A.N. Olenin. Archaeological museums were founded in Nikolaev (1803), Theodosius (1811) and Kerch (1826). The discovery of a rich Scythian burial mound at Kul-Oba near Kerch in 1830 attracted the attention and interest of the Emperor Nicholas I, who started at that time to spend money on excavations on a regular basis. The most striking and interesting finds from these excavations entered the imperial court's museum (the Hermitage), which only in 1852 received the status of a public museum. In 1854 a magnificent book in three volumes, in Russian and French, called *Antiquités du Bosphore Cimmérien conservées au musée impérial de l'Ermitage* was published at the Emperor's personal expense. In 1820 a Pole living in Russia, Z. Dolenga-Khodakovskiy, created a study programme for Slavic antiquities. His ideas were further developed later by a professor at St Petersburg University, I.I. Sreznevsky.

Nineteenth-century archaeologists

In the mid-nineteenth century the organisational structure of Russian archaeology started to take shape. In 1839 the 'Odessa Society of History and Antiquities' was founded, followed in 1846 by the 'Archaeological and Numismatic Society' in St Petersburg. In 1851 the 'Imperial Russian Archaeological Society' was set up, with three divisions: Russian and Slavic archaeology; Classical, Byzantine and Western European archaeology; and the Orient. Until 1917 the Chairmen of this Society were members of the ruling Romanov family: Duke M. Leuchtenberg, Grand Duke Konstantin Nikolaevich, Grand Duke Konstantin Konstantinovich and Grand Duke Georgy Mikhailovich. The Society sponsored excavations of the barrows in the vicinity of St Petersburg, in the Fortress of Staraya Ladoga, and at significant sites in the southern Caucasus. The publication of scientific literature was considered a priority by the Society, and it achieved great success in this area.

Tsar Alexander II in 1859 established in St Petersburg the Imperial Archaeological Commission within the framework of the Ministry of the Imperial Court. Until 1882 this Commission was headed by Count S.G. Stroganov, who looked on archaeology as the study of Classical antiquities. Accordingly, in this period, archaeological excavations were organised by the Commission mainly in the south of Russia, and only occasionally were expeditions sent to other regions. Preferential attention was paid to burial sites. The necropolises of the Bosphorus cities of Panticapaeum and Nymphaeum were excavated, as well as royal Scythian and Sarmatian burial mounds on the Dnieper and Don (Chertomlyk, Alexandrapol, Bol'shaya Bliznitsa, Khohlach).

In 1886, Count A.A. Bobrinsky was appointed Chairman of the Commission. He was well known, thanks to the excavations of mounds on the territory of his huge estate on the Middle Dnieper. He was able to increase the staffing and finance of the Commission and excavations were carried out in many regions of the European part of Russia, as well as in Siberia and Central Asia. From 1887 onwards the Commission conducted systematic excavations at the ancient Greek and Byzantine city of Chersonesos in the Crimea and from

1901 at the Greek polis of Olbia. The Russian archaeologists studied fortification systems, urban neighbourhoods and cemeteries. During the excavations of Olbia, for the first time in Russia, B.V. Farmakovsky used the technique of laying out a grid of squares, which he had previously seen on excavation sites in the eastern Mediterranean. A great archaeologist, A. Spitsyn, began to work for the Archaeological Commission in 1892 and did important work in the systematising and dating of archaeological material in Eastern Europe, from the Stone Age up to the Middle Ages. For the first time in Russia, he applied mapping methods and managed to reconstruct the settlement of Eastern Slavic tribes according to the dissemination of certain types of temple rings. Another member of the Commission, the Orientalist professor N.I. Veselovsky, carried out excavations on the northern coast of the Black Sea and in the North Caucasus, where he dug many Scythian burial mounds, for example that of Solokha in 1913 and the Maikop kurgan of the Early Bronze Age. Kiev amateur archaeologist V. Hvoyka discovered in Ukraine the settlements and tombs of the Eneolithic Trypillian culture, the Chernjakhov culture and the Zarubineckaja culture of the first centuries AD.

In 1889 the Imperial Archaeological Commission received a permit to monitor and supervise all excavations in the lands of the State, the Church and in public ownership. The Commission granted permits to these excavations and collected reports about them. The most striking and interesting finds were passed to the Imperial Hermitage Museum and the Historical Museum in Moscow; the rest were distributed among other museums or returned

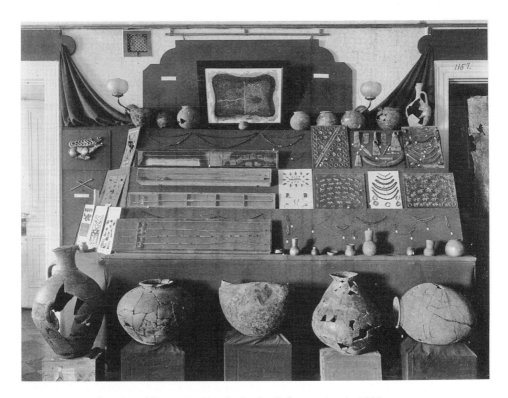

FIGURE 9.1 Artifacts found by N. Veselovsky in the Kuban region in 1897.

to the initiators of the excavation. Finds made on private lands were left to landlords and owned by them. Despite a series of government decrees banning treasure hunting and calling for the protection and collection of antiquities (1805, 1826, 1837, 1848, 1866), no specific, clear law was developed in Tsarist Russia for the preservation and protection of the archaeological heritage. At the beginning of the twentieth century this specific issue was discussed several times in the Russian parliament – the State Duma – but the law was never passed.

In 1864 Count A. Uvarov (Box 9.1) founded the Moscow Archaeological Society, which from 1869 onwards organised regular archaeological congresses in different cities of Russia: Moscow (1869), St Petersburg (1871), Kiev (1874), Kazan (1877), Tiflis (now Tbilisi) (1881), Odessa (1884), Yaroslavl (1887), Moscow (1890), Vilna (now Vilnius) (1893), Riga (1896), Kiev (1899), Kharkov (1902), Yekaterinoslav (now Dnepropetrovsk) (1905), Chernigov (1908) and Novgorod (1911). The sixteenth congress was scheduled for August 1914 in Pskov, but was cancelled due to the outbreak of the World War. The organisation of the congresses in the different cities was a brilliant idea, because it contributed to the study of monuments and to the development of archaeology in these regions. For example, the fifth Archaeological Congress in Tiflis spurred archaeological research in the Caucasus, and in 1888 the Moscow Archaeological Society published a special edition of 'Materials on the Archaeology of the Caucasus'. Unfortunately, due to bad personal relations between Counts Uvarov and Stroganov, the Society opposed the Imperial Archaeological Commission in St Petersburg and constantly competed with it. This situation worsened after Uvarov's death, when his widow, Countess Uvarov, became Head of the Moscow Archaeological Society.

BOX 9.1 Count Aleksey Sergeevich Uvarov (1825–84)

Count Aleksey Sergeevich Uvarov was born in St Petersburg into the family of the President of the Academy of Sciences and the Minister of Education Sergei Uvarov. He was educated at the Department of History and Philology of St Petersburg University, graduating in 1845, then attended lectures at the universities of Berlin and Heidelberg. In 1848 he conducted his first excavation in the northern Black Sea coast, with the results being published in Russian (1851) and French (1855): Ouvaroff, A. 1855–60. *Recherches sur les antiquités de la Russie Méridionale et des côtes de la Mer Noire*. 2 vols., Paris.

In 1851–2 Uvarov, together with the orientalist and archaeologist P. Saveliev, excavated more than 7500 burial mounds in the vicinity of Vladimir and Suzdal. Having examined the materials of these excavations, Uvarov defined them as a culture of the Finno-Ugric tribe Merya, and in 1872 published a monograph 'Meryane and their way of life according to the burial mound excavations'. Subsequently the St Petersburg archaeologist A. Spitsyn accused him of poor-quality excavation. This accusation of dilettantism continued throughout the Soviet period, but an objective analysis of Uvarov's field diaries and reports shows that the excavation and recording of finds were of a high standard for the time. In 1853–4 he carried out excavations in Olbia, Neapolis (known as 'Scythian Naples') and Chersonese. In the latter he discovered the largest medieval church in the Crimea – the basilica, which has since been named after him.

FIGURE 9.2 Count Aleksey Sergeevich Uvarov.

In 1869 he participated in the International Congress on Prehistoric Anthropology and Archaeology in Copenhagen, where he met many famous European scientists, for example, R. Virchow, J.J.A. Worsaae and C. Vogt. In 1877 Uvarov discovered and investigated one of Russia's first Upper Paleolithic sites on his estate of Karacharovo on the Oka River. In 1881 Count Uvarov published the book *Archaeology of Russia. Vol. 1. Stone Age*, which took into account almost all the finds of the Stone Age known at that time in Russia. This book became one of the first syntheses of the information and materials from the Stone Age in Russia. Uvarov also studied the history of Byzantine art and Christian symbolism, aiming to trace their evolution from the first centuries AD to medieval Russia. Archaeology was understood by Uvarov as the science of ancient everyday life, which studied the ancient tribes and nations using all available sources. He therefore included in archaeology ethnographic observations as well as written sources.

A.S. Uvarov distinguished himself as a talented organiser of science. In 1864 he founded the Moscow Archaeological Society, which since 1869 has organised all-Russian archaeological congresses in different cities. He also became the initiator and founder of the Historical Museum in Moscow (now the State Historical Museum, located on Red Square).

By the end of the nineteenth century regional archaeological societies and committees had been established in many cities of Russia. But all these societies had a much broader view of archaeology than today, seeing it as the study of all antiquities, including historical written sources. The activities of the largest of them were funded and controlled by the state. In 1894 the Russian Archaeological Institute in Constantinople was established, with the support of the Ministry of Foreign Affairs, and started its archaeological research in Asia Minor and the Balkans. The main theme of its studies was the Archaeology of Byzantium.

It was in the mid-nineteenth century that Russia began development of prehistoric archaeology. Most of the first explorers of the Stone Age were representatives of the natural sciences – biologists, geologists, anthropologists. In 1859 the biologist academician K. Baer made a presentation to the Russian Geographical Society, calling for the collection of information about Stone Age finds in Russia and the creation of an Archaeological Museum. A large collection of Stone Age tools from Western Europe and Russia was acquired by A.M. Raevskaya, daughter-in-law of a hero of the 1812 Patriotic War. With the help of a Swiss Professor, A. Morlot, she managed to buy the diary and an atlas of the mining engineer, J.G. Ramsauer, who had carried out the excavations at the Hallstatt cemetery.

In the proceedings of the Russian Archaeological Society P.I. Lerch published a survey of European finds from the Stone Age, the three-age system, the achievements of the Scandinavian school, and Neolithic tools from Karelia and the north of Russia. The Scandinavian scholar J.J.A. Worsaae, when taking part in the first All-Russian Archaeological Congress, stated that in the East European plains there were no Palaeolithic sites, due to the fact that there were no caves. But in 1871 a Palaeolithic site was discovered in Irkutsk; another in 1873 in the village of Gonzu in the Ukraine; and in 1877 at Karacharovo, on the estate of Count Uvarov, near Murom. In 1879 Ivan Polyakov discovered Kostenki on the Don, near Voronezh, and K. Merezhkovsky found a series of Palaeolithic sites in the Crimea. In 1879 the Museum of Anthropology and Ethnography was established within the Russian Academy of Sciences and began to acquire collections from Prehistory, mostly artifacts of the Stone Age along with ethnographic collections.

In the early 1880s the first books were published, generalised collections of information and material on the Stone Age: *Archaeology in Russia. Vol. 1. Stone Age* by A.C. Uvarov and *Prehistoric Stone Age man on the banks of Ladoga Lake* by A.A. Inostrantsev. At the beginning of the twentieth century two palaeoethnological schools were formed: one in St Petersburg, founded by F.K. Volkov, a student of G. de Mortillet, and the other by D. Anuchin in Moscow. Volkov and his students carried out excavations at the Palaeolithic site of Mezin near Chernigov, where they found unique art objects made of mammoth ivory. Both schools considered prehistoric archaeology to be a discipline in natural science, separate from history but closely associated with anthropology, ethnography, geography and geology. Their research centres were in the St Petersburg (Russian Anthropological Society) and Moscow Universities (Society of Naturalists, Anthropology and Ethnography). In 1892, on Anuchin's initiative, the XIth International Congress of Prehistoric Anthropology and Archaeology was organised in Moscow, and was attended by many European archaeologists, while Russian archaeologists also took part in congresses abroad.

V.A. Gorodtsov, the head of the Archaeological Department of the Historical Museum in Moscow, developed a system for describing pottery and systematised the materials from the Bronze Age burial mounds in southern Russia into three consecutive cultures, based on differences in the shape of the graves (pit grave, catacomb grave, timber grave).

FIGURE 9.3 F. Volkov and his students during classes on anthropology c. 1910.

University professors had been using the archaeological materials for their lectures since the middle of the nineteenth century; and by the start of the twentieth century the universities were already providing special courses in archaeology. For example, at St Petersburg University M. Rostovtsev, S. Zhebelev and B. Farmakovsky lectured and conducted seminars on Classical and Scythian archaeology, F. Volkov on Prehistoric archaeology, and A. Spitsyn on Slavic-Russian archaeology. The Archaeological Institute was established in St Petersburg even earlier, but it educated mostly archivists. In the Moscow Archaeological Institute, which was founded later, one of the teachers was V.A. Gorodtsov, who wrote a textbook on archaeology.

At the beginning of the twentieth century Archaeology in Russia was developing rapidly and dynamically in close contact with the whole of European archaeology. The greatest achievements took place in the study of Classical and Oriental antiquities, Scythian culture and the nomads. Studies of prehistoric and medieval archaeology were also carried out. Fieldwork in the western part of Russia was suspended due to World War I and the Russian October Revolution.

Archaeology in the USSR

The formation of its organisational structure and the expansion of field research in the 1920s

The Revolution of 1917 changed the organisational structure of Russian archaeology significantly. The archaeological societies were closed down, while the land and all archaeological heritage were declared state property and placed under state control. In April 1919 the former Imperial Archaeological Commission was transformed into the Russian Academy of the History of Material Culture (RAIMK; from 1926 the State Academy of the History of Material Culture, GAIMK) after one of Lenin's decrees. Its staff increased considerably, because all the leading archaeologists of Leningrad (as St Petersburg was named from 1924 to 1991) and Moscow become members. The Orientalist academician N.Y. Marr was elected Head of RAIMK–GAIMK. Marr was known for his pre-revolutionary excavations of Ani, the medieval capital of Armenia; but having become the Head of the central archaeological institution in Russia and the USSR, he stopped his archaeological activities and became fully engaged with 'a new language doctrine' (or Japhetic theory), invented by himself. This theory tried to link the development of language with the Marxist theory of socio-economic formations and was opposed to traditional comparative historical Indo-European linguistics. Later, Marr joined the Communist Party (the only member of the old Imperial Academy of Sciences to do so), and his teaching, despite the lack of supporting evidence and the absurdity of many proposals, was declared a dogma for philology and became popular among young Marxist-minded archaeologists. But in the 1920s Marr paid little attention

FIGURE 9.4 Founding members of the Russian Academy of the History of Material Culture, 1919. From left to right: sitting: V.V. Bartold, B.V. Farmakovsky, I.E. Grabar', S.F. Oldenburg, V.V. Latyshev, N.J. Marr, A.A. Vasil'ev, A.A. Shakhmatov, V.K. Malberg, N.P. Sychev; standing: P.K. Simoni, M.V. Farmakovsky, A.S. Raevsky, A.A. Miller, S.S. Lukjanov, K.K. Romanov, V.K. Shilejko, I.I. Tolstoy, P.P. Pokryshkin, D.A. Zolotarev, B.A. Turaev, N.P. Likhachev, N.V. Baklanov, I.A. Orbeli, A.M. Efros, J.M. Shokalsky, I.J. Krachkovsky, V.V. Bogdanov, S.P. Jaremich, B.F. Adler, S.N. Trojnicky, V.A. Schavinsky, I.I. Meschaninov, A.A. Il'in, S.G. Eliseev, A.K. Markov, V.K. Nikolsky.

to the affairs of GAIMK, which was led by his deputies, the Vice Presidents S.A. Zhebelev, V.V. Bartold and the Academic secretary B.V. Farmakovsky. The Academy was divided into three sections: the ethnological (five chairs), the archaeological (eleven chairs) and the art-historical. The Archaeological Institute of Technology was established within the Academy and began to study archaeological material in terms of production and technology. The GAIMK structure also included art critics and historians.

N.I. Veselovsky, F.K. Volkov, Y.I. Smirnov, A.S. Lappo-Danilevsky and V.V. Latyshev died from hunger and infections during the years of Revolution and Civil War. The director of the Kerch Museum of Antiquities, V.V. Shkorpil, and the Siberian archaeologist A.V. Adrianov were killed. Counts A.A. Bobrinskiy and P.S. Uvarova, and Professors M.I. Rostovtsev and N.P. Kondakov left Russia and went into exile. In the 1920s, in Prague, Kondakov organised the so-called Seminarian Kondakovianum, which united Russian historians, archaeologists and art historians in exile and regularly published collections of articles. Rostovtsev, who was later appointed a Professor at Yale University in the USA, led a major expedition and excavated the ancient city of Dura-Europos in Syria, and also trained many students. But most archaeologists stayed in the Soviet Union and continued to work there.

During the first decades after the Revolution, archaeology was not a subject of special interest to Bolshevik ideologists, who were busy tuning the humanities and social sciences to the Marxist mode, so archaeologists were able to work more or less in peace. Marxist understanding of the historical process was based on the theory of changing socio-economic formations (prehistoric or primitive, slave-owning, feudalism, capitalist, socialist) and the idea of class struggle as the main driving force of social development.

Trained in these Marxist principles, a group of young Moscow archaeologists, who were students of Gorodtsov – A.V. Artsikhovsky (see Box 9.2), A.Y. Brusov, S.V. Kiselev and A.P. Smirnov – in the second half of the 1920s called for the construction of a 'Marxist Archaeology'. They stated that 'archaeology has the right to exist only if its aim is to reconstruct the culture of socio-economic formation on the basis of research into the monuments of material culture'. According to their view, it was possible to achieve this by studying the implements of labour and the economic structure of settlements. The analysis of material from burials also provided information that could be used to reach conclusions about the level of a population's socio-economic development. The supporters of Marxist Archaeology were greatly influenced by the idea that the implements of labour are a basic determinant of productive forces – an idea that was owed to N.I. Bukharin, one of the theoreticians of Soviet Marxism, who was later executed by Stalin.

By the mid-1920s excavations that had been interrupted by the Revolution and Civil War were restarted. B.V. Farmakovsky continued excavating at Olbia, which became a school of Classical archaeology for Soviet archaeologists. Excavations in Kerch and Chersonese were also continued. The first major archaeological conferences of the Soviet era took place in Moscow and Kerch in 1926 and in Chersonese in 1927. Soviet archaeologists took part in the International Congress of Archaeologists in Berlin in 1929, and published their papers in *Seminarium Kondakovianum* and *Eurasia Septentrionalis Antiqua*. Western archaeologists came to the Soviet Union to carry out excavations and to participate in joint projects and the exchange of books was intensified. Local studies were actively developed, while new regional museums and societies were founded and undertook excavations. In 1922 the archaeological institutions in Petrograd (St Petersburg) and Moscow were consolidated and served as a basis for the archaeological departments in the universities, which began the systematic training

BOX 9.2 Arthemy Vladimirovich Artsikhovsky (1902–1978)

Arthemy Vladimirovich Artsikhovsky was born in St Petersburg into the family of a well-known botanist. In 1922 he enrolled at the Moscow State University and studied under V.A. Gorodtsov, trying to master Marxist methodology and apply it to archaeology. His PhD thesis 'Vyatich Barrows' (1929) introduced into science a new method based on the principles of mathematical statistics.

Artsikhovsky headed the Department of Old Russian archaeological research in the State Historical Museum, where in 1929 he developed a new museum exhibit on Old Russia, showing a broad historical panorama through the rich variety of the artifacts. In 1930 he was appointed Head of the archaeological team during the construction of the Moscow Metro. The success of this work was due to the creative combination of the interests of science and the construction workers – the first example of such a combination in the USSR.

In the late 1920s Artsikhovsky also selected a vast new historical and archaeological research topic – Novgorod the Great. The story of the Novgorod archaeological expedition began in 1932. An optimal technique of investigating the urban cultural layers, was developed: the excavation of broad areas that made all the neighbourhoods of the ancient city the subject of archaeological research; the stratification system and chronological scale were designed according to dendrochronology. In 1951 the expedition, led by Artsikhovsky, discovered the first birch-bark letters – a fundamentally new source of historical information. The seven-volume academic publication of the Novgorod birch-bark letters in 1951–76 is an example of a brilliant synthesis using different sources.

FIGURE 9.5 Arthemy Vladimirovich Artsikhovsky.

FIGURE 9.6 Troicky (Trinity) pit (excavation area) in Novgorod, 2005.

Artsikhovsky's article 'The archaeological study of Novgorod' (1956) presented a programme of a complex and synthetic approach to the study of the medieval city.

In the course of the Novgorod expedition, he managed successfully to bring together many talented scientists. The expedition started the academic career of his best students, particularly V.L. Yanin. Artsikhovsky was involved not only in archaeological studies, but also in studies on the history of medieval Novgorod and applied arts studies (such as questions of heraldry and numismatics). His doctoral dissertation 'Old Russian miniatures as a historical source', submitted in 1940, also became the fundamental piece of research on that topic.

A.V. Artsikhovsky's life and work were associated with the Moscow State University, where he taught from 1927 and where in 1939–78 he directed the Department of Archaeology. In 1952–7 he acted as Dean of the Faculty of History. The author of one of the first essays on the history of Russian archaeology, he was for a long time the chief editor of the scientific journal *Soviet Archaeology*. He also published a popular textbook, *Fundamentals of Archaeology*. His phrase 'Archaeology is history armed with a shovel' is well known. Despite some glaring speech defects (Artsikhovsky could not pronounce some letters), his lectures were extremely popular with students. He had a phenomenal memory and could remember the names of all the students and the alumni of the Department of Archaeology. On his initiative, a basic course on archaeology was incorporated into the educational programme of the Historical Faculties of all Russian universities and pedagogical institutions.

and education of professional archaeologists. In Leningrad all teachers in the University's Archaeological Department were at the same time employees of the GAIMK. This made it possible for students to take part in the expeditions and scientific activities of the GAIMK.

The palaeoethnological school achieved great success in the 1920s. Its members made many remarkable discoveries and carried out field-study programmes. S.A. Teploukhov, like Gorodtsov, developed a cultural and chronological periodisation of the Southern Siberian monuments of the Age of Metal, separating out the Afanasiev, Andronovo and Karasuk cultures. A culture was seen as a unit of classification and its divisions as stages. To the specified group of cultures was added the Minusinskaya barrow culture, which included four consecutive stages. The scheme's development was completed in 1929, when Teploukhov divided all the monuments on the Minusinsk steppes into twelve chronological groups. In the same year, an expedition, led by S.I. Rudenko (see Box 9.3), discovered the Pazyryk mounds in the Altai Mountains, with organic remains that were particularly well preserved due to the permafrost. Crimean Palaeolithic sites were studied in their natural environment by G.A. Bonch-Osmolovskiy. In the cave of Kiik-Koba he discovered the burial of a Neanderthal. Under the leadership of P.P. Efimenko the Palaeolithic sites at Kostenki on the Don River were excavated and new sites were opened up. Excavations were carried out over large areas, which enabled him to reveal the Palaeolithic dwellings.

Archaeology in the national republics of the USSR was actively developed. In Ukraine in 1924 the Ukrainian Archaeological Committee (VUAK) was founded; it became a major archaeological institution in the Republic and launched a large-scale field study on its territory. In 1927–32 major archaeological expeditions were undertaken within the project of the construction of the Dnieper HPP (Hydro Power Plant); on the construction site of

BOX 9.3 Sergey Ivanovich Rudenko (1885–1969)

Sergey Ivanovich Rudenko was born in Kharkov into a family of hereditary nobles. In 1904 he enrolled at St Petersburg State University and until 1909 studied in the Department of Geography and Ethnography under F.K. Volkov.

Rudenko's first expedition and research papers were associated with the study of ethnic history and anthropology of Bashkir. In 1908 he took part in the research at the Mezin Palaeolithic site in the Ukraine. In 1909–10 he collected ethnographic and anthropological material in north-west Siberia and excavated a Samoyed burial on the Lower Ob River.

In 1913–14 he visited Turkey, Syria, Palestine, Egypt and Italy, and for a year attended lessons and studied anthropology in Paris. In 1919–20 he taught at the Tomsk State University. He also worked as Head of the Ethnographic Department of the Russian Museum and at the same time as Head of the Department of Anthropology and Ethnography of the Petrograd State University. He made one of the most brilliant discoveries in Soviet archaeology during his investigations of the first Pazyryk mound in 1929. This barrow provided material that was unprecedented in its state of preservation and its quantity. Because of the permafrost wooden objects, remnants of felt carpets and leather goods were beautifully preserved. With the horse burials he found saddles, bridles, unique masks for horses made of leather, felt and fur, and other artifacts.

However, Rudenko's work in archaeology was interrupted for fifteen years, because in 1930 he was arrested in the course of a case fabricated by the NKVD (later the KGB) against scientists from the Academy of Science. During his imprisonment he worked on the construction of the White Sea–Baltic Canal, where he was seriously engaged in hydrology.

In 1945 Rudenko explored the coast of the Chukotka Peninsula – this was the first professional archaeological expedition to that peninsula and numerous settlements of the Eskimo (Inuit) were discovered. Rudenko put forward a theory about an Asian, not American, origin for the Eskimos (Inuit), contrary to what was assumed previously. According to his view, the Eskimos came to the Bering Sea from the Pacific, and then they populated Chukotka, Alaska and the Arctic coasts of Canada and Greenland.

Rudenko systematically investigated the mounds of the southern Altai mountains and unearthed numerous artifacts: clothing, jewellery, textiles, household utilities, horse harnesses and artistic and cult objects. This was the first time that ancient Near Eastern and Chinese fabrics and carpets of high artistic and historical value were excavated.

To determine the age of the Altai barrows he used methods from the natural and hard sciences. In 1955 he established a laboratory of archaeological technology at the Leningrad Branch of the Institute of Archaeology. Research on radiocarbon dating was also carried out here. Rudenko presented his research results in several monographs, which were also published in English: *Gold Guarding Griffins: Southern Siberia in Scythian times* (1965), and *Frozen Tombs of Siberia: The Pazyryk burials of Iron age horsemen* (1970).

FIGURE 9.7 Sergey Ivanovich Rudenko.

the Azovstal plant in Mariupol an Eneolithic cemetery was discovered. In accordance with the new legislation owners of land selected for construction were obliged to undertake an archaeological survey of the area before the start of the project. This opened up great opportunities for archaeology. The practice was called 'novostroechnye', which is equivalent to the concept of 'rescue (or salvage) excavation'.

Separate centres of archaeological research were founded in the Republics of the Caucasus (Georgia, Armenia, Azerbaijan) and in Central Asia. There were large-scale expeditions, which discovered numerous new sites. In general, by the end of the 1920s, archaeology in the USSR had developed quickly and successfully.

Interwar years: The destruction and crisis of 1929–37

By the end of the 1920s the Bolsheviks' ideological pressure on archaeology had significantly increased. The Communist Academy, which was established by the Bolsheviks as a counterbalance to the Academy of Sciences, delegated a team of Communist Academy employees to the GAIMK.

Among them were S.N. Bykovsky and F.V. Kiparisov. Though they had absolutely no experience in archaeology, they soon became the actual leaders of the GAIMK and otherwise began to embed Marxism into the spirit of the school of M. Pokrovsky, which was a substitute for real historical events and processes of abstract sociological schemes. Migrations of ancient populations were declared an invention by bourgeois scientists. Only autochthonous development, based on unilinear evolutionism, was recognised. This led to the absurd (from a modern point of view) assertion that a single people underwent different stages in its development, for instance being transformed from Cimmerians into Scythians, and then Sarmatians, Goths and Slavs.

The typological method and, soon, archaeology itself were declared 'bourgeois' and hence a subject for elimination. Such a decision was made by the All-Union Archaeological and Ethnographical Meeting in 1932. It dramatically decreased the quantity and quality of field research. Instead of specific studies of archaeological material, the GAIMK published articles on abstract schemes of development. Signs of class struggle had to be sought everywhere. Thus, for example, a slave revolt in the Bosphorus Kingdom, led by Savmak, was invented on the basis of unclear sources. In reality it was a struggle for power, but information about a revolt was included even in school textbooks, while the most popular sports clubs were named after Spartacus, the famous leader of Roman slaves.

In 1929 repression of archaeologists began. The Palaeoethnological school was totally destroyed, because its research into the natural environment did not correspond to Marxism. S.I. Rudenko, A.A. Miller, S.A. Tepluokhov, M.P. Gryaznov and G.A. Bonch-Osmolovskii were arrested in Leningrad, and B.S. Zhukov and B.A. Kuftin in Moscow. The RANION – the Moscow Centre of Archaeology – was closed down and its staff members Y.V. Gautier, A.A. Zakharov, I.N. Borozdin and A.S. Bashkirov were repressed. Gorodtsov was expelled from the Moscow State University and the State Historical Museum. Humanities departments were separated from the universities, creating independent institutions, which in fact destroyed the system of training professional archaeologists. For example, the Leningrad State University lost all its archaeological collections.

World War II and post-war developments: Overcoming the crisis and stagnation in 1937–91

Under Stalin's command–administrative system any discussions became mortally dangerous and therefore ceased. Many participants in those discussions were repressed. In 1936, the party leaders of the GAIMK, Kiparisov and Bykovsky, who had connections with the opposition to Stalin within the Communist Party, were arrested and executed. The sociological approaches of Pokrovskiy's school were declared hostile and inconsistent with Marxism. This led to the elimination of the GAIMK in 1937 and its transformation into the Institute of the History of Material Culture within the Academy of Sciences.

I.A. Orbeli was appointed Director of this Institute. He was also the Director of the State Hermitage Museum. Busy with the affairs of one of the largest museums in the world, he did not appear for months at the Institute, and dismissed many of the leading archaeologists, thus damaging the Institute's work. In this situation the Institute team rebelled against the director and won the decision that M.I. Artamonov would be appointed Director of the Institute – an unprecedented case in Stalin's time. Artamonov was far removed from the world of political campaigns and managed to organise the Institute's work in the field of studying the ancient history of the USSR. On his initiative the Institute began to publish not only the scientific magazine *Soviet Archaeology* but also other periodicals: *Brief Messages* and *Materials on the Archaeology of the USSR*. A branch of the Institute was also established in Moscow.

In the second half of the 1930s archaeological education in the universities was restored. The Faculties of History were opened in 1934 in the Leningrad and Moscow State Universities. In 1936 at the Leningrad State University a Chair of Archaeology was created. It was occupied by V.I. Ravdonikas, who, two years later, managed to form an Archaeological Department and combined the training of archaeologists with specialisation in prehistoric, Classical, Slavonic-Russian, Central Asian and Caucasian archaeology. M.I. Artamonov (see Box 9.4), P.I. Boriskovsky, P.N. Tretyakov, M.K. Karger, E.Y. Krichevsky and V.F. Gaidukevich were among the professors and teachers there. In 1938 Ravdonikas started large-scale excavations at Staraya Ladoga. Earlier he had studied the Oleneostrovsky burial ground and petroglyphs in Karelia. In 1939 a Department of Archaeology was organised by A.V. Artsikhovsky in the History Faculty of the Moscow State University. Expeditions under his leadership carried out excavations at Novgorod. Departments of Archaeology at the universities were located within the Faculty of History, and there were two lecture courses, the Fundamentals of Archaeology and the History of Primitive Society, which were compulsory for all students in the Faculty of History. This contributed to perpetuating notions of archaeology in the USSR as part of a historical science.

During World War II excavation activities were interrupted, with only one expedition in Central Asia continuing its work. During the siege of Leningrad, many archaeologists died of starvation or were killed at the Front. The activities of the leading Institute in Leningrad were paralysed, so the management of the IIMK moved in 1943 to Moscow, although the Leningrad Branch remained there.

In 1950 Stalin criticised the teachings of Marr, and this position contributed to the liberation of linguistics and archaeology from his erroneous ideas. Six years later the famous Western archaeologist G. Childe criticised Soviet archaeology in its entirety, pointing out the poor excavation techniques, the technical backwardness of laboratories compared with Europe, the terrible level of publications, and the lack of supporting evidence for the chronological schemes. Childe's letter was only published after the collapse of the USSR.

BOX 9.4 Mikhail Illarionovich Artamonov (1898–1972)

Mikhail Illarionovich Artamonov was born in the Tver Region to a peasant family. At the age of nine he was brought to the country's capital at that time, St Petersburg, where he had his secondary education. He worked in different offices and studied painting under the guidance of Kuz'ma S. Petrov-Vodkin. He participated actively in the military and revolutionary tumult of 1917. He studied at the Academy of Fine Arts and at the Archaeological Institute, which was included in 1922 in the organisational structure of Petrograd University. Among his teachers were the historian of art N.P. Sychev, and the archaeologists A.A. Spitsyn and A.A. Miller. His first scientific paper was devoted to the miniatures in the Koenigsberg chronicle. In 1929 Artamonov arranged his first expedition – an exploration of the Lower Don Region – and discovered one of the largest fortifications in Khazaria, the Sarkel. By studying written and archaeological sources, Artamonov produced the world's first systematic overview of the history of the Khazar Empire.

In 1939 on the initiative of the staff of the Institute of the History of Material Culture, Artamonov became Director of the Institute and succeeded in adjusting its work after the ideological defeat of the GAIMK. It was a unique situation for that time. He paid particular attention to publication of the results of field studies. Artamonov founded a periodical publication of summary articles *Brief Reports of the IHMC* and *Materials and Research on the Archaeology of the USSR*.

After World War II Artamonov worked as the Head of the Volga-Don archaeological expedition, the largest archaeological expedition in the USSR. For the first time, machines

FIGURE 9.8 Mikhail Illarionovich Artamonov.

were used for excavation of burial mounds and the main labour force was made up of GULAG inmates. From 1951 to 1964 he was in charge of one of the world's largest museums – the State Hermitage Museum – and paid a lot of attention to the creation of new archaeological exhibits, in which the principle of transparency was fundamental. During this period he was engaged in the study of Scythian art and published several books and albums in West European languages (*L'art barbare Scythe de la Sibérie à la mer Noire. Les origines du Farwest russe.* Paris, 1971; *Goldschatz der Skythen in der Ermitage.* Prague, 1970; *Treasures from Scythian Tombs.* London, 1969). Artamonov was removed from his post due to his intransigence in the face of interference from Communist Party functionaries in the management of the museum, in particular for his refusal to remove from exhibit the paintings of the 'bourgeois decadents', as Communist propaganda used to call the French impressionists.

From 1928 onwards he taught at the Leningrad State University and from 1949 until his death he headed the University's Department of Archaeology. Studying the origin of the Slavs, he called for 'archaeological realism', arguing against autochthonous concepts according to which, bizarrely, the ethnogenesis of the Slavic tribes was understood as more ancient, and which claimed that the Norsemen played a role in the formation of the Old Russian state. Artamonov's lectures on the basics of archaeology were as dull as his seminars were brilliant. During workshops and training sessions in special subjects, constantly with a cigarette in his hand, he presented to the students the latest results of his research, arguing with himself and stimulating responses from the students. Artamonov trained several generations of students, including S.A. Pletneva, L.N. Gumilev, A.D. Stolyar, I.I. Lyapushkin, L.S. Klejn, A.V. Gadlo, etc. He died in 1972 at his desk, editing a scientific article.

Soviet archaeologists undertook many major archaeological surveys and excavations in the various regions of the USSR. In the Caucasus B.B. Piotrovsky carried out the extensive excavations of the Urartian city of Teishebaini on Karmir-Bloor hill near Yerevan and wrote a history of Urartu. In Azerbaijan extensive archaeological material was derived from excavations of burial grounds near Mingechaura. Large-scale archaeological surveys were also undertaken in Central Asia. The Khorezm expedition, under the leadership of S.P. Tolstov, discovered in the lower reaches of the Amu-Darya River an ancient civilisation, which was completely unknown to science. Settlements of all ages from the Neolithic to Medieval times were opened up. For the first time in the Soviet Union aerial photography and aero-exploration were widely applied and contributed to the success of these expeditions. A.Y. Jakubowskiy, M.M. Dyakonov and A.M. Belenitskiy excavated remarkable monuments, including numerous fragments of paintings in the houses and temples of ancient Pyanjikent. In southern Turkmenistan M.E. Masson excavated Nisa, one of the capitals of the Parthian kingdom. A.N. Bernshtam carried out extensive research into Central Asian nomadic societies. In the south-east European part of the USSR the culture of the ancient agricultural tribes (Tripolye culture) was studied by T.S. Passek with unusual thoroughness and completeness: he accomplished the complete excavation of some settlements.

BOX 9.5 Boris Borisovich Piotrovskiy (1908–90)

Boris Borisovich Piotrovskiy was born in St Petersburg into a noble family with Polish roots, in which all men of previous generations were officers. When he was seven years old, his family moved to Orenburg and lived there until 1922. From early childhood he was interested in the history of ancient Egypt. On his return to Petrograd, he attended classes in the Hermitage Department of Antiquities and then continued to study Egyptology at the Leningrad State University.

In 1929 Piotrovskiy obtained a position in the Academy of the History of Material Culture (Institute of Archaeology of the Academy of Sciences), in the language section headed by academician N.Y. Marr, and in 1931 he also started to work at the Hermitage Museum as a Researcher. From his student years onwards, Piotrovskiy took part in archaeological expeditions to the North Caucasus under the leadership of A.A. Miller. In 1930, on the initiative of N.Y. Marr, he went for the first time to Armenia to seek traces of the ancient state of Urartu. Archaeological study of the Urartian civilisation was for many years a major focus of his research activities. The excavations at the ancient city of Teishebaini provided valuable information on Urartu culture and art. Interpretation of chance finds was replaced by the systematic study of the culture and art of the Urartu Kingdom. The results were presented by Piotrovskiy in the following publications: *The History and Culture of Urartu* (1944), *Karmir-Bloor* (1950–5), *The Van Kingdom (Urartu)* (1959) and *The Art of Urartu of 8–6th centuries BC* (1962).

FIGURE 9.9 Boris Borisovich Piotrovskiy.

In 1941–2 in Leningrad during the winter siege, Piotrovskiy wrote his major work *The History and Culture of Urartu* (published in 1944). For this book he was awarded the degree of Doctor of History (1944) and the USSR State Award (1946). After World War II Piotrovskiy continued his research at Karmir-Bloor. In 1961–3 he led an international archaeological expedition to Nubia, in the territories where the Aswan dam was constructed, and discovered a unique set of petroglyphs in Wadi-Alaq.

In 1953–64 Piotrovskiy was the Director of the Leningrad Branch of the Institute of Archaeology of the USSR. Later he became the Director of the State Hermitage Museum, remaining in this position for twenty-six years until his death. He used to combine a great deal of scientific and administrative work with his teaching and social activities. From 1966 onwards he headed the Department of the Ancient Near East at the Oriental Faculty of the Leningrad State University, and also lectured on the Archaeology of the Ancient East and the Caucasus in the Department of Archaeology. Piotrovskiy was a member of the Academy of Sciences of the USSR, a corresponding member of the Bavarian and the British Academy of Sciences, the Académie des Inscriptions et Belles Lettres in France, and an honorary member of another fifteen foreign academies and societies.

P.N. Tretyakov undertook a great deal of research into the origin and early culture of the Eastern Slavs. He associated a number of ancient archaeological sites with ancient Slavs. Old Russian crafts were specifically studied by B.A. Rybakov, who traced in some detail their techniques and the corresponding social organisation; and he discovered and proved their high level of development. Much attention was paid to the study of old Russian cities. An archaeological expedition led by A.V. Artsikhovsky to Novgorod discovered a number of unique birch-bark manuscripts – there are more than 1000 of these now. It was proved that Russian medieval towns had no specific commercial or administrative nature, and were (like the medieval towns of Europe and Asia) primarily handicraft centres. Excavations in the cities yielded proof of the high level of development of ancient Russian culture.

A. P. Okladnikov and his disciples opened up hundreds of new archaeological sites in Siberia. Because of large construction projects (reservoirs, canals, land reclamation) major expeditions were deployed in Siberia, the Urals, in the Kuban and in other regions of the USSR. By 1985 the annual number of expeditions had reached 700. Over one field season they would unearth hundreds of mounds of different chronological ages. Although not all the finds were duly processed and published, nevertheless the total number of archaeological publications significantly increased. While during the period 1918–40 a total of nearly 8000 books and articles on archaeology were published, in the 1980s the annual number of publications was more than 4000.

Since the 1960s Soviet archaeologists had primarily paid attention to the theoretical and methodological problems of archaeology. The level of Marxist dogmatism in the writings of archaeologists was drastically reduced. However, one necessary element remained – there had to be one or two references to the theorists of Marxism in the introductory part of publications. Discussions were held on the concepts of 'archaeological culture' and its relation to the ethnic group, according to the classification concepts of the 'type', of the 'archaeological source'. Contacts with foreign archaeologists were resumed. Soviet scientists began to participate in excavations in Egypt, Iraq, Syria, Afghanistan and Yemen. In northern Mesopotamia the expedition led by R.M. Munchaev discovered the ancient cult and administrative complex of Hazna Tell 1, with its monumental temple buildings.

The methods of the hard and natural sciences were widely introduced into archaeology: radiocarbon analysis, dendrochronology, magnetic survey, mathematical statistics, the study of ancient and medieval metallurgy using data from metallographic and spectral analyses, etc. During those years there was a decentralisation of the organisational structure of archaeology. Before the middle of the twentieth century the core team of archaeologists was concentrated in Moscow and Leningrad, but later a separate institution was founded by A.P. Okladnikov in Novosibirsk, and Departments of Archaeology were opened at the Kiev, Novosibirsk, Voronezh, Kazan and Kemerovo State Universities and in several cities of Siberia, in the Ural and Volga regions. This increased the number of professional archaeologists. The most significant discoveries of this time include the Upper Palaeolithic cave paintings in Kapova Cave in the Urals, and the excavation of a pair of children buried at the Upper Palaeolithic site of Sungir near Vladimir, both made by O.N. Bader's expedition.

Bringing the story up to date: Archaeology in modern Russia

Archaeology in Russia entered a new stage of development with the collapse of the Soviet Union and the onset of perestroika, which intensified the decentralisation. In 1991 the Leningrad Branch of the Institute of Archaeology was transformed into an independent Institute of the History of Material Culture in the Russian Academy of Sciences. To intensify contacts with foreign colleagues, Russian archaeologists have become involved in all major international congresses. A joint expedition of the State Hermitage Museum and the German Archaeological Institute opened a rich and fully preserved burial of a Scythian chief at Arzhan 2 in the Tuva Republic. Publication of new journals and periodical collections began. New research topics were formulated such as the earliest stages of human settlement in the North Caucasus, the dynamics of life and environmental conditions for the existence of Upper Palaeolithic settlement on the Russian plains, sites of mountain art in north-eastern Eurasia, the cultural situation of the Great Migration in the forest-steppe zone of the European part of Russia, the phenomenon of ancient villages in the pre-Mongolian period; and the archaeology of modern times (seventeenth to the nineteenth centuries).

However, many problems were also identified. The activities of Russian archeologists were mostly limited to the territory of the Russian Federation. In the 1990s state expenditure on excavation decreased sharply, to the point of almost complete cessation. In the last decade the situation has improved, and more than 1000 permits for excavation are now issued annually. Unfortunately, however, there has been a remarkable increase in the number of illegal excavations, treasure robbing using metal detectors has been revitalised and the illegal trade in antiquities has increased.

Some problems have arisen in the field of professional education, because of the transition to a two-tier system of higher education (i.e., a four-year Bachelors and a two-year Masters, instead of the previous five-year degree). The speciality of archaeology is not included in undergraduate and graduate programmes and the training of archaeologists is carried out within the speciality of 'History'. Nevertheless, Russian archaeology, with its rich historical traditions, is confidently moving forward.

FIGURE 9.10 The burial chamber of the Arzhan-2 barrow, 2001.

FIGURE 9.11 Pins with deer and a spoon found in the Arzhan-2 barrow.

Further reading

In English

Bulkin, V.A., Klejn, L.S. and Lebedev, G.S. 1982. Attainments and problems of Soviet archaeology. *World Archaeology* 13 (3): 272–95.

Dolukhanov, P.M. 1993. Archaeology in the ex-USSR: Post-perestroyka problems. *Antiquity* 67: 150–6.

Klejn, L. 2001. 'Russia', pp1127–45, in T. Murray (ed.) *Encyclopedia of Archaeology. History and Discoveries.* ABC-Clio: Santa Barbara.

Klejn, L.S. and Tikhonov, I.L. 2003. 'The beginning of university archaeology in Russia', pp197–207, in J. Callmerr, M. Meyer, R. Struwe and C. Theune (eds) *The beginnings of academic pre- and protohistoric archaeology [1890–1930] in a European perspective* (International meeting at Humboldt-University Berlin, 13–16 March, 2003). Marie Leidorf: Rahden.

Malina, J. and Vašiček, Z. 1990. *Archaeology Yesterday and Today. The Development of Archaeology in the Sciences and Humanities.* Cambridge University Press: Cambridge.

Miller, M. 1956. *Archaeology in the USSR.* Frederick A. Praeger: New York. (Unfortunately, there were many mistakes in this book, which first acquainted people in the West with the history of Russian archaeology.)

Mongait, A.L. 1961. *Archaeology in the USSR.* Pelican: Harmondsworth (second edition, translated and adapted by M.W. Thompson). (This was the Soviet ideological reply to Miller's book.)

Tikhonov, I.L. 2007. 'Archaeology at St. Petersburg University (from 1724 until today)'. *Antiquity* 81: 446–56.

Trigger, B. 1989. *A History of Archaeological Thought.* Cambridge University Press: Cambridge (Chapter 6, 'Soviet archaeology', pp207–43).

In Russian with English summary

Tikhonov, I.L. 2003. Archeologiya v Sankt-Peterburgskom universitete: istoriograficheskie ocherki (Archaeology at St Petersburg University: Historiographical essays). St Petersburg University Press: St Petersburg.

In Russian

Formozov, A.A. 1961. *Ocherki po istorii russkoj arkheologii.* 'Nauka': Moscow.

Formozov, A.A. 2007. *Russkie archeology v period totalitarizma.* Znak: Moscow.

Klejn, L.S. 2011. *Istorija arkheologicheskoy mysli* (2 vols). St Petersburg University Press: St Petersburg.

Lebedev, G.S. 1992. *Istorija otechestvennojj arkheologii 1700–1917 gg.* St Petersburg University Press: St Petersburg.

Tunkina, I.V. 2002. *Russkaja nauka o klassicheskikh drevnostjakh juga Rossii XVIII – seredina XIX vv.* 'Nauka': St Petersburg.

10

NORTH AMERICA

Philip Duke

The emergence of a discipline

In the mid-nineteenth century, as the United States was still expanding its territories in the western half of the continent, the emerging discipline of archaeology clashed with popular and effectively racist misperceptions about Native Americans and their past. This clash is exemplified in the so-called *Moundbuilder Controversy*, a protracted and bitter argument that lasted almost to the end of the century over who had constructed the thousands of prehistoric earthen mounds found from the American Midwest to the Eastern seaboard. The mounds are of two types. The first comprises small, conically shaped mounds that contained human burials, often with elaborate grave goods, and were constructed by the Adena and Hopewell Cultures in approximately 1000 BC to AD 500 (as a historical aside, Thomas Jefferson is credited with the first systematic excavations on the continent when he dug mounds on his Monticello estate). The second type consists of large, flat-topped mounds, sometimes called temple mounds, belonging to the Mississippian Tradition (approximately AD 700–1700). On the tops of the mounds were large buildings such as temples, chiefs' 'palaces' and other structures. At Cahokia, Illinois, a large Mississippian period city, the largest of the temple mounds is Monks Mound, over 30 metres in height.

The Moundbuilder controversy is of particular interest because it is an early example of how current ideology often intrudes into interpretations of the past. For if the mounds had been built by the ancestors of contemporary Native Americans, then the argument was undermined that they were 'savages' and needed to be civilised by the United States government. Those who believed that the ancestors of contemporary Native Americans could not have made the mounds include Caleb Atwater who in 1820 made the first accurate descriptions of the mounds in his state. In 1848, the Smithsonian Institution awarded funds to two antiquarians, Ephraim George Squier and Edwin Hamilton Davis, to publish the results of a comprehensive survey of the mounds in the Ohio and Mississippi River Valleys. *Ancient monuments of the Mississippi Valley* is a pioneering work in American archaeology, in that its authors not only meticulously described and classified the mounds, but also applied an elementary hypothesis-testing procedure to assess their origins.

FIGURE 10.1 Monks Mound, Cahokia. © Skubasteve834/Wikimedia Commons.

FIGURE 10.2 'Great Mound at Marietta, Ohio', Plate XLV from Squier and Davis, *Ancient Monuments of the Mississippi Valley*, 1848. Library of Congress Illus. in E74.M6S64.

Squier and Davis concluded that the Moundbuilders and contemporary Native Americans were not the same people. These studies were based on physical evidence and we should not denigrate them. However, other 'contributions' to the debate claimed that the mounds had been built by such folks as wandering Toltecs from Mexico, Hindus, Welshmen, Vikings and even people from the lost island of Atlantis. It is difficult not to conclude that there was a racist undercurrent to these arguments.

On the other side were those who believed that the mounds had been constructed by the ancestors of Native Americans. One such was J.H. McCulloh who, between 1813 and 1819, published a series of essays in favour of an indigenous origin. In 1838, the so-called Grave Creek tablet was found at the mound of the same name in West Virginia. This sandstone tablet bore a series of carved lines that were purportedly of some as yet undeciphered alphabet (expert opinions offered Celtic, Phoenician, old British and Canaanite, among others). One of the experts intrigued by the tablet was Henry R. Schoolcraft and he moved from the tablet itself to a wider consideration of the mounds. Although at first he followed standard belief, he later decided that the mounds were made by the ancestors of Native Americans. A slightly different tack was taken by Samuel Haven (1806–81) who concluded that the Moundbuilders were the ancestors of contemporary Native Americans, basing the theory on his belief that there was nothing spectacular about the mounds to begin with, and so there was no need to assign them to a separate race of builders.

The emergent discipline of physical anthropology was also deployed. In 1839 Samuel Morton, often called the father of American physical anthropology, initiated a study of human skulls recovered from the mounds. He concluded that the Moundbuilders and contemporary Native Americans were the same race. However, in order to explain the difference between the civilisations of Mexico and the less spectacular cultures of North America, Morton proposed that the American Indian race comprised two families: Toltecan and Barbarous (the Moundbuilders belonging to the former).

Using new archaeological techniques such as extensive field surveys and controlled excavations, Cyrus Thomas was hired in 1881 to investigate the mounds for the Bureau of Ethnology and built an unassailable case for indigenous origins. In 1894, the Bureau's twelfth annual report was dedicated to Thomas's final conclusions and it marked the end of the myth of the Moundbuilders. Of course, much ink and even more vitriol would have been saved had people listened to what contemporary Native Americans had to say: that there was no doubt that the mounds had been built by their ancestors.

Throughout the nineteenth century, archaeology, as it became more scientifically rigorous, increasingly became a discipline located in the universities and museums of the country. So, the Peabody Museum of Harvard University was founded in 1866 and in 1874 Frederic Ward Putnam (1839–1915), one of the founding fathers of American archaeology, became its Curator as well as the Peabody professor of American Archaeology and Ethnology. Archaeology still remained field-oriented as there was an all-consuming need, especially on the part of museums, to acquire objects for public display. Not surprisingly, the American Southwest was a prime target on account of its well-preserved Ancestral Pueblo sites like Mesa Verde and Chaco Canyon. A key early figure in Southwest exploration was John Wesley Powell (1834–1902), a decorated Civil War veteran and fêted explorer of the Colorado River. At his urging, in 1879 Congress put up $20,000 to publish studies on Native American artifacts collected by the United States Geological Survey. To administer this publication, the Smithsonian Institution set up a new department, the Bureau of American Ethnology, and

Powell was put in charge. He immediately initiated a study of the Moundbuilders, which led to Cyrus Thomas finally settling the debate, as we have already seen. He also sent Frank Hamilton Cushing to the Southwest in 1879 to study the Zuni, one of the Pueblo tribes in northwestern New Mexico. Cushing, who was only twenty-two years old at the time, stayed with the tribe for four and a half years and, although he was not a formally trained ethnologist, his work demonstrated the potential for anthropological research in the American Southwest. In addition to his ethnological work, Cushing also excavated a series of sites along the middle Gila River Valley of Arizona in 1886–7, an early example of how North American archaeology was becoming inextricably woven into the fabric of the wider field of anthropology.

The success of numerous expeditions throughout the continent led to an unexpected problem for museums, *viz.* how to systematically organise and present for public display the increasing amounts of material they were accumulating. The result was the concept of the *culture area*, a geographical area that is characterised by a broadly homogeneous culture. Examples of culture areas include the Arctic, the Plains, the Southwest. These became the basis for individual museum departments and displays. Interestingly, the culture area still partially defines the particular specialisation of American-trained archaeologists: one is a Plains archaeologist, or a Southwestern archaeologist, and so on.

The nineteenth century also witnessed amateurs and, later, trained archaeologists beginning to turn their attention to the vexed question of the origins of humans on the continent. The physician Charles Abbott (1843–1919) excavated on his farm at Trenton, New Jersey, in the 1870s in the hope of finding early human remains that dated to the end of the Pleistocene (the last Ice Age), 11,700 BCE. In the 1920s archaeologists intensified their search and important sites were excavated in New Mexico and Colorado that demonstrated conclusively that humans had been in North America during the Late Pleistocene, though how far before that was still unclear, and indeed today is still not decided. Sites like Lindenmeier and Dent in Colorado, and Blackwater Draw and Folsom in New Mexico, were the bases for the definition of the Clovis and Folsom periods, the earliest well-defined Paleoindian periods in North America, approximately dating to 12,000–11,000 and 11,000–10,000 years ago respectively. Many of these sites are what archaeologists today call *kill sites*, which comprise the butchered remains of the hunters' quarry, usually the now-extinct mammoth and giant bison, and the stone projectile points used to kill them.

Making sense of the past and the emergence of culture history

As the twentieth century dawned, the federal government began to involve itself directly in archaeology. The *Antiquities Act* of 1906 was the first attempt to protect archaeological sites on federal land. That same year, the country's first archaeological national park, Mesa Verde in southwest Colorado, was established in response to a public outcry over the looting of antiquities from its magnificent cliff-dwellings, which date to the twelfth century.

At the same time American archaeology began to make a fundamentally distinct turn from its European counterpart. In Europe, archaeology was now established as an independent discipline with its own academic departments in universities. Its closest academic ally was history. In North America, however, archaeology was formally subsumed as one of the sub-disciplines of the emergent field of anthropology, the others being cultural anthropology, physical anthropology and linguistic anthropology. The reason for this development,

FIGURE 10.3 The 'Cliff Palace' at the Mesa Verde National Park, Colorado. © Andreas F. Borchert/Wikimedia Commons.

foreshadowed for example by Cushing's work, was that anthropologists who studied contemporary Native American cultures reasonably saw archaeology as a means of understanding those peoples' distant past in that there lay a clear and discernible continuity between, say, the prehistoric pueblos and kivas of the American Southwest and contemporary Pueblo villages occupied by such tribes as the Zuni and Hopi. This institutional structure was imported into Canadian archaeology, with two notable and relatively recent exceptions, the Departments of Archaeology at the University of Calgary (Alberta) and Simon Fraser University (British Columbia), both of which offer degrees in archaeology from the bachelor's to the doctoral levels.

Nevertheless, despite these institutional divergences, American and European archaeologists continued to share information on new field techniques (see Box 10.1). For instance, the concept of stratigraphy had been devised by the Danish geologist Nicholas Steno in the seventeenth century, and archaeologists on both sides of the Atlantic realised its potential for understanding the chronology of archaeological sites. Excavators of prehistoric and historic shell-mounds along the coast of California in the early part of the twentieth century were important in refining the promise of stratigraphy for archaeological purposes. Archaeologists found they could recognise changes in the shellfish types and associated artifacts as they dug through the mounds, and thereby chart cultural and environmental changes though time. In 1916 Nels Nelson utilised the concept of stratigraphy in his interpretations of excavated material from archaeological sites in the Galisteo Basin of New Mexico. The technique was also used by Alfred V. Kidder, most notably in his excavations of Pecos Pueblo in New Mexico.

BOX 10.1 Excavation techniques

Excavation techniques evolved slowly, from a haphazard and often destructive process to the organised and systematic procedure employed by modern archaeology. Yet despite the technical advances made, excavation remains a labour-intensive and thereby expensive procedure.

Perhaps the earliest archaeological excavator was the sixth-century King of Babylon, Nabonidus, who uncovered ancient segments of his city and even put artifacts on display in a museum. But our story really begins in the eighteenth century. In England, antiquarians like Richard Colte-Hoare and William Cunningham systematically excavated hundreds of barrows in Wiltshire. In each of them they left behind a lead token indicating to future archaeologists when the barrow had been opened. On the other side of the Atlantic, Thomas Jefferson is credited with being among the first to use the stratigraphic method (see below) in his excavation of a burial mound on his Monticello estate in Virginia. Jefferson is sometimes called the Father of American Archaeology because of this. However, despite these laudable early attempts, in general too many sites were being destroyed and data lost by individuals interested only in artifacts. For instance, the infamous Giovanni Belzoni (see p73) did irreparable damage to Ancient Egyptian tombs in the early part of the nineteenth century, and even Heinrich Schliemann (p41) destroyed large parts of ancient Troy in his single-minded quest for the Homeric city.

But slowly, as archaeology became a scientific enterprise, so too did excavation techniques improve. Perhaps the most important innovation was what the American archaeologist Gordon Willey called the 'stratigraphic revolution'. Stratigraphy, the identification of vertical levels in an archaeological or geological site, was first put forward by the seventeenth-century Danish geologist Nicolas Steno. He formulated the Law of Superposition, which essentially says that, in a vertical profile, the lower one digs the older the deposits will be. This tool provided archaeologists with a means of observing changes through time at a site. John Frere, a British gentleman farmer, relied on this principle in 1797 in excavating Palaeolithic deposits at Hoxne in Suffolk. The nineteenth-century Danish prehistorian J.J.A. Worsaae complemented the Law of Superposition by developing the principle of association in which artifacts contained within a specific soil level are hypothetically the same age. These tools provided archaeologists with a means of observing changes through time at a site.

Today we can broadly identify two principal excavation strategies. The first, sometimes called 'telephone-booth excavation', involves digging small units through the site until 'sterile' deposits are found (no evidence of human activity). This strategy can tell the archaeologist if the site is single- or multi-component, i.e., whether it belongs to a single time period or was used over a larger span of time, and what different archaeological cultures are present.

The second strategy involves excavating over a much wider area of the site, even if the earliest deposits are not immediately located. This allows archaeologists to understand the context of the site at a particular time so that they can reconstruct settlement patterns, subsistence activities and so on. Interestingly, this strategy's potential was realised during the 1930s in Eastern Europe and Nazi Germany, when otherwise unemployed labourers were hired as diggers through government-funded unemployment relief programmes.

FIGURE 10.4 An example of archaeological stratigraphy from the excavations at Goosehill Camp in West Sussex, showing the different layers. © Ethan Doyle White/ Wikimedia Commons.

Of course, archaeologists routinely combine the two strategies. An early proponent of this was the British archaeologist, Mortimer Wheeler (p30). A specialist in pre-Roman and Roman period sites, during the 1940s and '50s Wheeler developed a system of excavating a site in large blocks, thus giving him a good idea of what was happening at a particular time, while keeping each block separated by baulks of earth that would provide stratigraphic control.

Regardless of the strategy, all excavation is meticulously carried out. Horizontal and vertical grids allow the archaeologist to describe the site's context, i.e., the spatial and temporal relationships of all artifacts and site features to each other. Moreover, archaeologists now routinely use a battery of remote sensing techniques such as resistivity and archaeomagnetic metering that allow them to examine sub-surface deposits without ever having to plunge a shovel into the dirt.

Further reading

Barker, P. 1986. *Understanding archaeological excavation*. Batsford: London.
Barker, P. 1993. *Techniques of archaeological excavation*. (third edition). Routledge: London.
Carmichael, D.L., Lafferty, R.H. and Molyneaux, B.L. 2003. *Excavation*. AltaMira: Walnut Creek.
Collis, J. 2004. *Digging up the past: An introduction to archaeological excavation*. Sutton: Stroud.
Harris, E. 1989. *Principles of archaeological stratigraphy*. (second edition). Academic Press: New York and London.
Wheeler, R.E.M. 1954. *Archaeology from the Earth*. Oxford University Press: Oxford.

After recognising the environmental and cultural homogeneity of the culture area, it did not take archaeologists long to investigate whether smaller geographical areas might also display cultural homogeneity, and this led to the emergence in the first decades of the twentieth century of archaeology's first distinct and theoretically informed paradigm, *culture history*. The primary goal of culture history is to organise the archaeological data into what is called a *spatio-temporal framework* so that, in a given area and time period, archaeologists can have confidence in assuming that, with only limited variation, sites and artifacts would be made the same way (e.g., all projectile points will have the same style and manufacturing techniques). Changes in material culture through time were explained by specific events. For example, the adoption of a new technology might be explained by the spread of ideas from one group of people to another, or the migration of a new people into an area.

There are, however, problems with the culture history paradigm that became increasingly difficult to overcome. First, the paradigm's so-called *normative* view of culture must of necessity downplay cultural variability; yet, as we know from our own culture, there is in fact a great deal of cultural variation at any given time. Another problem with this paradigm was the assumption that a homogeneous set of artifacts found within a particular area and time period represents the remains of an ancient people. We now recognise that homogeneity in material culture can be caused by many factors, of which ethnicity is only one. Nevertheless, for early archaeologists hankering for a way to organise their data, this culture-historical paradigm was an indispensable tool and it still remains the primary schema for North American archaeology.

It is not surprising that the methodology of culture-history was worked out in the American Southwest and the Southeast, because in these two regions archaeological sites contained an abundance of different types of artifacts that changed discernibly through time. In the Southwest, Alfred Kidder and a group of colleagues formulated the Pecos Classification in 1927 for material found in the Four Corners Region, one of the first attempts to organise the mass of archaeological data being accrued in North America. Emil Haury (see Box 10.2) further defined the system. In the Southeast the culture-historical paradigm flourished through the work of James A. Ford (see Box 10.3) who established the basic chronology for the whole region.

While archaeologists like Kidder, Haury and Ford did much to advance North American archaeology, like their counterparts elsewhere throughout the world they were hampered by the difficulty of assigning calendar dates to prehistoric sites and artifacts. One exception to this was found in the deserts of the American Southwest, where a fortuitous combination of factors (a dry desert environment that preserved the wood beams used by prehistoric builders in their pit houses and pueblos) allowed archaeologists to use dendrochronology, or tree-ring dating, to gain absolute calendrical dates for their sites. Developed by A.E. Douglass in the second decade of the twentieth century, tree-ring dating is based on the principle that the sequence of tree rings for a particular period and region will be unique in composition and thickness because of the particular climatic conditions. Therefore, an archaeologist can

---

BOX 10.2 Emil W. Haury (1904–92)

Emil W. Haury was a native of Kansas. His first archaeological fieldwork – at the age of twenty-one – was at the Mexican pre-Classic site of Cuicuilco. He then enrolled at the University of Arizona, the institution to which he devoted his professional life. In 1934 Haury completed his doctoral dissertation at Harvard under the supervision of Alfred Kidder and Alfred Tozzer. In 1936 he published *The Mogollon Culture of Southwestern New Mexico* – the first time a Mogollon culture separate from the Anasazi had been proposed. Haury also established the chronology for the Hohokam culture, which along with the Mogollon and Anasazi comprise the three major archaeological traditions of the American Southwest. In the 1930s he became Head of the Department of Archaeology at the University of Arizona (later the Department of Anthropology) and also Director of the Arizona State Museum.

Haury is best known for his work (1964–5) at the site of Snaketown in southern Arizona near the modern city of Phoenix (he had first worked on the site in 1934 for the Gila Foundation under the direction of Harold Gladwin, a wealthy archaeological philanthropist). The site is a large village on the banks of the Gila River, occupied from about 100 BC to AD 1450. The major architectural features are numerous semi-subterranean pit houses, a central plaza and enigmatic cleared areas that were originally designated as *ballcourts* in view of their similarity to Mesoamerican structures. Snaketown's inhabitants relied on the cultivation of maize, beans and squash, together with tobacco and cotton. Of particular significance is the complex of irrigation canals that brought water to the town's fields from the nearby Gila River. It was at Snaketown that Haury worked out the Hohokam chronological sequence still in use today, though the calendar dates he assigned have since been modified.

BOX 10.3 James A. Ford (1911–68)

James A. Ford was born in Mississippi. He received his bachelor's degree from Louisiana State University in 1936 and after a brief stint at the University of Michigan entered the doctoral programme at Columbia University in 1940. From 1948 until his retirement in 1966 Ford was employed by the American Museum of Natural History. He also served as the President of the Society for American Archaeology in 1963.

Among the first archaeological sites to whet Ford's appetite was the complex at Ocmulgee National Monument in Georgia, comprising a large temple mound, ceremonial and burial mounds, and defensive ditches, all of them dating to the Mississippian tradition of over 1000 years ago.

Although Ford worked in other parts of the world (for example, Alaska and Peru), he remained primarily a student of the lower Mississippi valley and he excavated extensively in the region throughout the course of his career. Like other contemporary archaeologists Ford relied on an encyclopedic knowledge of the artifacts and sites of his particular area, especially ceramics.

Ford is recognised as one of the greatest proponents of the culture-historical paradigm. It was said in his obituary in *American Antiquity* that he introduced 'the nerve of history' to the archaeology of the eastern USA and he took advantage of the 'stratigraphic revolution' that had earlier so strongly influenced the practice of Southwest prehistory.

FIGURE 10.5 Temple mound at Ocmulgee. Photo © Wayne Hsieh/Flickr.

He believed that people were the 'carriers' of culture. Unfortunately, he bore much of the critique of culture-history emanating from anthropologists who believed archaeologists had forgotten about the concept of culture in their quest to organise their data spatially and temporally. Despite this, Ford remains one of the great figures of North American archaeology.

remove a set of tree rings from a piece of timber preserved at an archaeological site (normally a small core running from the exterior to the interior of the timber) and compare it with a master chart of tree-ring sequences derived from the same region. Once a particular master chart has been assigned calendar dates (it must originate with rings taken from historic sites and stretch back to rings from prehistoric sites), the archaeologist can then establish calendar dates for his own sample.

Archaeologists in other areas were not so lucky and had to rely on a variety of techniques to provide a set of relative dates (i.e., older versus younger). Seriation is one of these and is based on the common phenomenon that through time the style of a particular artifact will often change (consider how automobiles have changed through time and can be 'relatively' dated according to their particular shape). The technique was first used in North America by Alfred Kroeber (1876–1960) in an analysis of Zuni potsherds published in 1916. Leslie Spier then applied it to other Zuni sites, and by the early 1930s James Ford was applying it to Mississippi Valley archaeology.

Although not primarily a relative dating technique, the *direct historical approach* allowed some temporal control on otherwise undateable sites. The direct historical approach, associated with two influential Plains archaeologists, William Duncan Strong (1899–1962) and Waldo Wedel (1908–96) (see Box 10.4), starts by locating a historic-period archaeological site occupied by a known Indian tribe. The archaeologist would excavate earlier and earlier levels at the site, all the while identifying artifacts or artifact assemblages that could be associated specifically with that tribe. It is assumed that the 'history' of the assemblage, in terms of its relationship to other assemblages in adjacent regions, is a reflection of the tribe's history. This strategy is often referred to as working from the known to the unknown.

Post-war transformations

It is not surprising that the war years saw a lull in archaeological activity, but the late 1940s and the decade that followed saw a veritable revolution in how archaeology was practised in North America. The impetus for this revolution can be laid at the feet of three distinct phenomena: the increasing dissatisfaction with the culture-historical paradigm; the invention of radiocarbon dating; and the rise of an environmental component to the explanation of past human behaviour.

North American archaeology, as we have seen, is a sub-discipline of anthropology. During the first half of the twentieth century, cultural anthropologists increasingly expressed unease with archaeology's concentration on artifacts rather than the people who made them. In this climate of criticism about the very point of archaeology as an anthropological enterprise, Walter Taylor, often described as archaeology's first Angry Young Man, radically proposed the essential

BOX 10.4 Waldo Wedel (1908–96)

Waldo Wedel is one of the great undervalued scholars of North American archaeology. A native of Kansas, he devoted his career to the archaeology of the Plains, that vast area of grasslands in the central portion of the continent. The Plains exist in the popular imagination as the home of the great bison-hunting cultures of the nineteenth century such as the Sioux and Cheyenne, but along the Missouri River of North and South Dakota the semi-agricultural tribes, the Mandan, Hidatsa and the Arikara, were also found.

Wedel's Master's thesis utilised the direct historical approach to investigate the archaeological remains of the Pawnee tribe. He was the first graduate to receive a doctorate in anthropology with a speciality in archaeology from the University of California, Berkeley. In his dissertation he switched his interests to the effects of the environment on prehistoric societies. His subsequent papers on this topic utilised Plains data and stood out in a North American archaeology that still very much devalued the importance of placing prehistoric peoples within their environmental context.

Wedel worked at first for the Nebraska Historical Society, but in 1936 he moved to the Smithsonian Institution where he remained until his retirement in 1976. He also served as the Field Director for the Smithsonian's River Basin Surveys, a monumental project that began just after the end of World War II and whose mandate was to archaeologically survey the huge Missouri River Basin to mitigate the effects of federal dam construction.

Waldo Wedel was instrumental in putting the Plains on the archaeological map. His career began in the formative years of American archaeology when the need to construct regional chronologies reigned supreme. His pioneering work on understanding the relationship between the natural environment and human behaviour presaged in many ways the processual movement of the 1960s.

dismantling of traditional archaeology. In his 1948 publication *A Study of Archeology*, Taylor emphasised that archaeologists had to go beyond the analysis of artifacts simply as a means of organising them into spatial and temporal categories, but rather had to understand the Indian who made them. Taylor advocated a *conjunctive* approach, whereby the totality of a past culture had to be studied in order to understand it fully. In essence Taylor was telling archaeologists to become anthropologists again.

However, none of these lofty goals could ever be fully realised unless archaeologists could free themselves of the intractable and virtually all-consuming problem of simply figuring out how old an archaeological site really was. The second great event of this period liberated them: the invention by the American Willard F. Libby (1908–80) of radiocarbon dating, the discipline's first universal absolute dating technique. Radiocarbon dating, in principle at least, is simple to understand (see Box 2.7). All living plants and animals have a constant, albeit small, amount of the radioactive isotope, Carbon-14. At death the amount of this isotope decreases at a known rate (the isotope's half life). Determining the amount of residual radioactive material allows scientists to determine how long ago the organism died. Once this technique became widely available, archaeologists could assign an accurate calendar date to organic material such as bone or wood, and were thus freed to devote more of their intellectual energies to answering other questions about the past.

The third event in the post-war revolution was an emerging interest in the relationship between past human societies and the natural environment. Although the 'ecological model' had a long tradition in Britain, it had been much less important on the other side of the Atlantic. As we have seen, as early as the 1930s Wedel initiated studies of the effects of the environment on human populations on the Great Plains but this approach did not immediately spread to the rest of the continent. During the 1950s, the shift to using the environment as an explanation for human behaviour and, moreover, couching this explanation in terms of general principles was stimulated by the anthropologists Julian Steward and Leslie White. Steward (1902–72) proposed that every culture had a core, which he defined as 'the constellation of features which are most closely related to subsistence activities and economic arrangements', and thus were very much conditioned by the surrounding natural environment. Leslie White (1900–75) argued that culture was 'primarily a mechanism for harnessing energy and of putting it to work in the service of man.'

It was out of this maelstrom of new ideas and techniques that there emerged the second great paradigm of American archaeology, the *New* or (later) *Processual Archaeology*. During the 1950s, Joseph Caldwell and others had begun to move towards an approach that emphasised understanding the *processes* by which cultures changed and the reasons for those changes. However, it was a young American archaeologist called Lewis Binford (1931–2011) who was to pull together all the threads of discourse over the past decade and confidently propose a fundamentally new way of doing archaeology. Binford's first article on the subject was published in 1962 and his position was then advocated in a series of persuasive and influential articles throughout the rest of the decade. Binford attracted many other young supporters, and the New Archaeology became a virtual juggernaut that for a time threatened to dominate the discipline entirely.

The goals of the New Archaeology were simple: archaeology was to make an independent contribution to anthropological understanding of human behaviour by developing itself as an explicit science, detached from the historical sciences that, according to Binford at least, had so far hampered its development. In order to accomplish this, he relied on four precepts: archaeology as a positivist science that tested hypotheses using the scientific method; heavy use of statistical techniques to manipulate data and draw inferences from them; reliance on Leslie White's conceptualisation of culture as a means of utilising and transferring energy through a society; and the use of systems analysis as an analogy for human society, in that changes to one element would potentially have a ripple effect through the rest of society.

Although these four core principles remained, some of Binford's followers took processual archaeology in slightly different directions. Some, like the Southwest archaeologist Fred Plog, believed that archaeology could establish universal laws of human behaviour. And in the 1970s Binford explored what he termed 'middle-range theory' as a means of identifying general principles that would help archaeologists understand the formation of the archaeological record (i.e., the material that archaeologists uncover from the ground) not just at the time it was originally made by prehistoric people but right up to the moment when it was uncovered by archaeologists in the course of their investigations.

Bringing the story up-to-date

Arguably the most important change to American archaeology in the past fifty years has been the development of Cultural Resource Management (CRM), the term for the private-sector

BOX 10.5 Locating archaeological sites

Before the development of reconnaissance survey, described below, antiquarians relied on a number of techniques to locate archaeological sites. Heinrich Schliemann (p41) carefully read the *Iliad* to point him to northwest Turkey in his search for ancient Troy. Also, the presence of ancient sites can sometimes be gleaned from modern-day place names. In southwest Europe, for example, archaeologists have been guided to prehistoric sites by maps that contain old words for tomb or stone. Even today many important archaeological sites are found accidentally, as a result of ploughing or urban development. Some sites have never really been lost, of course. An obvious example is the Great Pyramids.

Beginning in the eighteenth century, antiquarians in southern England began to ponder the relationship of Neolithic and Bronze Age barrows to the surrounding environment. This so-called Field Archaeology is really the basis for the most commonly used technique employed by archaeologists today, the reconnaissance survey. It is heavily employed in Compliance Archaeology or, as it is called in North America, Cultural Resource Management. Archaeologists walk large swaths of land examining the ground surface for even the faintest of ancient remains. The technique has changed little in decades: a crew of archaeologists will form a line and systematically cover the piece of land to be surveyed, stopping to record all artifacts and features. The environmental context of the site will also be recorded and sometimes soil samples will be taken and shovel test pits dug to determine the presence of buried material. The amount and types of artifacts collected from the site for further analysis will depend on the specific nature and goals of the survey.

Reconnaissance survey offers the archaeologist a number of advantages. First, it is much cheaper than excavation as a means of recovering data and is much less destructive. Second, it provides a very good overview of the types of sites found in the area as well as their age. Third, archaeologists can gain an accurate assessment of the different types of sites and their environmental setting and thereby gain insight into prehistoric settlement patterns. One thinks immediately of such classic settlement studies as those by Cyril Fox in Britain in the 1920s, Gordon Willey in Peru in the 1950s and William Sanders in Mexico in the 1960s.

In the 1960s archaeologists began to experiment with statistical sampling techniques and field survey was not immune to this trend. Archaeologists have always been fearful that in concentrating on only the large sites, smaller but equally important sites might be ignored. While the primary goal of archaeology was to recover the most visually impressive sites, this problem could be overlooked. However, it became increasingly insurmountable for archaeologists interested in human behaviour. In a statistically random survey, the region of interest is gridded into blocks, either uniformly across the region or by natural landforms (terraces, flood plains, etc.). Using a table of random numbers, specific blocks are chosen for field reconnaissance. It is assumed that the results found in the sample will accurately reflect (within an acceptable margin of error) the results if the whole region had been surveyed. Using statistical techniques also allows much wider coverage as only a small portion of the total area is actually surveyed.

Further reading

Ammerman, A.J. 1981. 'Surveys and archaeological research'. *Annual Review of Anthropology* 10: 63–88.

Banning, E.B. 2002. *Archaeological survey, manuals in archaeological method, theory and technique.* Kluwer/Plenum: New York.

Clark, A. 1996. *Seeing beneath the soil: Prospecting methods in archaeology.* (second edition). Routledge: London.

Mueller, J.W. (ed.) 1975. *Sampling in archaeology.* University of Arizona Press: Tucson.

Orton, C. 2000. *Sampling in archaeology.* Cambridge University Press: Cambridge.

industry concerned with the protection and study of archaeological sites on public land as required by federal, state and provincial laws. The impact of CRM on North American archaeology is incalculable. For one thing, it has massively increased the data bank available to archaeologists. Not only that, there is now a much better publication record of field projects, since federal law mandates that no project can be concluded (or final payment received for services rendered) until a final professional-quality report has been submitted to, and accepted by, the appropriate federal agency. For another, CRM is now the single largest employer of archaeologists in the USA and Canada, although the quality of those jobs, in terms of salary, benefits and security is still highly variable.

Fieldwork remains archaeology's principal means of recovering data, and many new techniques have emerged to help data recovery without expensive excavations. For example, ground-penetrating radar, the proton magnetometer and the resistivity meter are all now commonly used by archaeologists. These instruments allow the archaeologist to identify anomalies in the ground, giving them a pretty good idea of what caused the anomalies (e.g., a storage pit) and directing them to the most profitable area of the site for further investigation.

Other changes in archaeology, more theoretical in nature, have occurred not just in North America but beyond. In the 1980s many of these changes fell under the umbrella of the so-called 'postprocessual' movement, which was proposed as an antidote to the extreme 'scientistic' approach of processual archaeology. In North America, four trends are worth noting. First, archaeology has become much more sensitive to the rights of the indigenous peoples whose past is being studied (see Box 13.3 p237). Much of the initial debate revolved around the treatment by archaeologists of aboriginal buried remains, but this important issue is only one part of the overall problem of which interpretation should take precedence (scientific archaeology versus indigenous interpretations, for example). Intense and acrimonious charges from both sides coloured the debate. Compromises have, however, been reached. One such in the United States is the Native American Graves Protection and Repatriation Act (NAGPRA) of 1990. The law established procedures both for determining the ownership of Native American human remains and objects on federal or tribal lands, as well as those already stored in museums and universities, and for returning the material to the appropriate tribe. Canada does not have a federal equivalent of NAGPRA. Rather, each province has its own set of procedures. So, for example, in British Columbia the treatment of aboriginal burials is dealt with on a case-by-case basis through negotiations between the appropriate tribal band and museum.

Second, there has also emerged what might be termed a feminist or (to use a rather ugly neologism) an 'engendered' approach, which makes much more explicit both the role of women in past societies and the impact of how we describe that role in our understanding of women in today's society. Prior to this, it is fair to say that women were in many ways undervalued in archaeological reconstructions of the past despite the presence, albeit in the minority, of some important female archaeologists (see Box 10.6).

The third trend is the emergence of a greater interest in examining socio-economic class. Certainly, this interest is not so prevalent as indigenous and feminist perspectives, which are now common threads in North American archaeology, because many prehistoric societies on the continent are viewed as egalitarian hunting-and-gathering groups. It might also be the case that class as a category of social organisation tends to be somewhat overlooked in a country that prides itself on individualism and conservative ideology. Nevertheless, fertile ground for exploring socio-economic class is found in the ranked societies of the Midwest and the Southeast (the Mississippian Tradition, for example) or in the historic archeological record of the continent. One notable example of the latter is the work by the so-called Ludlow Collective on the Colorado Coalfield War Archaeological Project. During the first decade

BOX 10.6 Women in a man's world: Frederica de Laguna and H. Marie Wormington

Frederica de Laguna (1906–2004) was one of the continent's first female archaeologists. A graduate of Bryn Mawr, her initial interest in anthropology and archaeology was stimulated by seminars offered by the great anthropologist Franz Boas at Columbia University. Her subsequent dissertation investigated the possible links between Palaeolithic and Eskimo art. In 1930 she initiated fieldwork in Alaska, and this led to the publication of the *Archaeology of Cook Inlet, Alaska* (1934). She also worked in the Canadian Yukon, publishing her findings in *The Prehistory of North America as seen from the Yukon* (1947). She worked briefly on the Pima Reservation in southern Arizona, but suffered from sexist attitudes on the part of the male colleagues who were supposedly her employees (the only time in her career this happened, as she later acknowledged). After the end of World War II, she returned to Alaska. De Laguna did not draw a clear distinction between the sub-disciplines of anthropology, and her seminal work *Under Mount Saint Elias* (1972) relied on archaeological, ethnohistorical and ethnographic data. De Laguna founded the Anthropology Department at Bryn Mawr University and also served as President of the American Anthropological Association (1966–7).

H. Marie Wormington (1914–94) is an important figure in American archaeology for paving the way for other females to enter the field. Her first archaeological fieldwork took place in France where she helped excavate Palaeolithic sites. She then became a staff archaeologist at the Denver Museum of Natural History, but interrupted her tenure there in 1937 to begin graduate studies at Radcliffe and Harvard, becoming only the second woman admitted to the anthropology programme. Although she conducted numerous excavations, Wormington is perhaps best known for her synthetic works, especially *Ancient Man in North America* (first published in 1939). She also deserves credit for becoming the first female president (in 1983) of the Society for American Archaeology, the premier professional organisation on the continent.

of the new millennium, members of the collective studied the archaeological remains of a violent coalminers' strike that in 1914 virtually turned southern Colorado into a civil war zone. The project has tried to use its archaeological findings to make the public aware of this and other similar conflicts.

Finally, many archaeologists have engaged in the study and critique of how the archaeological past is portrayed at national parks or used in the promotion of tourism and in the so-called heritage industry. Of course, heritage parks and the like can serve a positive role by educating the public on the importance of archaeology. However, often the version offered in these contexts is seen as 'whitewashing' the past and indulging in an idealised re-creation. Archaeologists, as in the other three fields of interest, are now concerned with the contemporary political and economic impacts of how the past is studied and used.

Further reading

Bahn, P.G. (ed.) 1996. *The Cambridge illustrated history of archaeology*. Cambridge University Press: Cambridge.

Ceram, C.W. 1971. *The first American. A story of North American archaeology*. Harcourt Brace Jovanovich: New York.

Elliott, M. 1995. *Great excavations: Tales of early Southwestern archeology, 1888–1939*. School of American Research Press: Santa Fe, NM.

Kehoe, A. 1998. *The land of prehistory. A critical history of American archaeology*. Routledge: London.

Larkin, K. and McGuire, R.H. 2009. *The archaeology of class war*. University Press of Colorado: Boulder.

O'Brien, M.J. and Lyman, R.L. 1998. *James A. Ford: The growth of Americanist archaeology*. University of Missouri Press: Columbia.

Saitta, Dean J. 2007. *The archaeology of collective action*. University Press of Florida: Gainesville.

Trigger, B. 2006. *A history of archaeological thought* (second edn). Cambridge University Press: Cambridge.

Willey, G.R. (ed.) 1974. *Archaeological researches in retrospect*. Winthrop: Cambridge, Mass.

Willey, G.R. 1988. *Portraits in American archaeology. Remembrances of some distinguished Americanists*. University of New Mexico Press: Albuquerque.

Willey, G.R. and Sabloff, J.A. 1993. *A history of American archaeology* (third edition). Freeman: New York.

11

MESOAMERICA

Ann Cyphers

The saga of Mesoamerican archaeology is filled with dazzling tales of intrepid explorers, brilliant historians, dedicated anthropologists and bold archaeologists who broke the time barrier to reveal the story of ancient peoples. The archaeological record was their laboratory, a testing ground for facts and insights about olden times. Their discoveries were firmly anchored in a profound interest in the past as they relentlessly sought evidence of early behaviours in the mute testimony of bones, stones, potsherds, art and architecture. The success of their efforts is well illustrated by their great discoveries and, above all, by an exceptional comprehension of Mesoamerican archeology obtained from dedicated research.

The Mesoamerican past may be understood from different perspectives. As eloquently argued by Eduardo Matos, they include the self views held by the peoples who inhabited this region of the New World, the perceptions of Europeans and the archaeological interpretations. Yet these perspectives may not be kept separate when seeking to interpret ancient Mesoamerica since each one can potentially provide key information instrumental in the reconstruction of the past. Artistic objects, architecture and documents constitute prime sources for unravelling sacred myths and secular beliefs handed down through generations, which give vital insights about pre-Hispanic world views. Some European chroniclers faithfully documented aspects of Mesoamerican ways of life, while others projected their own beliefs onto the native cultures. On the other hand, archaeological interpretation often draws together multiple strands of historic and ethnographic information in conjunction with analyses of data obtained from field research.

Antiquarians

The sixteenth-century arrival of Europeans heralded the age of antiquarians, who sought to link past and present through the comparative study of isolated but beautiful objects. Emphasis was placed on artifact classification and artistic styles, as a way to understand the temporal placement and development of ancient cultures, but these approaches lacked scientific rigour and independent confirmation of the sequences of cultures.

Nonetheless, valuable eyewitness reports of Mesoamerican communities and customs were produced at this time. Hernán Cortés (1485–1547) and his followers wrote letters and chronicles of the native peoples and their customs. The work of Bernal Díaz de Castillo (1496–1584) is another well-known account. An important chronicler was the priest Bernardino de Sahagún (c. 1499–1590), who carefully documented many aspects of Mesoamerican life in his voluminous *Florentine Codex*. Other historians with an ethnological bent included Alva Ixtlilxochitl (c. 1568–1648), Diego Durán (1537–88), Francisco de Burgoa (c. 1600–81), Domingo Chimalpain (1579–1660) and Hernando Alvarado Tezozomoc (c. 1520–c. 1609). Diego de Landa (1524–79) took early steps towards deciphering the Mayan script for missionary purposes, a lengthy process that came to fruition in the mid-twentieth century with the milestone work of Yuri Knorosov (1922–99) and other scholars. Many codices were produced in order to preserve and disseminate information on the native cultures, and near the end of the sixteenth century the compilation of the *Relaciones Geográficas* made available a vast amount of information regarding the administration of the territories, with notations on population, agricultural production and commercial activities.

Importantly, numerous early scholars were firmly convinced of the developmental capacities and trajectories of native culture and struggled against the view that they were inferior to the great civilisations of other world areas. They dedicated their efforts to supplying evidence that the ancient civilisations had been created by the precursors of the contemporary natives.

The emergence of archaeology

The first study that was archaeological in nature was conducted at Palenque by the architect Antonio Bernasconi in 1785. It preceded by only a few years the 1791 publication of José Antonio Alzate (1737–99) on Xochicalco in which the acute observations of the author on the hilltop site gave the first indications of its fortifications. Only a year later, Antonio de León y Gama (1735–1802) published the iconographic study of the monumental Stone of the Sun and the massive Coatlicue statue, both now considered emblems of Mexican identity. With the blossoming of interest in the ancient cultures of the New World, the early discoveries ushered in the notion of the great pre-Hispanic past, which was used to show the participation in the universal development of civilisations and to refute ideas of inferior development such as the noble savage and primitivism.

The progressive accumulation of information contributed to a great awareness of the achievements of the pre-Hispanic cultures, thus providing the foundations for the development of systematic interdisciplinary studies. The assembled collection of historical documents, studies and reports formed the basis for comprehensive studies of the Mesoamerican past.

The late eighteenth and nineteenth centuries were dominated by explorers and collectors, such as Antonio del Río (c. 1745–c. 1789), Guillermo Dupaix (1750–1817), Lord Kingsborough (1795–1837), Count Waldeck (c. 1766–1875) and Alexander von Humboldt (1769–1859). Then, following the Mexican War of Independence (1810–21), historical studies by Francisco Paso y Troncoso (1842–1916), Alfredo Chavero (1841–1906) and Manuel Orozco y Berra (1816–81) dominated the scene, with their massive compilations of documents and data along with comparative studies. For the age of travel and exploration, John L. Stephens and Frederick Catherwood stand out as extraordinary explorers and scholars.

The efforts of Stephens and Catherwood in publicising the Mayan civilisation were achieved at a time when travel was difficult, had few amenities, and medicine and technology were scarce. It should not be surprising that Stephens and Catherwood were founders of the American Ethnological Society, since their works possess an analytical and objective quality

FIGURE 11.1 Drawing of the 'Stone of the Sun', in David A. Wells, *A Study of Mexico*, 1897, p.59.

BOX 11.1 John L. Stephens (1805–52) and Frederick Catherwood (1799–1854), pioneers of Mayan archaeology

John Stephens and artist Frederick Catherwood were early explorers of lost civilisations, seeking not just adventure and spectacular discoveries, but also an objective understanding of their ancient builders. Previous travellers had already reported some Mayan sites, but Stephens and Catherwood went beyond description and speculation to present analytical and impartial explanations of the meaning of Mayan ruins. They were the first archaeologically-oriented scholars to penetrate the Mayan region, and their multidisciplinary work has been the basis of much later research. The images drawn by Catherwood were the first faithful reproductions of these sites and their use of the daguerreotype, a then vanguard technology, reflects their concern with honest reporting. The lives of John Stephens and Frederick Catherwood were linked by their strong friendship and close collaboration. For this reason their names have become eternally merged as a symbol of their spectacular contributions to Mesoamerican archaeology.

Born in 1805, John Stephens grew up in New York City where he was educated as a gentleman. After pursuing a law degree, he did not immediately begin to practise the profession because the spirit of adventure lured him westward, first to the Illinois prairies and then southward to New Orleans. Upon his return to New York in 1825, he studied for a Master's degree, set up his law practice and became involved in politics.

He was a striking gentleman of the day with red bushy sideburns and fashionable knickerbockers and he smoked black cigars, a habit he acquired in his western journey. When his overly active lifestyle negatively affected his health in 1834, his doctors dispatched him to favourable European climates for recovery. His distant travels took him to exotic places such as Rome, Naples, Greece, Constantinople, Messolonghi and Petra. In Jerusalem he obtained a map of Petra drawn by Frederick Catherwood, but did not meet him despite the fact that he was working in the region at that time.

Catherwood was born in 1799 in Hoxton, in the London periphery. Having studied fine arts in the London Royal Academy, he was invited to collaborate in a study of Classical Roman architecture in 1821 and later joined the Duchess of Devonshire's excavations in the Roman Forum where he prepared his first archaeological drawings. A few years later Catherwood travelled the Nile for a year, drawing and mapping the sites. He joined Robert Hay's Nile research project and for the next ten years made drawings and maps of many sites such as Memphis, Giza, Thebes, Karnak, Luxor, Edfu and Elephantine. In 1833, he completed numerous drawings in Jerusalem, including the map that Stephens discovered in a bookstore in the Holy City. In 1835 Catherwood returned to England and began to work on a painted panorama of Jerusalem for a diorama.

Stephens visited the diorama, which is where he met Catherwood. It was the beginning of a great friendship, as each man recognised in the other a kindred spirit with similar curiosity and love of adventure and exploration. Catherwood introduced Stephens to a book entitled *Description of the Ruins of an Ancient City, Discovered near Palenque in the Kingdom of Guatemala*, by Captain Antonio del Río. Thus, the seeds of curiosity about the Maya were planted in their minds and later gave fruit to their incredible journeys through the Mayan region. Both men were immersed in the then current controversy about the Mexican ruins – whether they should be attributed to Phoenicians, Egyptians, Nords, Chinese or the tribes of Israel.

Stephens returned to New York where he published his book *Incidents of Travel in Arabia Petraea* in 1837, with *Incidents of Travel in Greece, Turkey, Russia and Poland* appearing the following year. With his literary fame guaranteed and having secured a diplomatic post, he used the royalties from these publications to finance his trip with Catherwood to examine the Mayan ruins.

They first proceeded to Copán in 1839. For Catherwood, the task of drawing the magnificent stone monuments was extremely difficult because he was not used to the art style, and also because the high jungle obstructed the sunlight. As trees were felled, Catherwood made drawings of fifteen stelae and the god of agriculture, Yum Kaax. He covered himself from head to toe, except for his eyes, to protect himself from the voracious insects and stood knee-deep in mud while drawing wearing gloves. His attempts to use the *camera lucida*, a device for superimposing a scene on the drawing surface, were unsuccessful.

8. STONE IDOL, 13 feet high, at Copan.

F. Catherwood.

FIGURE 11.2 Stone idol from Copán (Stele D). Drawing by F. Catherwood in J.L. Stephens *Incidents of travel in Central America, Chiapas, and Yucatan*, 1854.

After Stephens' journey southward to examine the possibilities of an isthmian canal, as charged by his government post, they journeyed to Palenque. By this time, they had contracted illnesses due to the unhealthy conditions, but nonetheless Catherwood was able to draw the Palace and hieroglyphics associated with the Temple of the Inscriptions, the latter noted as strikingly similar to those at Copán. Their Palenque work was the basis for their rejection of similarities with Egyptian remains.

Catherwood contracted malaria so they suspended their expedition and returned home. In his absence Stephens' business had flourished, and he found himself extremely well off when he arrived in New York – capable of financing the joint book with Catherwood, *Incidents of Travel in Central America*, which became a great success.

In 1841, they set off for another trip to Yucatán in the company of Samuel Cabot, medical doctor and naturalist. Catherwood took along a daguerreotype, which he used to take pictures of the local ladies. Returning to Uxmal, they elaborated maps and drawings of the ruins and monuments, and used the daguerreotype to capture images of the Nunnery building with the idea that they could create a replica once back home. Then they mapped Chichen Itzá, and Catherwood's drawings of the buildings known as the Observatory, the temples of the Warriors, the Jaguars, Kukulcán and Akab Dzib, the Nunnery, the Ball Court, the Monastery and the Church are counted among his finest work. From there they went on to the coast where they visited Isla Mujeres, Cozumel, Tulum and Izamal and then returned home, sailing via Habana, Cuba.

Stephens' next book, *Incidents of Travel in Yucatan*, included novel information from relatively unknown Spanish chroniclers such as Herrera, Cogolludo and Díaz de Castillo, as well as Pío Pérez's text on Mayan chronology. He concluded that the ancient vestiges were autochthonous. After writing hurriedly for only six months, he published the book in March 1843. His next book, *View of Ancient Monuments in Central America*, appeared in 1844, again promoting Stephens' conviction that the cultural expressions of Mexico and Guatemala were autochthonous.

Stephens, as a founder of the Panama Railroad Company, travelled on foreign business and on one such trip fell ill with malaria and hepatitis and subsequently died in 1852. After Stephens' death, Catherwood travelled back and forth between London and the United States. His ill-fortuned journey in September of 1854 on the ship *Arctic* ended with a collision with the French ship *Vesta*. The *Arctic* sank with 300 passengers aboard, including Catherwood.

that is characteristic of modern ethnology. Their rejection of prevailing diffusionist ideas included the explicit recognition of pre-Hispanic achievements and the lack of external influence. Their work was interdisciplinary, a novel concept for the era, since they used little-known historic and ethnohistoric sources to help them understand the jungle-covered ruins they had visited. For the first time, information obtained from local priests and scholars was made public. Stephens in particular possessed the capacity to recognise similarities among sites and to generalise beyond simple description, an incredibly complex task in *terra incognita*. The archaeological work conducted by Stephens and Catherwood had extraordinary value given the prevailing interests of the time and, due to its scientific value, continues to be used by scholars today.

Making sense of the past

The late nineteenth century witnessed another wave of anti-indigenous thought, spearheaded by Lewis H. Morgan's 1877 treatise *Ancient Society*, in which the ancient Mesoamerican cultures were classified in the 'barbarian' stage of development, a view that was rebutted by Alfredo Chavero, Edward Tylor (1832–1917) and Paul Radin (1883–1959). The search for knowledge intensified with unfounded speculation moving into the background. Numerous investigations and expeditions resulted in many well-illustrated volumes on archaeological sites, writing systems and related topics such as biology and language by outstanding scholars such as Alfred Maudslay (1850–1931), Ernst Förstemann (1822–1906), William H. Holmes (1846–1933) and Eduard Seler (1849–1922). Collecting artifacts continued to be a prime interest, as illustrated by the expeditions of Desiré Charnay (1828–1915) and Marshall Saville (1867–1935), which triggered intense discussions within the Mexican government about the ownership and exportation of archaeological pieces.

These were the first glimmers of archaeological heritage protection and the appropriation of the past to be used in the building of the nation. In testimony to this trend, Leopoldo Batres (1852–1926) began excavations at Teotihuacan and Xochicalco, to commemorate the upcoming hundredth anniversary of Mexican Independence. Although he has been greatly criticised for the improper restoration of the Teotihuacan Sun Pyramid and the use of dynamite in his fieldwork, Batres held the position of Inspector of Archaeological Monuments during the political regime of Porfirio Díaz (1876–1910), which allowed the documentation of the national archaeological patrimony in a way never done before.

Just after the Mexican Revolution, the first school of anthropology in Mexico was founded with the intense participation of Franz Boas (1858–1942), an ethnologist often named as the 'Father of American Anthropology'. His influence on Mesoamerican archaeology is undeniable because he was instrumental in forming the academic career of Manuel Gamio (1883–1960), the principal Mexican social anthropologist and archaeologist of the revolutionary period. Boas helped provide the first institutional link between teaching and research in Mexico through his active participation in the founding of the International School of Archaeology and Ethnology, which was the precursor of the current National School of Anthropology and History. His active promotion of the application of scientific methods in archaeology and the other sub-disciplines of anthropology underscored rigour, objectivity and high standards of evidence, thus transforming the discipline of archaeology into a respected scientific field, always stressing the need for empirical evidence and rejecting unfounded speculation.

Although not an archaeologist *per se*, Boas promoted archaeological field research in Mexico, which was supervised by archaeologist Manuel Gamio, who implemented the stratigraphic method encouraged by Boas. The introduction of the stratigraphic method in Mesoamerican archaeology was a methodological watershed that revolutionised the construction of chronologies. This method involves the careful recording and the separation of archaeological materials according to each superimposed layer of soil. Its application derives from the geological principle of superposition, in which the deepest remains are earliest and the shallowest more recent. New ways of recording and recovering data permitted the documentation and reconstruction of ancient sequences of activities. Gamio, who had previously conducted hundreds of excavations without stratigraphic controls, applied the new methods at highland sites such as San Miguel Amantla, Culhuacan and Copilco and thus obtained a sound basis for the first reliable reconstruction of the succession of cultures in the Basin of Mexico.

Gamio became an influential figure at this time, encouraging new perspectives on indigenous peoples who, for centuries, had been traditionally scorned. In the countrywide discourse, this was considered one of the great national problems. Archaeology's purpose shifted, departing from visions of a glorious past to recognise the cultural deadlock as the point of departure on the pathway to modernisation.

Post-revolutionary events led to the gradual centralisation of archaeological practice by government institutions. By the late 1930s the process crystallised with the creation of the National Institute of Anthropology and History (INAH) as the institutional vehicle for placing the practice and control of archaeology firmly under the aegis of the Mexican government. Mesoamerican archaeology witnessed systematic explorations of archaeological sites and regions and, importantly, the definition of culture areas. These culture areas were regionally identifiable and contained distinctive cultural manifestations. One example is the Zapotec culture of Oaxaca where archaeologist, epigrapher and historian Alfonso Caso dedicated several decades of his life to research at the great capital of Monte Albán.

The modern situation

By the second half of the twentieth century, the move away from migrations as explanation of culture change continued as interpretations turned to sociopolitical and economic processes. The concepts of cultural ecology promoted by anthropologist Julian Steward (1902–72) were

FIGURE 11.3 Temple at Monte Albán, Oaxaca. © Raymond Ostertag/Wikimedia Commons.

BOX 11.2 Alfonso Caso y Andrade (1896–1970), an intellectual giant among the ruins

Born to a middle-class family of Mexico City, Alfonso Caso followed in the family tradition of distinguished personages. The people who knew him stress his dynamic and multifaceted personality and firm convictions that were never overshadowed by the work of his famous older brother, Antonio Caso y Andrade, an eminent philosopher. Although Alfonso Caso did not support his brother's theories, he always gave him his place among the great Mexican thinkers.

Alfonso Caso was widely recognised as one of the *Siete Sabios* (Seven Wise Men) of Mexico, along with Antonio Castro-Leal, Manuel Gómez, Vicente Lombardo, Alberto Vázquez, Teófilo Olea y Leyva and Jésus Moreno, as a result of their founding of a society for promoting conferences and concerts among university students. This group of intellectuals frequently attended reunions in the home of their friend Vicente Lombardo, who was the brother of Alfonso Caso's future wife, María Lombardo. A famous writer in her own right, she had four sons by Caso. Following her death in 1966, he married her sister Aída.

Alfonso Caso obtained his law degree in 1919 at the tender age of twenty-three and immediately began a teaching career in the National Autonomous University of Mexico. He went on in 1920 to obtain another degree in philosophy. However, he did not find his true vocation in archaeology until his late twenties, which stemmed from a visit to the site of Xochicalco, Morelos. As a consequence, he began studies under Hermann Beyer and Eduard Seler at the International School of Archaeology and Ethnology in the period 1924–7.

Caso's driving concern was to show the *in situ* evolution of Mesoamerican civilisation, in juxtaposition to the earlier trends of diffusionist explanations. He began by studying iconography and epigraphy before initiating field-research projects with an interdisciplinary focus that included linguistics, ethnography, history and demography. His interests ranged widely across Mesoamerican cultures of all time periods. His work on the Aztecs culminated in the identification of deities and origin myths, and he produced landmark works on the Mayan and Mexica calendar systems as well as a correlation of the Aztec and European calendars.

His early work on deciphering writing, *Estelas Zapotecas (Zapotec Stelae)*, published in 1928, offered a catalogue of glyphs and was the first work to distinguish the Zapotec from the Mixtec manifestations and present a sculptural chronology from pre-Zapotec times to the Conquest. His documentation of the conquests of the Zapotec capital of Monte Albán through the decipherment of their writing system and iconography led to his proposal of Zapotec hegemony, which was highly criticised at the time. This interpretation was validated by later studies, even though he did not live to enjoy the vindication. He also interpreted the multicoloured Mixtec deer-skin codices that narrate origin myths and complicated genealogical information on rulers, priests and warriors.

His research in Oaxaca was motivated by his conviction that one of the hearths of Mesoamerican civilisation was to be found there. It included investigations of numerous sites, including Monte Albán, Mitla and Mixtec sites such as Yucuita, Yucuñidahui and Monte Negro. His lifelong work mostly centred on the great capital of Monte Albán, a task that was inspired by the need for stratigraphic excavations in order to clarify chronological relationships. Starting in 1930, his research continued for eighteen field seasons, a period in which he uncovered twenty buildings and 176 tombs. In 1932 he discovered Tomb 7, one of the richest sepulchres ever found in Mesoamerica. He diligently documented and studied the finds for more than three decades, an effort that culminated in 1969 with the publication of the book, *El Tesoro de Monte Albán* (*The Treasure of Monte Albán*).

The historical concern with showing the continuity of Mexico's archaeological heritage can be perceived as a guiding theme in Alfonso Caso's work. His deep interest in the discoveries and identification of the Olmec culture in the southern Gulf coast region of Mexico during the 1930s and 1940s led to his masterminding of the 'mother culture' concept in 1965. This concept served to expunge centuries-old formulations of migrations as the source of Mesoamerican civilisations and promote Mexican nationalism by tracing the origins of the modern nation to the Olmec.

Alfonso Caso was the leading figure in Mexican archaeology during the first half of the twentieth century as the first Director of INAH, Director of the National School of Anthropology and History and Rector of the National Autonomous University of Mexico. His visionary efforts were instrumental in the creation of national museums and the founding of the Mexican Society of Anthropology and the National Indigenist Institute. He is famous for a quote about evaluating '*al indio vivo, a través del conocimiento del indio muerto*' ('the live Indian, through knowledge of the dead Indian'), which illustrates his abiding interest in Mesoamerican cultural continuity.

FIGURE 11.4 Alfonso Caso and Martin Bazan exploring the west side of Tomb 7 at Monte Albán. Fondos Documentales Alfonso Caso, IIA-UNAM, no. 513.

BOX 11.3 Richard S. MacNeish (1918–2001), a household name in studies of agricultural origins

Richard (aka 'Scotty') MacNeish's dedication to the field of archaeology stemmed from unusual formative experiences. In a 1997 interview, he recalled an eighth-grade art history assignment, a notebook project on artistic traditions other than Greco-Roman art, for which he chose the Maya because his own name started with 'M'. Leaving the assignment until the last minute, he enlisted the aid of his family to cut out pictures from *Science Newsletter*, *National Geographic Magazine* and *Scientific American* to paste into the notebook. At the end of the semester when the project won a prize, his teacher, Miss Ives, made him give a talk about the Maya, so he was, after all, forced to read his own notebook project, which included material about the work of Alfred Kidder. This was his first introduction to Mayan archaeology and to one of its prominent archaeologists, who would later become an important figure in his life.

As a descendant of the signers of the Declaration of Independence and of the founders of Princeton University (on his mother's side), the young MacNeish was expected to go to college but did not enrol in Colgate College until 1936. There he won a Golden Gloves boxing prize. In 1938 he transferred to the University of Chicago, his father's alma mater. In 1940 he received his BA and in 1944 his Master's degree. Upon return from World War II Army service, his doctoral work in Chicago included archaeological fieldwork at the Kincaid site in Illinois, which was financed by WPA (Works Progress/Projects Administration), a government programme that was instrumental in training a generation of important archaeologists. It was his first experience in managing large-scale excavation.

At the time he was at Kincaid, archaeologists were interested in the idea that migrations from Mesoamerica might be responsible for Moundbuilder architecture, so his doctoral research focused on this problem through field research in the Mexican state of Tamaulipas. However, he found no evidence for the proposed migrations. Guided by his local pal, Pedro Lerma (whose last name was given to the Lerma projectile points characteristic of the Paleoindian period), he discovered dry caves with abundant perishable pre-pottery remains. A few years later in La Perra cave he experimented with excavation methods, first applying the WPA system of arbitrary levels and then switching to careful horizontal excavation by cultural levels, which allowed finer chronological control. Tiny corncobs were recovered in La Perra cave that dated to 2500 BC. This was the beginning of his enduring search for the origins of maize agriculture and sedentary life in Mesoamerica.

Encouraged by botanist Paul Mangelsdorf, he went on to excavate two productive caves in the Sierra de Tamaulipas that were named after the Mexican scholars who reported them, Javier Romero and Juan Valenzuela. Then, following a period of dedication to Canadian archaeology, he returned to Mexico in 1958 to continue his search for the origins of maize.

After fruitless searching in several places, such as Chiapas, Oaxaca and Guerrero, he arrived in the arid Tehuacán Valley of the state of Puebla, where he located promising dry caves. Pilot excavations recovered early maize cobs and provided the impetus for the design and realisation of a great interdisciplinary regional project involving archaeologists such as Melvin Fowler, Angel García-Cook and Antoinette Nelken, and botanists such as Hugh Cutler, Walton Galinat, Paul Mangelsdorf, C. Earle Smith and Thomas Whitaker. Specialists such as James Neely and Richard Woodbury approached the study of irrigation, and Kent Flannery identified the faunal remains. The studies by this landmark project focused on environment, subsistence, regional reconnaissance and excavations, artifact classification and chronology, ethnographic and historical analogy, and irrigation. The five published volumes of the project contain an enormous amount of meticulously reported raw data and the final tome presents the phase-by-phase reconstructions of ancient life in the Tehuacán Valley.

Data on the origins of agriculture were largely obtained through excavations in the dry caves. Of the fifteen caves that were tested, the most important was Coxcatlán, which is considered a world-class archaeological cave by Kent Flannery and Joyce Marcus, comparable in importance to Tabun and Kebara in Israel, Ksar Akil in Lebanon and Combe Grenal and Abri Pataud in France. It contains remarkable evidence of forty-two distinct occupations composing twenty-eight habitation zones and seven cultural periods spanning nearly 10,000 years, making it a key site for documenting the appearance of domesticated plants and the transition to agriculture. In fact, so transcendental was this discovery that excavation supervisor Melvin Fowler once remarked that the stratigraphic sequence of Coxcatlán Cave caused him to abandon his own religious beliefs because the occupational antiquity negated the *Book of Mormon*.

Mangelsdorf and MacNeish identified tiny cobs of 'wild maize' in the vast quantity of plant remains in Coxcatlán Cave and dated their appearance to the Coxcatlán phase, c. 6000–4000 cal BC. Considerably later, this hypothesis was rejected in favour of a teosinte ancestor, and direct dating of the cobs slightly reduced their antiquity to the lower end of the phase. Even so, other domesticates are present in the upper end of the phase, indicating the advent of agriculture.

MacNeish was also deeply interested in dating the arrival of humans in the New World. In the early 1990s, he excavated a site in southern New Mexico with a splendidly sassy Spanish name, Pendejo Cave, where he found evidence of pre-Clovis occupation dating to some 30 millennia before the present, including sixteen fingerprints. As always, MacNeish's findings again stirred up the debate with those who believed that the Clovis tradition (c. 11,000 BP) represents the first settlement of the New World. The mounting evidence for settlement transcending the 12,000 BP 'Clovis Barrier' includes not only Pendejo Cave but also sites such as Tlapacoya, Valsequillo, Rancho La Amapola, Monte Verde and El Bosque, among others. Genetic studies of human hair from Pendejo Cave show a match with Siberian DNA, which coincides with recent studies indicating that Native American populations originated in this region.

Scotty MacNeish was a tireless seeker of ancient human activities. His archaeological research in widely separated geographic areas included the United States, Canada, Mesoamerica, South America and China. Whether or not seeking the oldest remains was his driving concern, he always managed to unearth them and, by doing so, generated unending and productive debate.

taking hold in Mesoamerican archaeology. His perspective emphasised the ways culture changes are produced by human adaptations to the environment, and was embraced by archaeologists in order to interpret ancient human behaviour within a rigorously scientific framework with the use of testable hypotheses. Data were obtained in ambitious multidisciplinary research projects conducted in extensive study regions. One of the first of such projects was conducted in Puebla by Richard S. MacNeish in his search for the origins of agriculture.

Another archaeologist to apply the precepts of cultural ecology on a wide regional scale was William Sanders, who is recognised for his work in the Basin of Mexico during the 1960s. As one of the foremost cultural evolutionists of his time, he made significant theoretical and empirical contributions to the development of the cultural ecological approach, in which the relationships of humans to the environment took precedence over heredity. In this holistic and cross-cultural approach, adaptive responses to specific environmental conditions, particularly with regard to food production, are expected to produce shared cultural regularities among societies. Breaking with the time-honoured Mesoamerican tradition of gripping discoveries of unique tombs, offerings and artworks, Sanders preferred exploring the conditions and dynamics that led to their creation in order to seek cultural universals of human behaviour.

The research conducted by MacNeish and Sanders, as well as that of many of their contemporaries, left a clear mark on the trajectory, intensity and nature of archaeological studies during the latter part of the twentieth century. Their innovations in methods and theories, along with the trend of increased fieldwork and intense publication, helped shape a greater awareness of the cultural complexity of myriad societies, thus guiding Mesoamerican archaeology to the new intellectual horizons of the twenty-first century.

BOX 11.4 William T. Sanders (1926–2008), illustrious pacesetter in regional studies

William Sanders was born to working-class parents in Pachogue, New York, a village on the south side of Long Island and a place far distant from the area where he made his life's work. His lifelong interest in Mesoamerica was stimulated by his early readings. His uncle's gift of *The Book of Mormon*, first published in 1830, showed him a diffusionist view of the origins of Mesoamerican civilisations, and later his reading of William H. Prescott's 1843 *History of the Conquest of Mexico* was the definitive inspiration of his enthusiasm. Little wonder that his horizons expanded given that Prescott's romantic historiography was peppered with dramatic narrative and solid documentary research that elevated Hernán Cortés to the role of culture hero. Given Bill Sanders' love of controversy, he must have enjoyed this mid-nineteenth-century backlash against centuries-old mistrust of the Spanish that had been characteristic of the American colonies.

After finishing military service in the Navy during World War II, Sanders obtained his undergraduate and graduate degrees at Harvard University under the GI Bill in 1949, 1953 and 1957. His interest in studying at Harvard did not stem from its prestige but rather from the presence of Earnest Hooton, whose academic standing was rivalled only by Franz Boas and Ales Hrdlicka. In high school, he had read Hooton's works, which may

FIGURE 11.5 William T. Sanders (1962). Photo by Jeffrey Parsons.

have included ones with catchy titles such as *Up from the Ape* (1931), *Apes, Men and Morons* (1937) and *Man's Poor Relations* (1942). The comprehensive nature of these treatises and their pleasant literary style made them widely popular. His studies with Carleton Coon prompted his interest in comparative ethnography. When Gordon Willey became Bowditch Professor, Sanders signed up for his courses and was thus introduced to the landmark Virú Valley regional settlement survey (see p190), a method he refined and applied in later years in Mesoamerica.

Under Coon, Sanders presented his 1949 senior honours thesis, *The Urban Revolution in Central Mexico*, in which he applied V. Gordon Childe's cultural evolutionary model, which had been published in 1942 in the volume *What Happened in History*, to the great Aztec capital city of Tenochtitlán. Other scholars whose work exerted a strong influence on his thinking include Julian Steward, Karl Wittfogel and Leslie White.

In 1951 he attended the National School of Anthropology and History in Mexico City where he and fellow student Angel Palerm studied with the famous Mexican scholar Pedro Armillas, who was a former student of Alfonso Caso, Paul Kirchhoff and Pedro Bosch-Gimpera. Armillas was the principal proponent of Childe's ideas and their application to Mesoamerican studies.

In Willey's symposium about settlement patterns held in the 1950s, Sanders first presented his concept of the 'central Mexican symbiotic region'. He summed it up concisely in his 1956 publication: 'The study of settlement patterns is the study of the ecological and demographic motors. Settlement pattern is, in effect, human ecology since it is concerned with the distribution of population over the landscape and an investigation of the reasons behind that distribution'. The 'economic symbiosis' in central Mexico prior to the Conquest referred to the complex social and commercial interactions – symbiotic relationships – arising among the inhabitants of diverse ecological zones who used their resources in optimum and mutually beneficial ways.

During the same year of this landmark publication, and before receiving his PhD in 1957, Sanders took a faculty post at the University of Mississippi, where he finished writing his dissertation, *Tierra y Agua: A Study of Ecological Factors in the Development and Personality of Mesoamerican Civilizations*. In 1959, he accepted what was to become a permanent position at Pennsylvania State University. This happened just in time to benefit from the expanding interests of the National Science Foundation into Social Science research that followed close on the heels of the 1957 Sputnik launch.

The National Science Foundation and Pan American Union granted the funding for Sanders' 1960–4 Teotihuacan Valley survey, which occurred at a time when Mexico City's seemingly unstoppable urban spread began to negatively affect the region. In this project he upgraded previously existing survey methods and created new ones, including highly effective interpretations of aerial photography. The survey results were published in the milestone 1965 work, *The Cultural Ecology of the Teotihuacan Valley*. By the late 1970s it became possible to synthesise the results of numerous surveys in the now landmark regional analysis of sociocultural evolution over a period of 3000 years. This work, *The Basin of Mexico: Ecological processes in the evolution of a civilization*, published in 1979 by Sanders in co-authorship with Jeffrey Parsons and Robert Santley, has been dubbed 'The Green Bible' due to its far-reaching impact and bright green cover.

During the mid 1960s, Sanders was invited to present a talk at the 'Wednesday Seminar' held at the Anthropology Department of Columbia University, then headed by famous anthropologist Marvin Harris. His theoretical discourse, characterised by one observer as seemingly interminable, was the seedling of the 1968 book, *Ancient Mesoamerica: The evolution of a civilization*, which was written in co-authorship with Barbara J. Price, then a brilliant Columbia graduate student.

During the 1970s, Sanders and Joseph Michels began the Kaminaljuyú Project in highland Guatemala. The evidence of Teotihuacan connections at this Mayan trade centre in part explains Sanders' long move southward from his treasured area of study, central Mexico. Like Teotihuacan and Tenochtitlán, it was in danger of destruction from the urban expansion of Guatemala City.

In the 1980s, Sanders joined forces with another important Penn State University scholar, David Webster, to direct the second phase of the Copán Project in western Honduras. A major regional survey around this important Classic Maya centre was instrumental in understanding its regional development. They clarified the settlement history of Copán through the use of surveys, mapping and excavations in order to assess population changes. Sanders also studied modern subsistence and residential patterns that were important for comparative purposes in interpreting the ancient past.

Further reading

Alcina Franch, J. 1995. *Arqueólogos o Anticuarios. Historia Antigua de la Arqueología en la América Española.* Ediciones del Serbal: Barcelona.

Bernal, I. 1980. *A history of Mexican archaeology: The vanished civilizations of Middle America.* Thames and Hudson: London.

Caso, A. 1969. *El Tesoro de Monte Albán.* Memorias del Instituto Nacional de Antropología e Historia III. Secretaría de Educación Pública: Mexico City.

Ceram, C.W. 1960. *Dioses, tumbas y sabios, La novela de la arqueología.* Ediciones Destino: Barcelona.

Ferrie, H. 2001. An interview with Richard S. MacNeish. *Current Anthropology* 42(5): 715–35.

Flannery, K.V. and Marcus, J. 2001. Richard Stockton MacNeish, 1918–2001. *Biographical Memoirs* 80. The National Academy Press: Washington, DC.

Gamio, M. 1942. Franz Boas en México. *Boletín Bibliográfico de Antropología Americana* 6: 35–42. Instituto Panamericano de Geografía e Historia: Mexico City.

Godoy, R. 1977. 'Franz Boas and his plans for an International School of Archaeology and Ethnology in Mexico'. *Journal of the History of the Behavioral Sciences* 13: 228–42.

Güemes, L.O. and García M.C. (eds) 1988. *La Antropología en México.* 15 vols. Colección Biblioteca del INAH, Instituto Nacional de Antropología e Historia: Mexico City.

Herskovits, M. 1953. *Franz Boas.* Scribner: New York.

León-Portilla, M. 1973. Alfonso Caso 1896–1970. *American Anthropologist* 75(3): 877–85.

Matos Moctezuma, E. (ed.) 2001. *Descubridores del Pasado en Mesoamérica.* Antiguo Colegio de San Ildefonso: Mexico City.

Matos Moctezuma, E. 2001. Un poco de historia, pp15–29, in E. Matos (ed.) *Descubridores del Pasado en Mesoamérica.* Antiguo Colegio de San Ildefonso: Mexico City.

Parmenter, R. 1966. Glimpses of a friendship, Zelia Nuttal and Franz Boas, pp83–148, in J. Helm (ed.) *Pioneers of American Anthropology.* University of Washington Press: Seattle.

Robles García, N. 2001. Historia de la arqueología de Mesoamérica, Oaxaca, pp111–33, in E. Matos Moctezuma (ed.) *Descubridores del Pasado en Mesoamérica.* Antiguo Colegio de San Ildefonso: Mexico City.

Schavelzon, D. 1983. 'La primera excavacion arqueologica de America. Teotihuacan en 1675'. *Anales de Antropología* XX: 121–34.

Von Hagen, V.W. 1947. *Maya explorer, John Lloyd Stephens and the lost cities of Central America and Yucatan.* University of Oklahoma Press: Norman.

Von Hagen, V.W. 1976. *Alla ricerca dei maya, I viaggi di Stephens e Catherwood.* Rizzoli Editore: Milan.

Webster, D.L. and Evans, S.T. 2008. 'Even jades are shattered . . .', William Timothy Sanders, 1926–2008. *Ancient Mesoamerica* 19: 157–63.

Woodbury, R.B. 2002. 'Richard Stockton MacNeish (1918–2001)'. *American Anthropologist,* new series, *104*(1): 299–302.

12
SOUTH AMERICA

Enrique López-Hurtado

Early beginnings: First scientific missions in the New World (eighteenth and nineteenth centuries)

The beginnings of archaeology in the South American continent can be traced back to the first European scientific missions to the New World during the eighteenth and nineteenth centuries. Although usually headed by geologists, geographers and naturalists, these missions were multidisciplinary and holistic in nature. This new approach, which opened up European eyes to the exotic landscapes, flora and fauna of South America, also included accounts about the people and cultures of these remote lands both past and present. In this sense, along with detailed descriptions of new species of animals and accurate measurements of geographic features, these reports illustrated some of the most emblematic archaeological remains of South America.

The first and probably one of the most famous of these expeditions was the Spanish–French Geodesic Mission, also known as the Geodesic Mission to the Equator. This expedition left France in May 1735 towards what is now Ecuador, a country that was at that time under the control of Spain. Its main objective was to measure the roundness of the Earth at the Equator. However, as we will see, the study also included observations about the flora, fauna and geography, as well as the description of the most important archaeological remains of the region. Among the famous members of this expedition was the young Spanish scientist Antonio de Ulloa (1716–95) who, during the mission, recorded for the first time one of the most emblematic archaeological sites of northern South America: San Agustín de Callo.

Standing at the foot of the Cotopaxi volcano, in central Ecuador, San Agustín de Callo was one of the two most important settlements built by the Inka Empire in Ecuador. At the end of the fifteenth century the Inkas, whose capital city Cuzco was located a thousand miles to the south in the central Andes of Peru, conquered most of modern Ecuador. Some modern scholars argue that the site corresponded to one of the palaces of the emperor Huayna Capac, one of the last Inka rulers.

Ulloa's work at San Agustín de Callo included a thorough description of its buildings and their impressive stone architecture, as well as the first known map of the settlement. In 1748 he published *A Voyage to America*, an account of the geography, people and history of the

South American countries that he and his fellow traveller Jorge Juan visited during this expedition. In this publication Ulloa presents among other findings a description of the site, a brief essay about the Inka nature of the settlement, as well as a map of the distribution of its architectural structures. This publication served as a guide for the great German geographer and naturalist Alexander von Humboldt (1769–1859), who less than a century later visited the site again and produced detailed drawings of its noticeable stone-made architecture during his famous Latin American expedition of 1799 to 1804.

During the remainder of the eighteenth century, many other scientific missions followed the pioneering work of the Ecuadorian expedition. They included the French cartographer Jean Godin's (1713–92) pioneering exploration of the Amazonian jungle. Following the path forged by the Spanish–French Geodesic Mission, these expeditions maintained the same holistic and interdisciplinary approach and devotion to the study of some of the most important archaeological remains of the region.

Nineteenth-century archaeologists

There is no doubt that the pioneering descriptions, maps and illustrations produced by these travellers constituted important milestones in the history of the study of archaeological remains in South America. However the study of such remains was far from being the main goal of these scientific missions. This situation changed during the nineteenth century. Important political changes occurred in the South American continent that influenced the way in which archaeological remains were perceived and studied. In 1821 the Spanish Crown lost the vice kingdom of Peru, its last colonial stronghold in South America. For almost ten years before Peru declared its independence, former Spanish colonies in the continent were falling north and south of the Peruvian border. After a long and cruel independence campaign, these new nations faced the difficult task of defining their own identities. This was not an easy task because it required finding common ground for nations that, after having almost 5000 years of urban pre-Hispanic history, were forced to face abrupt changes derived from three centuries of colonial domination. How to conjugate the native pre-Columbian world with the European period in a nation's historical identity?

According to many historians, the political independence from Spain marked the origin of a period of self-discovery for most South American national elites. The road to independence meant for them, among other aspects, the search for a national identity and international recognition. In this context the demand for up-to-date information regarding the republic's territory, resources and history became one of the main tasks of the new political elites.

For this reason many of these countries launched exhaustive explorations and reconnaissance with the aim of locating, describing and inventorying the natural, cultural and historical diversity of their territories. The publication genre selected by the political leaders of the new South American countries was the Atlas. In the making of the first South American national atlases, the work of two individuals stands out: that of the Italian Agostino Codazzi (1793–1859) in Venezuela and Colombia, and the work by the Frenchman Claude Gay (1800–73) in Chile. The presentation of archaeological evidence is practically non-existent in the Atlas of Venezuela but there are a few places depicting Chilean antiquities in Gay's work.

In Peru, given the amount and size of the pre-Hispanic monuments located in its territory, the first atlas financed by the state displayed a previously unheard-of emphasis on its rich pre-Hispanic legacy represented by the Inka Empire. The atlas was called *Peruvian Antiquities* and it was published in Vienna in 1851. Edited by Peruvian scholar Mariano Eduardo de Rivero (1798–1857) and Swiss naturalist Johan Jakob von Tschudi (1818–89), *Peruvian Antiquities* constituted the first case in which a local scientist was one of the principal investigators of the project.

This atlas presents the Inka Empire as the ancient Peruvian nation. In this work it is possible to find studies about the art, language, religion, customs and the most important institutions of the Inka Empire. The atlas is illustrated with elaborate engravings depicting Inka artifacts and monuments. The publication of *Peruvian Antiquities* marked the starting point of the modern studies of the ancient history of the Andes.

It was in this context of revival of Andean pre-Hispanic past that the Italian geographer Antonio Raimondi arrived in Peru in 1850. Driven by his vocation for researching the land of the Inkas, Raimondi spent most of his life travelling through the Andes. His work represented the most extensive and exhaustive scientific exploration of Peru in the nineteenth century, including his famous evidence of Peru's pre-Hispanic past.

BOX 12.1 Antonio Raimondi (1824–90), a life dedicated to the study of the Andean region

Antonio Raimondi was born in 1824 in Milan, Italy. Trained as a naturalist at the botanical gardens of Brera and the Natural History Museum of Milan, Raimondi arrived in Peru in 1850 at the age of twenty-six. On his arrival he established contact with the famous Peruvian physician Cayetano Heredia. Heredia quickly recognised the potential of the young Italian scientist and provided him with lodgings and work as a teacher at the Independence College, which would later become the oldest medicine school of Peru.

In 1851 Raimondi started a series of state-funded scientific expeditions that marked the beginning of nineteen years travelling across Peru. During his travels he covered the arid deserts of the Peruvian coast and the mountains and valleys of the Andean cordillera, as well as the Amazonian jungle. These intensive scientific expeditions collected data about the nation's geography, geology, botany, zoology, ethnography and archaeology.

As a man of science, accurate observation and meticulous description formed the basis of his research methods. However, it was the quality of his illustrations, be it in the form of drawings or watercolours, that constituted a central component of Raimondi's work. In this regard he wrote that 'a naturalist is not complete if he does not know how to draw with exactitude the objects which he studies'.

The vast richness of Peru's archaeological monuments is omnipresent throughout Raimondi's notes and illustrations. From the funerary towers of Sillustani located more than 4000 m above sea level in the Lake Titicaca region, to the pre-Hispanic coastal city of Chan Chan, the location and characteristics of all the archaeological sites he encountered during his travels were accurately recorded. However, in contrast to the naturalists of the eighteenth and nineteenth centuries, Raimondi's archaeological studies were not limited to the detailed description of these monuments. Based on the wide range of sites he systematically recorded, Raimondi was able to detect important architectural and stylistic differences between them. Starting from these empirical observations he was the first person to challenge the popular idea that all archaeological

FIGURE 12.1 The so-called 'Raimondi Stela', depicting Chavín's main deity, the staff god. Photo © Johan Reinhard.

FIGURE 12.2 One of the most important monoliths found at Tiwanaku named after American archaeologist Wendell Bennett. Photo © Johan Reinhard.

remains in the Andes corresponded to the civilising action of the Inka Empire. In this sense he was the first to postulate a pre-Inka period in South America's past.

It was the extensive study of one of these pre-Inka monuments that is recognised as his most important archaeological contribution. The site of Chavín is located in the northern Peruvian highlands at more than 3000 m above sea level and dates back to the year 1200 BC. It consists of a massive flat-topped pyramid surrounded by lower platforms. Inside the temple, walls are decorated with sculptures and carvings depicting a pantheon of fierce anthropomorphic and zoomorphic creatures. Modern archaeologists argue that the site was the centre of a pan-Andean cult that congregated elite members from nearby regions to be initiated during ceremonies that often included the consumption of hallucinogenic substances.

At this site Raimondi produced drawings and traces of the stone sculptures and motifs that decorate the external walls and subterranean galleries of the pyramid. However, it was at a nearby village that he made one of the most important discoveries in Peruvian archaeology: a seven-feet-high carved stone stela depicting Chavín's main deity, the staff god. The piece, nowadays called the Raimondi Stela in honour of the Italian scientist, is recognised as one of the most emblematic pieces of Andean archaeology. It is currently exhibited in the courtyard of the National Museum of Archaeology, Anthropology and History of Peru.

Raimondi's scientific work was published in an ambitious encyclopedic series called *El Perú* (1874–9). This work received the backing of the Peruvian state, which bought his collections and oversaw the publication of the volumes. On 26 October 1890, affected by a long illness, Raimondi died in the northern Peruvian town of San Pedro de Lloc.

Raimondi's contributions to the study of the Andean past provided the basis for the emergence of scientific archaeology on the South American continent. His work constituted an inspiration to other contemporary scientists with an explicit interest in archaeology, such as the American diplomat Ephraim Squier (1821–88) whose work on the Inka Empire (1873) incorporated some of Raimondi's illustrations. The German geologist Alphonse Stübel (1835–1904), mentor of the great German archaeologist Max Uhle, explicitly incorporated Raimondi's chronological assessments in his study of the pre-Inka city of Tiwanaku in Bolivia (1892).

Late nineteenth/early twentieth century or before World War I

The beginning of the twentieth century coincided with a period of formalisation of archaeological research in South America. Unlike the naturalist's approach, archaeological monuments were not understood any longer as peculiar components of the natural landscape, but as a main source of information for the history of South American societies. As a consequence, archaeological studies in this new era departed from the realm of the natural sciences like geology and became more related to ethnology and history. From this point of view, the reconstruction of the cultural history of a given region was perceived as the main goal of archaeological research.

In order to be able to address the cultural history of a region the main objective for archaeologists became the establishment of regional chronological sequences. In the absence of modern techniques that assess the antiquity of archaeological remains in absolute terms, such as radiocarbon dating, the reconstruction of regional chronologies was a very difficult task. To this end two main methods were used, the construction of typological sequences and the record of stratigraphic columns.

Typological sequences are built around two basic premises. The first is that the artifacts produced during a given period and place have a distinct and recognisable style. The second premise is that stylistic change is quite gradual, even evolutionary. In other words, particular artifacts like ceramic vessels produced during the same period are often alike. In contrast, artifacts produced several centuries apart will be stylistically different due to centuries of change.

The record of stratigraphic columns used in conjunction with typological sequences provides a temporal direction for observed stylistic changes. The main principle of stratigraphy indicates that in an archaeological deposit the underlying layers are older than the ones deposited over them; and artifacts found in association with each other in the same stratigraphic layer are considered to be contemporaneous. In contrast, artifacts found in different layers are considered to have been produced earlier or later depending on the order of the deposition.

Among the earliest studies that applied these methods in South America one can cite the work of Ricardo Latcham (1869–1943) in northern Chile (1897). However, without any doubt, the most important figure of this period was the German archaeologist Max Uhle who carried out archaeological research in Ecuador, Peru, Bolivia and Chile. Based on his work in these four countries he proposed the first chronological sequence of the Andean region.

Uhle's chronological sequence provided the framework for the development of systematic archaeological research in the region. Archaeological sites began to be selected for research based on their potential to contribute to the reconstruction of a master sequence that would ultimately account for all the chronological periods in Andean prehistory. To achieve this goal many scholars followed Uhle's methodology in their research. This was certainly the case in the work by the famous American anthropologists Alfred Kroeber (1876–1960) and Duncan Strong (1899–1962) from the University of California (Berkeley) during the 1940s. Similar work was conducted by Wendell Bennett (1905–53) in the Lake Titicaca basin, especially at the site of Tiwanaku during the same years. This same task was continued during the 1960s and 1970s through the work of John Rowe (1918–2004), whose master sequence of cultural horizons and intermediate periods, developed for the Peruvian Southern Coast, was to a large extent based on Uhle's pioneering work.

These first specialised archaeological researchers made significant progress towards the systematic study of South American prehistory. The work of Max Uhle in Ecuador, Peru, Bolivia and Chile provided the basis for this endeavor. Following his stratigraphic methodology, similar research was conducted in many regions of these four countries and contributed to the reconstruction of the cultural history of each region.

Interwar years

As we have seen, during the nineteenth and the beginning of the twentieth century, archaeological research in South America was mostly centred on the Andean region. After the first three decades of the twentieth century this situation changed. The new period was marked by a growing awareness of the geographic variability in the archaeological cultures

FIGURE 12.3 Chavín stone sculpture. Photo © Johan Reinhard.

of the continent. Although the establishment of cultural chronologies continued to be one of the objectives, these new studies were more interested in defining archaeological cultural regions. To this end researchers started to focus on areas that were hitherto conceived as peripheral in relation to the Andean region.

As the twentieth century was unfolding, previously unstudied areas were emerging as the focus of archaeological research in South America. Such was the case of the work of the Spanish archaeologist Perez de Barrada, who in 1937 began excavations at San Agustín, one of the most important archaeological sites of Colombia. He concluded that the civilisation responsible for the construction of the megalithic stone statues that characterised the site of San Agustín did not have its origin in the Central Andes but was the product of early migrations from Mesoamerica.

A similar situation occurred in Venezuela at the northern extremity of the South American continent. Archaeological research in Venezuela was almost non-existent before the first half of the twentieth century. It was not until the 1930s that internal political circumstances caused

BOX 12.2 Max Uhle (1856–1944), the father of scientific archaeology in South America

Max Uhle was born in Dresden, Germany on 25 March 1856. Widely recognised as the father of Andean archaeology, Uhle received a doctorate degree in philology from the University of Leipzig in 1880. In 1888 he left the Royal Museum of Zoology, Anthropology and Ethnology of Dresden to start a new position as assistant curator at the Royal Ethnographic Museum of Berlin. It was in this institution that he first became acquainted with South American archaeology while studying the cultural materials collected by German geologists Reiss and Stübel.

In 1892 he travelled to South America to conduct research in Argentina and Bolivia on a mission sponsored by the Royal Ethnographic Museum of Berlin. During the years of 1892 and 1893 he visited archaeological sites in Bolivia and northern Argentina. Inspired by the early work of Stübel, Uhle conducted a brief field season at the site of Tiwanaku. Although he planned to continue research there, the unstable political situation in Bolivia at that time forced him to leave the country the same year.

Uhle returned to South America in 1896 for what turned out to be his most important field campaign. Sponsored by the University of Pennsylvania Museum of Archaeology and Anthropology, he conducted excavations for ten months at the religious centre of Pachacamac on the central coast of Peru. Uhle's work at Pachacamac represented the first archaeological excavations conducted in South America using stratigraphic principles. Based on his excavations at this important site he proposed the first cultural chronology for the Central Andes.

During the next twenty years Uhle dedicated his research to the development of similar chronological sequences for archaeological sites and regions in Ecuador, Peru, Bolivia and Chile. Uhle's ambitious goal was to connect these regional chronological sequences based on the presence of two widely distributed styles: the Inka and Tiwanaku. Uhle's reconstruction of the first chronological sequence for the Andes represents an intellectual achievement of the first order. To achieve this goal he recovered and analysed over 90,000 artifacts from many different sites spanning over 3000 years of Andean prehistory. Moreover, the introduction of chronology to South American archaeology marked a milestone for historic research in this continent. The basic principles of Uhle's sequence are still in use in current Andean archaeology.

In recognition of his intellectual merits Uhle was asked to participate in the development of several research institutions in the region. In 1905 he was commissioned by the Peruvian state to assist in the formation of the Museum of National History, an institution that he directed until 1910. After his tenure here he travelled to Chile, invited by the University of Chile where he stayed for eight years until 1919. In Chile Uhle conducted extensive research and founded and directed the Museum of Ethnology and Anthropology. In 1920 he travelled to Ecuador where he conducted research with Ecuadorian archaeologist Jijón y Caamaño (1890–1950). In 1933 he returned to Germany where he dedicated the next ten years to the synthesis and publication of the results of more than forty years of research in South America. Max Uhle died in Germany at the age of eighty-eight in 1944.

BOX 12.3 Julio C. Tello (1880–1947), the first indigenous archaeologist of the Americas

Julio C. Tello was born in 1880 in the Andean village of Huarochirí in the central highlands of Peru. Son of a modest peasant family, his first language was Quechua, the most widely spoken indigenous language in the nation. He moved to Lima, the capital city, where he completed his Bachelor's degree in medicine at the National University of San Marcos in 1908. While still a student, Tello became interested in pre-Hispanic medical practices and pathologies. His Bachelor's thesis, entitled 'The Antiquity of Syphilis in Peru', is considered one of the first studies on palaeopathology in the world. Already recognised as a promising man of science he was awarded a scholarship by the Peruvian government to continue his studies at Harvard University, where he obtained a doctoral degree in anthropology.

In 1913 Tello returned to Peru and began an almost thirty-year career dedicated to the study of Andean pre-Hispanic societies. Tello did fieldwork in many regions of Peru, but his two most important excavations were at the site of Chavín in 1919 and the necropolis of Paracas in 1925. Chavín was already known due to the work of the nineteenth-century naturalist Antonio Raimondi (see Box 12.1) but it had never been systematically excavated. Based on his excavations at the site, Tello proposed Chavín as the centre of a culture that lasted several hundred years.

In 1927 Tello excavated 429 mummy bundles in the Paracas Peninsula. The necropolis contained ritual burials, in which corpses were placed in baskets in a sitting position. Each of the bodies was covered with large textiles, works of woven cotton that had been embroidered with wool to create elaborate designs. Tello and his team recovered a total of 394 of these textiles, and gained funding from the Rockefeller Foundation for their preservation.

As a militant member of the *indigenismo* movement Tello was the most adamant defender of the autochthonous origins of Andean culture. It is no surprise that he strongly opposed Uhle's theory about the Mesoamerican origin of Andean civilisation, which dominated the international academic landscape during that time. He proposed that, instead of being influenced by early migrations from Mesoamerica, Andean culture developed entirely independently and without any outside influence. He presented the Chavín Culture, centred on the eponymous site, as the 'matrix' culture from which civilisation spread out to the whole region.

Tello was the major force behind the creation of a law for the protection and preservation of archaeological monuments, one of the first of its kind in South America. He was also responsible for the creation in 1929 of the National Patronage of Archaeology and the Regional and Provincial Inspectors that functioned until 1968. These governmental institutions were in charge of the regulation and supervision of archaeological projects. Similar institutions are now functioning in almost every South American country.

Tello died in 1947 at the age of sixty-seven. He was buried, according to his request, in the gardens of the National Museum of Archaeology and Anthropology.

an approach between American archaeologists and the Venezuelan government. This approach was to a great extent the responsibility of the Venezuelan amateur archaeologist and politician Rafael Requena (1879–1946). During the years 1930 to 1933 Requena was appointed chief of staff of Venezuela's dictator, General Juan Vicente Gomez. As a consequence of Requena's interest in the past, from 1932 onwards the Venezuelan government invited some outstanding American archaeologists to conduct research in the Caribbean region. The first guest archaeologist was Wendell Bennett, from the American Museum of Natural History, whose visit was followed a year later by Alfred Kidder II (1885–1963), from the Peabody Museum of Harvard University, and by Cornelius Osgood (1905–83), of the newly founded Caribbean Archaeological Program.

As a result of the visits by these researchers, several works were produced, including the first chronological table for Venezuela published by Kidder II in the influential *Handbook of South American Indians* published in 1948. For the first time, Venezuelan archaeology was placed in a continental perspective and within the same parameters as in the Andean region. The main idea was that the reconstruction of the cultural history and chronology of the South American Caribbean region would contribute greatly to the understanding of the relationship between Mesoamerica and the Andean region.

The presence of American archaeologists during the 1930s and 1940s was very important for training and establishing a little group of Venezuelan archaeologists. In those years, the first systematic excavations by Venezuelan archaeologists were carried out, especially by Walter Dupouy, Antonio Requena and Jose Cruxent. Later, they became members of the Caracas Group, a research council under the chairmanship of the Smithsonian Institution. The foundation of the Caracas Group and the Caribbean Archaeological Program provided the basis for the rapid development of Venezuelan archaeology.

The rise of nationalist archaeology

The rapid development of South American archaeology during the first half of the twentieth century was mainly propelled by the work of foreign scholars, mostly from the United States. However, from the 1920s onwards, a growing number of local archaeologists were starting to make their voices heard. These local archaeologists were concerned with the role of foreign scholars in the reconstruction of their national archaeological past. The rise of nationalist archaeology in South America has its roots in the *indigenismo* movement during the 1920s. This movement was a major manifestation of nationalism in South American countries, glorifying their archaeological past in order to legitimise their unique Indian identity.

The *indigenismo* movement had several manifestations in South American societies of the early twentieth century. From the political sphere, to literature and theatre, the main objective was to denounce oppression and mistreatment of the indigenous population during the colonial and the early republican periods, as well as to press for a greater social and political role for these groups. In archaeology the movement advocated the indigenous origin of pre-Hispanic civilisations, but it did not depart from the reconstruction of chronological sequences and regional cultural histories introduced to the continent by foreign researchers. The movement also advocated a bigger involvement of national governments in archaeological research as well as in the control and supervision of research by foreign archaeologists. Government involvement was channeled through national institutions whose functions were the control and supervision of foreign archaeological projects, the protection of archaeological patrimony and the development of archaeological research headed by local scholars. Examples of this type of institution can be seen in Peru in 1929, founded by Julio C. Tello in Chile during the 1960s in the form of regional museums, and the National Institute of Ethnology in Colombia in 1941.

Among the earliest nationalist archaeologists we can count Jijón y Caamaño in Ecuador. Caamaño carried out excavations in the Ecuadorian province of Manabí between 1912 and

---

BOX 12.4 Junius Bird (1907–82) and his work in South America's Pacific Coast

Junius Bouton Bird was born in 1907 in Rye, New York. When he was only twenty-four years old he was appointed curator of South American Archaeology at the American Museum of Natural History. In this capacity Bird organised in 1933 his first South American expedition. He headed to southern Chile where he surveyed the north shore of Navarino Island and excavated the site of Puerto Pescado. In a subsequent expedition that lasted from 1935 to 1937 Bird excavated in Palli Aike and Fell's Caves located at the southern extremity of the South American continent in the Straits of Magellan. Here he discovered human artifacts in clear association with bones of extinct fauna such as paleo-horses and sloths. These findings represented a crucial advance in South American archaeology because, based on the association between human artifacts and extinct animal species, it was possible to establish the presence of human population in this region as early as 9000 years BC.

During the years 1941–2 Bird embarked on another expedition for the Museum. This time he conducted research in the Atacama Desert of northern Chile, where he excavated at various sites. His work here resulted in the creation of a long chronological sequence for northern Chile.

In 1946 Bird returned to South America, this time to do research at the site of Huaca Prieta, a late pre-ceramic mound located in the Chicama Valley on the north coast of Peru. The site of Huaca Prieta was the earliest site excavated in Peru at that time, and also the first in the continent that was dated using the recently discovered radiocarbon method. The study of Huaca Prieta addressed for the first time the existence of a period of pre-ceramic farmers and fishermen who dwelled in semi-subterranean rooms around 2500 BC. The most important findings relate to the beginning of the famous Andean textile tradition. Remnants of cotton fabrics containing beautiful iconographic representations, including the famous image of the Condor of Huaca Prieta, were recovered at the site. Based on the evidence recovered at this site, Bird was able to propose Huaca Prieta as the earliest presence of social complexity on the South American continent.

Bird returned to Peru and Chile several times after Huaca Prieta but only for short-term field campaigns. During the 1950s, '60s and '70s he revisited some of the sites he excavated early in his career to collect carbon and pollen samples. Bird's fruitful career was widely recognised while he was alive and many academic awards were given to him such as The Viking Fund Medal for Archaeology in 1956 and the Order of the Peruvian Sun of the Peruvian State in 1974. In 1961 he was elected president of the Society for American Archaeology. Junius Bird died in New York in 1982, he was seventy-five years old.

1925, and was responsible for the foundation of the National Academy of Historic studies. In Bolivia, Carlos Ponce Sanjinés (1925–2005) organised the Tiwanaku Archaeological Institute in 1957. But the most emblematic figure in the rise of nationalistic archaeology in South America is without doubt the Peruvian Julio C. Tello, who is considered the 'father of Peruvian archaeology' and who was America's first indigenous archaeologist.

World War II and post-war developments

The years from 1946 to 1948 mark a milestone in Andean archaeology. In this short period of time, some studies had an important impact on later archaeological projects not only in South America but the whole world. Among these studies the most important was certainly the Virú Valley Project, developed on the north coast of Peru and headed by the American archaeologist Gordon Willey (1903–2002) from Harvard University.

The Virú Valley project was an attempt for the first time in archaeology to put to work ideas that identify not just archaeological sites, but also how sites fit into the context of the physical landscape, available resources and other sites in the region. In a 1999 edited volume in commemoration of the fiftieth anniversary of the Virú valley project, Willey wrote that at the beginning of this adventure he wasn't sure about what he was going to do. The whole project was developed as the result of a suggestion made by senior archaeologist Wendell Bennett. Bennett argued that post-war archaeological research in Peru should concentrate archaeologists from several institutions in a single coastal valley. It was actually Willey's friend Julian Steward who introduced him to the concept of 'settlement ecology'. This new approach consisted of the study of the regional distribution of sites rather than the isolated analysis of individual settlements.

Following Steward's suggestion Willey recruited some of the best archaeologists from different American and Peruvian institutions such as Thomas Ford and Julio C. Tello. Willey's research strategy was to undertake a meticulous survey of the entire Virú valley in order to address the way in which each settlement interacted with the others. The study combined the use of aerial photography, architectural observations and regional maps of site distributions to reconstruct not only chronological sequences or cultural boundaries but the sociopolitical organisation of the study region. This new theoretical and methodological approach was called 'settlement patterns study' and it is today one of the core concepts in archaeology.

While Willey's Virú Valley project marked an important moment in the practice of archaeology around the world, another American archaeologist, Junius Bird from the American Museum of Natural History, made an important discovery that challenged previous notions about the origins of Andean civilisation. From 1933 on, Bird's interest in pre-Columbian textiles and the early societies of the western hemisphere led him to conduct research at early pre-ceramic sites in southern and northern Chile. However it was at the site of Huaca Prieta on the north coast of Peru that he made his most important discovery.

The last milestone of the post-war era in South American archaeology was the development of Brazilian archaeology. Despite the vast amount of archaeological research conducted in Colombia, Ecuador, Peru, Chile and Argentina, in Brazil it was not until 1961 that archaeological investigations assumed a protagonist role in Brazilian social sciences. The development of Brazilian archaeology during the 1960s was greatly influenced by the work of foreign archaeologists, in particular by the research of Betty Meggers (1921–2012). Early in her career, this prominent American scholar centred her research on the Island of Marajo at the mouth of the Amazon River. Here she established the cultural sequence of the region.

BOX 12.5 The rise of Latin American social archaeology

The legacy of Tello, as the continent's first indigenous archaeologist, propelled the development of nationalist archaeologies in the region. This movement extended beyond the Andean region into northern Venezuela, Colombia and even Brazil. Along with this movement, a new theoretical perspective, centred on the works of Gordon Childe (p25) and Karl Marx, replaced the old cultural historical paradigm.

This new movement was called Latin American Social Archaeology and it was born in the midst of the Cold War during the 1970s. This new school of thought was conceived primarily as a political reaction against American imperialism in Latin America. Members of this movement advocated a social role for archaeology in the vindication of the oppressed groups of the past and present. It is no surprise, therefore, that the main advocates of this movement also played important political roles in their countries. It is necessary to remember that the 1970s were a very convoluted decade in Latin American politics. Two main political factors favoured the emergence of this new school of thought. First, the increasing popularity of Marxist political ideology during the 1960s and '70s in Latin America was strengthened by the emergence of a series of national revolutionary movements and by the regional impact of the Cuban revolution. Second, for the first time in the continent socialist movements and parties achieved power in certain South American countries like Venezuela, Peru and Chile. This political context favoured the formation of a series of Marxist archaeologists who found for the first time a friendly political environment and the resources to develop their ideas.

From a theoretical point of view they rejected the cross-cultural comparisons present in American research, developed during the Virú Valley project, regarding them as a form of colonialism. They argued that Latin American pre-Columbian history should be studied as a unique cultural process and for that reason it should be interpreted on its own terms. To this end Marxist theory was adapted to the study of ancient societies. Marxist concepts such as historic materialism and class struggle were used to understand changes in past societies, and a great emphasis was placed in the investigation of pre-Columbian modes of production.

One of the main preoccupations of Latin American Social archaeologists was to establish a connection between their academic works and political action. According to this school of thought, archaeology should seek to contribute from its own ground the production of knowledge about the past, with the political struggle of the oppressed masses of the present. From this point of view archaeological research should not be conceptualised as a neutral endeavour but as another battlefield for class struggle.

Among the most notable contributors to Latin American Social Archaeology are the Chilean archaeologist Felipe Bate, the Peruvian Luis Lumbreras and Venezuelans Mario Sanoja and Iriada Vargas.

BOX 12.6 Juan Schobinger (1928–2009), opening up new paths for research

Juan Schobinger was born in Switzerland in 1928 and moved to Argentina very early in his life, when he was three years old. He studied Philosophy and Humanities at the University of Buenos Aires as an undergraduate. He later specialised in South American prehistory and his dissertation discussed the evidence of early rock art in the Argentinean province of Neuquen.

In the late 1950s he accepted the position of Professor of Prehistoric Archaeology at the Faculty of Arts of the National University of Cuyo, Argentina. Here he served as Director of the Institute of Archaeology and Ethnology and also as a member of the National Council of Scientific and Technological Investigations. His studies focused on early hunter-gatherers and rock art, but his greatest contribution was in the realm of Inka high-altitude shrines, a subject that he pioneered.

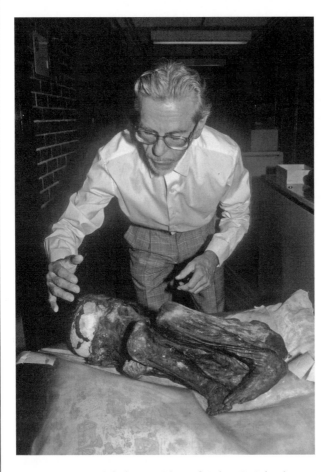

FIGURE 12.4 Juan Schobinger. Photo © Johan Reinhard.

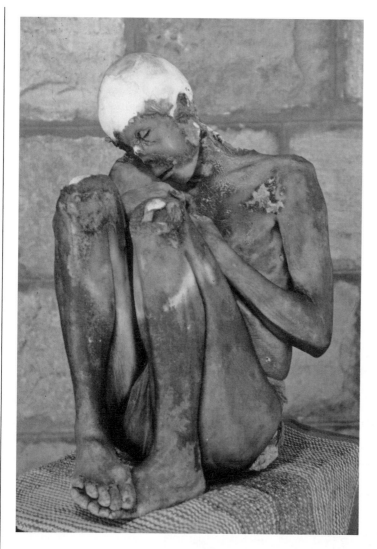

FIGURE 12.5 The mummy of Cerro El Toro. Photo © Johan Reinhard.

Schobinger's interest in Inka shrines began in 1964 when two climbers discovered, on the summit of Cerro El Toro, a mountain ice peak, located in the Argentinean province of San Juan, what looked like a pre-Hispanic mummy. They contacted Schobinger who organised a rescue expedition. This find was a milestone in Schobinger's career and allowed him to introduce for the first time to the academic community the existence of what he called 'high-altitude Inka shrines'.

He proposed that the Inkas climbed many of the highest peaks of the Andes to deposit offerings on their summits. The offerings at the high-altitude shrines were dedicated to state deities and local mountain gods, and involved a wide range of objects, ranging from gold and silver figurines, shell necklaces and high-quality textiles to pottery and food items. Human sacrifices were also performed on some of the more important peaks. One of the most interesting characteristics of these remains is the extraordinary preservation of the bodies and organic materials in the cold, dry environment of the snow peaks.

After the finds on Cerro El Toro, Schobinger conducted the systematic survey of the Aconcagua Mountain, the highest in South America, located in the Argentinean province of Mendoza. In 1985, the frozen body of a seven-year-old boy was found at about 5300 m above sea level. The mummy and its associated offerings were rescued and studied by a team of scholars led by Schobinger, revealing that the child had been presumably killed by a blow to his head. The bundle contained several textile mantles, a feathered headdress, as well as figurines made of gold, silver and seashell. Schobinger also participated in research on the Chuscha Mountain and the Llullaillaco Volcano on the border between Argentina and Chile.

As a member of the Argentine National Academy of History during his career, Schobinger received numerous distinctions including honorary membership of the Argentinean Anthropological Society. He was also recognised as a committed teacher and his work was respected and influential beyond South America's borders. In 2009 Juan Schobinger died at the age of eighty-eight.

Meggers was also responsible for the formation of an important generation of Brazilian archaeologists. She and her late husband Clifford Evans (1920–81) conducted seminars where they taught survey techniques geared towards elaborating chronological sequences and regional cultural histories. The American couple, along with Brazilian colleagues, created the National Program of Brazilian Archaeological Investigations. This research group produced an outline of the archaeology of eleven littoral states of Brazil, providing the basis for the development of modern archaeology in that country.

The modern situation

During the 1970s many intellectual and political aspects of the international panorama were marked by the Cold War, and South America's social sciences were no exception. Here, based on the nationalistic and *indigenismo* movements from the 1930s and 1940s, a new school of archaeological thought was developed: Latin American Social Archaeology. Unlike previous important episodes in the archaeology of this region, this time the main proponents of this new school of thought were scholars born and educated in Latin America.

The vast amount of both foreign and local projects created a fertile ground for the proliferation of archaeological research. Since the 1970s, despite the debate introduced by the Latin American Social Archaeology, there have been more collaborative projects in South America. Local and foreign collaboration, research on specific areas, and the emergence of sub-disciplines like palaeozoology or ethnobotany have greatly contributed to a better understanding of the past. In Brazil, for example, one of the countries in South America where scientific archaeology was not developed until the 1960s, there are now more than 100 archaeological projects every year.

A noticeable example of this new spirit of specialisation and interdisciplinary collaboration is the work of the Argentinean scholar Juan Schobinger. During his career he became the leading expert in the study of high-altitude Inka shrines, including in his research insights from new archaeological disciplines such as bioarchaeology.

Schobinger's research, along with the work of other archaeologists such as the American Craig Morris (1939–2006) from the American Museum of Natural History, or the Peruvian Ruth Shady from San Marcos University, has opened the field to a new era of research in South America. In addition to a notable increase in international and interdisciplinary collaboration, nowadays almost every South American country has doctorate programmes in Archaeology and Anthropology. In addition, every year more South American archaeologists opt to enrol in doctorate programmes in the universities of North America and Europe. In this context the beginning of the twenty-first century certainly looks very promising for South American archaeology.

Further reading

Abal, C.M. 2009. Juan Schobinger (1928–2009). Nuestro Adiós a un 'Caballero de la Ciencia'. *Chungará, Revista de Antropología Chilena, 41*(2): 179–82.

Burger, L.R. (ed.) 2009. *The life and writings of Julio C. Tello: America's first indigenous archaeologist.* University of Iowa Press: Iowa City.

Fernandéz, J., Panarello, H.O. and Schobinger, J. 1999. 'The Inka mummy from Mount Aconcagua: Decoding the geographic origin of the "Messenger to the Deities" by means of stable carbon, nitrogen, and sulphur isotope analysis". *Geoarchaeology, 14*(1): 27–46.

Gasson, R. and Wagner, E. 1994. 'Venezuela: Doctors, dictators and dependency (1932–1948)', pp124–38, in A. Oyuela-Caycedo (ed.) *History of Latin American Archaeology.* Athenaeum Press: Newcastle.

Jaramillo, L.G. and Oyuela-Caycedo, A. 1994. 'Colombia: A quantitative analysis, pp49–68, in A. Oyuela-Caycedo (ed.) *History of Latin American Archaeology.* Athenaeum Press: Newcastle.

Kaulicke, P. (ed.) 1998. *Max Uhle y el Perú Antiguo.* Pontificia Universidad Católica del Perú Fondo Editorial: Lima.

Matos Mendieta, R. 1994. 'Perú: Some comments', pp104–23, in A. Oyuela-Caycedo (ed.) *History of Latin American Archaeology.* Athenaeum Press: Newcastle.

Mérida Aliaga, S.M. and la Torre Silva, R. (ed.) 2006. *Antonio Raimondi en el Perú.* Termil Editores: Lima.

Oyuela-Caycedo, A. (ed.) 1994 *History of Latin American Archaeology.* Athenaeum Press: Newcastle.

Raimondi, A. 2004. *Oro del Perú. Compilación y Estudio Introductorio de Luis Flipe Villacorta Ostolaza.* Fondo Editorial Universidad Nacional Mayor de San Marcos: Lima.

Rivera, M.A. and Orellana, R.M. 1994. 'Chile: Institutional development and ideological context', pp36–48, in A. Oyuela-Caycedo (ed.) *History of Latin American Archaeology.* Athenaeum Press: Newcastle.

Rivero y Ustáriz, M.E. and von Tschudi, J.J. 1971. *Peruvian antiquities.* Kraus Reprint Co.: New York.

Safier, N. 2008. *Measuring the New World: Enlightenment and South America.* University of Chicago Press: Chicago.

Schmitz, P.I. 1994. 'Brazil: Tendencies and growth', pp22–35, in A. Oyuela-Caycedo (ed.) *History of Latin American archaeology.* Athenaeum Press: Newcastle.

Schobinger, J. (ed.) 2001. *El santuario incaico del cerro Aconcagua.* Editorial de la Universidad Nacional de Cuyo: Mendoza.

Tantaleán, H. 2013. *Peruvian Archaeology. A Critical History.* Left Coast Press: Walnut Creek, CA.

Uhle, M. 1903. *Pachacamac. Report of the William of the William Pepper, M. D., LL. D., Peruvian Expedition of 1896.* Department of Archeology, University of Pennsylvania: Philadelphia.

13

AUSTRALASIA

Caroline Bird

Earliest beginnings

The first encounters of European explorers with the peoples of Australasia in the eighteenth century took place against the backdrop of the Enlightenment and the beginnings of empirical science. The cultures of the Pacific provoked curiosity about the nature of primitive human societies and what could be learned about the nature of humanity, as well as stimulating ideas about social evolution. Acquiring information about Pacific cultures featured in the scientific aims of voyages of exploration such as those of England's Captain Cook and the French expeditions led by La Pérouse and Baudin. The rich descriptions, artifacts and drawings that resulted not only provide an unparalleled record of these cultures, but also shaped the development of the emerging discipline of anthropology. Archaeology, however, was a relatively late development in Australia and the Pacific.

The origins of the cultures of Australia and the Pacific were the subject of considerable speculation throughout the nineteenth century. However, prevailing social evolutionary views ensured that they were mainly viewed as exemplifying the lower rungs on the 'ladder of human progress'. Australia particularly was seen as a cultural backwater and the home of 'relic savages'. The anthropologist Baldwin Spencer (1860–1929), for example, wrote:

> Australia is the present home and refuge of creatures often crude and quaint, that have elsewhere passed away and given place to higher forms. This applies equally to the Aboriginal as to the platypus and kangaroo. Just as the platypus, laying its eggs and feebly suckling its young, reveals a mammal in the making, so does the Aboriginal show us, at least in broad outline, what early man must have been like before he learned to read and write, domesticate animals, cultivate crops and use a metal tool. It has been possible to study in Australia human beings that still remain on the culture level of men of the Stone Age.

Similarly, in the Pacific, it was generally assumed archaeology would merely duplicate ethnography and thus recording material culture and oral traditions was of more value. There was little intrinsic interest in investigating cultures that were viewed as essentially static and lacking history, and thus little room for archaeology. Although Governor Phillip's investigation of a burial mound in 1788 is credited as the first excavation in Australia, or indeed the Pacific region, most attempts at excavation over the next century tended to be aimed at determining the function of specific sites or investigating palaeontology. As late as 1928, R.W. Pulleine (1869–1935) could deny there was any point in archaeological investigation, famously characterising Aborigines as 'an unchanging people living in an unchanging land'.

Nevertheless there was speculation about origins, particularly of the Aborigines in Australia and the Polynesians in the Pacific. The differences between Australian and Tasmanian Aborigines were recognised early on: mainland Aborigines were assigned to a 'Neolithic' stage of development because they had domesticated dogs (dingoes) and ground stone tools. The Tasmanians lacked both and were assigned to the 'Palaeolithic'. This two-stage model implied that the human occupation of Australia was of considerable antiquity. Greater precision, however, was impossible as there was no means of dating Aboriginal remains. Variation in the shape of Aboriginal stone tools was thought to be due to raw material rather than style or function, and this meant that there was no way of building up a cultural sequence on the basis of a succession of different artifact types. It was known that there were several extinct species of large marsupial, which had once occupied Australia, but proof that Aborigines and megafauna had coexisted remained elusive.

In New Zealand speculation focused on the origins of the Maori. Walter Mantell (1820–95) is credited with the first excavation at the Awamoa site in North Otago in 1852. The remains of the extinct flightless birds known as moa had already been excavated at several sites, but Mantell was the first to show that people had hunted them. By the 1870s, evidence of moa hunting had been found at six sites, and it seemed that the giant birds had been extinct since at least the sixteenth century. This raised questions about the antiquity of the sites and the identity of the hunters, and a lively debate ensued, largely stimulated by Julius von Haast (1822–87), a German geologist who arrived in New Zealand in 1858 and became the first Director of the Canterbury Museum. Haast himself investigated several sites and was able to recognise two distinct periods of occupation. Influenced by European discoveries of extinct animals associated with flaked stone tools, Haast proposed that the Maori occupation of New Zealand, which he equated with the 'Neolithic', had been preceded by a 'Palaeolithic' people who lacked polished stone tools and domestic dogs. It was these more 'primitive' people who were the moa hunters. Haast's views were controversial and his critics soon came up with evidence of the survival of the moa into recent times as well as moa-hunter sites with polished stone tools. Haast finally modified his views as a result of excavations at Moa-bone Point Cave, near Christchurch, where polished stone tools were found in moa-hunter layers dating back at least 600 years.

However, these early interests in Pacific archaeology were not followed up. The Polynesian Society was founded in 1892 to record what were thought to be the remnants of a dying and disappearing culture, and the Maori scholar Peter Buck (Te Rangi Hiroa) (1877–1951) took the lead in developing a new synthesis of New Zealand and Polynesian prehistory, largely based on a doubtful body of Maori oral tradition. This remained dominant until the middle of the twentieth century when scholars began to question the historical accuracy of Maori accounts of the colonisation of New Zealand and cleared the way for a more modern and rigorous approach incorporating archaeological evidence.

Early archaeologists

In the first half of the twentieth century, museums provided the base for the development of archaeological investigation throughout the region. In Australia, Norman Tindale (1900–93) at the South Australian Museum and Frederick McCarthy (1905–97) at the Australian Museum in Sydney were the key figures. Although neither was an archaeologist by training, both recognised the potential of archaeological investigation to illuminate the Aboriginal past and both conducted pioneering excavations – Tindale at Devon Downs in 1929 and McCarthy at Lapstone Creek in 1936 – which allowed them to propose rival interpretations of prehistoric culture change in Australia. In New Zealand, the ethnologist H.D. Skinner (1886–1978), based at the University Museum of Otago, focused on comparative material culture studies and strongly encouraged field archaeology. His most prominent student was Roger Duff (1912–78) at Canterbury Museum. He conducted major excavations at Wairau Bar and showed that the occupants were Polynesian in their physical characteristics and that there was no evidence for any population preceding the Maori. Duff's work culminated in a major synthesis of New Zealand prehistory.

In the wider Pacific region, most of the work conducted before World War II was field survey and material culture studies rather than excavation. At the beginning of the nineteenth century there were several mainly ethnographic expeditions to Melanesia and Micronesia and, in 1913–16, a major investigation of Easter Island by an intrepid Englishwoman, Katherine Scoresby Routledge (1866–1935). From about 1920, attention particularly focused on Polynesia and H.E. Gregory (1869–1952) and later Kenneth Emory (1897–1992), both based at the Bishop Museum in Hawaii, conducted major field recording programmes in several island groups. Finally, in the late 1940s E.W. Gifford (1887–1959) excavated several sites on Fiji and demonstrated a sequence of changing pottery styles.

Post-war transformations

With the 1950s came a period of radical change in methods and approaches to archaeology throughout the region. The impact of the new technique of radiocarbon dating was one important factor, opening up at last the possibility of reliable chronology. But new ideas and methods, particularly the emphasis on rigorous excavation techniques introduced to the region by pioneers such as John Mulvaney in Australia, Jack Golson in New Zealand and Robert C. Suggs in the Marquesas, laid the foundations for radical new approaches.

In 1954, Golson came from Britain to take up the first university lectureship in prehistoric archaeology anywhere in the region, in the anthropology department at Auckland University, and embarked on a programme of excavation and training. By the time he left for Australia in 1961, he had transformed New Zealand archaeology, both from a practical and theoretical perspective, improving field standards and introducing studies of settlement and subsistence to complement material culture studies. His successor at Auckland was Roger Green (1932–2009), an American archaeologist and student of Gordon Willey. He strongly advocated a settlement system approach and in turn influenced the development of archaeology in New Zealand and the Pacific.

In Australia, John Mulvaney started as a historian at Melbourne University but went to study at Cambridge, intending to return with a sound training in modern archaeological methods that could be applied in Australia. On his return he introduced a course in prehistory at Melbourne University and embarked on a vigorous programme of field survey, excavation

FIGURE 13.1 Professor John Mulvaney excavating at Fromm's Landing, South Australia. Photo ©
National Library of Australia.

and critical analysis of earlier work, as well as documentary research into Aboriginal history. His first excavation was at Fromm's Landing in 1956, only a few miles from Tindale's pioneering excavations at Devon Downs. In 1961, Mulvaney published a comprehensive review article entitled 'The Stone Age of Australia'. This was highly critical of the earlier syntheses of Tindale and McCarthy and marks a clear break with the past and a new beginning for Australian archaeology. Mulvaney's new broom swept so clean that Australian archaeologists have felt little need to pay attention to the efforts of his predecessors.

The 1960s saw an explosion of interest in the archaeology of the region, coinciding with significant expansion of university education. In both Australia and New Zealand, there was an influx of archaeologists trained in Cambridge under the influence of Grahame Clark's economic view of prehistory – one of the most important of these was Rhys Jones (see Box 13.1). The 'new archaeology' from the USA was also an important influence. American archaeologists Richard Gould and Brian Hayden conducted important ethno-archaeological

---

BOX 13.1 Rhys Jones (1941–2001)

Rhys Jones was one of several young archaeologists, many of them Cambridge-trained, who took up positions in Australia as part of the expansion of universities in the 1960s. He was born into a Welsh-speaking family in North Wales, attended grammar school in Cardiff and read Natural Sciences and Archaeology at Cambridge University. He took up a Teaching Fellowship at the University of Sydney in 1963, where he completed a PhD on the Rocky Cape site in Tasmania. He moved to the Research School of Pacific Studies at the Australian National University in 1969, where he spent the remainder of his career.

The use of ethnography as a source of models for interpreting the past strongly informed Jones' archaeological work. He characterised Aborigines as active managers of their environment through coining the phrase 'firestick farming'. His detailed study of early Tasmanian ethnographic records, particularly of French explorers, was complemented by his work with the Anbarra people of Arnhem Land, in association with his partner Betty Meehan.

Much of Rhys Jones' research focused on questions of chronology and the initial colonisation of Australia. At Rocky Cape, he confirmed that occupation there pre-dated the separation of Tasmania from the mainland by rising sea levels. He promoted the development of new dating methods based on luminescence, resulting in claims for the age of human colonisation as far back as 60,000 years.

Rhys Jones was an eloquent, charismatic and often controversial communicator. His inspirational skills as a speaker and teacher led him into film making and broadcasting. In the 1980s Jones played a key role in the discovery of Ice Age sites in southwest Tasmania and the campaign to save them from the damming of the Franklin River. He had a flair for the dramatic, once famously announcing his land claim over Stonehenge as a Welshman and descendant of its builders. He succeeded in putting Australian archaeology firmly on the international stage through his passionate belief in its distinctive contribution to the broader human story and the potential it held for the development of theory in the study of hunter-gatherer societies.

research in Australia. American archaeologists, such as Roger Green, were particularly active in promoting a settlement pattern approach to sites in the Pacific.

The result was an explosion of information about the peopling of Australia and New Guinea. In 1960, the oldest confirmed radiocarbon date for an Australian site was 8700 BP. In 1963, Mulvaney's excavations at Kenniff Cave, in Queensland, had produced a stratified series of dates back to 16,000 years ago. By the end of the decade, the discovery of human remains, stone tools and animal bones at Lake Mungo, western New South Wales, had pushed occupation back beyond 30,000 years ago. The next decade saw the discovery of several other Pleistocene sites in Australia and New Guinea, ranging from Devils Lair in the southwest corner of the continent to Kosipe in the highlands of New Guinea; and by 1980, 40,000 years was widely accepted as the date of first colonisation. By the end of the century, sites of this age had been found over almost the whole continent and Pleistocene occupation of the near Oceanic islands had also been demonstrated. How much earlier Australia was first occupied remains controversial. Luminescence dating has resulted in age estimates of up to 65,000 years ago for occupation at several sites, but not all have been accepted.

The establishment of an Ice Age antiquity for the occupation of Australia led to a number of other discoveries that challenged traditional Eurocentric views of archaeology. These included finds of ground stone axes in northern Australia, and art and underground flint mining at Koonalda Cave on the Nullarbor Plain, both about 20,000 years old. At the same time, the New Guinea highlands emerged as a centre for the early development of agricultural systems dating back some 10,000 years. Although Polynesia remained the main focus of archaeological research, fieldwork in New Guinea stimulated interest in the western Pacific, and particularly in Melanesia. Finds of dated Lapita pottery increasingly suggested the possibility that the Lapita cultural complex might be associated with the ancestors of the Polynesians. The 1970s and 1980s saw concentrated research in Melanesia, providing not only a large amount of data on the spread of Lapita, but also unexpected evidence of occupation dating back more than 30,000 years in the Bismarck Archipelago.

One of the most important events in Polynesian archaeology was the expedition to Easter Island and other islands led by Norwegian adventurer Thor Heyerdahl in the 1950s. The members of the expedition carried out pioneering work in excavation and interpretation, and foremost among them was William Mulloy (see Box 13.2).

The 1960s also saw the emergence of legislation to protect Aboriginal archaeological sites and, later, historic sites and shipwrecks. All Australian states had some legislation by the mid-1970s and the federal government had established the Australian Heritage Commission. In New Zealand, legislation to protect archaeological sites was passed in 1975. Heritage legislation in the United States affected Hawaii and other US territories from the 1960s and independent Pacific states have also established similar laws. This has resulted in the growth of consulting archaeology and, in a number of areas, a large increase in resources and thus data collection. Although there have been significant contributions, much of this work receives only limited publication and the sheer volume of it means that incorporating the new information into regional syntheses is slow.

The use of archaeology to investigate historic sites and shipwrecks also began in the 1960s. Much of the early focus was on colonial settlement with a strong though not exclusive emphasis on the nature and spread of European settlement. With rising public interest in heritage and the growth of cultural tourism, this has been a rapidly developing area.

BOX 13.2 William T. Mulloy (1917–78)

William Mulloy was an American archaeologist, best known for his investigations into the enigmatic monumental statues on Easter Island (Rapa Nui). He was born in Salt Lake City and graduated from the University of Utah. After an interval in the US Army during World War II he joined the University of Wyoming and conducted field research on the archaeology of the Plains Indians and of the Southwest.

In 1955, Mulloy was invited to join a team of specialists assembled by the Norwegian adventurer Thor Heyerdahl (1914–2002) to investigate the archaeology of Easter Island and other parts of Eastern Polynesia. Mulloy undertook excavations at the major platforms of ahu Vinapu, as well as in the ceremonial village of Orongo. The results of the

FIGURE 13.2 William Mulloy at Ahu Akivi in 1961. © Brigid Mulloy/Wikimedia Commons.

preliminary investigations of this expedition were published in 1961. Mulloy quickly saw the archaeological potential of the area and subsequently made Easter Island his life's work. In 1968 he developed an archaeological inventory project aimed at a complete record of the island's sites. This was a vast undertaking aimed at effectively preserving the archaeological record. As well as investigating major site complexes, Mulloy also began the major work of restoring the monumental architecture of the island, starting with the ahu Akivi, a row of seven moai statues on a low platform, one of the few such platforms located inland instead of along the coast. He also restored platforms at Tahai, as well as the village of Orongo. Mulloy saw his restoration of the monuments as a means of reaffirming the identity and dignity of the islanders. He also proposed important ideas about how the statues were transported from the quarry to the platforms.

His work laid the foundations for our knowledge of the environmental decline that hit the island a few centuries ago: having encountered root moulds in the soil at Akivi, he rightly deduced that Easter Island had once been covered by quite large vegetation. In two papers, he set out his theory that the island's environment had been progressively depleted by man since human occupation. Unfortunately he had no idea of the scale of the island's deforestation or any precise data about what constituted its forests, and he died before pollen analyses and other studies provided the supporting evidence for his deduction. He also narrowly missed out on discovering the eyes that were sometimes placed in the eye sockets of statues on the platforms – he found an almost intact specimen made of white coral during his work at Vinapu, but alas it was very eroded, and its round shape led him to think it was a fragment of a 'beautifully made coral dish'.

FIGURE 13.3 The seven restored moai at Ahu Akivi. © The Power of Forever Photography/istock.

Mulloy's work on Easter Island laid the foundations for the declaration of the Rapa Nui National Park as a World Heritage site. On his death, his ashes were buried on the island; the plaque on his tomb says: 'By restoring the past of his beloved island he also changed its future'. His archive and library were also left to the island, where they are now housed. Over the past few decades, most new research on Easter Island has been carried out by people who studied under, or were otherwise inspired by, William Mulloy.

Bringing the story up to date

From the 1980s on, archaeology in the Australasian region has become increasingly self-conscious in terms of both practice and theory. Theoretical debates in the region reflect broader debates in archaeology generally about the nature and interpretation of archaeological evidence and the explanation of cultural change. In the post-colonial world the practice of archaeology in Australia and the Pacific has increasingly been questioned and critically examined by Indigenous people (see Box 13.3). Reconciliation remains a challenge for archaeologists in the twenty-first century.

With the broad outlines of the timing and spread of human populations through Australasia apparently established, attention has turned to more detailed regional studies. In Australia, for example, these have highlighted local and regional variability. The idea of a relatively homogeneous archaeology for much of the period of human occupation with regional diversity emerging only in the late Holocene is now coming into question. However, much of the region remains poorly known, as recent startling discoveries, such as a new species of hominin in Flores and unexpected finds of Lapita pottery in the Papuan Gulf, remind us.

The practice of archaeology in the region is increasingly associated with resource development. The pressures of development are particularly problematic in areas that are still relatively unexplored archaeologically, such as much of Papua New Guinea and the Pilbara region of Western Australia. While this has stimulated archaeological research in new areas, what is done is often just the minimum required by law, and the pioneering nature of the research means that there is little context within which to evaluate the results. The political and economic pressure to proceed with development is often overwhelming. As a result there is a large and growing 'grey' literature.

From the great European voyages of discovery until about the 1940s, archaeology struggled to contribute to understanding the cultures of this vast region since they were seen as unchanging and peripheral. The achievements of archaeologists in the last fifty years have transformed this preconception and shown that the long and complex history of the dispersal of humanity into Australia and the Pacific is not only intrinsically fascinating but can contribute to broader theoretical debates.

BOX 13.3 Archaeology and Indigenous peoples

The history of archaeology is intimately bound up with European colonisation. The encounter with Indigenous peoples stimulated speculation and debate about the nature of human society and social evolution even as they themselves were dispossessed and marginalised by the colonising powers. If archaeologists working in North or South America, Africa, Asia and Oceania paid any attention to living descendants of ancient peoples, it was as ethnographic examples of people at more primitive stages of cultural development, or sometimes simply as labour. Indigenous beliefs and sensitivities about places of cultural significance and human remains were widely ignored. The second half of the twentieth century saw the retreat of the European colonial powers and the emergence of new nations. At the same time, dispossessed Indigenous peoples in the settler societies of North America, Australia and New Zealand began to demand recognition and restitution, while new nations in Africa, Asia and the Pacific also moved to take control of the interpretation of their own past. In all these areas, the challenge by Indigenous people has broadly followed a similar pattern with archaeology viewed not as detached and objective science but as a colonialist enterprise contributing to the objectification and dehumanisation of Indigenous people.

In Australia, archaeology had matured in the post-war period just as the discipline was reframing itself as a scientific and objective inquiry. However, Indigenous peoples rather saw archaeology as at best irrelevant and at worst complicit in the colonial enterprise. During the 1980s, Australian archaeology became increasingly caught up in the Aboriginal struggle for social justice and political recognition. The campaign for land rights was a critical part of this struggle, but Aborigines also asserted ownership over their heritage, accusing archaeologists of complicity in their continuing dispossession. As a consequence Australian archaeologists had to reconsider their relationship with Aboriginal people and how they conducted their practice. The most public and bitter area of dispute has generally been the treatment of human remains. Aboriginal people made no distinction between 'scientific' excavation and the indiscriminate robbing of graves to collect anatomical specimens, which had been common practice in the nineteenth and early twentieth centuries. State and Federal bureaucracies moved to involve Aboriginal people in the management of sites and new heritage legislation explicitly acknowledged this. At the same time, many academic archaeologists began to build relationships with Aboriginal people and develop a more collaborative approach to archaeological research. By the early 1990s, both the Australian Archaeological Association and the Australian Association of Consulting Archaeologists developed codes of ethics that explicitly recognised the interests of Indigenous people in their heritage and required members to conduct appropriate consultation.

In 1992, the High Court recognised the existence of native title in the Mabo case. This landmark decision had far-reaching implications and has required all non-Aboriginal Australians to re-examine their relations with Aboriginal and Torres Strait Islander people. One result is that consultation with traditional owners or native title claimants is now part of the approval process for a range of land uses, such as minerals exploration and mining. Land-use agreements between mining companies and traditional owners commonly deal with the identification and protection of sites, and can also include archaeological research. Archaeologists have also played a role in some native title cases and there is increasing interest in the archaeology of contact sites. Some Aboriginal groups have been active in inviting archaeologists with whom they have built relationships to conduct archaeological research, although it remains to be seen how far these projects truly involve shared power.

FIGURE 13.4 Representatives of Aboriginal communities in western Victoria, Australia, discussing the results of archaeological research in the Grampians region, 1996. Photo © David Frankel.

Further reading

Anderson, A. 1989. *Prodigious birds: Moas and moa-hunting in prehistoric New Zealand.* Cambridge University Press: Cambridge.

Colley, S. 2002. *Uncovering Australia: Archaeology, Indigenous people and the public.* Smithsonian Institution Press: Washington, DC.

Du Cros, H. 2002. *Much more than stones and bones: Australian archaeology in the late twentieth century.* Melbourne University Press: Melbourne.

Furey, L. and Holdaway, S. (eds) 2004. *Change through time: 50 years of New Zealand archaeology.* New Zealand Archaeological Association Monograph no. 26: Auckland.

Horton, D. 1991. *Recovering the tracks: The story of Australian archaeology.* Aboriginal Studies Press: Canberra.

Kirch, P.V. 2000. *On the road of the winds: An archaeological history of the Pacific Islands before European contact.* University of California Press: Berkeley.

Langford, R. 1983. Our heritage – your playground. *Australian Archaeology,* 16: 1–6.

Lilley, I. (ed.) 2000. *Native Title and the transformation of archaeology in the postcolonial world.* Oceania Monograph 50. Left Coast Press, Walnut Creek, CA.

Lilley, I. (ed.) 2006. *Archaeology of Oceania: Australia and the Pacific Islands.* Blackwell Publishing, Oxford.

MacFarlane, I., Mountain, M.J. and Paton, R. (eds) 2005. *Many exchanges: archaeology, history, community and the work of Isabel McBryde.* Aboriginal History Monograph 11. Canberra.

McNiven, I.J. and Russell, L. 2005. *Appropriated pasts: Indigenous peoples and the colonial culture of archaeology.* AltaMira Press, Walnut Creek, CA.

Mulvaney, J. and Kamminga, J. 1999. *Prehistory of Australia.* Allen & Unwin: St Leonards.

Mulvaney, J. 2011. *Digging up a past.* University of New South Wales Press, Sydney.

Watkins, J. 2005. 'Through wary eyes: Indigenous perspectives on archaeology'. *Annual Review of Anthrolopogy,* 34: 429–49.

CONCLUSION

The future of archaeology

Colin Renfrew, McDonald Institute for Archaeological Research, Cambridge

Archaeology has a great future. As long as there are people on earth, the places they live in and the artifacts they use will leave traces. The archaeologists of the future will always have work to do! There are so many new research techniques becoming available, and so many discoveries being made today that our understanding of the past is becoming richer all the time. As the chapters in this volume clearly set out, in many parts of the world the techniques of archaeology already allow the past history (and prehistory) of a country to be pieced together: built up and established on the basis of the material remains, even when written records are not abundant or lacking altogether. In most other areas that position will be reached in the next twenty or thirty years.

The basis of archaeology anywhere, good archaeology, is systematic excavation, which is careful to give attention to stratigraphy and to respect and study the context of discovery. In each of the lands reviewed in this volume the story has followed much the same pattern. The European geologists of the eighteenth century who came to understand the principles of stratigraphy were the precursors. They opened the way for the founders of systematic archaeology in the nineteenth century. These in turn applied those principles to the study of the remains of the human past in many lands by means of careful stratigraphic excavation. Those early excavators had their precursors, of course, but it was the pioneers of the Three Age System in Europe who led the way. And they were followed in North America and beyond in creating an outline periodisation of the past. The application of those principles led, in every part of the world, to the establishment of local sequences, local prehistories and histories, based upon the actual material finds. It became possible for every region and every country, indeed every locality, to have its own prehistory and history, based on an understanding of the local finds, as represented in secure stratigraphic contexts. This is already the reality in many areas, and will soon be so everywhere.

Then came radiocarbon! When Willard Libby, the American chemist, invented (or should we say discovered?) radiocarbon dating in 1949, he opened the way towards a universal, or at least a global archaeology. For then it became possible to link these local pasts in different parts of the world together into a single coherent picture. It has taken archaeologists several decades since then to produce an outline of that picture, which in some areas is still under construction. But with radiocarbon dating it at last became possible to establish the dates and the ages of things in different parts of the world in a standardised way. The prehistory of Australia, for instance, could be compared to that of France or of North America, all on the same basis and using the same timescale. That is what made it possible at last to have a real world archaeology, which is based upon the material evidence and not upon assumptions about cultural priority or upon prior ideas about how history ought to be. To construct that world archaeology, at a detailed level, across the continents, is one of the tasks that lie ahead.

But radiocarbon dating does have its limitations in terms of accuracy and scope. So before about 40,000 years ago other dating techniques have to be used: radiocarbon cannot be used much beyond that. But the principles of radioactive decay, on which radiocarbon dating relies, apply to other elements also, allowing the application of other radiometric dating methods, such as potassium/argon dating, for earlier time periods. So the good news is that archaeologists can now do dating. There are margins of error to take into account, of course, and many specialisms are involved in the growing field of archaeological science. But, armed with the principles of stratigraphy and with the techniques of radiometric dating, world archaeology has now become a reality.

The grand narrative: Enter DNA

The broad outlines of the human past are thus only now becoming clear. Already in the early twentieth century it was becoming evident that Africa was the cradle of humankind. But only in the past twenty years has the broad narrative of the out-of-Africa expansion of our species emerged. It does now seem that the earlier expansions of our hominin ancestor *Homo erectus*, who peopled much of the globe (but not the Americas) from a million years ago, did not lead to successors surviving today. Only in Africa were there survivors whose descendants evolved to our own species, *Homo sapiens*, and so became the ancestors of us all. For only now do we understand (and it is not beyond dispute in some quarters) that all surviving humans today are the result of the expansion of our own species *Homo sapiens* out of Africa some 60,000 years ago. But how many earlier, and presumably ultimately unsuccessful, expansions were there? That has not yet been securely established. The application of the study of the DNA of living humans has allowed the broad picture to be built up, using mitochondrial DNA and then Y-chromosome DNA. And the picture was clarified further by the successful sampling of ancient DNA from preserved skeletons of Neanderthal hominins. The application of DNA studies, and particularly the study of ancient DNA, which is only now taking off, will soon clarify several aspects of this grand narrative of humankind. They will one day establish just when the Americas were first peopled, which is still in dispute. The story is emerging in its broad outlines, but the details are not yet clear.

It is now realised that the development of food production, with the domesticating of plants and animals, was a particularly decisive step. The great archaeologist Gordon Childe understood that, already before World War II, when he formulated his concept of the 'neolithic revolution'. The origins of food production are now a major focus of study in every part of the world. And while pioneering projects in the Near East in the later twentieth century established some of the broad outlines, and also in Mexico, major discoveries are still being made in China, in Peru and in other key areas, which are clarifying understanding of that revolutionary transformation.

It was Gordon Childe also who highlighted the 'urban revolution', focusing again mainly on the Near East. We see now, however, that the origins of complex society followed rather different paths in different parts of the world. These are elements of the Grand Narrative that are still being worked out, and which will become clear over the next few decades.

DNA studies are still in their infancy, still relying too much on contemporary data (from modern populations) to build up an imagined picture of earlier times, which is, in effect, projected back onto the past in the process of interpretation. It is here that ancient DNA, taken from well-stratified and well-dated human remains, can in favourable circumstances offer an insight into the genetic make-up of the human population at the times and places in question. There are technical difficulties here that have yet to be overcome. But already in the study of prehistoric Europe it is beginning to be possible to study the demographic processes that took place, using evidence which derives from the times in question. That will soon be possible in other areas also.

So one development that we can soon look forward to is the construction of a demographic history for each continent and each area, from the time of the out-of-Africa dispersals of our species down to the present day. Clearly this will depend on finding human remains datable to the relevant periods, and on the successful extraction of ancient DNA from them. But this is more than a dream: it is already beginning to happen. From this we can expect to learn about initial population dispersals and also of subsequent migrationary episodes if they occurred.

The broad outlines of the rise and fall of civilisations are thus already being reconstructed using the traditional archaeological techniques of stratigraphic excavation, supported by sound chronology. This process will continue in the future. The origins of urban society can be established for each region. Those areas that have been neglected archeologically until recently will also tell their story. We can look forward to a much richer world history.

Thick description: Languages and peoples

The grand narrative offers us the outlines of what happened in history in each part of the globe. But that overview, that objectified account, is not enough. Sometimes we need more personal insights into what life was like. We would like to know what people thought. Sometimes the depictions that they produced of the world, which we often today designate as 'art', allow us to glimpse something of that. Yet the best way to achieve this is to read what they themselves have written – when such an account is available. And early written records are available in regions where literacy developed early. The archives of some of the great sites of the Near East have been discovered – such as Boğazköy and Kültepe in Turkey and Ebla in Syria. But many inscribed clay tablets have still to be read, and more is to be learnt there. Then there are still undeciphered scripts – the writing of the Indus Valley civilisation, or the Minoan Linear A script of Crete, or the inscriptions of ancient Elam. In many such cases the problem is that there are insufficient texts available to permit a decipherment. But one may hope that in some cases additional texts will soon be found, perhaps preserved in waterlogged deposits. The wonderful success of the Maya decipherment in recent decades (see Chapter 11) offers hope that, with the discovery of more epigraphic material, further comparable advances can be made in other areas.

Yet even without newly found ancient texts, progress is possible. The astonishing linguistic diversity in the modern world is studied by historical linguists who can use the relationships among languages to establish language families. These are groups of related languages, with similarities in vocabulary, grammar and phonology, and which in many cases are thought to be descended from an ancestral proto-language. The great language families of the world must have had earlier origins, reaching back to the days before writing was developed. The origins of these families have been much discussed, and often widely disputed. The extent to which archaeological evidence can be used to clarify the patterns of linguistic dispersals and developments in different areas is an issue not yet resolved. Yet there is growing interest today in the possibility of better understanding the prehistory of languages. The origin of the Indo-European language family, for example, is an old problem that has been much debated. Very promising work has been undertaken on other continents, for instance, in Peru.

When we are speaking of different peoples, in the modern world, a crucial factor is indeed language. Very frequently those speaking a specific language or even a dialect think of themselves as a separate people. This is a major component of what is meant by ethnicity. So that while in Europe or North America there are just a few languages, each with millions of speakers, in other parts of the world – in South America or New Guinea – there are languages each with only a few thousand (or even a few hundred) speakers today. This is part of the rich diversity of humankind; these peoples have their own histories, and potentially their own archaeologies.

The future narratives of world archaeology will thus be written from many different perspectives. The ones that you yourself will read may depend to some extent on who you are, who your parents are, on the languages you speak and on where you live. Of course if you live in South America, the world looks very different when compared with the view from Europe. The archaeology can loom even larger when there is not much written history to supplement it, and written history in the Americas does not begin until the late fifteenth century AD (apart from those important Olmec, Maya and Aztec documents already mentioned). It naturally feels different also if you are personally a descendant of Native Americans or (speaking of Africa) if you are yourself of African descent. Ancestry has a powerful influence upon what seems relevant and important. And so does the language we speak, especially our own mother tongue.

These comments are not intended as an argument for relativism. The archaeologies of different lands and different peoples do not contradict each other. They accept, however, that the view you have depends upon the standpoint of the viewer. The archaeology of the future, or better the local archaeologies of the future, will recognise this. They will be written in different languages and from different perspectives. And they will focus upon what interests their readers.

Heritage and its enemies

The term 'heritage' has several different meanings. Each one of us has a genetic inheritance, passed on to us by our parents. The mechanisms of transmission of that genetic inheritance are now, thanks to the recognition and study of DNA, relatively well understood. As noted above we also have a linguistic heritage in the language or languages that we have learnt from our parents and those that we have subsequently acquired from others. The cultural heritage also involves the ways we do things: the clothes we wear, the things we like to eat, and our special behaviours, like song and dance, which we learn as we grow up. That heritage also has material components, and it is there that archaeology comes into its own. The buildings in which we live, especially the traditional ones, are also part of that heritage. For these reasons, conservation is important to many of us. We value those surviving records of the past and we seek to conserve its most notable products. So it is that in Britain and in Europe the great mediaeval cathedrals are such a valued feature, and why they are conserved, and restored, sometimes using public money. This is true of the great mosques of Islam and of the temples of the religions of the East, including the Hindu and Buddhist faiths. Many organisations, like the appropriately named 'English Heritage' in England, have a duty to conserve the built heritage.

Fortunately as this volume narrates, our interest is not restricted to the monuments and evidences of the country in which we are born. The history of archaeology, as these pages indicate, has been written through the efforts of travellers and explorers, and also scientists, who take the wider view. That is how it is possible to construct the archaeology and the history of humankind. But the record of the past, the material record, is often fragile. Every day across the world, new developments involving fresh construction works inevitably destroy some of those traces of the past. Urban archaeology, which developed mightily after World War II, began in the bombed-out ruins of some of the great cities of Europe. The notion of rescue archaeology or salvage archaeology or cultural resource management was encouraged by the success of those post-war urban excavations, which revealed so much of the archaeology and history of the urban centres in question. The same logic was soon applied to rural developments – that the developer should pay for Cultural Resource Management – for the management of the cultural resources that are threatened in the course of new developments. So it is that, all over the world, new highway developments have revealed important archaeological remains, and the investigation of these has increasingly been undertaken in a systematic manner. So much of the future of archaeology will be public archaeology – that is to say archaeology undertaken as a public obligation by future developers, private as well as civic.

But there will always be those who are willing to bulldoze ancient monuments for private gain and who are willing to disregard the heritage of the past. Those are the first enemies.

Strangely, however, the most dangerous enemies of our shared cultural heritage are not those who ignorantly disregard the preserved heritage of the past. Often the very people who are responsible for the destruction of archaeological sites are precisely those who claim to value the past. These are the unscrupulous collectors. Often they are willing to pay large sums of money to secure ownership of significant antiquities obtained illegally and illicitly from archaeological sites, and to gather them together in private collections. And, strangely, there are directors and curators in major museums who are willing to put these illicit antiquities on public display.

This is one of the paradoxes of archaeology today and, I fear, for some time in the future. Modern archaeology, as this book narrates, has gradually built up the techniques of investigation that allow a coherent picture of the past to be established by careful archaeological excavation, by publication and by study. It can then be made public by scholarly publication and by popularisation, by television and other means of dissemination. It has always been the case that the artifacts deriving from such excavations, the 'antiquities' as they are termed, have excited curiosity and wonder. That curiosity attracted private collectors in the early days of archaeology and has led to the formation of public museums. Yet with the growth of modern archaeology, as this book describes, it has gradually been realised that what matters most is the information that these finds bring with them, above all when considered in context.

It is through them and their contexts, as described in this volume, that our knowledge of the early human past has been formed. In the nineteenth century major expeditions, some of them sponsored by the great museums of the world, resulted in the discovery of new sites and the recognition of new civilisations. They are described in nearly every chapter above. They led on to some of the great museum collections of the Western world: to the great altar from Pergamon in the Pergamon Museum in Berlin, to the winged bulls of the Palace of King Sargon II at Khorsabad in the Louvre, to the stone reliefs from the palace of King Ashurnasirpal II at Nimrud in the British Museum. In the twentieth century too there were scientific expeditions led by skilled archaeologists, like Sir Leonard Woolley (see Chapter 6), which enriched the Museum of the University of Pennsylvania in Philadelphia as well as the British Museum and the National Museum in Baghdad. But those days are now past. Today the expeditions of Sir Aurel Stein in the 1920s to what was Chinese Turkestan and is now the Xinjiang Autonomous Province of the People's Republic of China, which so enriched the British Museum as well as the National Museum in New Delhi, is viewed with disfavour in China, just as the activities of Lord Elgin at the Parthenon in Athens, which so enriched the British Museum, are now deplored in Greece. These episodes now lie in the past, however, although they have led to claims for restitution that will go on to generate controversy in the future.

Much more serious for the future of archaeology is the on-going looting of archaeological sites. The looters who undertake these illicit and damaging excavations represent the greatest threat to the future of archaeology. For the archaeological record is fragile and it is finite. Once destroyed it cannot be replaced. If the developers who destroy the record of the past in the course of their construction work are the first enemies, these looters and those who finance them constitute the second and greater enemy. And the irony is that those who fund them are the very private collectors who hold the resulting 'antiquities' in high esteem, and the museum directors and curators who aid and abet them.

It is now more than forty years since UNESCO adopted its Convention on the Means of Prohibiting and Preventing the Illicit Import, Export and Transfer of Ownership of Cultural Property of 1970, which has now been ratified by most advanced nations in the world. It was ratified by the United Kingdom in 2002 (although the UK has still not ratified the 1954 Convention on the Protection of Cultural Property in the Event of Armed Conflict). Fortunately in many countries the leading museums have now adopted acquisition policies that prevent their acquiring, even by gift, antiquities that have appeared on the market after 1970 (the year of the Convention) and which might therefore derive from illicit excavations. The British Museum adopted such a policy in 1998. The J. Paul Getty Museum adopted a well-formulated ethical acquisition policy in 2006, but only after a major international scandal, when its former curator of antiquities, Marion True, was charged by the Italian authorities for conspiracy to traffic in illicit antiquities. More than twenty major antiquities were soon returned to Italy and to Greece. The Metropolitan Museum of Art in New York was similarly obliged to return looted antiquities to Italy. These were positive steps, but the looting of antiquities continues worldwide.

At first sight the museums might now seem to be behaving more ethically, and in some countries they are. The Association of Art Museum Directors (of the USA) in 2008 at last adopted a policy that required them, before acquisition, to establish a clear ownership history dating back to 1970. Yet the Association went on to contrive a glaring loophole by establishing an 'object list' on its website permitting museums in special circumstances to avoid (i.e., subvert) that principle. For many archaeologists a significant and perhaps defining issue has been the position of the Metropolitan Museum of Art in New York, which during the directorship of Philippe de Montebello resisted the new acquisition code. It was adopted only on his retirement in 2008, after years of questionable acquisitions. For many years the Met has had on display items from the collection of the late Leon Levy and his wife Shelby White (a Trustee of the Museum), some of which do not appear to conform with that clear principle underlying the 1970 UNESCO Convention. Will the Met continue to display these anomalous, perhaps illicit items? And will it even eventually accept them as a gift or bequest? That is seen as an acid test by many archaeologists. The Miho Museum in Japan is another example of a rich institution that apparently fails to follow an ethical collecting policy.

It is clear that the looting will not stop, or even diminish, while major museums continue to acquire illicit antiquities, and while collectors can obtain tax benefits, or even sometimes supposedly favourable publicity for their supposed generosity in donating them to such museums.

The threats to the future of archaeology come therefore from several directions – from unregulated development, and from looting funded indirectly by private collectors and even major museums. The aspiration of a world archaeology, available to everyone, and relevant to every country in the world, is threatened today by commercial forces that have not yet been effectively controlled.

Who owns the past? Whose past? Who tells the story? Whose story?

The implication that emerges from the chapters in this book, taken together, is that the past belongs to everyone. It is part of the heritage that we can all share. Archaeology is the means by which that past is recovered and revealed to us, as these pages so clearly show.

Of course there are many different ways to tell a story, using the evidences revealed by the techniques of archaeology. I have referred above to the Grand Narrative, the broad sweep of the story of human origins and dispersals, of the developments of food production, of the rise of complex societies and of the development of literacy. But this story too can be told in different ways. Gordon Childe, one of the most eminent story tellers, was much influenced by Marxist thought. As we have seen in Chapters 8 and 9 respectively, Marxist thought was prevalent in Russia in the days of Stalin, and in China during the Cultural Revolution. It is still influential in archaeology in many ways, and indeed many aspects of Marxist thought in archaeology are still fruitful and productive. But other philosophies and world views can be brought to bear with equal validity. In Anglo-American archaeology in recent years there has been a debate between processual archaeology (formerly 'the New Archaeology') and interpretive archaeology (formerly 'post-processual' archaeology). The kinds of archaeology written by the protagonists on the two sides of this debate were in practice rather different. That debate ran along different lines from the analysis of the forces of production and of the class struggle favoured by Marxist thinkers, and has perhaps now run its course. Other fashions in theorising about the past will no doubt follow.

These controversies, in a way, illustrate the greatest strength of archaeology. There is no one, official story. The evidence of archaeology is mute. It has to be excavated, analysed, summarised and interpreted. Any good interpretation will be based on the evidence, but many interpretations are possible from any specific set of data. Those who come to archaeology already inspired by a specific religious faith or a persuasive political doctrine will draw one set of conclusions. Others will wish to see how their own particular view of the world fits in. Archaeological scientists will emphasise the importance of the techniques that they themselves utilise. Yet in the end, archaeology is not subject to any of these doctrines or philosophies or methodologies. That is its particular and special strength. It has developed, as the chapters in this book reveal so clearly, its own preferences and interpretive styles, in many parts of the world. The methods of investigation available to archaeology are growing and developing all the time. It offers a perspective in which everyone can seek and find their place in the world and in world history. There is no demanding doctrine that determines which narrative or integration should be followed. That is its greatest strength.

INDEX